GAZA

PREPARING FOR DAWN

DONALD MACINTYRE

ONEWORLD

A Oneworld Book

First published by Oneworld Publications, 2017
This paperback edition published 2018

Copyright © Donald Macintyre 2017, 2018

The moral right of Donald Macintyre to be identified as the Author of this work has been
asserted by him in accordance with the Copyright, Designs, and Patents Act 1988

ISBN 978-1-78607-433-1
eISBN 978-1-78607-107-1

Maps © Erica Milwain

Photographs: Disengagement © Quique Kierszenbaum; Abed Rabbo Aziz © Osama Hatem/
Independent; Gaza City coastline © Marcin Monko; Playground, Abdel Salem al-Shobaki, and
Mousa Sweidan © Heidi Levine; Nabil Shurafa © *Independent*; Nader al-Masri © Associated
Press/Rex Features; Wreckage of Home in Beersheba and IDF artillery unit © Israel Defense
Forces; Hamas rally © ZUMA Press, Inc./Alamy; remaining photos courtesy of the author.

Every effort has been made to trace copyright holders for the use of
material in this book. The publisher apologises for any errors or omissions
herein and would be grateful if they were notified of any corrections that
should be incorporated in future reprints or editions of this book.

Typeset by Hewer Text UK Ltd, Edinburgh
Printed and bound in Great Britain by Clays Ltd, Elcograf S.p.A.

Oneworld Publications
10 Bloomsbury Street
London WC1B 3SR
England

MIX
Paper from
responsible sources
FSC® C018072

PRAISE FOR GAZA

'Donald Macintyre skilfully picks his way through the tangle of accusations that surrounds Gaza's tragedy. This is a lucid, essential guide. Highly recommended to anyone who wants to understand the conflict between Palestinians and Israelis.'

Jeremy Bowen, BBC Middle East editor

'A brilliant and incisive account of this tiny, vibrant, but embattled enclave. With the two million people of Gaza struggling to survive . . . this is a must-read.'

Jon Snow

'Donald Macintyre's *Gaza* is a deeply informed and elegant portrait of this small but profoundly important and misunderstood part of the world. Not only are Gaza's history and politics made compellingly accessible, so too are her sight, sound and smell. In this way Macintyre challenges any notion of Gaza's irrelevance and perhaps more importantly does what few authors writing on Gaza have done: elevates the ordinary in a manner that will endure, helping the reader understand that no matter who we are and where we are from, in Gaza we can recognise ourselves. This book speaks to something greater than Gaza's pain; it speaks to Gaza's soul.'

Sara Roy, Senior Research Scholar,
Center for Middle Eastern Studies, Harvard University

'Donald Macintyre has written a remarkable political panorama about Gaza today. In cool prose he exposes the history of the conflict and the discussion that has surrounded it. Anyone interested in understanding the situation between Hamas, the Palestinian Authority and Israel should look at the conclusion of this book. Anyone who wants to feel a little bit how people live in this narrow strip of land on the Mediterranean coast must read the whole work.'

Shlomo Sand, Professor of History, Tel Aviv University,
and author of *The Invention of the Jewish People*

ABOUT THE AUTHOR

Donald Macintyre was the *Independent*'s Jerusalem bureau chief for eight years between 2004 and 2012, and before that its political editor and chief political commentator. He is a former presenter of BBC Radio 4's *Week in Westminster*. Macintyre won the Next Century Foundation's Peace through Media Award in 2011 and has previously been shortlisted for the Orwell Prize for Journalism and for the Martha Gellhorn Prize for Journalism. He lives in Clapham, south London.

To Ofri

Contents

PART TWO

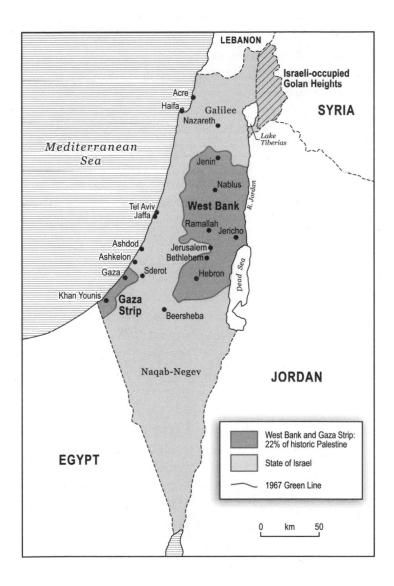

LEBANON

Israeli-occupied
Golan Heights

SYRIA

Acre

Haifa

Galilee

Nazareth

*Mediterranean
Sea*

*Lake
Tiberias*

Jenin

Nablus

Tel Aviv

Jaffa

West Bank

R. Jordan

Ramallah

Jericho

Ashdod

Jerusalem

Ashkelon

Bethlehem

Dead Sea

Gaza

Sderot

Hebron

Khan Younis

**Gaza
Strip**

Beersheba

Naqab-Negev

JORDAN

EGYPT

West Bank and Gaza Strip:
22% of historic Palestine

State of Israel

1967 Green Line

0   km   50

Prologue: Shakespeare in Gaza

L EYLA ABDUL RAHIM HAD COME TO the line in Act IV of *King Lear* where the blinded Gloucester laments, 'As flies to wanton boys are we to th' gods. They kill us for their sport.' Or, rather, the paraphrase offered in the textbook *English for Palestine*: 'We are like flies and the gods are like cruel little boys. They torment us and kill us for fun.' The teacher described children pulling the wings off a fly. 'So the gods torment us for fun, to laugh, to play, okay?' she said, quickly adding: 'This is not related to our religion. It is away from our Islam. Allah doesn't torment us, of course.'

It was tempting to point out from the back of the class that God isn't supposed to do that in other monotheistic religions either. But that would have been an abuse of Mrs Abdul Rahim's generous invitation to sit in on her Grade 12 English class at Bashir al-Rayyes High School for Girls in Gaza City. And the thirty students – preparing for the *tawjihi*, the high school matriculation, for which *King Lear* was a set text – were enjoying themselves. Hands shot up and there were repeated cries of 'Miss, Miss' whenever Mrs Abdul Rahim tested her seventeen-year-old charges, all but one in the standard uniform of pale blue smock, jeans and white headscarf. 'Goneril is now in love with Edmund. He's evil. He's like her exactly. Do you think Goneril respects her husband?' (Chorus of 'no'.)

When Mrs Abdul Rahim ended the lesson, the girls burst spontaneously into applause. After the class, Khulud al-Masharawi said in English that she liked the play because 'Lear began to feel sorry for people other than himself. He thought about people who had no home, or are on their own.'

It took a moment to remember that this classroom tour de force had taken place in an isolated, overcrowded 140-square-mile strip of territory corralled by concrete walls and electronically monitored fences, ruled by an armed and proscribed Islamic faction, and succinctly described in recent memory by Condoleezza Rice as a 'terrorist wasteland'. Gaza, as often, was failing to conform to its stereotype.

I had been brought to the *Lear* class by another English teacher, Jehan al-Okka. It was fair-minded of her, because she harboured doubts about the suitability for Gaza schoolgirls of Shakespeare's tragedies, a sentiment clearly not shared by her colleague. For Jehan, *Lear* was at least an improvement on *Romeo and Juliet*. She had been among a group of Gaza teachers who staged a successful mini-uprising against a decision to include *Romeo and Juliet* in that year's English curriculum for the *tawjihi*. (Despite the schism between Hamas and the Fatah-dominated Palestinian Authority since Hamas's seizure of control in June 2007, the PA continued to supervise the syllabus from its Ramallah base for Gaza as well as the West Bank.) Jehan was convinced that *Romeo and Juliet* was the wrong play at the wrong time. 'It encourages suicide and disobeying parents,' she said. Jehan was also concerned that some of her pupils, upon learning that they were to study the play, had downloaded the film version; more, she thought, for the 'immoral scenes' rather than any educational purpose. She was relaxed about university students studying the play but felt it was unsuitable for impressionable teenagers.

As it happened, *Romeo and Juliet* had been part of the high school syllabus from the years when Gaza had been under Egyptian control and then after the Six Day War and Israeli conquest in 1967. But Jehan, who wasn't in Hamas, saw a 'contradiction' between Islamic culture and 'the things that Shakespeare is trying to convey in his tragedies'. She spoke of the conditions in Gaza: the ten-year Israeli blockade crippling Gaza's economy which, she believed, had led to a rise in crime. 'I'm not saying *King Lear* is encouraging it, but we are trying to reduce violence in our country. And for people who have psychological problems this makes it looks glamorous . . .' When she was teaching *Lear* she said she was careful to warn her pupils: 'this is not in our culture. None of you will do this.'

Despite her doubts, Jehan took pride in the conscientiousness with which she taught the play. And she was popular. Abir, one seventeen-year-old in the science stream class Jehan took for English, gently defied her teacher by saying she wouldn't mind studying *Romeo and Juliet* instead of *Lear*. When we discussed the right age to get married, none of the girls wanted to do so before their twenties, despite the tradition of early marriage prevalent in some sections of Gaza society. But the independent-minded Abir suggested the highest age of all: twenty-eight. Jehan explained that some two-thirds of science stream pupils wanted to be doctors – 'It's a dream,' she said. But Abir wanted to be an engineer. Were there many women engineers in Gaza? 'Yes, many,' the teacher said crisply, 'without jobs. Unemployed.'

Back in the principal's office we returned to the subject of the English set text. 'Why give the students something that is full of misery?' she asked. 'The students, when someone dies – they are all like, "why is he doing this, the writer?" Everyone dies by the end and the lovely Cordelia dies. Some of the students cried when I said Cordelia died. When I studied at university I was old enough to understand the value. For children, when they read something they take the image – killing, suicide, treason. And life in Gaza is bad enough not to increase that misery.'

This was the most challenging of Jehan's points. She was right, for example, that suicide among young Gazans seemed to be on the rise. Are there societies so under pressure that they cannot safely absorb Shakespearean tragedy?

Whatever Jehan's concerns, the prevailing Gaza answer to that question appeared to be no. At Gaza City's al-Mis'hal Cultural Centre, a staged version of *Romeo and Juliet* ran to appreciative audiences for eight nights in early May 2016. The prominent Gaza writer Atef Abu Saif and the director Ali Abu Yassin had set the play in modern Gaza with the star-crossed lovers Yousef and Suha belonging to each of the main rival Palestinian factions Hamas and Fatah, instead of to the Montagues and Capulets. It opened in a café where a clean-shaven Fatah doctor and a bearded Hamas businessman fall into an argument until they are thrown out by the owner. The café owner represented the Gazan everyman, enraged by the split between the two factions that had deformed Palestinian politics since 2007.

But the ending differed from Shakespeare's. Warned by the café owner that Suha's family will never accept Yousef as an in-law, the young man, with the cries of Suha imploring him to stay ringing in his ears, leaves for Egypt through the tunnels to catch a boat for Europe, just like the dozens of Gazans believed to have drowned on a fatal voyage to

Malta in September 2014. Nor did the denouement resolve the split between the two factions, as it had in the original. After years of futile meetings aimed at Fatah–Hamas reconciliation, such a finale would probably be too implausible for an audience of Palestinians now deeply cynical about the prospects of such a desirable outcome.

Nor was this the only Gaza commemoration of Shakespeare's death in the summer of 2016: students at the Nusseirat refugee camp in the middle of the Strip mounted their own video performance of *Lear*. It was advertised outside the Education Ministry's local Cultural Centre by a handsome poster of James Barry's eighteenth-century painting, *King Lear Weeping over the Dead Body of Cordelia*.

True, Cordelia's (very modest) décolletage had been Photoshopped to leave an orange blur in its place. But this was the only concession to the socially conservative sensibilities of Gaza's Hamas rulers. The show was an imaginatively produced series of drawn and photographic tableaux with a voiceover by the high school pupils in faultless English and some entertaining visual effects. Lear's palace was Blenheim, while Regan's home was Buckingham Palace, complete with ceremonial troop of Grenadier Guards representing her visiting father's unwelcome entourage. There were no Arabic subtitles. But as it was condensed into thirty-one minutes with every plot development intact, none of the parents who had loyally turned out for the evening seemed to mind.

First, there were speeches. Dr Kamal Ghunaim, an Islamic University professor and chairman of the Centre's trustees, was convinced that Shakespeare had read the Qur'an and suggested that *Othello* had 'contextualised' the work of the ninth-century Arab poet Deek al-Jinn al-Homsi, who talked about killing his wife after being told to do so by his cousin.

Dr Ghunaim explained that the *Lear* project 'aims to help bridge the gaps between Palestinians and other nations'. Yet before we sat down for the evening, I had asked the Ministry's Head of English whether the British Council had been involved in the event. No, he said sadly. The Ministry's contact with the Council had stopped in 2006, when Hamas was elected. The international political and economic boycott of Hamas was a cultural boycott, too.

Jehan al-Okka, the Bashir al-Rayyes High School Shakespeare sceptic, was thrilled in 2016 to be awarded a place on a US government-backed international six-week Excellence and Achievement Programme for teachers at Bowling Green State University, Ohio, coupled with a visit to Washington, DC. Among the programme's aims was the building of 'lasting relationships that promote mutual understanding and collaboration between the United States and international teachers and students through educational and cultural exchanges'. Except that in an experience wearily familiar to Palestinians in Gaza, Mrs al-Okka was refused by both Israel and Jordan the permits necessary for her to be able to leave.

Maybe she wouldn't have been converted to *Romeo and Juliet* as a high school text. But you couldn't help thinking of the lively insights this spirited and engaging woman would have brought to discussions about teaching English in the Arab world. Amid the convulsions of the Middle East, from Syria to Libya, from Iraq to Yemen – and that of Gaza itself over the last fifteen years – a crushing mid-career disappointment inflicted on a high school teacher unable to improve her skills abroad seems trivial. But it was part of a larger story: Palestinian, Israeli and international, a story of how and why a population of two million at the south-east corner of the Mediterranean became so beleaguered and isolated from the outside world.

PART ONE

1

FROM OTTOMANS TO OSLO, 1917–1995

R EACHED BY A SANDY TRACK THROUGH tall cypresses, the Common-
wealth War Graves Commission cemetery is the most tranquil
spot in the whole of the Gaza Strip. These days its vast lawn and carefully tended beds of geranium and rosemary are a refuge for picnicking
families and those who simply want to meditate quietly in the shade of
the cemetery's oleander and jacaranda trees. But the neat rows of 3,217
graves are also a reminder of Britain's pivotal role in shaping modern
Gaza.

After terrible losses in the French trenches of the First World War,
the new Prime Minister David Lloyd George wanted a quick, high-
profile victory over the Germans' Ottoman allies, the imperial power in
the Middle East for five centuries. What better conquest than Jerusalem?
Following in the footsteps of great leaders of the past – Thutmose III,
the great Egyptian warrior Pharaoh in the fifteenth century BCE;
Saladin, the general who led the Arabs against the crusaders; and
Napoleon – the only route into Palestine was through Gaza. Sir
Archibald Murray established a major camp at Deir el Balah ('Dear old
Bella' to the British Tommies) but twice failed to take the city in the
spring and summer of 1917.

Under Sir Edmund Allenby, who replaced Murray, the imperial
forces broke through the Ottoman lines between Gaza and Beersheba
despite fierce resistance; Allenby's troops marched into Gaza City
unopposed in November 1917. Within a month, Allenby was in

Jerusalem, realising Lloyd George's dream of capturing it by Christmas. Gravestone after gravestone – more than 700 of them inscribed with the anonymous 'A soldier of the Great War: Known unto God' – commemorate the men of the Egyptian Expeditionary Force killed during the three assaults. Eighty-year-old Ibrahim Jaradeh, the gardener awarded the MBE for looking after the cemetery with his family over more than half a century, said the British had always been good to him although, 'of course, my job here made me hate war. These soldiers lost their lives when they were young.' For a man who hated war Jaradeh had seen a lot of it: as well as caring for the graves of thousands who had fallen in the 1917 military campaign for Palestine, he himself had lived through an even more epic turning point for his nation thirty years later.

Five days before Allenby's troops had entered Gaza City, the British government had taken a momentous step, setting in train a process that would eventually culminate in that second war. In a letter to Lord Rothschild, the Foreign Secretary, Lord Balfour wrote: 'His Majesty's Government view with favour the establishment in Palestine of a national home for the Jewish people, and will use their best endeavours to facilitate the achievement of this object, it being clearly understood that nothing shall be done which may prejudice the civil and religious rights of existing non-Jewish communities in Palestine or the rights and political status enjoyed by Jews in any other country.'

While the Balfour declaration was a response to the long-standing Zionist urgings for a national home in Palestine after centuries of anti-Semitism and persecution in Europe and Russia, it was largely dictated by what the British government determined were its strategic interests. It held out the prospect of persuading Jewish leaders abroad to stiffen the resolve of the US, whose hesitant entry into the war was disappointing British expectations. At the same time, the secret Sykes–Picot negotiations with France to carve up the Middle East between the two powers after the war had been unable to reach agreement on Palestine, deciding it should be run by some form of postwar international administration. Following Allenby's decisive victory, the British were now anxious to retain control. As the historian Eugene Rogan put it: 'On the face of it, Lord Balfour was offering Palestine to the Zionist movement. In fact Lloyd George's government was using the Zionist movement to secure Palestine for British rule.'¹

In doing so, however, it cut directly across the promises of independence from foreign rule with which Britain had enticed the Arab leadership to rise up against the Ottomans in the First World War – aspirations which would be further encouraged by US President Woodrow Wilson's dramatic pledge at the 1919 Paris conference of 'an absolutely unmolested opportunity of autonomous development' in the region. It was hardly surprising that the increase in Jewish immigration between the two world wars would meet with stiff resistance, expressed in the Arab riots of 1929 and a full-scale revolt in 1936. Britain, now exercising power in Palestine under a League of Nations mandate, would prove unequal to the task of reconciling the two conflicting aims of providing a 'national home' for the Jews while preserving the rights of its 'non-Jewish' – overwhelmingly Arab – 'communities', who were in the clear majority. Palestine would gradually become enmeshed in a triangle of rising and lethal violence between the Arabs, the Jewish underground and British forces. As David Ben-Gurion, who would become Israel's first Prime Minister, had clear-sightedly remarked after the 1929 riots: 'Politically speaking it is a national movement . . . The Arab must not and cannot be a Zionist. He could never wish the Jews to become a majority. This is the true antagonism between us and the Arabs. We both want to be the majority.'²

By the end of the Second World War the monstrous events which had unfolded in Europe – Hitler's murder of some six million Jews in the Holocaust – immeasurably strengthened the case for a Jewish home in Palestine. Unable to find the basis of a peace agreement, Britain handed the problem to the UN, which in 1947 proposed a Palestine of two states: a Jewish one covering fifty-six per cent of the land and an Arab one on forty-four per cent. Most nations, including the US – after intial hesitation – and the Soviet Union, supported the partition proposal. But Arab leaders, both in Palestine and outside it, flatly rejected it. They saw partition of Palestine as requiring them, after having lived peacefully in earlier centuries with a local Jewish minority, and despite the promises of independence made by the Western powers during and after the First World War, not only to accept on their land, but also on a large part of it become subject to, a

state controlled by immigrants from Europe – albeit including those
fleeing persecution and now survivors of Hitler's genocide. In 1947
the Arabs were still a two-thirds majority in Palestine. Cities like Haifa
and Jaffa, designated as part of the Jewish state by the UN partition
resolution, had large Arab majorities; the Arabs owned ninety-four
per cent of Palestinian land and eighty per cent of its arable
farmland.[3]

In fact a minority of Palestinians did support partition. A heavily
autobiographical novel, *Would They Ever Learn?* by Mustafa Abdel
Shafi, a Palestinian surgeon from an old Gaza family, gives a rare glimpse
of Gaza in the 1940s and early '50s. The life and loves of his hero, a
conscientious and ambitious doctor named Basil, are set against the
turbulent political background of the period. Coming from a family
untainted by anti-Jewish prejudice – his father had been horrified by
the Arab massacre of Jews in Hebron and elsewhere in 1929 – Basil (like
the author and his more famous brother Haidar, in real life) is among
those who had very reluctantly taken the (almost taboo) view that they
should accept the partition resolution. 'The plan is painful and unfair . . .
but we cannot resist it,' Basil says at a family discussion. 'Let's suppose,
for argument's sake, that we had the military power. Would the powers
that be sit hand-bound and watch us frustrate what they had schemed
for so diligently? . . . They would invoke shameful incidents, of which
we are completely innocent, to justify their action. They would remind
the whole world of the atrocities of Auschwitz, Treblinka and Dachau to
justify their determination to create a national home for the Jews in
Palestine. We should follow the common saying "If you cannot beat
them join them." Let's brace up, build our own state and let the future
take care of itself.'[4]

In view of subsequent events, this was far sighted, seen from the
vantage point of a twenty-first century in which Palestinians are struggling for a state on twenty-two per cent of the land, half of what they
were offered in 1947. But if rejection of the partition plan was as
great an error as it is often described in hindsight – an 'Arab mistake as
a whole' as the Palestinian President Mahmoud Abbas, twelve at the
time of the UN resolution, put it in 2011[5] – then the UK's Labour
government had done little to discourage it. Britain was drained militarily and economically by the Second World War, and armed insurrection – terrorism, as the British classified it – by Jewish groups had

hardened public opinion at home against staying in Palestine.* Britain abstained in the General Assembly vote. And having already decided to wind up its Mandate in May 1948, it did not seek to enforce the UN resolution.

On the day the Mandate ended David Ben-Gurion declared Israel an independent state. The first major foreign leader to recognise the fledgling country was US President Harry Truman (the second was Stalin). Truman had ignored the advice of his own State Department, which had been seeking a postponement of Ben-Gurion's declaration in the hope of averting war between the Jews and their Arab neighbours. With a domestic election campaign only six months away, Truman had an eye on Jewish support – which could hardly be other than enthusiastic about the new state of Israel after the horrors of the Holocaust. As when the Americans had voted with the majority at the UN Assembly the previous November, Truman's recognition of the new nation – especially when contrasted with the slowness of Britain – would indelibly reinforce the Israeli view that the US was its most important supporter. Though occasionally complicated by serious disputes, the US–Israel relationship would deepen significantly over the next half-century.

BY NOW GAZA HAD BECOME, LIKE the rest of Palestine, engulfed in what became, for Israel, the War of Independence; and for Palestinians the *nakba*, or catastrophe. The military 'Plan D' evolved by the Hagana, the paramilitary Jewish defence organisation which became the Israel Defense Forces after Israel's birth, was to secure territory allocated to the Jewish state in the UN partition plan, 'as well as settlements outside those areas and corridors leading to them so as to provide a solid and continuous basis for Jewish sovereignty'. A few years later, 'Basil', who, despite his reluctant backing of partition, remains a nationalist to his core, tells a Jewish audience in the American town where he is by then working that 'they planned to occupy as much Arab territory as they

---

* Three examples were the assassination by Lehi of Lord Moyne, the British minister in Cairo, in 1944, the blowing up of the King David Hotel, Jerusalem (where the British administrative headquarters was), by Irgun in 1946, which killed ninety-one Britons, Jews and Arabs, and the hanging of two hostages, British police sergeants, in 1947 when the authorities refused to commute death sentences on two Irgun members. The leader of Irgun at the time, Menachem Begin, and the joint leader of Lehi, Yitzhak Shamir, both later became Prime Minister of Israel.

could, trying to evacuate it of its rightful inhabitants'. Basil goes on to cite 'the notorious massacre of Deir Yassin where scores of innocent unarmed men, women and children were killed in cold blood'. This, he says, was 'aimed at terrorising other Arab villagers, to make them leave their homes . . .'[6]

Whether or not it was the 'aim', the April 1948 massacre at Deir Yassin, a village outside Jerusalem (which was in turn followed by the retaliatory killing of seventy-three Jews in a convoy travelling to the Hadassah Hospital-Hebrew University complex in Jerusalem) did indeed give a 'powerful push to the flight'[7] of Arabs from their homes elsewhere.

In fact there were two wars, or a war of two phases. The first civil or 'ethnic' war between the Jews and Arabs of Palestine lasted from the UN partition resolution in November 1947 until Ben-Gurion's declaration of the state in May 1948. The second, from May 1948, was between the newly founded Israel and the armies of neighbouring Arab states that arrived to support the Palestinians: Jordan, Syria, Iraq and Egypt, the last of which, for obvious geographical reasons, formed a southern front that included Gaza and its surrounding countryside.

According to Uri Avnery, who fought as a commando on the Jewish side in the 1947–8 war and later became a pioneering left-wing peace activist, it was in the second phase that 'a deliberate policy of expelling the Arabs [living in Palestinian towns and villages] became an [Israeli] war aim on its own'.[8] As Avnery also pointed out, no Jews remained in the land the Arabs conquered[9] – like the Jewish quarter of Jerusalem's Old City. But that hardly compared with over 700,000 Arabs driven by the Jewish advances from their homes into permanent exile, internal or external, or with hundreds of Palestinian villages which (unlike the handful of Jewish neighbourhoods conquered by the Arabs but recovered twenty years later after the Six Day War) were subsequently destroyed.

Refugees poured into Gaza not just from the surrounding villages but from major towns like Jaffa, Ashdod, Majdal (now Ashkelon, where Mustafa Abdel Shafi had been a GP) and Beersheba as they fell to the Israeli forces. The Gaza cemetery gardener Ibrahim Jaradeh's family fled Beersheba, which was repeatedly hit by strafing and bombing by the Israeli air force on the nights of 19 and 20 October 1948. Israeli ground troops moved into the town on 21 October, in a conquest 'accompanied by the execution of a handful of Egyptian POWs and wholesale looting by individuals and military units'.[10] Aged eleven at the time, Jaradeh remembered the journey by camel to Hebron where they were eventually given temporary housing through the winter of 1948. 'So it wasn't only the immigration, God also made it harder with the cold and snow, we used to sleep next to each other, holding the [younger] kids to make them feel warm with the very light blankets.' Then the family, plus two camels, and, said Jaradeh, a monkey, made for Gaza. His younger brother travelled in one of the camel's saddle bags. Sixty-nine years later he told his British visitor that Ethel Mannin's *The Road to Beersheba* was an authentic account of how 'Israel stole our land', but then added quietly: 'God willing things will be for the better, we ask God for peace for the Jews and for the Arabs.'

Many refugees, including Jaradeh's family (and indeed Gamal Abdel Nasser, who served as an Egyptian officer in the Gaza district during the war), blamed Egyptian failures for the loss of territory. Attia Hijazi was twenty-two and living in Deir Sneid, only half a kilometre from the Gaza district kibbutz of Yad Mordechai. His father was the village *mukhtar* (local leader). 'We had good relations with them [the Jews] before the war. They were Palestinian Jews and immigrants. My father regularly visited the Jews' *mukhtar*. We were connected by the common interest of agriculture.'

When the war started, the residents were determined to prevent the village from being captured. But, said Hijazi, 'when the Egyptian army came during the war they told our fighters they could take a rest, saying, "We'll do it."' The Egyptians occupied Yad Mordechai after a five-day battle in May during which the local kibbutzniks, aided by a Hagana unit, had held out under heavy Egyptian bombardment, allowing Israeli forces time to halt the Egyptian army's northern push. Hijazi said that when the Egyptians started to fall back to Deir Sneid, 'the Jews attacked them, and we understood that the Egyptian army was covering its withdrawal, not fighting. By October, they left us all with no protection whatever and the Jews bombarded the place. My brother was injured. When we saw the Egyptian flag coming down at Yad Mordechai [in November], we left for Beit Lahiya [in Gaza].'[11]

By the winter 13,500 refugees were sheltered in a former British Army camp at Bureij, south of Gaza City. 'They had staked out little cubicles for themselves using rags or flattened gasoline tins. Everyone was very dirty and cold. In one cubicle we saw a group of ten people

ranging in age from infancy to about seventy looking at an old woman
on the floor who had just died . . .'[12]

By then Basil/Abdel Shafi had become the only doctor at a clinic
servicing refugees in Khan Yunis and agitating against the 'unacceptable' insanitary conditions in the camp, where, according to an
International Committee of the Red Cross (ICRC) estimate, children
were dying at the rate of around ten a day.

The war ended with an armistice signed by Israel and Egypt in
February 1949, followed by similar agreements with Syria and Jordan in
the succeeding months. These divided what had been Palestine into
three separate parts: first the new state of Israel, of course; second, a
landlocked 5,640-square-kilometre territory under Jordanian control
which contained East Jerusalem (including the Old City) and a sector
that became known as (and still is) the West Bank (of the Jordan river);
and, finally, the 'Gaza Strip', which came under Egyptian control and
was cut off from the Jordanian-run East Jerusalem and the West Bank
by what was now southern Israel. Israel had been offered fifty-six per
cent of Palestine under the UN partition plan. It now held seventy-eight
per cent; the rest was made up of Gaza, East Jerusalem and the West
Bank.

The armistice brought little relief for the now 200,000 refugees in
Gaza, numerically overwhelming the existing population. (There were
up to 750,000 Palestinian refugees in all from what was now Israel:
280,000 in the West Bank, and most of the rest in Syria, Jordan and
Lebanon.) A new body, the UN Refugee and Works Agency (UNRWA),
had taken over from Quakers and others who had been caring for them
voluntarily. A year later Sir Ronald Storrs, who had been Britain's first
military governor, launched a series of appeals for clothing to be donated
to UNRWA for refugees who had 'fled their homes of more than 1,000
years', quoting a UN official at one camp describing 'children by the
hundred, most of them half naked – shoeless, shivering . . .'[13]

Uri Avnery always believed the moment that determined the subsequent history of the conflict was not so much the expulsion and flight of
the refugees itself; rather, that 'the real decision was taken after the war:
not to allow the 750,000 Arab refugees to return to their homes'. The
decision was ruthlessly enforced. Mustafa Abdel Shafi's autobiographical novel describes his own indelible memory of carrying out post-
mortems of impoverished refugees shot dead by Israeli forces on the

new armistice line as they tried to get back to the villages where 'they had earned their living by hard work', if only to retrieve a few belongings: 'There was a dead man, riddled with bullets and his intestines were exposed, for the first time Basil saw maggots in action; it was a ghastly scene . . . On the way back he wondered when the massacre of these innocent, ignorant and unarmed people was going to stop.'[14]

The plight of many of Gaza's non-refugees was hardly better. The Gaza Strip was now under Egyptian control, but the armistice lines made it far narrower than the old Gaza district under the British Mandate; forty-one kilometres long and a mere twelve at its widest point. As a result peasant farmers whose land lay beyond the armistice line, and therefore in Israel, simply lost their livelihoods. Nor were they afforded even the rudimentary provision for refugees; their woefully undernourished children were sent begging, and some of the poorest were reduced to selling the doors and windows of their houses and even timber from the roofs. D. C. Stephen, the district officer of UNRWA, which became and still is to this day responsible for the education and welfare of the refugees, pointed out that the native Gazans had previously 'made a fair livelihood according to standards generally accepted in the Middle East'. 'They are of a proud race and it is as degrading for them as it would be for us to be in their present position . . . The setting of the present boundary by the "Powers that Be" means that the people of Gaza have completely lost their only means of existence.'[15]

Over the following eighteen years, Gaza – now under Egypt's control – played a pivotal part in the hostilities between Israel and its Arab neighbours, which culminated in all-out war in 1967. The 1955 Gaza Raid, authorised by then Defense Minister David Ben-Gurion after Palestinian infiltrators killed an Israeli cyclist, and led by twenty-seven-year-old paratroop officer Ariel Sharon, killed thirty-seven Egyptian soldiers at a cost of eight IDF lives. It almost certainly put paid to a secret dialogue between Egypt's Gamal Abdel Nasser and Israel's dovish Prime Minister Moshe Sharett, which might have dented the unremitting hostility of Arab countries towards the eight-year-old Israeli state.[16] Instead, after the raid Nasser, who had hitherto restrained Palestinian *fedayeen* – nationalist volunteer militants mostly from refugee families – allowed them to carry out commando raids across the Gaza border.[17]

Ben-Gurion, who soon became Prime Minister again, in turn adopted a much more confrontational policy towards Egypt. The secret partnership between the United Kingdom, France and Israel to confront Nasser after he decided to nationalise the Suez Canal in July 1956 ended in disaster for the first two governments, causing head-on confrontation with US President Eisenhower and leaving the Canal in the hands of Nasser, whose prestige in the region greatly increased in the wake of the Anglo–French fiasco. But, at least in the short term, it was a military triumph for Israel, which overran both Gaza and the Sinai Desert in Egypt. Although Ben-Gurion too was forced to bow to US pressure, in his case to withdraw from both Gaza and the Sinai, and he did not succeed in overthrowing Nasser as he wanted, nevertheless the Israeli military destroyed the main *fedayeen* bases in Gaza during its four-month occupation of the Strip.[18] And he secured a US guarantee that Egypt would allow free passage for ships bringing Iranian oil for Israel through the Straits of Tiran.

In the following decade, which passed without military conflict between Egypt and Israel, Nasser moved to bring Palestinian nationalism under the wing of the Arab states, and Egypt in particular. He took the lead in the Arab League's formation in 1964 of the Palestinian Liberation Organization (PLO) with its military arm, the Palestinian Liberation Army; their stated aims were the 'restoration of the Palestinian homeland' – including the return of the 1948 refugees to their original homes in what was now Israel. In practice the PLA came under the strict control of its Egyptian, Iraqi and Syria sponsor governments.[19] Nasser was also seeking to curb the activities of the more militant and independent Fatah.[20]

On 22 May 1967 Nasser decided to close the Straits of Tiran to Israeli shipping. This was a dangerously provocative step, though it is unlikely Nasser intended it to lead to war. The Six Day War, which did indeed break out a fortnight later, on 4 June, was arguably the only Arab–Israeli war that 'neither side wanted'.[21] Nasser was under mounting Arab pressure to show solidarity with Egypt's ally Syria, whose border with Israel was the focus of an escalating series of incidents culminating in an aerial battle in which six Syrian MIGs were shot down in April. The historian Avi Shlaim has persuasively depicted Nasser as having embarked 'on an exercise in brinkmanship that was to carry him over the brink', while also rejecting a widespread Arab view that Israel deliberately provoked the war to expand its territory.[22] The huge expansion that did indeed follow Israel's stunning military victory against the forces of Egypt, Jordan and Syria, was a consequence rather than a specific war aim.

This did not make it any less traumatic for the Palestinians in the conquered territory. Israel now occupied all the land that since the 1949 armistice had been controlled by Jordan (the West Bank and East Jerusalem, including its holy sites) and by Egypt (Gaza).* By 1967, the tents and makeshift huts in the still crowded and impoverished refugee camps set up in 1948 had largely been replaced by UNRWA with more solid housing. But the somewhat better conditions added to the bleak sense of permanent displacement among refugees, now reinforced by the catastrophic defeat of the Arab states. For the refugees it meant being controlled by the very forces who had driven them from their homes – sometimes on land that, painfully, they could still see from inside the Strip – nineteen years earlier.

Mohammed Kardash, who was thirty-three and living in Jabalya at the time, remembered with disgust forty years later the bombastic claims of Ahmed Said, the Egyptians' propagandist-in-chief, who declared Israeli warplanes were 'falling like flies', when in fact Egypt's air force was destroyed on the first day of the June war. 'We huddled round the radio all the time to listen to him. I believed what he was saying and so did everyone else. He said, "I congratulate the fish of the Mediterranean because they will eat the flesh of Jews."' Still furious at the deception, Kardash added: 'There is a stain of shame in the way he was talking.'

After the war, Kardash, who had originally been brought to Gaza in a Turkish boat by his parents fleeing from his native Jaffa in 1948, would now be a refugee again, this time in Jordan, part of a limited and ill-starred scheme by then Israeli Prime Minister Levi Eshkol to evacuate (with some money) refugees from Gaza after the 1967 war. (In fact, Kardash had hidden two rifles for his brother who had been in the Palestine Liberation Army. After what he said was a beating, 'the [Israeli] army gave me a choice,' he says, 'to go to prison or to leave Gaza'. He never revealed the whereabouts of the rifles.)[23]

---

* The defeat of Syria also left Israel controlling the Golan Heights, which, like the West Bank, East Jerusalem and Gaza, it still occupies fifty years later, and the Sinai Peninsula, which Israel ceded back to Egypt under the Begin–Sadat Peace Treaty of 1979.

It was after the Six Day War that Fatah, the secular resistance organisation founded by Yasser Arafat ten years earlier, began its ascendancy in the Palestinian liberation movement. In 1969 it joined and immediately dominated the PLO. Arafat, whose chequered *keffiyeh* and battledress would become the global symbol of Palestinian struggle, had been born in Cairo to Palestinian parents. He had studied in the Egyptian capital, fought in the 1948 war and founded Fatah in the early fifties in Kuwait with a group including two Gaza-based refugees, both to become prominent PLO leaders.*

The militancy repressed by the occupation of 1956 resumed in Gaza after the Six Day War. Within a few months of the war ending, the military occupying authorities began to allow Palestinians out through Erez, the Strip's northern crossing, to work in Israel. This would begin what was to be for three decades a major source of income for tens of thousands of Gaza's families, albeit one entirely dependent on Israeli goodwill and the demand for cheap labour. As a boy growing up in the poor and overcrowded Shaboura district of the Rafah refugee camp, Fathi Sabbah, who would later become an activist and later still a leading journalist, remembered armed militants throwing grenades at Israeli buses transporting the workers, as well as ambushing soldiers in the camps' narrow alleys and attacking military bases. 'There was a saying that the Palestinian militants were ruling Gaza at night and the Israeli army in the daytime,' he recalled.[24]

In 1971 Ariel Sharon – by now in charge of the IDF's Southern Command – moved large forces into the refugee camps in a remorseless operation to crush the nascent resistance. Hundreds of Palestinians were killed in Gaza in 1971–2 and thousands more detained and sometimes deported. His troops conducted house-to-house searches under curfew, bulldozed thousands of houses to create buffer zones and widen the roads to allow armoured vehicles easier movement through the camps.[25] In Shaboura, Sabbah recalled, 'the only street that was paved with asphalt was for security reasons, not for helping people. It wasn't easy for their vehicles to withdraw. So they destroyed hundreds of houses and they deported people from Shaboura to the Canada and Brazil camps.' Those two camps – named after the UN national

---

* These were Khalil Ibrahim al-Wazir and Salah Khalaf, better known by their respective *noms de guerre* Abu Jihad and Abu Iyad.

contingents that briefly patrolled the border immediately after the 1956 Sinai campaign – were located on either side of what would much later – in 1982 – become a new border, cutting Rafah in two and leaving thousands of Palestinians permanently stranded on the Egyptian side. Now in 1971 – after the mass exodus of 1948 and further displacements in 1967 – refugees were on the move again.

Sharon's draconian tactics were successful. Elsewhere in the region, the following decade was turbulent: the 'Black September' conflict between the PLO and Jordan, the massacre of athletes at the Munich Olympics in 1972, the 1973 Yom Kippur War, Anwar Sadat's decision to address the Knesset in Jerusalem in 1977, the Israel–Egypt peace agreement in 1979 and Sadat's subsequent assassination in 1981. But Gaza was relatively calm. Defence Minister Moshe Dayan's 'invisible' occupation policy of trying to ensure 'that areas of friction between the two peoples are minimal' was intended to dilute Palestinian nationalism; but it had financial benefits. The opening of the borders to daily migrant workers was one; another was allowing farmers and manufacturers to trade with Israeli companies, though with restrictions to ensure their exports did not adversely compete with Israeli business (while no such restrictions applied to imports from Israel to Gaza). Exports abroad – beyond Israel and the West Bank – were invariably handled by Israeli agents. But when a generation later exports of goods and labour were barred and unemployment shot up above forty per cent, and above sixty per cent for youth, older Palestinian civilians often looked back on the 1970s as – paradoxically – something of a silver age.

MUNIR DWEIK STARTED WORK IN ISRAEL at the age of fifteen. He had grown up in a desperately poor family of refugees in the Jabalya camp. His parents had been peasant farmers from Batani al-Gharbi, east of Ashdod, one of the villages targeted – and in most cases mortared – by incoming Israeli troops in May 1948 during the IDF's Operation Lightning, under which the Givati Brigade was ordered to deny 'the enemy a base for their future operations . . . by creating general panic'.[26] In a circuitous flight typical of the times, the Dweik family fled to Gaza through neighbouring villages, moving on as each also fell. With his father unable to find regular work, his steadfast and resourceful mother decided that *tourmos* – lupin beans, a regional staple and universally popular in Gaza – could provide a living for the family.

Four decades later, now a fifty-two-year-old taxi driver, Dweik recalled every detail of the process. First his mother bought a sack of lupin beans and boiled them in a large saucepan; then she decanted the beans into half a dozen separate earthenware pots filled with sugary water to counter their natural bitterness. She changed the water three times a day, over several days, until they tasted good enough to eat. At 8 a.m., Dweik and his father would carry them in sacks 2.5 kilometres from the refugee camp to Beit Lahiya to sell, shouting 'tourmos, tourmos' when they arrived; if they could find a wedding, they might sell out by noon; if not they stayed into the afternoon. Dweik remembered the journeys back to Jabalya in summer on the scorching sand. His father had plastic shoes but he had none; sometimes to cool his feet he would sit on the ground and put his legs in the air. 'It was boiling. Sometimes I was making a pee, and then put my feet in the pee to cool them, after that I was running, running to find some shade and wait for my father.'

A school friend suggested Dweik join him working as a chicken plucker and cleaner for a shopkeeper in Tel Aviv during the summer holidays. The boys took the bus through Erez early in the morning from Monday to Thursday, earning about 150 shekels a week. When he was sixteen, Dweik decided to work in Israel full-time; his mother resisted strongly because she wanted him to stay at school and complete his education, despite the parlous state of the family finances. 'This is your future, you should continue studying and learning – maybe you could become a teacher or a doctor,' his mother told him. Remembering his mother's warmth and selflessness, Dweik put his hands over his face to cover his tears.

From 1981 until restrictions were imposed on Palestinian workers in Israel during the 1990–91 Gulf War, Dweik worked full-time in Israel. As he improved his skills and became fluent in Hebrew, he worked for several Jewish employers, each of whom successively poached him with higher pay, till he was earning around 450 shekels a week. Dweik remembered nearly all his employers with affection.

By now the right-wing Likud government elected in 1977 and led by Menachem Begin had begun to expand Jewish settlements in occupied territory. Like Palestinian refugee camps, settlements are the object of a frequent popular misconception. The camps now consist not of tents but residential buildings, even if usually ramshackle and heavily over-crowded, set along dusty narrow alleys. Similarly, settlements are not normally the remote, hastily assembled barbed wire-protected hilltop clusters of caravans the word conjures in the foreign imagination. Such outposts – many illegal even in Israeli law – have always existed, and usually as an embryonic settlement or the expansion of an existing one. But most settlements proper, essentially colonies in occupied territory, would in time become well-planned communities, often close to Palestinian villages or towns, and typically comprised red-roofed villas, often with shops, synagogues and leisure centres, making ample use of local water and land for agriculture and domestic purposes. The rural ones were and still are normally protected from the Palestinians (to whom they were such a daily affront) by their own armed security details, and by IDF troops stationed in the vicinity. Not only did the Palestinians see their land, including pastures and olive groves, swallowed up by the settlements and their surrounding military security zones, but they themselves, unlike the settlers, who enjoyed normal civil rights as Israeli citizens, were subject to the Israeli military justice system. The biggest settlements, those bordering the 1949–67 'green line', like, say, Maale Adumim, close to Jerusalem, or Ariel, a great residential finger stretching through the West Bank from east to west, became essentially dormitory cities, many of whose breadwinners would work in Israel itself.

The settlement building in Gaza and the West Bank had started, albeit falteringly, after the Six Day War under a Labour government, despite the written opinion of the Israeli Foreign Ministry's own legal adviser, submitted in secret to ministers, that it contravened international law, especially the Fourth Geneva convention, for a country to transfer civilians to occupied territory. That might be less significant had the lawyer not been Theodor Meron, who rose to become one of the world's most eminent international jurists and President of the International Criminal Tribunal for the former Yugoslavia. A Holocaust survivor, Meron has never recanted, and in 2007 confirmed that this was still his opinion.[27] Yet despite that legal view, widely shared by most Western governments, settlements steadily multiplied during the seventies in the West Bank and Gaza – where the most rapid growth would take place in the eighties. And that in turn convinced many Palestinians that Israel felt no real international pressure to end the occupation.

For this and other reasons, the relative calm in Gaza in the early 1970s could not last indefinitely. The Palestinian sense of abandonment increased with the 1979 Egypt–Israel Treaty; Sadat effectively subordinated the Palestinian cause to Egypt's own interests and Begin had little intention of implementing even the severely limited provisions for Palestinian autonomy contained in the treaty terms. At the same time, the factions were beginning to stir again. Fathi Sabbah recalled that when he joined the Popular Front for the Liberation of Palestine (PFLP), a smaller leftist faction within the PLO, in 1981 as a nineteen-year-old, he was part of a consciousness-raising group. 'Our main duty was to read about what happened in the *nakba* ... then we make a presentation to the group about it.' The group then passed on what they had learned to high school students and others. The PFLP was rooted in the left and, unlike the Communist Party, had not rejected armed struggle. Its members studied Marx, Engels, Maxim Gorky, Che Guevara. They idolised Ghassan Kanafani, a PFLP official and among the greatest of Palestinian twentieth-century writers, assassinated by Israel in 1972 at the age of thirty-six. The PFLP also ran social programmes, including food donations, house repairs and street cleaning.

There were repeated clashes during the 1980s between students and others against Israeli soldiers. In 1986 Yitzhak Rabin as Defense Minister revived long-dormant emergency administrative detention regulations used by the British in the 1930s. These allowed detention without charge (still in force today), under which thousands of Palestinians were gaoled.

In December an Israeli truck plunged into a line of vehicles in Jabalya, killing four Palestinians, a spark that ignited huge protests across the Strip. It was an accident, but was swiftly rumoured to be deliberate retaliation for the killing of a settler.

The mass uprising – the First Intifada – started, and to a large extent continued, as a wave of spontaneous and fearless throwing of stones and improvised firebombs at Israeli targets, led by the *shabab*, unarmed young men. While a local leadership later emerged to organise the protests, and diversify them into strikes, boycotts and mass demonstrations, the Intifada did not lose its popular character. A first-hand observer recalled a typical incident:

> It was astonishing to see young and old women coming out of houses
> to join the men in street protests. On one occasion from inside Shifa
> hospital in Gaza city, I watched a crowd of young men who were

pelting an Israeli army unit with stones. The soldiers were trying to get inside to arrest some of the Palestinians who had been injured in clashes earlier in the morning. Girls and women had formed a human chain to keep the *shabab* at the front line, the faces of the young men masked by *keffiyehs*, supplied with small rocks and pieces of jagged masonry. As tear-gas was fired into the hospital, older women provided an onion to ease the stinging pain.[28]

A rumour persisted that Rabin, early in the Intifada, declared that Israeli forces should 'break the bones' of Palestinian participants. Rabin denied it, but the Israeli military counter-measures were certainly harsh: shootings, arrests, deportations, assassinations,* tear gas, daily curfews, school and university closures. Television footage of an army firing at stone-throwing teenagers or beating women and children was not only bad for Israel's image but helped to propel Palestinian demands for independence and an end to the occupation into the international spotlight. In one form or another, the Intifada lasted until 1991. Among much else, the factions tried to halt the flow of Palestinian workers to their jobs in Israel, which they saw as undermining the resistance. In 1989 Israel issued magnetic cards without which Palestinians would not be allowed out to work; activist Fathi Sabbah remembered the PFLP confiscating, sometimes by force, between 20,000 and 30,000 such cards from their owners. But it was hard to withstand the tide of economic necessity. Munir Dweik, for his part, would remember that, like tens of thousands of other Gazans, he would simply go and get another from the Israeli military authorities, lying low in Tel Aviv for a night or two if the card-collecting campaign was particularly vigorous.

It was early in the Intifada that Hamas emerged as another force in Palestinian politics. It was a descendant of the Muslim Brotherhood, founded in Egypt in 1928 as a religious, educational and charitable institution that was also opposed to British imperial rule. More directly it was an offspring of the Mujamma, or Islamic Centre, formed in 1973 by Brotherhood adherents led by the quadriplegic and charismatic Sheikh Ahmed Yassin, and including several future Hamas leaders like Mahmoud Zahar and Abdel Aziz Rantissi. The movement did not

---

* Including that, in Tunis, of Arafat's long-time comrade Abu Jihad. He was shot by Israeli agents in front of his wife and children.

originally espouse violent insurrection in Israel. Indeed, Islamic Jihad was formed in 1981 as a breakaway precisely because of its fellow Islamists' refusal to do so. The Mujamma's functions lay mainly in Islamic social, charitable and educational work. The Israeli authorities gave it considerable leeway as a counterweight to the nationalist PLO, which the Mujamma's leaders opposed, as they increasingly opposed other secular organisations. In 1980, the Mujamma's followers, for example, attacked the offices of a vital civil organisation, the Palestinian Red Crescent Society, an equivalent of the Red Cross, which had been formed by Haidar Abdel Shafi, the brother of Mustafa, a widely respected secular nationalist and leftist. Abdel Shafi's close friend and ally, the psychiatrist Eyad Sarraj (who later founded the Gaza Community Mental Health Programme), recalled that Islamists advanced on the Red Crescent offices: 'thousands of people with beards' shouting slogans like 'Liberation of Afghanistan', while nearby there was 'an Israeli military jeep which did not interfere'. Sarraj later saw Brigadier Itzhak Segev, the Israeli military governor in Gaza, and told him, 'You are playing with fire, this could really come back to you in a violent way.' He said that Segev had assured him, 'Don't worry. We know how to handle things. Our enemy today is the PLO.'[29]

Even in 1988, when the recently formed Hamas was participating in the Intifada – though from outside the uprising's joint leadership – it remained, as its Islamist forebears had been, a point of contact for Israeli politicians deeply hostile to the PLO. On the one hand, Hamas indicated that it would consider a long-term truce in return for Israel's withdrawal from the territory it occupied in 1967, a proposal that Israel rejected. On the other, in the summer of 1988 it issued its notoriously anti-Semitic charter, which also defined the whole of mandatory Palestine – including what was now Israel – as sacred Muslim territory. In 1989, in one of its first militant operations, it captured and murdered two Israeli soldiers; Israel arrested 300 of its leaders, including Yassin and Zahar, broke off all contact and made it an offence to be a member of Hamas.

In August 1988, however, the PLO,* from what it saw as a position of relative strength because of the successes of the Intifada, formally

---

* The formal decision was taken by the 'legislative' arm of the PLO, the Palestinian National Council.

accepted the idea of a permanent two-state solution: a Palestinian state based on Gaza, the West Bank and East Jerusalem living side by side in peace with Israel. Arafat publicly recognised Israel, renounced terrorism and endorsed a peace settlement based on the post-Six Day War UN Resolution 242, which called for Israeli withdrawal from the Occupied Territories. Though taken for granted in retrospect, this was in fact a historic compromise; the Palestinian leadership was abandoning its claim to the whole of historic Palestine, now accepting the notion of a state on twenty-two per cent of its land (and half of what they had been offered in 1947) with Israel occupying the rest on borders that the PLO was ready to recognise. The PLO thus met the conditions set for it by the US, which eventually agreed to contact with it. The breakthrough, as it initially seemed to be, brought real hope of a solution. In Gaza, 'people celebrated by dancing in the streets, defying curfew (and thereby risking their lives) as soldiers stood at a distance, watching in stunned disbelief'.[30]

Although it took another three years of tortuous diplomatic negotiations, these events eventually led to a US-brokered international peace conference in Madrid. Israel's far-right Prime Minister Yitzhak Shamir agreed to attend only when faced with a clear US threat by President George Bush (Sr) to cancel $10bn in loan guarantees to the Israeli government. Bush's threat was unusual for a US President. Although his predecessor Ronald Reagan had faced severe differences with Israel over the 1982 invasion of Lebanon, his policy had mainly been to strengthen an already close relationship by advancing loan guarantees and granting an annual $3bn in military assistance, which would become permanent. There would be other reasons in later years but one was strategic – the view summed up by Alexander Haig's remark in the early 1980s that 'Israel is the largest American aircraft carrier in the world that cannot be sunk, does not carry even one American soldier, and is located in a critical region for American national security'.[31] Since the early seventies, it had understandably been to the US that Israel had looked for mediation with its Arab neighbours; but Bush was now flexing his muscles as a mediator.

At the Madrid Conference, Shamir had no intention of agreeing to a Palestinian state because he was deeply committed to Jewish settlement in the Occupied Territories – including Gaza – and the idea of Greater Israel stretching from the Jordan to the Mediterranean. Cleaving, like the Israeli right, to its claim of the whole of mandatory Palestine, Hamas opposed Madrid, but wholly failed to rally support in Gaza against Palestinian participation in a summit that appeared to offer the first real chance of an Arab–Israeli peace. The summit went ahead, though Arafat was absent. Shamir had refused to negotiate with the 'terrorist' PLO leader.

The upshot of Arafat's absence was to thrust into the international limelight Gaza's Haidar Abdel Shafi, whose opening speech to the conference was the most eloquent, forward-looking and peace-seeking presentation of the Palestinian case ever given. In one passage of his speech the imposing seventy-year-old doctor said: 'In the name of the Palestinian people, we wish to directly address the Israeli people, with whom we have had a prolonged exchange of pain; let us share hope instead. We are willing to live side by side on the land and the promise of the future. Sharing, however, requires two partners willing to share as equals ... Your security and ours are mutually dependent, as inter-twined as the fears and nightmares of our children.'[32]

To the great dismay of Shamir, the Americans now insisted on detailed negotiations between both sides in Washington, with the Palestinian delegation led by Abdel Shafi in the opening stages. The on-off talks in Washington proved to be extremely tough, even after the 1992 Israeli election, which brought Labour's Yitzhak Rabin to power on a mandate for peace talks with the Palestinians.

In December a Hamas operative abducted an Israeli border police-man, demanding the release of Ahmed Yassin, the organisation's founder and 'spiritual leader', as the price of the policeman's return. Israel refused; the policeman's body was found several days later. Rabin's reprisal was to deport 415 Hamas activists to a makeshift encampment in southern Lebanon. The talks broke up for the eighth and penultimate time when the Arab delegations, including the Palestinians, walked out. When the talks resumed, the going was still tough. Bill Clinton, newly elected as US President, was seen by the Palestinians – not unjustly – as being more favourable to Israel than his predecessor.[33]

It was now that a back channel opened up between Arafat and the Israeli government, courtesy of Norway. Rabin's decision to sanction direct, though secret, talks in Oslo with the PLO was a major reversal of previous Israeli policy. It was also a time when Arafat had been damaged by his ill-considered support of Saddam Hussein after Iraq's 1990 invasion of Kuwait, the PLO was running badly short of funds, and – according to his highly critical biographer Said Aburish – the PLO leader was determined that he rather than the Washington negotiators should be the architect of any peace accord. Otherwise, he feared, 'despite all the evidence to the contrary', Palestinian negotiators in Washington would 'wrest the leadership from him and the Tunis PLO'.

The resulting Oslo Accord prescribed that Israeli forces withdraw initially from Gaza (except the thousands of troops to protect the settlers), Jericho and other Palestinian cities, while maintaining control of sixty per cent of the West Bank. It envisaged a transitional Palestinian Authority running services like education, health and welfare, pending talks on a final agreement which would begin within two years and be completed in five.

As the first ever agreement between Israelis and Palestinians, it was historic. But how bankable was it? The terms did not commit Israel to a Palestinian state, even after the specified five years had elapsed; they did not define how much of the West Bank Israel would eventually with-draw from; they deferred the difficult issues of the return of 1948 refugees and Jerusalem, the eastern, Arab, part of which the Palestinians wanted as their capital; they did not tackle the fate of 10,000 Palestinian prisoners. Again and again the Palestinian and other Arab leaders had been berated, and not only by Israel, for their rejectionism. After the Six Day War, the Arab League's Khartoum summit had issued its famous three 'nos' to recognition, negotiation or peace with Israel.[34] Despite Israel's own record of rejecting or avoiding diplomatic solutions to the conflict, Israeli Foreign Minister Abba Eban's aphorism that the Palestinians 'never missed an opportunity to miss an opportunity' had resonated down the years. Yet was it possible that at Oslo Arafat, rather than demanding too much, had actually accepted too little? The danger was that by conferring a measure of autonomy in the Occupied Territories without the promise of a state, Israel was transferring to the Palestinian leadership responsibility without power. At the very least it would need an unstoppable momentum to fulfil Haidar Abdel Shafi's dream of 'two partners sharing as equals'.

The original 'Declaration of Principles' was signed at the famous ceremony where Rabin and Arafat shook hands in Washington on 13 September 1993. Among much of the Palestinian public, including those in Gaza, the initial reaction was, alongside wariness, relief, celebration and hope that a lasting peace might at long last be on the way. This was reinforced by the huge international profile given to the ceremony on the White House lawn; the ferocious opposition of an Israeli right wing, led by two future Israeli Prime Ministers, Benjamin Netanyahu and Ariel Sharon, to a deal it saw as paving the way for the abandonment of 'Greater Israel' and the establishment of a Palestinian state; Arafat's extravagant spin on the accords;[35] and the genuinely historic mutual recognition embedded in the agreement. (Even if the Palestinians were recognising Israel as a state while Israel was merely recognising the PLO as the 'representative' of the Palestinian people.) Among Palestinian opponents was Hamas, which, in a mirror image of the right-wing opposition in Israel, charged that Arab claims to all of Palestine were being abandoned. Arafat sent a Fatah emissary, Jibril Rajoub, to the Hamas leaders still exiled in Lebanon, in the hope of some welcome for Oslo, however lukewarm. The overture was swiftly rebuffed.[36]

There were also objections from Palestinians who had nothing to do with Hamas fundamentalism; indeed, some of those critics had advocated co-existence and two states for longer than Arafat. The official negotiating team (Feisal Husseini,* Hanan Ashrawi† and Haidar Abdel Shafi) had been completely unaware of the PLO's separate, secret track. They were all committed to reaching a deal, which they had been pursuing zealously in Washington. But that also gave them an exceptional insight into the flaws of the Oslo agreements. As Abdel Shafi told Arafat at a heated meeting in Tunis, when the negotiators were shown the initial 'declaration of principles' before the signing ceremony, it would allow Israel to go on expanding Jewish settlements in occupied territory in the transitional period. As well as being a constant goad to Palestinians who lived next to them, such expansion would pose a continued threat to the final partition of land between Israel and the Palestinians. When they confronted Arafat in Tunis, the Washington negotiators were 'subjected to their leader's screams of "we're broke, we couldn't

---

* A pragmatic and widely respected leading Jerusalemite, advocate of co-existence with Israel, and Palestinian nationalist, one of the first to begin exploratory talks with Israel. Once considered a possible successor to Yasser Arafat, he died in 2001.

† A Christian Palestinian from Ramallah who rose to prominence as the articulate spokesman for the Palestinian delegation at Madrid. She wrote Haidar Abdel Shafi's speech to the conference. Later head of the PLO's Cultural Department.

continue." [37] The three leading negotiators resigned; Ashrawi would later say she was sure they could have eventually secured better terms in Washington. [38]

The deeply disappointed Abdel Shafi returned to Gaza, where he criticised the agreement in measured terms while making clear that he would not agitate against it or condone violence in response. [39] Out of loyalty Husseini and Ashrawi later rescinded their resignations and the Israeli withdrawals from Gaza and Jericho happened as envisaged. Arafat made a triumphant return through the Egyptian border to Gaza, with large welcoming crowds lining the roads. Palestinian police were deployed in Gaza and Jericho, and progressively in the main West Bank cities. The Palestinian Authority was set up. In 1995, Rabin was subjected to virulent personal abuse by his right-wing opponents; Likud's Benjamin Netanyahu appeared at rallies during which protesters brandished posters depicting Rabin as a Nazi. Then, on 4 November 1995, the Prime Minister was assassinated by an extreme right-wing Israeli fanatic, Yigal Amir, at a rally in Tel Aviv in support of the agreements.

Whether Rabin would have been able to lever the Oslo accords, for all their defects, into a final peace agreement is one of the great counterfactuals of Middle East history. What is clear is that without him the chances were greatly diminished. Late in his life Rabin had taken a real risk – in the end a fatal one – to reach an understanding with the Palestinians. And as a security-minded general, with a formidable military reputation dating back to 1948, he would have had a unique authority to end the occupation of Gaza, the West Bank and East Jerusalem had he been willing to do so. He was mourned by many Israelis – and not a few Palestinians.

2

PEACE CANCELLED: FROM HOPE TO INTIFADA, 1995–2003

ON A CHILLY, GREY SUNDAY AFTERNOON in January 2003, we were standing outside what had been, until the night before, Mahmoud al-Bahtiti's vehicle engine repair shop in the southern Gaza city neighbourhood of Zeitoun. The previous night Israeli tanks, supported by Apache attack helicopters, had rumbled along the main north–south Saladin road, ramming three buses – which still lay mangled and skewed across the road – setting market stalls on fire and flattening three houses identified by Israeli intelligence as belonging to the families of Palestinians who had launched attacks across the border. Eleven of the twelve Palestinians killed that night were militants who had rushed onto the streets to fire their AK-47s on heavily armoured Israeli troops. The incursion, which followed the firing of ten homemade Qassam rockets into Israel, albeit without causing injuries, had ended before dawn. As the fifty-year-old al-Bahtiti nodded towards the smoking ruins of his metal workshop, one of more than a dozen destroyed overnight, he shrugged and a brief grin flitted across his face. 'So Abu Ammar said Gaza was going to be the new Singapore,' he said.

The sardonic – and characteristically Gazan – joke was a reference to Yasser Arafat's portentous prediction nine years earlier of a Gazan renaissance, and it summed up how the expectations raised by the PLO leader's triumphant return to Gaza from Tunis in 1994 had gone the way of al-Bahtiti's workshop. That day in January 2003 the Israeli military said it had destroyed 100 lathes that had been or could be in the future used to make rockets. Al-Bahtiti insisted he had never made a single rocket; his premises had been used only to fix car engines. Either way Gaza was not morphing into Singapore any time soon.

It was my first visit to Gaza, but the scene inside Shifa hospital would become bleakly familiar: tired doctors in white coats and nurses in dark green scrubs weaving through anxious or bereaved relatives in the corridors, the wards' yellowing walls needing a fresh coat of paint. Lying on his bed a twenty-three-year-old called Azzam said: 'For every Palestinian bullet, there were two Israeli tank shells. But we taught them a lesson. We forced them to leave.' I didn't yet realise this was bravado: the Israeli troops had withdrawn after a few hours as they surely had always intended, and on this occasion without casualties.

It was now almost a decade since the 1993 Oslo Accord. Instead of the peace that Rabin and Arafat had envisaged would be entrenched by then, this was the third year of the Second Intifada, far deadlier than the first.

In 1996 Arafat had been elected Palestinian Authority President (Hamas had not participated in the elections). Once in power Arafat cracked down on Hamas and other dissidents, especially in Gaza; as early as November 1994 ten demonstrators had been shot dead outside a Gaza mosque, and hundreds of Palestinians were detained and often tortured in the gaol once used by the Israeli occupying forces. Complaints about PA corruption began to surface.

The task in Israel of pursuing the lasting peace envisaged in the accords was now that of the new Prime Minister Shimon Peres, who lacked Rabin's authority. In the election campaign of 1996, Peres promised to stick to Oslo, but made blunders. The first was to ignore an agreement between Yossi Beilin, the minister closest to Peres, and Mahmoud Abbas, the senior Fatah figure who had signed the Oslo Accord on behalf of the PLO in 1993. The document was intended as a blueprint for negotiations to end the conflict and on which Peres could have fought the election. Peres's second mistake was to agree to an ill-fated proposal from Shin Bet, the domestic intelligence agency and Israel's equivalent of MI5, to assassinate a leading Hamas militant, Yahya Ayyash, in Gaza.[1] Known as 'the engineer', Ayyash had organised from Gaza several lethal suicide bombings by Hamas; though, at the time he was killed, Hamas had informally agreed with the PLO to suspend attacks in the run-up to the 1996 Palestinian elections and Ayyash was said to be in hiding.[2]

Suicide bombings directed at Israeli civilians were a departure for Hamas, which, during the first Intifada, had targeted only soldiers and settlers in occupied territory. The bombings undoubtedly helped to undermine progress in implementing the Oslo accords, which Hamas itself continued to oppose. Hamas had first used such bombings, a technique borrowed from the Shiite Lebanese group Hezbollah, after the massacre by local Jewish settler Baruch Goldstein of twenty-nine Palestinians in Hebron's Ibrahim mosque in February 1994, though it may also have become a covert technique to destabilise its PLO rivals.[3] Nevertheless Ayyash's funeral was attended by hundreds of thousands of Palestinians in Gaza; Hamas promised revenge, duly carried out in a series of terrible suicide bombings in Ashkelon, Jerusalem and Tel Aviv, killing sixty Israelis and injuring many more. The veteran former chief of Israel's Military Intelligence, Shlomo Gazit, said Yasser Arafat later told him that he had been unable to restrain the 'extremists' after Ayyash's assassination.[4]

The political consequence was the strengthening of Peres's opponent, Benjamin Netanyahu, who narrowly won the 1996 election, helping to stall a peace process against which he had consistently fought in opposition. Yet after three years in which Netanyahu deeply frustrated Western leaders – including Clinton – by his obdurate lack of interest in maintaining the process started by Oslo, Israeli public opinion was still keen to see an end to what Rabin had begun. In 1999, the Labour leader Ehud Barak, a much-decorated general like his military and political mentor Rabin, was decisively elected in Netanyahu's place. It seemed a new beginning was possible.

Barak articulated with lapidary clarity the benefits to Israelis as well as to Palestinians of ending the occupation of the territory conquered in 1967. 'Every attempt to keep hold of this area as one political entity leads, necessarily, to either a nondemocratic or a non-Jewish state. Because if the Palestinians vote, then it is a bi-national state, and if they don't vote it is an apartheid state.'[5] It was hard to find a better case for what is commonly known as the two-state solution: a division of the land between Israel and a Palestinian state along borders agreed by both sides and recognised by the rest of the world. In contrast to Oslo, moreover, Barak did not envisage some dangerously long-drawn-out process towards this goal, but, rather, a lasting end to the conflict achieved in a single negotiation. The talks with Arafat took place under Bill Clinton's chairmanship at Camp David in July 2000.

They covered all the issues central to such a solution: the Palestinian aspiration for a state on the pre-June 1967 borders – just twenty-two per cent of what had been historic Palestine – on Gaza and the West Bank, full sovereignty over East Jerusalem, including the Old City, and, at least in theory, the right of the 1948 refugees and their families (some 4.5 million are now registered with the Palestinian refugee agency UNRWA) to choose between returning to their original homes in what was now Israel or compensation. The scope for negotiation lay, as it does today, in the possibility of 'land swaps', under which Israel would retain at least part of the more populous West Bank settlement blocs, arrangements allowing both Jews and Arabs to worship at the holy sites, and a more limited right that would allow a symbolic return of tens of thousands of refugees to Israel and others to the new Palestinian state.

Although no agreement was reached on the other issues – Barak's final offer at Camp David was ninety-one per cent of the West Bank – the main point on which the talks eventually foundered was Jerusalem, and in particular the holy site (Haram al-Sharif to the Arabs, the Temple Mount to the Jews) of the Wailing Wall (sacred to Jews) and the plaza containing the al-Aqsa mosque and the Dome of the Rock (sacred to Arabs). Arafat accepted Israeli sovereignty over the Wailing Wall but not of the longer Western Wall of which it was a part; nor did he accept a last-minute proposal by Clinton for the Palestinians to have 'custodial sovereignty' over the Haram/Temple Mount while Israel would maintain 'residual sovereignty'.[6] Clinton then wound up the talks.

Although Arafat insisted the Palestinians were ready to continue negotiations, both Barak and Clinton heaped public blame on Arafat for the failure of Camp David and of the later attempts after Clinton belatedly unveiled his own 'parameters' for a peace deal towards the end of his presidency in December 2000. The ferocious Barak/Clinton spin was all the more persuasive because Barak had indeed gone much further than any Israeli leader before him in offering a Palestinian state in Gaza, (most of) the West Bank and East Jerusalem. There was, Barak now concluded, 'no partner' on the Palestinian side with whom to talk peace. It was a message which most Israelis internalised; the collapse of the initiative did more than any other single event to weaken the peace camp in Israel.

A very different view gradually emerged, including from some of the Americans most prominently involved in the negotiations.[7] This held that the summit and its aftermath were underprepared, ill-conceived, and badly timed, and also that an 'aloof' Barak had refused to meet Arafat directly at crucial points.[8] Nor had any prior effort been made to involve the Arab states, a *sine qua non* of reaching any agreement on the vexed issue of Jerusalem. Clinton proposed that four to six per cent of the West Bank – comprising the territory occupied by the largest Jewish settlement blocs – should be annexed by Israel, and the equivalent of two to three per cent of Israeli land should be transferred to the Palestinians in a partial swap. Amos Malka, the head of Israeli Military Intelligence, believed that Arafat would have accepted an offer better than, but not necessarily radically different from, the Clinton parameters.[9] Moreover, Israel's 'reservations' about Clinton's December proposals on Jerusalem were arguably at least as strong as the Palestinians'.[10] But this revisionist reading has never embedded itself in the popular Israeli consciousness.

Palestinian disappointment at the Camp David outcome was compounded by the realisation that since the Oslo Accord in 1993, far from fundamental conditions improving, the number of Jewish settlers, along with all their attendant security apparatus, had more than doubled in Gaza to 6,700 and increased from 117,000 to 200,000 in the West Bank,[11] still further restricting the lives and livelihoods of three million Palestinians. This was just what Haidar Abdel Shafi had predicted.

Into this polarised post-Camp David atmosphere opposition leader Ariel Sharon, who had adamantly opposed Barak's offer to Arafat, decided to assert what he saw as Israel's sole right to sovereignty over Jerusalem's Old City, including its holy sites, Muslim as well as Jewish. On 28 September 2000, he made a high-profile tour to the Western Wall, the sacred remainder of the old Jewish Second Temple destroyed by the Romans, and to the al-Haram al-Sharif esplanade where the Dome of the Rock and the al-Aqsa mosque are sited. Sharon's trip, under the protection of around 1,000 policemen, was deeply symbolic at a time when he was facing competition from a younger rival, Benjamin Netanyahu, for the leadership of his right-wing Likud party. Nor was Sharon just any politician on the make. He was, after the death of his political opponent Yitzhak Rabin, the only remaining veteran among major political figures of the 1948 war, in which he had been badly wounded. Courageous, enterprising, often insubordinate as an army officer, he was every inch a warrior – the word was indeed the title of his autobiography – known for his deep mistrust of Arabs throughout his career as a general and a politician. As a major in the commando unit 101 he led a notorious raid on the West Bank village of Qibya in 1953, which destroyed forty-five houses and killed sixty-nine civilians. And, of course, he knew Gaza well: as the head of the IDF's Southern Command he had been responsible for the punitively lethal operations in 1971–2 to crush the nascent Palestinian resistance. He had been dismissed in 1982 as Defense Minister after being censured by an (Israeli) official commission of enquiry into the first Lebanon war 'for not taking appropriate measures to avoid the bloodshed' in a massacre by Christian militiamen of 800 Palestinians in the Sabra and Shatila refugee camps in Beirut. And he was the politician who had most actively promoted Jewish settlements on Arab land – in both Gaza and the West Bank – where he had once exhorted, 'Everybody has to move, run and grab as many [Palestinian] hilltops as they can to enlarge the [Jewish] settlements because everything we take now will stay ours.' In other words the more 'facts on the ground' Israel could establish in occupied territory, the more difficult it would be for a more left-wing government to end the occupation.[12]

For Palestinians at least, Sharon's presence at Jerusalem's holiest Muslim site was, to put it mildly, an aggravation. Arafat warned of the potentially lethal consequence of the tour, but Barak allowed it. Barak subsequently explained that he could only stop Sharon on grounds of national security – grounds that would, as it subsequently turned out, have amply justified a prohibition.[13]

The reaction came the following day, after Friday prayers. Palestinians began hurling stones from al-Haram al-Sharif onto Jewish worshippers at the Western Wall below. Israeli police stormed the compound and in subsequent clashes killed four Palestinians and injured many more, as the rioting spread into the West Bank and Gaza. While the initial uprising was generally unarmed, it met with a heavily armed response. The Israeli academic Ahron Bregman argues that, knowing that its vast military superiority would always give it the advantage if the Palestinians resorted to armed conflict, the Israeli military 'massively overreacted' to the rioting – firing 1.3 million bullets in the first month – because it wanted to provoke the Palestinians into firing back.[14]

If that was its purpose, it was successful. But even if it wasn't, the Israeli forces certainly did little to prevent the crisis escalating, while setting a pattern in which Palestinian casualties would heavily outnumber those of the Israelis. Despite the extensive experience of the First Intifada, neither the police nor the army showed any sign of readiness for civilian crowd control rather than a concerted military response, which included the use of live ammunition against unarmed protesters as well as Palestinian gunmen.[15]

On the second day of the Intifada the first iconic martyr was created in Gaza. Film shot by a Palestinian news cameraman that instantly ricocheted around the world showed twelve-year-old Mohammed al-Dura crouching, terrified, with his civilian father before he was shot and killed in crossfire between Palestinian snipers and Israeli soldiers beside the main Saladin road, close to the settlement of Netzarim.

The firefight started after Israeli troops used tear gas to contain stone-throwing demonstrators who were protesting against Sharon's tour of the holy sites. Jamal al-Dura was returning with his son from a car auction. While the argument raged about who was responsible, Mohammed's death quickly became a visual symbol of Palestinian suffering at a time when the Palestinian death toll across the West Bank and Gaza would reach 100 in a fortnight.

Less than two weeks later, on 12 October, two Israeli reserve soldiers, Yosef Avrahami and Vadim Norzich, mistakenly drove into the centre of Ramallah as thousands of angry Palestinians were gathering to mourn Khalil Zahran, a seventeen-year-old who had been killed by Israeli forces two days earlier. The soldiers were stabbed by a violent mob who invaded the local Palestinian police station where they had been in PA custody. The mutilated body of one of the reservists was hurled through a first-floor window and then paraded through the streets of Ramallah. Also captured on film (by a passing Italian TV crew), this horrific event powerfully resonated with Israelis, including many who had been actively in favour of reaching a solution with the Palestinians.

Each of these incidents had helped to accelerate the rapid slide into protracted armed conflict, which militated against rescuing the negotiations from the debacle of Camp David, despite a narrowing of the gaps between the two sides at last-ditch negotiations in January 2001 at the Sinai resort of Taba, as Barak's and Clinton's periods of office were running out. Neither of their replacements, George W. Bush or Ariel Sharon, who was first elected as Prime Minister in March 2001, had seen a continuation of diplomacy as offering any way out of the crisis engulfing Israelis and Palestinians as they took over.

Sharon was elected again in January 2003, two days after Mahmoud al-Bahtiti's workshop had gone up in smoke. In March, forty-eight Palestinians were killed in Gaza alone. Two Britons, the pro-Palestinian International Solidarity Movement activist Tom Hurndall and James Miller, a cameraman making a documentary, were also killed that spring. But the moment that probably drew most international attention to the conflict in the Strip was when Rachel Corrie, a twenty-three-year-old American activist who was also in the International Solidarity Movement, was crushed to death when she tried to stop an Israeli bulldozer engaged in the widespread house demolitions taking place near the Egyptian border in Rafah during March. Sharon promised Washington a 'thorough, credible and transparent' investigation, but no action was taken on what the IDF called a 'regrettable accident'; the US State Department believed the investigation had not fulfilled the promise. After arriving in Rafah in late February, the idealistic student had emailed her mother Cindy saying: 'I'm witnessing this chronic, insidious genocide and I'm really scared, and questioning my fundamental belief in the goodness of human nature. This has to stop. I think it's a good idea for all of us to drop everything and devote our lives to making it stop.'[16]

Denied any redress the family, seeking a symbolic $1 compensation, brought a civil action. In a Haifa courtroom in 2010 a fellow activist of Corrie's, British landscape gardener Richard Purssell, described how Corrie, wearing a fluorescent orange jacket, had climbed almost to the top of an earth mound being created by a fifty-six-tonne D9 Caterpillar bulldozer, with her feet just below the top of the pile.

'She is looking into the cab of the bulldozer,' Purssell recalled. 'The bulldozer continues to move forward. Rachel turns to begin coming back down the slope . . . As she nears the bottom of the pile, something happened to cause her to fall forward. The bulldozer continues to move forward and Rachel disappeared from view. The bulldozer moves forward approximately another four metres before it stops . . . I heard a lot of people shouting and gesturing to the bulldozer to stop' – then 'it reversed back in the tracks it had made, in a straight line; Rachel is lying on the earth'. The judge in the case ruled that Corrie 'was accidentally killed in the framework of a "war-related activity" . . . [and] the state bears no responsibility for the damages inflicted on the plaintiffs resulting from a war-related action'. Corrie had 'put herself in a dangerous situation'. The judgment was later upheld by Israel's Supreme Court.

As the Intifada wore on Hamas increasingly resorted to suicide bombings, killing mainly Israeli civilians. Gradually such attacks would also be carried out by Fatah loyalists and other factions, competing with Hamas for support among militants. In the first of two attacks in early 2001, twenty-one Israelis – mostly teenage girls of Russian origin – were killed by a Hamas suicide bomber outside the Dolphinarium discotheque in Tel Aviv; in the second, fifteen Israelis were killed at the Sbarro pizzeria in downtown Jerusalem. These were only a precursor to many more before suicide bombing was largely abandoned as a means of killing Israeli civilians by Hamas in 2004, and by the smaller Islamic Jihad at the end of 2005.

Few of the suicide bombings were carried out from Gaza because of the extreme difficulty of leaving the Strip. But since Hamas's Palestinian leadership was in Gaza, Israel frequently launched targeted strikes there, sometimes with significant 'collateral' casualties among non-involved civilians.[17] They also targeted some of the faction's most prominent military and political leaders.

By 2004 such assassinations reflected a systematic effort by the Sharon government, as his military Chief of Staff Shaul Mofaz would put it much later, to 'liquidate the terrorists' from Hamas.[18] They in turn provoked – or provided the pretext for – further suicide bombings. Targeted killings attracted criticism from abroad because of doubts about whether they conformed to international law. But the more telling charge against them was that they were on occasion used to sabotage actual or potential ceasefires. These truces might have increased the international pressure on Israel to take important practical steps towards a negotiated two-state solution, particularly after 30 April 2003.

That was the day the Middle East 'Quartet' of the EU, Russia, the UN and, most important, the document's actual authors the US, produced its 'Road Map' to Middle East peace. The document envisaged phased progress to a 'final and comprehensive permanent status agreement that ends the Israeli–Palestinian conflict in 2005 . . .' It was put in the hands of Sharon and Mahmoud Abbas, who was sworn in that very day as Palestinian Prime Minister – the job which Washington had demanded Arafat create as he himself had been in effect declared *persona non grata* by the Israeli government.

A long-time associate of Arafat's, though possessing none of his flamboyance and little of his charisma, Abbas had been recruited to Fatah in the early sixties when it was still an essentially paramilitary organisation. Unlike Arafat he was a 1948 refugee, his family having fled when he was twelve from the Galilee hill city of Safed to Syria. He also had serious negotiating experience. Though based with Arafat in Tunis at the time, he had been closely involved in the Oslo process. And in 1995 he had drafted with the Israeli politician Yossi Beilin the framework agreement which Shimon Peres declined to promote in his failed 1996 election campaign. From the outset of the Second Intifada he had stood out by publicly opposing violence. If anyone on the Palestinian side could steer this new international initiative to a successful outcome, Abbas seemed a good candidate.

The Road Map was in many respects a by-product of the Iraq war, a *quid pro quo* for such allied support as Washington had been able to muster for the invasion, and in particular that of British Prime Minister Tony Blair and King Abdullah of Jordan, both of whom had pressed George W. Bush to balance the destruction of Saddam Hussein's regime with a positive initiative to end the Israeli–Palestinian conflict.

Its first phase was as ambitious as the subsequent rapid, if cloudily delineated, steps it envisaged towards a final resolution of the conflict. From the Palestinians it required not only 'an end to violence and terrorism' but 'the dismantlement of terrorist capabilities and infrastructure'. On the Israeli side, it stipulated a withdrawal of Israeli forces from the substantial areas of occupied territory they had operated freely in since the beginning of the Intifada (most lethally in West Bank cities during Operation Defensive Shield, launched after the massacre of Israelis during Passover at the Park Hotel in Netanya in March 2002), and an immediate freeze of 'all settlement activity' including 'natural growth' – a euphemism for expansion serving the Jewish settlers' ever-increasing population.

The problems, from the first, lay in interpretation. The Israeli Cabinet's highly qualified acceptance of the Road Map a month after it was unveiled was an ideological departure since it signified, at least in principle, assent by a Likud-dominated government to partition of what had once been mandatory Palestine into two states, which the party, like Hamas on the Palestinian side, had historically opposed. Sharon was also by now talking freely of the 'occupation' – a word that had hitherto been taboo in Likud circles and would be again a decade later – and the need for a 'political settlement' to 'free ourselves from control over three and a half million Palestinians whose numbers are rising all the time'.[19] This was anathema to the Likud right wing, still clinging to the idea of a greater Israel from the Jordan to the Mediterranean. Seven of the party's ministers, including then Finance Minister Benjamin Netanyahu, either abstained or voted against the Road Map.

The Israeli Cabinet issued fourteen 'reservations' on the document – which Abbas had approved without qualifications – and they went a long way to blunting the decision's impact.

Since the Road Map had been first mooted in 2002, Sharon had applied considerable diplomatic pressure to ensure that nothing would have to change on his side, including a settlement freeze, until the Palestinians had fulfilled their stated obligations on security.[20] His diplomacy had failed, at least on paper, since the text required that 'in each phase the parties are required to perform their obligations in parallel'.

But then the Cabinet insisted that 'the first condition for progress will be the complete cessation of [Palestinian] terror, violence and incitement'. Among several other reservations, this suggested Sharon was still determined that the moves on either side would be sequential, with the Palestinians going first, rather than in parallel, whatever the Road Map said. The cheerful assessment years later by Dov Weisglass, Sharon's Chief of Staff and closest lieutenant, did little to contradict this interpretation: 'Sharon's brilliant gambit – and I say this with the utmost lack of modesty – is that we agreed [the Road Map] knowing that the result would be different . . . Theoretically if the Palestinians had fully implemented the first stage, we could have been in permanent status negotiations with Arafat by the end of 2003 . . . And in fact they did nothing.'[21]

However, it was not quite true that the Palestinians 'did nothing'. Mahmoud Abbas, now a strong opponent of armed struggle, immediately set about negotiating a ceasefire with the other factions, notably

Hamas, ahead of a summit in Aqaba convened by George Bush and the King of Jordan, at which Abbas would state baldly: 'The armed intifada must end.'[22] Such words might not have meant much had Hamas not already indicated it would accept the ceasefire – for the first time.

It was clear that this would not be enough for Sharon's government, which wanted Abbas to launch a final military reckoning with Hamas. Israeli officials frequently reached back in this period to a parable from the earliest days of their state – David Ben-Gurion's *Altalena* moment'.[23] In June 1948 Israel's first Prime Minister ordered the newly formed Israel Defense Force to shell an old US Navy vessel heavily loaded with arms intended for Irgun, which was led by Menachem Begin and had for many years been a more extreme and violent organisation than Hagana, which Ben-Gurion himself headed. After being hit by a shell off the Tel Aviv coast, the ship went down with most of the arms and forty Irgun members were killed.[24] The *Altalena* episode ensured the final dissolution of Irgun into the new Israel Defense Forces. For Irgun then read Hamas now, the Israeli message went, for the IDF/Hagana Fatah. But for all its symbolic importance and traumatic overtones of inter-Jewish bloodletting, Ben-Gurion, leading a state and an army, had been in a vastly stronger position to sink the *Altalena* than Abbas was to launch a civil war to dismantle an entire armed faction. Abbas, only number two in the Palestinian Authority, was being urged by Israel, and increasingly by the US, to eliminate Hamas as a martial force – exactly what Israel itself, with massively greater military resources, had failed to do.

In such circumstances, the three-month ceasefire that Abbas secured from the main Palestinian factions, including Hamas and the much smaller Islamic Jihad, appeared his only realistic option. Despite the doubts freely expressed in Washington as well as Jerusalem about its bankability, Israel refrained for the moment from the targeted assassinations, and the ceasefire largely held throughout July. Most Israelis dated the moment it ended to the horrific suicide bombing of a bus, by a Hamas activist from Hebron on 19 August, which killed sixteen mainly ultra-orthodox adults and seven children in West Jerusalem. In fact it had begun to unravel before then. The bombing came after the fatal shooting of Mohammed Sidr, head of Islamic Jihad's military wing in Hebron, on 14 August. Israel said Sidr had been planning a terrorist attack – that he was, in a favourite phrase of the security forces, a 'ticking bomb'. If so, wrote Amos Harel, *Haaretz*'s military commentator,

more information should be given than 'generic statements' since otherwise 'there will always be those who suspect it is Israel that is stirring up
trouble in order to free itself of the yoke of the concessions demanded
by the Road Map'.[25]

This was perhaps the last moment that the Road Map, and its ambitious goal of a speedily negotiated end to the conflict, could have been
kept on track. So dangerous was the crisis that Abbas finally secured a
go-ahead from Arafat to move against Hamas and Islamic Jihad, at least
in Hebron, by arresting those responsible for the Jerusalem bombing
and closing schools and medical facilities run by the factions.[26]

But Israel was not going to wait. On 21 August 2003 Israeli helicopters fired five missiles at a white Volkswagen, killing one of Hamas's top
leaders, Ismail Abu Shanab, and his two bodyguards in Gaza City.
Hamas immediately declared the truce finished, as did Islamic Jihad
and Fatah's al-Aqsa Martyrs' Brigades in Gaza, while Abbas himself
warned, 'this for sure will affect the whole [peace] process and the decision taken by the Palestinian Authority [to confront Hamas]'.[27]

The previous year Israel had assassinated the head of Hamas's military wing, Salah Shehadeh, by dropping a one-ton bomb on a house in
Gaza where, according to intelligence, he was staying with his wife and
aides. The strike also killed his daughter and thirteen uninvolved civilians – ten of them children, the youngest a two-month-old baby – in the
apartment block next door. An outcry had resonated around the world
including among many Israelis. And that sense of revulsion returned in
August 2003 when people heard what Dan Halutz, head of the air force,
said when asked how he felt about such a bombing. He answered: 'I feel
a slight bump to the plane as a result of the release of the bomb. After a
second, it passes. And that's it . . .'[28]

This time, when Abu Shanab was assassinated, there was only one
'collateral' death, a seventy-year-old woman who died from shrapnel
wounds a week later.[29] But the choice of target was widely regarded,
especially in Gaza, as highly significant, because Abu Shanab, a political
rather than military Hamas figure, had been among the less extreme
members of the faction's Gaza leadership and had played a big part in
securing the truce. The *Guardian*'s Chris McGreal wrote from the scene:
'Ariel Sharon could not have been in any doubt that killing Abu Shanab
would wreck the ceasefire. He was widely seen as more pragmatic than
fellow leaders. He broke a taboo within Hamas by recognising that there

would have to be a Palestinian state alongside Israel not in place of it.'[30] The White House reacted to Abu Shanab's assassination with a routine observation that 'Israel has the right to defend itself', while mildly venturing that Israel should also 'take into account the effect that actions they take have on the peace process', and again urging Abbas to take 'immediate steps to dismantle terrorist capabilities'.

Whether Sharon had deliberately targeted Abu Shanab because of his relative moderation or was merely indifferent to it, the assassination now made that task impossible. If Arafat had approved moves against Hamas before the assassination, he was not going to do so now. Abbas's appointment as Prime Minister – and, indeed, the creation of the office, which had not previously existed in the Palestinian Authority – had arisen directly from Sharon's deep personal hostility to Arafat and George Bush's landmark speech in June 2002 (which Sharon's lieutenants had been intimately involved in drafting)[31] insisting on a 'new and different Palestinian leadership'.

But Abbas's premiership was consistently undermined by Israeli policy. This did not just stem from the disparagement by the Sharon camp of Abbas as a 'chick that's not yet grown feathers' or Sharon's own leaked comment that 'Abu Mazen,* too, is still an Arab'.[32] Settlement building continued. And the handful of settlement outposts that Sharon had promised to dismantle turned out to be either empty shacks, which the settlers helpfully volunteered to pull down for effect, or were simply restored to life the day after photographers had recorded their evacuation. The separation barrier that the Israeli military had started to build on Sharon's orders was already beginning to cut into the West Bank, a de facto annexation of Palestinian territory theoretically opposed by the US.

Above all, Sharon was obdurate in the face of Abbas's repeated requests for the release of prisoners, the granting of which would have enhanced Abbas's credibility with the Palestinian public. While eventually Israel released around 400 prisoners, most were serving short

---

* The 'Abu' or 'father' formulation is a *kunya*, often used as a term of familiarity or respect and usually based on the named person's eldest son. Thus, because Mahmoud Abbas's firstborn son was Mazen, he becomes 'Abu Mazen'. But the *kunya* can occasionally be a non-familial *nom de guerre* like Arafat's 'Abu Ammar' in which the reference to Ammar is to a companion of the Prophet Mohammed.

sentences already near their completion. Otherwise Sharon stuck rigidly by the formula that prisoners with 'blood on their hands', i.e. who had been convicted for direct involvement in attacks on Israelis, should not be freed. Yet, as Abbas continually reminded him, that ruled out the release of many prisoners who had been detained before the Oslo agreement and had long passed the age at which they posed a threat. The now resolutely anti-violence Abbas pointed out to Sharon – to no avail – the contradiction that he was now sitting round a table with the Israeli Prime Minister yet was unable to secure the release of men whom he himself had sent out on militant operations against Israel long before Oslo.[33] Unsurprisingly, Abbas resigned on 6 September, blaming disagreements with Arafat over security control but also, at some length, Israel and the Americans.

The Road Map could only have succeeded if the international community, and especially the US, had pushed the parties into reinforcing and building on the admittedly fragile ceasefire, ensuring that Israel curbed its policy of targeted assassination and started to fulfil some of its own Phase One obligations. But this did not happen. In their instructive 'How-to and How-not-to' guide to Middle East peacemaking, Daniel Kurtzer, who was US ambassador to Israel at the time, and Scott Lasensky, state bluntly: 'Backed by the so-called Quartet of the US supported by the EU, Russia and the UN, the Road Map was released with fanfare just after the overthrow of Saddam Hussein ... But no sustained attempt was made to implement the initiative. Its ambitious goals and timelines were effectively abandoned.'[34]

Before the day of Abbas's resignation was out, an F16 had launched a 250kg bomb at a house in which the primary founder and undisputed leader of Hamas, Sheikh Ahmed Yassin, was lunching with his close associate Ismail Haniyeh and other Hamas members. The house was badly damaged but no one was killed. The following day, the quadriplegic Yassin, who had been only slightly injured in the attack, serenely held court to a steady stream of well-wishers in a white robe from a bed in his home in Gaza City, the room festooned with Hamas and religious posters, his wheelchair parked against a wall. 'God saved us,' he said.

Two days later, on 9 September, fifteen Israelis were killed in two more suicide attacks. The bombings were too well planned to be retaliation for the attempt on Yassin; rather, they were to avenge Abu Shanab's and others' assassinations. Eight Israelis, mostly off-duty soldiers, were blown up at a well-known bus and hitchhiking stop on Route 44, close to an army base outside Tel Aviv. The scene could hardly have been bleaker. The bomb had blown body parts twenty feet above the ground onto the bus shelter's roof, which was spattered with blood. Ninety minutes after the blast a leg still lay on the ground and a dismembered limb could be seen dangling from the roof of the bus shelter, as rescue workers collected the remains of the victims in sterile bags.[35]

A few hours later, seven Israeli civilians, including Dr David Applebaum, the head of the emergency centre at Jerusalem's Shaare Zedek Hospital, were killed outside the popular Café Hillel in the city's German Colony neighbourhood. Also among the victims were the café's twenty-two-year-old security guard Alon Mizrahi, who had spotted the bomber and stopped him from entering and causing even more destruction. One young woman was killed by a bolt from the nail bomb as she walked along the pavement some twenty-five yards from the café. It was another reminder of the price 'ordinary' Israelis as well as 'ordinary' Palestinians were paying for the collapse of the ceasefire and the diplomatic breakdown.

Sharon's reaction was immediate: the next day in Gaza City the Israeli air force bombed the house of the Hamas leader Mahmoud Zahar, killing one of his sons and a bodyguard. At the same time the Israeli Prime Minister, breaking off relations with the PA, took a resolution through the Cabinet pledging to 'remove' Arafat, who they saw as the main 'obstacle', 'in the manner and time of our choosing'.

Recalled in hindsight, the period inevitably takes on the character of a seemingly unstoppable cycle of violence. In fact, in Israel as in the Occupied Territories, life continued. In Gaza, shops and markets were open, couples got married, students went to school (when they were not closed because of the conflict), factories functioned, cargo crossed the border both ways. But the economic damage was great: Gaza had shared with the West Bank in an economic slump – from an already low level – since the beginning of the Intifada, which had seen Palestinian unemployment climb to thirty-seven per cent, with real incomes forty-six per cent lower than in 1999. Poverty, defined by having to live on less than $2.10 a day, now afflicted sixty per cent of the population.[36] Never affluent – never mind being a Singapore – the Strip's economy was much more restricted than it had been before the Intifada started in 2000.

The Second Intifada had, albeit at terrible human cost, some success in focusing international attention on the conflict. But unlike the First Intifada, which was followed by the Madrid summit and eventually the Oslo process, the second produced highly negative consequences for the Palestinians, recognised in hindsight by some of its participants.[37] Whereas the defining global images of the first had been that of well-armed Israeli troops shooting at children throwing stones, that of the second had too often been the horrific deaths and wreckage inflicted on defenceless Israeli civilians. Most importantly, it enabled Sharon to identify the Israeli–Palestinian conflict with the US-led 'war on terror' after 9/11, despite its fundamentally different root causes, and to persuade the Western powers to do so too. For many Western politicians, especially in the US, *terrorism* was now the story of the Intifada. It eclipsed another reality: an oppressive military and civilian Israeli occupation of Gaza, the West Bank and East Jerusalem, which had been in place for well over a quarter of a century before the first Palestinian suicide attack.

Suicide bombing is abhorrent. Nor was the abhorrence – shared by many Palestinians – much relieved by the standard justification deployed by those sending often impressionable young perpetrators to their deaths; namely that for Palestinians, lacking the weapons of Israel's modern first-world military force, it was the only alternative capable of inspiring terror in a perceived enemy. But it had a context. No doubt the young men – and less often women – bombers acted from a mixture of motives, which included the 'honour' of sacrifice to a cause, obsessive religiosity, the prospect that their often indigent families would be compensated (including, until his fall in the Iraq war, by the Iraqi dictator Saddam Hussein), and revenge for the killing by Israeli forces of a relative. But it's impossible to believe that so many would have volunteered without the sense of despair and powerlessness generated by the corrosive social and economic impact on an unenfranchised and increasingly impoverished population of an occupation, with its attendant checkpoints, land seizures, lack of freedom of movement, unemployment and the relentless control exercised over their day-to-day lives by an ubiquitous and, to the Palestinians, foreign army.

This might not have justified terrorism any more than during the British Mandate, when both Arab and Jewish groups repeatedly conducted terrorist operations. But it was sometimes better understood in Israel than it was abroad. It had been the then future Prime Minister Ehud Barak, who in 1998, after the wave of suicide bombings that had helped to dislodge his own Labour party from power, admitted: 'If I was [a Palestinian] at the right age, at some stage I would have entered one of the terror organisations and have fought from there, and later certainly have tried to influence from within the political system.'[38] Nevertheless Sharon's conflation of Palestinian terror with its global counterpart dissipated any pressure on the Israeli Prime Minister to seek a diplomatic solution and freed him to crush the uprising by draconian military means.

The price of Sharon's course was high; the death toll would mount steadily in the first five years of the century. Among the dead were twice as many Palestinians as Israelis.[39] In Gaza the deaths overshadowed another impact of Israeli incursions into the Strip, one which would set a pattern for future years: the systematic destruction of farmland, including the uprooting of orchards and olive groves, usually justified by the need to protect Israeli settlers from militants who might be using them as cover. Local estimates were that between the beginning of the Intifada and the end of July 2001 alone over 3,300 acres or seven per cent of Gaza's farmland had been destroyed.[40] Noam Hayut, a young Israeli officer cadet serving in Gaza early in the Intifada, recalled, 'as a farmer's son who knew the value of an old orchard', seeing a distraught old Palestinian emerging at dawn with his grandson to see his trees cut down 'kneeling in the sand and crying. All I could do was use the little Arabic we knew, and shout "get out of here".'[41]

The death toll included hundreds of uninvolved civilians on both sides, including children. Mourning his fifteen-year-old daughter Malka, who had been a stalwart protector of her severely handicapped sister, and was killed in the Sbarro pizzeria bombing in Jerusalem in 2001, the Israeli Arnold Roth said: 'I want people to know she isn't just another statistic.'[42] It was a sentiment the Palestinian al-Daour family would share. In August 2003 Israeli attack helicopters launched three missiles at a white Renault 5 on a busy road in a heavily populated area west of Jabalya Town in northern Gaza. While the three militants in the car escaped and ran off before another two missiles hit the car and incinerated it, others were not so lucky. Ten-year-old Sana al-Daour was sitting in the back seat of a Mercedes taxi with her parents and sister on a trip to buy books for the new school year. The taxi was overtaking the Renault at the moment the missiles struck and Sana was showered with shrapnel; she died in Shifa hospital eight days later. Two days after that, her grieving father Jamil was receiving condolences at the mourning tent. As relatives handed out the customary dates and coffee in little cups to mourners, Jamil al-Daour gave a quietly caustic reply to the question of whom he blamed for the cycle of violence that had claimed Sana's life: 'I blame my daughter for getting into the car.'

3

'NOT A JEW LEFT IN GAZA': DISENGAGEMENT, 2004–5

THE THIRTY OR SO POLICEMEN WHO came for Sarit Cohen that blisteringly hot afternoon in August 2005 looked away in a kind of shame as she bent to claw at the desert sand, and let it slip through her fingers for all to see. Staring fixedly at the sombre-looking men in uniform waiting to take her away with all the gentleness they could muster, she wailed: 'You are leaving this soil to the people who want to kill us.'

Her family of fourteen – children, spouses and grandchildren – sang their last prayers outside the house, with its neat garden and red-tiled roof. Two of her daughters were weeping. And then the old matriarch, dressed in a pillbox woollen hat and a long, flowing skirt, and clutching an enormous embossed black bible, led the reproachful little party to the waiting bus, pausing to denounce the policemen and the soldiers standing behind them for betraying their fellow Jews. When they reached the bus, a middle-aged man, the Cohens' friend and neighbour, ripped his shirt. Later he would explain this ancient biblical gesture of mourning by lamenting that, as he saw it, rightful inhabitants of this corner of 'the land of Israel' were being forced to retreat because their state no longer had the stomach to protect them after years of Palestinian attacks. 'This is a beautiful family who has never hurt anybody and had a life project,' he said. 'To give a prize for terror, to show that terror works, that is not what the world needs.'

Another Cohen, no relation of his outraged neighbour and name-
sake, was not so passive. Shmuel Cohen, a black-bearded bear of a man,
fought so fiercely on the fifteen-metre journey from his house to the bus
that it took seven soldiers to force him onto the vehicle. His wife and
several of his tearful children struggled, too; four women police officers
were required to carry her. The officer in charge of the operation, Major
Sagy, explained that many of the apparent resisters wanted to be carried
out so they would not have to say they left voluntarily, but 'we visited
this family in the morning and we realised that unfortunately we would
have to use force'.

There was something theatrical about this enforced leave-taking –
and indeed about the whole Israeli withdrawal from Gaza. Here in Neve
Dekalim, founded in 1983 and the most populous among the Gush
Katif bloc of Jewish settlements, the eviction of 350 or so families who
had failed to leave voluntarily was just one scene in the drama. Many of
the settlers had been here for two decades or more, enticed by Israeli
government discounts on housing, the beaches and the prospect of
lucrative agriculture. Their pain was real, reinforced by anger and frustration that it was Prime Minister Ariel Sharon, the politician who,
more than any other, for years promoted Israeli settlement, who had
now declared that by the end of 2005 there would 'not be a Jew left in
Gaza'.[1] In a symbiotic symmetry, the claim that disengagement from
Gaza was a 'prize for terror' was matched by the boasts of Hamas that
Gaza had been 'liberated' by the 'resistance'.

It was hard amid all this emotion to remember that in a strip of land
with a population of 1.4 million Palestinians, a mere 8,500 Israeli settlers
had controlled twenty-five per cent of the territory including roads for
their sole use, military posts, security zones and checkpoints, along
with forty per cent of the arable land and access to some of the best
water sources.[2] Or that they were being compensated by the state with
payments to each family of between $200,000 and $450,000; or that a
democratically elected government was removing settlements judged
illegal in international law by most countries, including every EU
member state.

Equally, the dire predictions that had been made for months, of a
civil war and armed violence by the settlers, were not fulfilled. In Neve
Dekalim the following day the troops forced their way into one of the
two synagogues and removed about 800 young anthem-singing,

kicking and screaming settler supporters, mainly infiltrators from the West Bank. In Kfar Darom, where they put up the strongest resistance, police said twenty-seven officers had been moderately injured, some by acid thrown in their faces, and one policeman fell two floors after slipping on oil deliberately left on the stairs by demonstrators. But there were no deaths or even serious injuries arising directly from the forced evacuation. The shouts of 'Nazi' and 'gestapo' from far-right demonstrators, the graffiti on the soon-to-be bulldozed houses – 'Goodbye, my sweet home', 'We hate you Ariel Sharon' – and the incessant chants of 'a Jew does not expel a Jew' were expressive enough. But for all the rhetoric, even the most militant settlers and their allies were unable to deliver serious resistance in the face of the combination of state power in the form of 40,000 soldiers and police and a compensation package worth $1bn.[3]

There are few more dynamic built environments in the world than the occupied Palestinian territories. Tunnels and 'bypass roads' to protect settlers from the Palestinians, many driven through hillsides; concrete walls and fences with electric sensors to separate Israelis from Palestinians; checkpoints that more closely resemble international border terminals; Israel's continued construction of buildings (usually Israeli) or demolition of buildings (usually Palestinian) – all serve a military or political goal. Even by those standards, the operation that began on 17 August 2005 in the Gaza Strip was momentous, not least because the houses being destroyed were those of Israelis. Within eight days the Sharon government withdrew 8,500 Jewish settlers and the military's big D9 armoured Caterpillar bulldozers began reducing their 2,800 houses to rubble in the first withdrawal from occupied Palestinian territory since the 1967 Six Day War.

THIS WAS ALL A MERE THREE years since Sharon had promised that the Gaza settlements were here to stay, declaring 'the fate of Tel Aviv is the fate of Netzarim'. Because Netzarim, isolated and only five kilometres from Gaza City, was the Gaza settlement most vulnerable to Palestinian attacks, and therefore the most heavily protected by the IDF, there could hardly have been a more dramatic way of reassuring the Israeli residents of the strip. If Netzarim was not going to be disbanded then, they could reflect, the permanence of all the other settlements was guaranteed. So what had led the old warrior, the politician who had devoted so much of his life to promoting Israeli colonisation of occupied territory, to abandon the promise he had made in April 2002, and to his first disengagement announcement in December 2003?

While many settlers had believed the right-wing national religious rabbis who told them God would not allow it to happen, some were convinced that Sharon had an ulterior motive: keeping at bay a scandal over election funding that had threatened to engulf his son Omri. 'In the Bible, it says our forefather Abraham was prepared to sacrifice his son for the nation', a sardonic Gush Katif resident explained at the time. 'Sharon has sacrificed the nation for his son.' Nor was this view confined to the settlers: Moshe Yaalon, the IDF Chief of Staff at the time of the announcement, also thought Sharon was chasing national and international acclaim to insulate himself from possible scandal.

But if this were true it was not the only motive. A remark repeatedly attributed to him after he became Prime Minister was: 'What you see from here you don't see from there.' Part of what he saw 'from here' was the political unsustainability of the status quo. He had fought the January 2003 election on a platform of 'peace with security' and by the following autumn significant sections of the Israeli public were demanding moves towards the first as well as the second goal.

Sharon was publicly dismissive of two unofficial but detailed blueprints for a two-state deal agreed by prominent Israelis and Palestinians. One was the Geneva Accords reached between Yossi Beilin and Arafat's lieutenant Yasser Abed Rabbo; the other by Sari Nusseibeh, the urbane president of al-Quds University who had been active in the First Intifada, and Ami Ayalon, a former head of Shin Bet. But it was less easy to ignore a widely publicised letter in September 2003 from twenty-seven pilots in the air force reserves, which announced that, while they would willingly continue to serve on any genuine mission needed to defend Israel, they objected 'to carrying out illegal and immoral attacks . . . in the [occupied] territories', and that the 'continuing occupation mortally damages Israel's security and its moral strength'.[4]

At least as powerfully, four former heads of Shin Bet, including Ayalon, gave a joint interview in the mass circulation *Yedhioth Ahronoth* in which they, too, castigated the occupation. Avraham Shalom, who had led the intelligence service in the 1980s, declared: 'If we don't give up the goal of "Greater Israel" and if we don't stop treating the other side in the disgraceful way we do and if we don't start understanding that he, too, has feelings and that he, too, is suffering, then we're on the way to the abyss.'[5]

Especially topical was the criticism by all four securocrats of the key element of Sharon's approach to the Road Map – that there could be no progress to negotiations until the Palestinian leadership had 'crushed terror'. When Carmi Gillon, the Shin Bet head in the mid-1990s, said this was a mistake, Shalom corrected him. 'No you're wrong. It's an excuse.'[6]

Shalom's analysis was perceptive; Sharon had by now abandoned any belief in the Road Map. One of the main attractions of unilateral disengagement from Gaza was that it could be presented to Washington as an alternative to the Road Map, one that required no negotiations with Arafat and left the Israeli occupation of the West Bank intact. Indeed, Sharon had been explicit about superseding the Road Map when he had first floated the idea to the Deputy National Security Adviser Elliott Abrams at a meeting in his hotel in Rome during an official visit. Abrams, an able Bush ally and a self-confessed 'neo-con', was the US official whom Sharon most trusted.* As the Israeli Prime Minister devoured a large plate of what to his startled fellow Jew looked suspiciously like ham,[7] Sharon, by his own account, told the American 'that in the absence of a partner I saw a danger to Israel and it was therefore imperative to free ourselves of the "Road Map" and go to a different term'.

Sharon's allies also deployed a demographic argument in favour of disengagement. In the whole of the Holy Land there were 5.4 million Jews and 4.6 million Palestinians, if Arab citizens of Israel were included. But the Palestinians were increasing in numbers – particularly in Gaza, where the population growth rate was then four per cent per year. If a point was reached when there were more Arabs than Jews it would be increasingly difficult, if not impossible, to maintain that the 'Greater Israel' beloved of settlers and right-wing parties was actually Jewish, let alone democratic. Sharon 'started to see the strength of the left's argument that Israel could not hold on to all the occupied territories and keep its Jewish identity'.[8]

---

* In early 2017 Abrams was considered as a Deputy Secretary of State but was rejected by Trump because of his criticisms of the future President during the election campaign.

Finally, Gaza disengagement could be levered into extracting a reward from Washington. Despite Sharon's de facto abandonment of the Road Map, the Bush administration gave the 'bold and historic initiative' its blessing. And, in a stunning diplomatic coup for the Israeli Prime Minister, it granted his request for a *quid pro quo*. This was a letter from Bush – formally handed over to Sharon on his visit to Washington in April 2004 – which appalled the Palestinian leadership and Arab governments, and infuriated officials in Europe. In a break with long-standing and bipartisan US policy, the letter went a long way towards prejudging the terms of any future two-state solution very much in Israel's favour.

It expressed support for Israel holding on to the main Jewish settlement blocs – or 'existing major Israeli population centres', as the letter put it – in the West Bank. The Fatah-dominated PA negotiators understood that some populous settlements close to the border would probably fall to Israel in return for a land swap in any final status negotiations, but this deprived them of even the little left to negotiate about. Sharon immodestly claimed later that the letter had been seen by the Palestinians as their 'greatest blow' since the 1948 war. It was easy to believe Israeli media reports that he had telephoned Condoleezza Rice while the plane taking him to the crucial Washington meeting was still on the tarmac at Ben-Gurion airport, threatening to call the visit off unless the wording was just as he wanted it.

Sharon's closest lieutenant, Dov Weisglass, provided an explanation to *Haaretz* in October 2004:

> Effectively, this whole package that is called the Palestinian state, with all that it entails, has been removed from our agenda indefinitely. And all this with authority and permission. All with a presidential blessing and the ratification of both houses of Congress . . . We educated the world to understand that there is no one to talk to. And we received a no-one-to-talk-to certificate. That certificate says: (1) There is no one to talk to. (2) As long as there is no one to talk to, the geographic status quo remains intact. (3) The certificate will be revoked only when this-and-this happens – when Palestine becomes Finland. (4) See you then, and shalom.[9]

This gloss, among other things, gave rise to the widespread view that Sharon's real purpose in pulling out of Gaza was to consolidate Israel's grip on the occupied West Bank. On the other hand, Sharon's biographer David Landau made a persuasive case that the Prime Minister intended further, if gradual, unilateral withdrawals from the West Bank.[10] But the two readings are not mutually exclusive. It was a safe bet that any future withdrawal Sharon envisaged from the West Bank would leave the three main settlement blocs intact, and at most would mean abandoning land east of the separation barrier. Because the barrier cut into the West Bank at various points, swathes of Palestinian land would be left in Israeli hands.

While the polls repeatedly showed that a majority of the Israeli public supported withdrawal from Gaza, Sharon faced consistent opposition from those within his own right-wing Likud party who depicted it as a surrender to the militants. This was one reason why he and Shaul Mofaz, now Defense Minister, were determined throughout 2004 to make it 'brutally clear that the army would not be scurrying out of Gaza as it had – in their view at any rate – out of South Lebanon in May 2000'.[11] In March 2004 a suicide bombing in Israel mounted, unusually, from inside Gaza killed ten port workers. The retaliation came a week later, on 22 March, amid threats from the Cabinet to kill all Hamas leaders. The first of three Hellfire missiles fired from an Apache helicopter killed Ahmed Yassin along with two bodyguards and seven bystanders as he returned in his wheelchair from dawn prayers at a mosque in Gaza City's Sabra neighbourhood.

Sharon called Yassin 'the mastermind of Palestinian terror', but he was a provocative choice of target. His funeral procession, estimated locally at around 200,000-strong, was accompanied by large formations of Qassam Brigades fighters carrying AK-47s and RPGs, chanting: 'The assassination of Sheikh Yassin is the beginning of the end of Israel.' Yassin had been admired for his shrewdness, physical courage and ascetic lifestyle beyond the ranks of the Islamic faction. As the leader who had sanctioned Hamas's suicide bombings, he had offered Israel, through Jordan's King Hussein, to call them off in return for a long-term truce back in 1997.[12]

Abdel Aziz Rantissi was immediately named as successor to Yassin as the Hamas leader, only to be assassinated by another Hellfire missile attack on 17 April. Another mass funeral, more bloodcurdling threats of retaliation, more volleys of gunfire as armed, balaclava-wearing pallbearers carried the open coffin, with Rantissi's pallid, bearded face uncovered by the green Hamas flag draped over his body, through a dense, swaying crowd. The megaphones blared: 'Your leader? Rantissi. Your way? Resistance. Your movement? Hamas. Your hope? To be martyrs.'

This time, Hamas took the precaution of not publicly naming Rantissi's successor, a little-known imam by the name of Mohammed Sham'ah, in a bid to prevent another assassination. But this was not the only precaution taken by the movement's consultative council, the Majlis al-Shura. It approved a secret, Egyptian-brokered deal with Israel, according to one well-informed account: no more assassinations of Hamas leaders; no more suicide bombings by Hamas.[13] This would explain why Israel did not carry out its threat to wipe out the entire Hamas leadership in Gaza, and why suicide bombings in Israel were now discarded as a tactic by Hamas (though not by Islamic Jihad, not a party to the deal).

Yet the month following Rantissi's assassination was one of the bloodiest in Gaza since the beginning of the Intifada. On 2 May, Israeli settler Tali Hatuel and her four daughters were shot dead while driving out of Gaza. Eleven soldiers were killed in two days when armoured personnel carriers were hit by mines in Gaza. One was the twenty-year-old son of one of Israel's most celebrated stage actors, Shlomo Vishinsky. As mourners gathered for the soldiers' funerals at Jerusalem's Mount Herzl cemetery, Vishinsky said bitterly that his son had been a 'patsy' for the governing party. He wrote in *Yedhioth Ahronoth*: 'It's clear that no one wants to be in Gaza except the members of the Likud.'[14]

The deaths of the soldiers deepened the resolve of the 150,000 Israelis who demonstrated their support for the Gaza pull-out at a rally in Tel Aviv's Rabin Square. Alon Ashkenazy, the father of a soldier killed in Gaza the previous year, moved many when he addressed his son: 'I'm your father and I love you . . . You told me after every Israeli incursion, after every targeted killing, that we should leave Gaza.'

The rally was rich in ironies. Many of those present were adherents of the Israeli peace movement who found themselves in the unaccustomed role of supporting, however reluctantly, a plan of Ariel Sharon's. Some had been among the 400,000 who had come to the same square twenty-two years earlier to express their rage against Sharon, then Defense Minister, after the Israeli military had allowed Phalangist gunmen to perpetrate the massacre of hundreds of Palestinians in the Lebanese refugee camps of Sabra and Shatila. The square was also where the right-wing fanatic Yigal Amir had shot dead Prime Minister Yitzhak Rabin at a peace rally in November 1995. The assassination followed a two-year political campaign in which the right wing had vilified Rabin for negotiating the Oslo Accords with Yasser Arafat, a campaign in which Sharon and Netanyahu had played a prominent part.

The rally represented an uneasy alliance between those who backed unilateral disengagement from Gaza as a limited step and those – probably a majority that evening – who wanted Sharon to go much further and negotiate with the Palestinians an end to the occupation of Gaza, the West Bank and East Jerusalem. There was a tremor of excitement, a hope that withdrawal from Gaza might lead to something bigger. As the crowds dispersed, dozens of white balloons were released into the air to the strains of John Lennon's 'Give Peace a Chance'.

The military's response to the soldiers' deaths was predictably ferocious. In Operation Rainbow, launched in Rafah refugee camp on 12 May, aerial and ground forces killed more than fifty Palestinians, razed hundreds of homes and, in an oddly macabre twist, laid waste the local zoo. The IDF and the Palestinians disputed the number of civilians killed, but visiting Rafah's small and overflowing al-Najar hospital I saw dead and injured children. Ahmad Mughayer, fourteen, and his sixteen-year-old sister Asmaa had been on the roof of their apartment block when they were shot, apparently by an Israeli sniper. Ahmad had been feeding pigeons, while his sister was taking in the washing. So full was the morgue there was only room for Asmaa. As the bombardment continued, Dr Ahmed Abu Nkaira, the busy deputy director of the hospital, took the *Guardian*'s Chris McGreal and me to a flower nursery where, in the refrigerated storage room beside a bed of white carnations just beginning to bloom, Ahmad's body had been laid out with those of twelve other victims. Eight were obviously militants, draped in the colours of their factions: green for Hamas, black and yellow for Islamic Jihad, yellow for Fatah's al-Aqsa Martyrs' Brigades.

The IDF claimed the children had been accidentally killed by Palestinian explosives, but Dr Nkaira removed a sheet to show us a small wound where a bullet had entered just above Ahmad's hairline. Then he pointed to the exit wound, identical to his sister's, a much larger and bloodier hole in the back of his head. The experienced casualty medic had no doubt it had been caused by an Israeli bullet. 'This is the 'accident" that the Israelis are talking about,' he said. 'This is how the Israelis talk all the time. I am sorry the Europeans and the Americans believe these kind of stories.'

The Rafah operation was at least as controversial because of the systematic demolition of homes, particularly in the Brazil neighbourhood of the refugee camp. One morning late in the operation, forty-year-old Ibrahim Abu Hamad stood in front of the rubble and concertinaed concrete slabs which had once been his home to describe the surreal experience he had had when it had been destroyed. Abu Hamad was in the house with his wife and seven children when an armoured bulldozer smashed its way into the front of the building. At that moment, he was on the telephone to his Israeli employer, for whom he had worked as a builder for fifteen years. The Israeli, Meir Grimstein, who did his military service in Gaza, had phoned to ask how his employee was managing amid the chaos of the military operation.

'When I told him the bulldozer had started to demolish my house, he said: "I don't believe you. I know where your house is. It isn't near the border." ' When Abu Hamad persuaded him otherwise, 'he said "how can I help you?" I told him: "You can't help me. The bulldozer is already here. It's too late." ' By now the bulldozer had lumbered to a halt within five metres of the rear wall, leaving the family room to escape as they waved a white cloth in the hope that it would stop troops shooting at the sand around their feet. It was fairly obvious both that Abu Hamad, who had an Israeli permit to cross through Erez to his job in Israel, was no militant, and that there was no tunnel under what had been his house. The irony of seeing his home destroyed in a short few minutes was not lost on Abu Hamad. 'I build houses in Israel, and the Israelis destroy my house here,' he said.

House demolitions had been going on in Rafah since early in the Second Intifada; Rachel Corrie had been trying to stop a bulldozer from embarking on such an operation when she was killed in 2003. A roughly 300-metre strip of houses along the Gaza side of the border with Egypt had been cleared. But by June 2004 demolitions had accelerated from about fifteen homes a month to a hundred. More than 15,000 people – over ten per cent of Rafah's population – had lost their home in the previous four years. Tommy Lapid, the Israeli Justice Minister and leader of the secular centrist party Shinui, said – to the fury of some of his Cabinet colleagues – that the television footage of an old Palestinian woman scrabbling for her medicine in the rubble of her home during Operation Rainbow reminded him of his own grandmother (who had died in Auschwitz).*

The IDF's routine justification was the need to destroy tunnel shafts used to bring in weapons and to protect Israeli troops patrolling the heavily fortified 'Philadelphia corridor' along Rafah's border with Egypt. But a detailed report by Human Rights Watch (HRW) challenged both explanations, pointing out, for example, that the military had admitted after destroying 166 homes during Operation Rainbow that, of three tunnels it said it had found, one was an incomplete shaft and another was outside Rafah altogether. It also noted the progressive expansion of the corridor by demolishing houses if anything exposed the troops to 'risks subsequently invoked to justify further demolitions'. HRW – and the UN Secretary General Kofi Annan – concluded that indiscriminate demolition of houses like Hamad's violated international law because it was 'not required by military necessity'. HRW speculated that it had been 'intended as retaliation for the killing of five Israeli soldiers in Rafah on 12 May, as well as a show of strength'.[15]

Beyond the questions of international law, however, there was also a wider political question, identified by David Shearer, the country director of the UN's Office of the Co-ordination of Humanitarian Affairs (OCHA) at the time (and later leader of the New Zealand Labour Party). He and lawyer Anushka Meyer argued that, as the occupying power, and irrespective of the legality of the demolitions, Israel had a responsibility to repair damage it caused and rehouse the homeless.

While the EU presidency condemned Israeli actions in Rafah as 'completely disproportionate' and showing 'a reckless disregard for human life', it and other international donors paid up in response to a $15m appeal from UNRWA to rehouse Palestinians living in territory occupied by Israel and left homeless by that same Israeli military action. As Shearer and Meyer put it: 'Although international law is cited to condemn demolitions, so far it has not influenced international aid policy.'[16]

This was a microcosm of a much larger question about aid to the Palestinians. The Palestinian politician Mohammad Shtayyeh liked to

---

* Lapid, who partly grew up in a Budapest ghetto during the Second World War, was quick to assert he was not drawing a comparison with the Holocaust.

point out that a bridge on the road to Beit Hanoun had been bombed three times, and each time had been rebuilt with EU funds. Wouldn't it be cheaper to stop Israel bombing the bridge? And were such payments not subsidising the occupation? Shearer and Meyer suggested that if Israel were 'presented with the . . . bill' for Rafah's reconstruction, it might 'prompt a rethinking of military strategy'.

This approach carried dangers for Palestinians since, while 'donors wait for Israel to assume its obligations as occupier, human suffering will go unalleviated'. But, Shearer and Meyer concluded, 'it is time for donors to examine how $1bn a year might be used more effectively – with imposed conditions – as a lever for peace rather than being suckered into simply buying the sticking plasters'.

Towards the end of 2004 there were hopes in Western capitals that peace might be in sight without any need for such levers. One reason was Sharon's willingness to withdraw from settlements, if only in Gaza. The other was Yasser Arafat's death in November 2004. This isn't the place to speculate on the causes: the near-universal suspicion among Palestinians that he was poisoned by collaborators acting on behalf of Israel has always been adamantly rejected by Israel itself. By accepting the historic compromise of a two-state solution in 1988, Arafat had set the Palestinians on a course towards self-determination and a negoti- ated end to the conflict. Yet Sharon continued, as he had since the 1980s at least, to treat him implacably as the enemy. Arafat's likely replace- ment by Mahmoud Abbas, who had set his face against armed struggle, seemed to offer the chance of a new beginning in Israeli–Palestinian relations.

On the ground, however, the year ended as bloodily as ever. As if to underline that the demolition of houses earlier in the year had been ineffective in stopping the digging of tunnels, on 11 December Gaza militants from Hamas and the 'Fatah hawks'* used one under the Egypt–Gaza crossing point at Rafah to detonate 1,500kg of explosives which killed five Israeli soldiers, all of them Bedouins (who had long been allowed to volunteer for military service). The militants claimed the attack was in retaliation for Arafat's 'assassination'. But it was clear that, just as Sharon and Mofaz maintained their efforts to prove that Israel was not running away from Gaza under fire from Hamas, so the

---

* The name had been used by Fatah militants during the First Intifada.

armed factions – especially Hamas – were intent on proving they were doing just that. Each side sought to show to their supporters – and doubters – that they held the initiative: the extensive media coverage in both Israel and Gaza of every military advance on either side reinforced the two viewpoints.

Hamas also resorted to another method: agit-prop street art. Abed Amr worked at a commercial sign-writing and graphic design business in Khan Yunis. The day before the attack, the twenty-year-old (politically unaffiliated) draftsman took a call from a local Hamas official confirming an earlier order – worth $36 a day – for Khan Yunis walls to be covered with murals and graffiti commemorating the seventeenth anniversary of Hamas's foundation in December 1987. The Hamas man now insisted on the urgency of the task. 'Don't take any other jobs,' he said, adding, only half jokingly: 'If Sheikh Abdel Aziz Rantissi himself rises from the dead and asks you to work for him, don't!' Only later did Abed realise that Hamas wanted the murals on street walls by the time Khan Yunis woke up to the explosion.

In Northern Ireland, during the Troubles, there was similar visual propaganda. But in Gaza, the sheer range – from painted sheet-metal 'martyr portraits' of Palestinians killed in the conflict, through murals of famous Palestinian leaders, to instant but elaborate 'calligrafitti' – was greater, the iconography more complex. When Rantissi was killed, a vibrant piece of spray-painted calligraphy appeared on a wall near his home proclaiming: 'You got what you wanted, Abu Mohammed, You won'. At first sight it seemed a sardonic commentary on the Hamas leader's remark in an interview a few months earlier that he would rather be killed by an Israeli Apache helicopter than die from a heart attack. In fact, all the signs were that it was commissioned propaganda, seeking to offset the public impact of a grave blow to Hamas.

In the years of the Second Intifada, examples of propaganda included the single blood-red Arabic word 'Jabahywoun' or 'Fronters' on a whitewashed wall in a refugee camp, with the symbols of the armed uprising – a *keffiyah*, a masked face, an AK-47 and a grenade – woven into lettering denoting the Popular Front for the Liberation of Palestine. Or a weeping eye with Jerusalem's al-Aqsa mosque reflected in its pupil; or a portrait of Yahya Ayyash, revered by Hamas supporters as 'the engineer', shown beside his grisly handiwork: a bombed Israeli bus, bodies flying into the air, a corpse dangling from a window, a severed hand.

The factions took turns for wall space. 'We paint a wall for Hamas for one week, then whitewash it and do the same for Fatah the next week,' explained Abed. While they worked for free for a bereaved family paying for a funeral themselves, charging only for paint if the family could afford it, work for the factions was strictly commercial. For Fatah commissions at least, there was a new face to perfect, less colourful than Arafat, less well known in Gaza, and without the trademark *keffiyah*. In a January 2005 election that Hamas did not contest, Mahmoud Abbas was duly elected President, raising international hopes that with an avowed moderate succeeding Arafat an agreement to end the conflict might at last be in sight.

The new President almost immediately travelled to Gaza. At the end of January, he secured agreement from the armed factions for one month of 'calm', or *tahdiya*. Within a day of the month-long 'calm' ending, an Islamic Jihad suicide bomber killed five Israelis. Abbas denounced the attack as 'an act of sabotage' against the peace process, offered a joint Israeli–Palestinian investigation into the atrocity, and returned to negotiations with the armed factions. In March, he persuaded them once again to agree to an open-ended 'calm' if Israel reciprocated, which would now largely hold until the summer.

Abbas's strategy was to persuade the factions that such a respite would give him the space to open serious peace negotiations with Sharon. In other circumstances, this would have been the moment for the US-led Quartet to press for such a move. But Sharon, fully focused on the planned disengagement from Gaza, did not see it that way. He continued to insist on the implausible condition that a voluntary cease-fire was not enough and that Abbas had to confront Hamas and eliminate the 'terrorist infrastructure'.

Even Elliott Abrams, the US official most sympathetic to and trusted by Sharon, admitted the 'calm' was actually helpful to the Israeli Prime Minister, writing to Stephen Hadley, then his immediate boss as the National Security Adviser: 'There is optimism in the region, but there is also a dilemma. Israel complains that Abbas is not confronting Hamas and is pressing him to do more. His [Abbas's] slow and non-confrontational approach produces quiet, about which the Israelis then complain, but which helps Sharon in his own internal political battle. Confronting Hamas would produce more violence, which neither Abbas nor Sharon want right now.'[17]

Sharon, now determinedly unilateralist in his approach, was not seeking negotiations with Abbas even on the practicalities of Gaza disengagement, let alone as part of a wider peace process. And the US was not going to press him, at least before the withdrawal from Gaza, which it regarded, in a phrase beloved of diplomats, as 'the only show in town'.

Sharon gave the new Palestinian President little help in boosting his authority among grassroots Palestinians in other ways, despite encouragement from the Bush administration to do so. Once again a promised release of prisoners was confined to 900 – out of 7,500 – many convicted of criminal rather than political offences, or close to their time of release. The IDF strained 'the calm' to the limit – for example, in April 2005, by shooting dead three Palestinian boys playing football close to the Gaza border with Egypt. The incident triggered a predictable series of mortar attacks by militants on the Gush Katif settlements. And Sharon failed to carry out his promise to the Americans to dismantle West Bank settlement 'outposts' – often no more than a few caravans established, in defiance of Israeli as well as international law, as the nucleus of further expansion.

By July 2005, it was nevertheless dawning on increasing numbers of Israeli settlers in Gaza that disengagement was going to happen. True, Neve Dekalim beach, long closed to Palestinians, still presented a vivid tableau of Israeliness. One morning, when the sand was so hot it burned underfoot, there was an Orthodox Jew in a heavy black coat and wide-brimmed hat; a circle of teenage settlers sharing a hubble-bubble of sweetly apple-scented tobacco; a pair of armed and uniformed policemen patrolling the shore; two off-duty soldiers reading newspapers in their swimming trunks, their M16s embedded in the sand and pointing upwards beside them; two or three surfers 'lining up' in the waves; an Israel Defense Forces post surrounded by razor wire, its radar antenna circling continually in the remorseless search for potential Palestinian attackers and Palestinian fishing boats rash enough to stray beyond the narrow strip of in-shore water to which they were restricted. Meir Amshik, surfer, lifeguard and deeply religious Yeshiva student, was wrapped in a Chilean poncho but with a white embroidered prayer shawl on one shoulder as he studied a large Torah.

Amshik compared the settlers' eviction from Gaza to the biblical flight of the Jews to exile in Egypt, and thought that Arabs leaving the

Holy Land altogether would not only be the 'best option' but 'may happen when the Messiah comes'. Amshik had nevertheless come to the conclusion that God would not stop the withdrawal happening. So had his more secular and less dogmatic friend and fellow lifeguard Lior Barda, who said he wouldn't oppose disengagement if it would end 'all the killing and shit'.

Once it was all over, and the surfers had packed their boards, Palestinians in Gaza at last had something to celebrate. On 12 September, the Israeli military – troops, bulldozers, tanks and all – finally left the interior of the Strip. Israel still controlled the borders, airspace and territorial waters beyond the six nautical miles fishermen were allowed to work in (as opposed to the twenty allocated to them under the Oslo agreement). But the withdrawal removed some of the internal restrictions – and risks – posed by more than two decades of Gaza settlement. One was the hated Abu Houli checkpoint, which effectively bisected the Strip north of Khan Yunis. With level-crossing-style gates flanked by fortified military watchtowers, Abu Houli had been a constant source of frustration for Palestinians, who were obliged to queue in cars and trucks for hours, even days.[18]

As dawn broke the green flags of Hamas and the black and yellow of Islamic Jihad had been planted in a mountain of rubble. Explaining why these, rather than the national Palestinian flag, were flying among the ruins, a young Islamic University student and Hamas supporter, Ehab al-Baz, said: 'The settlement was liberated by resistance weapons and not negotiations. And we got here first.' As if to underline his point, an ostentatious six-vehicle convoy of masked Islamic Jihad militants brandishing AK-47s drove into the heart of the settlement as he was speaking.

Meanwhile, a single Palestinian Authority bulldozer driver was trying to demolish the solid concrete wall of the domed synagogue which, like all the others in Gaza's twenty-one settlements, Sharon had decided to leave standing, whether for religious reasons or to tempt the Palestinians into destruction which his government would later condemn as 'barbaric'. The site foreman Haitham Ghanim said he was acting under orders; but, unlike al-Baz, he added that, welcome as it was, disengagement was 'fifty per cent resistance and fifty per cent an Israeli decision. Let's not kid ourselves.' The dividing line between al-Baz and Ghanim over whether the 'resistance' in general and Hamas in particular had driven the Israelis from Gaza would be exactly that between Hamas and Fatah in the elections five months later.

Tens of thousands of Palestinian men, women and children poured out of nearby Khan Yunis, Gaza's second city. Units from Islamic Jihad's al-Quds, Hamas's Izzedine al-Qassam and Fatah's al-Aqsa Martyrs' Brigades planted more banners in the rubble celebrating 'the victory over Zionism'. One al-Aqsa squad tried to burn down one of the settlement's two synagogues. But most were civilians; some came to scavenge among the rubble, some to wonder at the devastation, others simply for the sheer novelty of strolling in once-forbidden territory without fear of being shot. 'I never believed my feet would ever touch this ground,' fifty-year-old Rasmiya al-Najar said, as, with hundreds of other curious, hopeful, celebrating Palestinians, she walked the street into the settlement. 'I never imagined it.' The scavengers brought donkey carts to load up with doors, light fittings, sinks, glass and anything else they could grab from the council office and other public buildings left intact. Arriving from Khan Yunis at 7 a.m., fourteen-year-old Basil Quweida made straight for the ruins of the once solid red-roofed residential villas on a more homely quest. In one of the synagogues, echoing to the crashes of men using metal bars to detach the window frames and hurling strips of aluminium onto the floor from the gallery above, he proudly showed off the contents of the carrier bag he had been filling all morning: a football, a baby's rattle, a large blue toy car, a child's yellow plastic helmet, a kettle. He would give them all to his mother, he explained, beaming, adding that the toys were for his five younger siblings, aged from two to thirteen.

Thousands of other Palestinians from Khan Yunis simply wanted to see, and plunge into, the sea from beaches just two miles away from home, but which had long been closed to them. (For six Palestinians, this had tragic consequences: they drowned.)[19] Nine-year-old Mohammed Hijezi, who had never seen the sea before, ran all the way from his home as soon as he had dressed and had breakfast. 'I was supposed to go to school,' he said. 'My parents don't know. I was dreaming of swimming. The water is very beautiful and very cold.'[20]

Yet for all the immediate rejoicing among the Gazan public, disengagement would not yield the political dividend Mahmoud Abbas had expected when he had been elected back in January. Sharon could have involved him publicly in negotiations regarding disengagement before it happened. He could have staged a symbolic public handover of the settlement sites to the Palestinian President. He could have ordered the IDF visibly to coordinate the passing of control over them to Abbas's security forces. Such a move might have encouraged sceptical Palestinians to think that non-violence and negotiations had a future. But he chose not to. In his sympathetic portrayal of Sharon in this period, David Landau, a strong supporter of disengagement, wrote: 'Even though his basic strategic decision was that Israel must act unilaterally there was room – and need – for close coordination on a tactical level with the Palestinian Authority. Sharon's disdain for "the Arabs" meant that he did not sufficiently apply himself to this aspect . . . Israel could have done much more to help ensure that the PA security forces took firm control of the Gaza Strip in the wake of the IDF's departure.'[21]

Landau linked the failure to coordinate disengagement with Abbas to Sharon's much earlier comment that 'Abu Mazen [Abbas], too, is still an Arab', which Landau thought gave 'an unguarded glimpse into the deep reservoir of [Sharon's] distaste and distrust for the neighbouring nation'. So far from unilateralism being the 'last resort in the absence of a credible negotiating partner' it was 'in a very profound way for Sharon . . . a policy of first resort, even of first choice'.[22]

Sir John Jenkins, then the British Consul General, had been to a 2005 meeting in the West Bank with Saeb Erekat and others where 'they said "they're [Israel] going to disengage and we've got this security plan . . . we're going to coordinate with them and put a security cordon around the former settlements, greenhouses and so on, and we'll make sure they're protected."' When Jenkins expressed scepticism, 'they said "they have to"'; they were convinced the Israelis had to do it and they couldn't otherwise get the settlers out. They were hapless really, the PA.'

While sharply critical of Palestinian officials for the sketchiness of their 'security plan', Jenkins added: 'I think [Sharon] was damned if he was going to coordinate with the PA. This took the PA by surprise. Could the Israelis have coordinated more with the PA? Of course they could. They could have enabled Abu Mazen [Abbas] to have claimed the credit. I just think Sharon was absolutely determined the Palestinians were going to get absolutely nothing for free.' As for the possibility that Hamas would instead be able to benefit, arguing that they had driven the Israelis out: 'I don't think he cared.'[23]

Politically flawed although its execution was, Sharon had been true to his reputation as 'The Bulldozer'. Disengagement did not lead to negotiations on a final peace settlement; nor was it intended to. But Sharon had overcome the opposition of his most dangerous political rival, Benjamin Netanyahu, who would later head Israel's most right-wing government ever as Prime Minister. And he had set a momentous precedent which showed that Jewish settlers could be uprooted, if there was an Israeli leader with the desire, the will and the authority to do so. When and whether another would emerge able and ready to apply these attributes to the far larger task of withdrawing the settlers from, and ending the occupation of, the West Bank was much less certain.

4

'THE DREAM TURNED INTO A NIGHTMARE': POST-DISENGAGEMENT, 2005–6

THREE LANES OF HONKING TRAFFIC GRIDLOCKED the disused east–west sandy road between Rafah and the flattened military base which, until now, had blocked access to the sea. Palestinians here were also celebrating the Israeli army's withdrawal from Gaza's borders a month after the settlers had left, and it seemed as though every person in the Strip's southernmost town – more violent and ravaged in the past five years than any other – was shouting. Every vehicle moved at a crawl, pick-ups carried squads of masked and armed Hamas militants, donkey carts creaked with anything useable or saleable from the abandoned detritus, cars bulged with families curious to inspect the ruins and gulp the sea air at last. Mohammed Mahulain, a thirty-three-year-old construction worker, had rushed out of his house in pyjamas at dawn after hearing the Israeli army had left the settlement of Rafiah Yam. Later, dressed in an immaculate grey *dishdash*, he stood outside his apartment block, which was pockmarked with bullet holes, and watched the traffic jam, an irrepressible grin on his face. Yes, he worried that the settlement would be used to build summer houses for important PA officials rather than to rehouse thousands of residents whose homes by the border had been destroyed in the last five years. But he wasn't going to let that spoil the day. 'I'm in a good mood,' he chuckled.

The following day, some Rafah residents were even able to leave Gaza briefly, although the official crossing remained closed. During the previous five years, to stray anywhere near the eight-metre steel barrier had been to invite shelling or machine-gun fire from the heavily fortified military posts along its length, or from the tanks and armoured vehicles patrolling the Philadelphia Corridor on its other side. With the army gone, hundreds of jubilant Palestinians clambered on ladders over the barrier or through gaps left by the abandoned gun turrets and across the international frontier which had bisected the town since the 1979 Egypt–Israel peace treaty, thrilled by the opportunity to visit relatives and buy cheap Egyptian goods. One middle-aged resident, Ala Adin Fodeh, joked he had trouble sleeping without the sound of repeated explosions and gunfire, while Mohammed Said Abu Marahil, a sixty-year-old egg merchant on his way to visit his seventy-five-year-old sister for the first time in ten years, said: 'This is the real proof that we have peace.'

The Palestinian hopes for the future were as nothing compared to the the international welcome. For Sharon, the weeks that followed the withdrawal were 'an untrammelled splurge of *gloria mundi*. At the UN General Assembly in New York [in September 2005], which Sharon addressed for the first time, statesmen from dozens of countries literally vied for face time and a photo op with the Israeli leader, who by universal consensus had taken the Middle East a giant step forward.'[1]

It was a consensus, moreover, sharply reinforced by the strong, sometimes almost hysterical, opposition Sharon had faced from critics on the extreme nationalist end of the Israeli political spectrum. If those far-right critics had been so antagonistic to Gaza withdrawal, foreign leaders reasoned, his policy must be correct (Sharon eventually jumped clear of his internal critics by announcing on 21 November that he was going to form a new party, later named Kadima, or 'Forward').

In the end, however, the assertion of the egg merchant Abu Marahil was wrong. That he could visit his sister in Egypt proved nothing. The border was swiftly sealed after strong complaints by Israel to both Egypt and the Palestinian Authority about a grave breach of security. More fundamentally, the expectations raised by disengagement among Gazan civilians, like those of the Oslo Accords more than a decade earlier, would prove to be illusory. Disengagement was indeed a historic precedent. The paradox was that it also marked the beginning of a crippling decade-long economic blockade of Gaza and three military onslaughts by Israel more devastating than any in the territory's turbulent history.

From the outset disengagement was subject to myth-making on both sides. Hamas lost no time exploiting the 'liberation' of the Gaza Strip, erecting banners proclaiming that Jerusalem and the West Bank would follow. Mahmoud Zahar said: 'No one can claim the disengagement was a unilateral step and a gift from Sharon. It was a crushing defeat to the dignity of the Jewish state.'[2] This was a shameless overstatement. While the move partly reflected a growing intolerance of the loss of soldiers' lives in a dangerous corner of historic Palestine that most saw as of zero strategic value, the outcome was much less of a defeat than Hamas claimed.

For their own purposes Hamas might claim that Gaza had been 'liberated' and Israel that its occupation of the Strip had ended. But Israel still patrolled the air space and the territorial waters, enforcing whatever limits it chose on Gazan fishermen; Israel authorised each ID card and logged every birth in its Ministry of Interior computer, and it dictated who could leave Gaza for Israel or the West Bank. Freedom of travel within Gaza had been restored and, for the first time since the Six Day War, there were no Israeli troops within its borders. But travel from Gaza to the outside world did not become easier; instead, it soon became even harder. In the hindsight of the left-wing Israeli commentator Gideon Levy: 'The gaoler pulled out of the gaol and was now holding its prisoners captive from without.'[3] And the troops would soon be back, if not permanently, at least frequently.

The settlers' denunciation of Sharon's 'betrayal' neatly mirrored the militants' depiction of their 'victory'. Yet the mainstream Israeli reading was more dangerous for the Palestinians. Most believed Israel had presented Gazans with an unprecedented opportunity to order their own lives, to use the land and other resources abandoned by the departing settlers, and live in prosperity and peace; but all it had got in return was the firing of rockets and the transformation of Gaza into an impoverished wasteland for which the world unaccountably held Israel responsible.

The reality was different. The argument that Israel's security would have been better preserved had the settlers stayed in Gaza does not stand up to scrutiny. While the rockets used by Hamas increased in effectiveness and range after disengagement, actually 162 Israelis and foreign workers were killed in the five years before disengagement compared to 140 in the ten years afterwards.[4]

The idea that in Gaza the settlers had left behind a potential oasis of prosperity is also deeply flawed. The previous year, the World Bank had warned that with the Palestinian economy having 'lost all economic dynamism and experienced a recession of historic proportions' since the beginning of the Intifada, the Gaza disengagement alone would 'not alter this dangerous, unsustainable situation'.[5] It would have little impact on Palestinian livelihoods, which had fallen by a third since 2000, leaving half below the poverty line,* unless there was a major easing of the closures and restrictions introduced since the beginning of the Intifada.

Even when the main cargo crossing at Karni was open, traders faced serious obstacles like the archaic system of 'back to back' loading and unloading of goods for export and import. Yet there were readily available scanners which would have sped up the passage of goods without manual searches while guaranteeing security. Arguing that the failure to speed up the process in Karni was itself contributing to Palestinian business failures and consequent unemployment, the normally dry and understated World Bank warned this ran counter to Israel's own interests: the impoverishment and alienation of young Palestinians, said the Bank, was 'undermining the credibility of the PA, increasing the popular appeal of militant factions and threatening Israel's security'.

Instead an Israeli policy of 'separation' of Gaza from both Israel and the West Bank, the two main markets for its goods and labour, had started months before disengagement. Separation between Israel and the West Bank was under way with the 440-mile 'separation barrier' which Sharon had authorised, taking in occupied territory in many parts of its route and cutting off thousands of Palestinian farmers from their land in border areas. Now Sharon's government took steps to cut even more severely the already limited links between Gaza and Israel.

THEY ARRIVED IN BEATEN-UP OLD SUBARUS and Peugeots, five or six to a car, at around 4.30 a.m. to queue for admission to work. Although they were among the lucky few to have both the prized Israeli magnetic cards and the Israeli-stamped employer permits, they still had to lift their shirts to the neck and their trousers up to the knees to show the soldiers guarding the zone they were not carrying explosives. All this to enter a zone that was within Gaza's borders. 'We can have work without dignity,'

---

* $1.90 a day at 2016 prices.

joked thirty-eight-year-old carpenter Mohsen Ashur, 'or we can have dignity without work.' But the mood was good; it was another moment of hope for Gaza: the reopening of the thirty-year-old Erez industrial zone, under Israeli control but just inside Gaza, with its Israeli and Palestinian businesses – from furniture to car repair – accessible to both nationalities. These businesses had employed some 4,000 Palestinian workers until work at the industrial zone had been suspended after a series of attacks in April 2004. Now it was February 2005 and two days after Ariel Sharon and the new Palestinian President Mahmoud Abbas had both declared their commitments to a ceasefire at a Sharm El Sheikh summit. Another worker, Fahmi al-Bahtiti, had, like many of those queueing in the dark, watched the summit on Al Jazeera. 'It was a good conference. We want to live in peace with Jews,' he said. 'I hope the cease-fire will work. The next step should be to implement the road map.'

But the men who had lined up that morning didn't know they were making history – and not in a good way. For these were the very last group to work in the industrial zone, for so long the main physical interface between Gaza and Israel. In June 2005 Ehud Olmert, then Industry Minister, closed the zone for good, announcing that the Israeli companies would now be relocated to Israel, and given subsidies to cover the higher wages they would now have to pay to Israeli employees.

Olmert cited 'security reasons' for closing the zone. But given that the ceasefire which Abbas had, true to his promise at Sharm, negotiated with all the armed factions in March was holding well, it looked as if there was another reason: what was now explicitly acknowledged to be the Israeli government policy of separating Gaza from Israel and the West Bank. As Giora Eiland, chairman of Israel's National Security Council, put it, disengagement was 'meant to separate Israel from the Palestinians both politically and for security purposes, and this requires economic separation as well'.[6]

The first steps were already under way to do just that. Israel announced its intention to stop issuing permits for Palestinians to work in Israel from 2008. But for Gaza this came much more swiftly – not just in the industrial zone but in Israel itself. The closure was the culmination of a gradual process since 1991, when Israel changed its policy of free move-ment and began to limit the permits issued to Palestinians for travel – to work, study or visit relatives. In better circumstances it would make far more economic sense for Palestinian workers to be employed in productive industry in Gaza, rather than provide cheap labour to Israel. But that would also have required a radical rethink of a closure policy that was already starting to cut off Gaza from the outside world.

The 2004 warnings from the World Bank that disengagement alone would not ease Gaza's economic travails had been signed off by James Wolfensohn, the seventy-two-year-old Jewish Australian-born head of the Bank. In April 2005 George W. Bush chose Wolfensohn as the first envoy of the international Middle East 'Quartet', comprising the US, EU, Russia and the UN.

Wolfensohn made a heroic effort to lever disengagement to advance progress towards a negotiated peace – and in the process to revive the Gaza economy. He ignored an ominous warning from his friend, the experienced US Middle East diplomat Martin Indyk, that he was being 'used' by both the US and Israel. Elliott Abrams, the US neo-conservative point man on the Israeli–Palestinian issue and a pro-Israel hawk, was 'laughing' at him behind his back; and Sharon had 'zero interest' in a deal with the Palestinians and was only open to talks with Wolfensohn to show 'progress', while confident that his ideas would not be carried out.[7]

Undaunted, Wolfensohn saw himself on a mission, part of which was to ensure the Palestinians benefited from what had been the Gaza settlers' greatest economic asset: the greenhouses growing for export a wide range of produce, from bug-free lettuce for the Jewish ultra-orthodox market to cherry tomatoes and geraniums. Some of the plastic marquee-like greenhouses scattered through the twenty-one Gaza settlements were high-tech, with sophisticated temperature control and irrigation systems, and their turnover was between $75m and $100m a year. Acquiring them was a race against time; despairing of receiving what they saw as inadequate compensation for the greenhouses, the settlers had by mid-July dismantled about half, leaving about 500 acres of greenhouse farming intact.[8] Wolfensohn raised $14m from US philanthropists – including $1m of his own money and a $10m grant from the Bill and Melinda Gates Foundation – to pay for the greenhouses left by the settlers to be transferred intact to the Palestinians.

Wolfensohn's idealistic dreams were never fulfilled. One standard explanation is that greenhouses left by the settlers were destroyed by looting and the opportunity was thrown away by the Palestinians themselves.[9] Certainly, immediately after the pullout, the PA police failed to prevent scavengers from helping themselves to water pipes and other useful components from many of the greenhouses. According to Ayed Abu Ramadan, who ran the 'ex-settlement project' on behalf of the Palestinian Economic Development Corporation, some of the looting was encouraged by private owners of land that had been expropriated by Israel for the settlements and which they were now seeking to recover.[10] Equally, some of it was fuelled by a belief that the settlements would be taken over by the PA or its agencies for the direct benefit of its leaders. The leading Gaza economist Omar Shaban suggested:

> The refugees, those who were victims of the occupation, they felt that, oh we didn't get anything out of our struggle, even this land which we liberated was given to those bad people. And the refugee camp in Khan Yunis, the most miserable camp, it's 200 metres from a nice area, [and] the people in the camp were looking at the water for the greenhouses for the nice villas, while they don't have water. There was a lot of anger. So people went in at midnight to steal everything. Not because people are looters or they like to steal, but because they believe these assets belong to them and somebody will take them again.[11]

Nevertheless, Wolfensohn noted that after 'a day or two of looting' which had done 'some damage', the greenhouses 'came through essentially intact'.[12] When he toured Gaza with PA Finance Minister Salam Fayyad, he found the security forces were protecting the greenhouses and 'everywhere people were excited about building hotels, fostering tourism, and creating a thriving economy'.

Moreover, the greenhouse project rapidly gained traction despite its shaky start and the absence of inventories or instructions from the Israeli owners, employing 4,500 day labourers, 300 supervisors and a range of subcontractors for irrigation and managing water wells. Strawberries, tomatoes, cherry tomatoes, bell peppers and herbs were planted with the first crop harvested in November and a second planting begun. The problem was getting the fruit and vegetables out of Gaza and through Israel to the European markets for which they were intended. The cumbersome 'back to back' regime, in which highly perishable produce had to be laid out on the tarmac for often lengthy security inspections, meant significant parts of the few consignments allowed through had rotted by the time they left Gaza.

The delays compounded the endemic corruption at Karni. The less the crossing was open, the higher the bribes demanded by Israeli officials to allow trucks to enter Gaza.[13] But the system also applied to the few trucks allowed out of Gaza, prompting a pained Wolfensohn to remark wryly that the bribes were the 'best example of Israeli-Palestinian cooperation at the official level.'

For Abu Ramadan:

> The dream turned into a nightmare. It was like having an elephant in a gaol which you can't feed and you can't let out. You don't know what to do with it. It's a fortune, you have greenhouses worth millions of dollars, capable of providing jobs for thousands of people. But if you plant you can't sell it in the local market because [the amount] is too huge. And Israel won't allow you to export it or imposes delays. And then we had the elections [won by Hamas in January 2006] and the Israelis were even more reluctant.

Wolfensohn, seeing that a disaster was imminent, and despite being gradually forced out of the Bush/Rice circle, had persuaded Rice to use her authority to negotiate two agreements between Israel and the Palestinians to open the borders, ensuring, among much else, that the harvested crops could leave Gaza. One would provide for movement of goods and people through Israel and to the West Bank; and the other was aimed at providing Israel with security guarantees which would allow the free movement through the Rafah crossing, to be operated jointly by the PA and Egypt but monitored by EU officials in a new 'Border Assistance Mission' (EUBAM).

Rice arrived in Jerusalem in November 2005 for talks on an Access and Movement Agreement for Gaza (AMA). In his illuminating account of the period, Elliott Abrams acknowledged that, three months after disengagement, the 'expected advantages to the Palestinians' were 'invisible' and they could not 'conduct normal export and import activity'.[14] But he also depicted the Secretary of State as needing a short-term diplomatic achievement to repair the public relations damage inflicted by the wholesale failure of a US–Arab summit on democracy in Bahrain earlier in the same Middle East trip. Israel was evidently reluctant to sign the Wolfensohn-drafted agreement during the negotiations at Jerusalem's David Citadel Hotel. Around midnight on the night of 14–15 November Abrams telephoned Sharon's closest aide Dov Weisglass and told him: 'Look, Condi needs this agreement ... I explained about Bahrain and the press. Tell the Prime Minister [Sharon] this is personal. This is a favour to her; she needs to have a victory here. He got the point quickly and said he'd do what he could.'[15]

This boded well for the signing of the agreement, but much less so for its implementation. There was a dramatic sideshow, in which Wolfensohn threatened resignation and vented his fury on Abrams – 'Look, Elliott, I think you are a son of a bitch' – at being kept on the sidelines during the negotiations on what was essentially his own plan.

A central provision had been that 'on an urgent basis, Israel will permit the export of *all* agricultural products from Gaza during this 2005 harvest season' (my italics). In the event the UN estimated that just four per cent of the season's harvest was exported. For Wolfensohn, whose health suffered in the process, it was the 'biggest personal disappointment during my mandate'.[16]

He was not alone. Barakat al-Boh had been recruited in September 2005 to the Wolfensohn-inspired Gaza Agriculture Project, harvesting green peppers and tomatoes in greenhouses that had belonged to the departed Jewish settlers of Gannei Tal. Al-Boh was an experienced nurseryman who had been a foreman for more than twenty years, until the Intifada started in 2000. He had been unemployed since then, and was delighted to get the job. 'It wasn't much money, frankly, just sixty shekels (then £7.30) a day, not really enough to make a living. But we were happy to be going to work. We were even more productive than the settlers, I can tell you. It was Palestinian, the project belonged to us, and we wanted to prove to the world that it could succeed.' In May 2006 he and his brother, who had joined him, were laid off when the project closed, unable to sustain its heavy losses in the absence of revenue. 'We were really hurt when it closed,' said al-Boh. 'When we heard the lorries were getting to Karni and then not being allowed across, we went nuts, crazy.'

Raji Sourani, the head of the Palestinian Centre for Human Rights (PCHR), and in many ways the leader of Gaza's civil society, got to know Wolfensohn well. When they first met, Wolfensohn had said, ' "Raji: I know you know nothing about economics. What's your dream economy-wise?" I said: "I want freedom of movement for goods and individuals between Gaza and the West Bank and the outside world. This is my dream. If this happens, super-fantastic." He said "this is ipso facto an economy. No economy can exist without freedom of movement of goods and people."' Sourani said that at the end of his term as Quartet envoy Wolfensohn had sadly apologised to him for failing to provide Gaza with its 'ipso facto economy'.[17]

If implemented, the AMA would have been a major advance on what had gone before for Gazan civilians. Not only would they have had the freedom of passage to the West Bank denied them since the beginning of the Intifada, but outlets for Gazan industry and agriculture would have seen a major expansion; it envisaged 400 export trucks leaving Karni every day including a daily convoy passing to the West Bank from 15 January 2006. It held out a real hope for jobs and for an easing of the social and psychological pressures of closure by providing for a similar daily bus convoy of passengers by 15 December 2005. While the Rafah crossing into Egypt remained open nearly every day, with 'third party monitoring' by the EU, until the capture of the Israeli soldier Gilad Shalit by militants in June 2006, the rest of the agreement was stillborn. The actual number of trucks in 2006 averaged around twelve a day; and the convoys simply never happened.[18]

As usual, Israel cited security concerns to explain the agreement's non-implementation. This was not seriously challenged by either the Bush administration or the EU, despite arguably good grounds for doing so. Israel's cancellation of talks with the PA to discuss implementation followed a suicide bombing which killed five people and injured around fifty in Netanya on 5 December; but this was perpetrated from the West Bank and by Islamic Jihad (which, unlike Hamas and the other factions, had violated the ceasefire declared in March three times since July). It was true that, in a clumsy attempt to cover up its responsibility for the explosion of a Qassam rocket in one of its military displays in September which had killed twenty Palestinians, Hamas, as well as Islamic Jihad, had earlier fired dozens of rockets into Israel, causing minor injuries to five Israeli civilians. This triggered a fierce response from Israel, which fired artillery rounds into Gaza for the first time, killing an Islamic Jihad operative. But that was two months before the AMA was signed. And Hamas had reverted to the ceasefire.

Moreover, according to the UN's special Middle East representative Álvaro de Soto, it was envisaged that talks on implementing the agreement would not be 'contaminated by events'.[19] That was not how Israel saw it. Its official position after the Netanya bombing was that it would not talk about access and movement with the PA until it had done more to clamp down on terrorism (even though the PA's security forces claimed to have arrested around twenty Islamic Jihad members in previous weeks).

But Israel's demand raised the question once again of how Abbas was supposed to succeed where Israel itself had failed to eliminate by force the threat posed by determined militants – a question which exercised even Condoleezza Rice. A year later, when Rice urged the team around Ehud Olmert, Sharon's successor, to embark on serious peace negotiations with Abbas, they insisted that they could not do so until Abbas first 'stopped terror'. Rice candidly retorted: 'They [the PA] can't stop terror . . . we can't either, in Iraq or Afghanistan.'[20] This revealingly honest remark exposed the unreality of the doctrine that Israel had stuck with since 2003. But in November 2005, it still held firm.

Beyond that were two conflicting views about what would in the long term be the better guarantee of Israel's security – the punitive and military approach espoused by its leaders, or some hope of normal life and work for Gaza's residents, as Wolfensohn believed.

The year 2005 had started on an optimistic note. The replacement of Arafat by Abbas seemed to promise an end to the four-year period in which Israel had insisted it had 'no partner'. Despite the weakening of the PA both by Israel's reprisals against the Intifada and its own internal quarrelling, Abbas had secured a ceasefire in Gaza. Disengagement had briefly generated some hope of wider progress. But virtually none of those hopes were realised. In Gaza, freedom of movement within the confining barriers that kept it isolated from the outside world had proved the only tangible benefit. For all the enthusiastic welcome it had received, Israeli disengagement had inflicted further damage on Gaza's stricken economy; the abortive AMA had been the last hope of repairing that damage.

So 2005 ended in pessimism, reinforced by episodes of anarchy and violence. The Fatah-dominated PA security forces in Gaza were unable to prevent a 100-strong armed militia from storming the home of one of its senior figures, Musa Arafat, a rival of Mohammed Dahlan, and shooting him dead.* Then on 28 December, a dedicated Arabic-speaking Briton, Kate Burton, who was on secondment to the respected Al Mezan human rights agency, was kidnapped with her visiting parents on a trip to southern Gaza. They were forced at gunpoint into a white Mazda by two masked members of a maverick extremist group calling themselves 'The Brigades of the Mujahadeen-Jerusalem'. The family was released in the early hours of New Year's Eve, but only after the cool and competent Ms Burton had been forced to stand by one of the gunmen as he made a video denouncing Britain's record in the Middle East and threatening the kidnap of EU monitors coming to Gaza for the Palestinian elections, now less than a month away.

In Gaza to cover the kidnapping, I had gone with a British colleague, as we often did in those days, for a drink at the UN Beach Club. Dating from the 1950s, it was the only establishment still serving alcohol in the Strip. With wood panelling, armchairs and a welcoming fire in winter, it was presided over by an amiable if somewhat lugubrious Christian Palestinian, who would occasionally offer his regulars an illicit joint when it was not too busy at the end of the night. Officially only for foreigners, it was also visited by some Palestinians, including a veteran bearded former member of Arafat's Naval Police, who regularly nursed his beer at the corner of the bar.

It would be the last drink any of us would ever have there. The following night, at around 2 a.m., when the bar was closed, five unidentified armed men arrived at the seafront club, tied up the security guard, hit him with a rifle butt and planted explosives in the bar, which they detonated by remote control, blowing the ceiling off and severely damaging the rest of the club's rooms. With hindsight, both the Burtons' ordeal and the blowing up of the Beach Club were portents of the turbulence ahead.

Historic and desirable a precedent as it was, disengagement had left civilian Palestinians in Gaza facing not only a continued Israeli occupation, albeit in another form, but also a mounting economic and

---

* The murder was attributed to the Popular Resistance Committees, a grouping of dissident Fatah militants along with some ex-Hamas and ex-Islamic Jihad adherents, and led by the former 'Fatah Hawk' Jamal Abu Samhadana, whom Hamas would later put in charge of its new paramilitary police – the 'Executive Force' – after winning the 2006 elections.

humanitarian crisis, and the stark new dangers posed by lawlessness and inter-Palestinian conflict. Meanwhile, if Sharon's intention was to follow withdrawal from Gaza with an equally unilateral pull-back from parts of the occupied West Bank, it would never be realised. In January 2006 he suffered a massive stroke which left him in a coma from which he would never recover. Within weeks Israel would have a new prime minister. And so would the Palestinians.

5

'A BEAUTIFUL PICTURE TO THE WORLD': ELECTIONS, 2006

THE GREEN TRIANGULAR PENNANTS FLUTTERED FROM every lamp post on the main road into Beit Hanoun, their presence all the more striking for belonging to an organisation that had never before fought an open election. It was January 2005, and the flags were a testament to the campaigning energy of Hamas's thirty-nine-year-old would-be mayor, Mohammed Nazeq al-Kafarna, a polite but determined university lecturer in religion. These elections, the first to be held under the presidency of Mahmoud Abbas, were municipal contests which took place a year before the momentous 2006 parliamentary ones.

Beit Hanoun was one of fourteen Gaza councils taking part in the first local elections in occupied Palestinian territory for nearly thirty years. Then, groups represented by the PLO – mainly Fatah but also some communists – swept to a resounding victory with eighty-five per cent of the seats. Now, Hamas hoped that the 2005 local contest, a dress rehearsal for the more fundamental parliamentary elections a year later, would produce a similarly radical result, this time in its favour.

Al-Kafarna had to work for his votes. To the deep distress of local farmers, the Israeli army had felled many of the town's orange groves, in response, they said, to the firing by Hamas of Qassam rockets into the nearby Israeli border town of Sderot. To an outsider it seemed strange, then, to see Hamas – an Islamic organisation readily associated in Israel and abroad with lethal militancy – plunge into small-town politics. But al-Kafarna's campaign was all about road sweeping, water and sewage, and he promised to cut out the 'middle men' who ensured that those with connections got benefits, from jobs in the municipality to building permits. 'Hamas is not only resistance. It is also a social and political movement,' he said on the eve of polling day.[1]

Without ignoring the appeal of Hamas's new-found enthusiasm for pavement politics, however, Fatah's campaign manager Meher Shinbari thought it would not be the deciding factor. Pointing out that Beit Hanoun had recorded a seventy-five per cent majority for Mahmoud Abbas in the presidential election a fortnight earlier (in which Hamas had not taken part), he said: 'The majority are with Abu Mazen and his efforts to stop the Qassam rocket attacks. The voters will be swayed first by politics of the Israeli–Palestinian conflict, second by the family factor, and third by local services.'

He was wrong on all counts. Hamas took ten out of thirteen seats in Beit Hanoun the following day, in a landslide repeated across the Gaza Strip. Of the total of 118 seats in contention, Fatah took thirty-nine, while Hamas – campaigning as the 'Change and Reform List' – won seventy-six. Voters in Beit Hanoun told me that local issues had swayed their decision. Four months later, Mohammed Ali, a sixty-four-year-old long-time Fatah supporter, paid handsome tribute to the new Hamas council for providing the dusty lane where he lived on the edge of the town with a street light and a bus service that took his grandchildren to school, instead of the hour-long walk they had been subjected to before. 'It's all about honesty,' he said. 'All these years, where did the money go? We haven't seen any of it. Hamas is straightforward . . .'[2]

Nor was the 'family factor' as much of an electoral motivator as Shinbari had predicted. Clan loyalty is a major feature of Gazan life, and two dominant clans in Beit Hanoun were the Kafarnas and the Masris. In a spectacular case of road rage, a conflict between the two broke out later that year when a donkey cart owned by a Masri scratched an SUV belonging to a better-off member of the Kafarna clan. The following two months of armed feuding cost nine lives. But elections were different. Political division cut directly across the clans; Hamas had been careful to put a Masri as well as a Kafarna on its ticket, while most candidates were members of neither family.

With hindsight it seems curious, given the scale of Hamas's munici-pal successes, that its victory in the Palestinian Legislative Council

(PLC) elections a year later came as such a shock. Had Western governments taken more seriously the prospect of Hamas winning a majority in the PLC, they might have thought more deeply about their subsequent actions.

There was no shortage of expert advice to Western diplomatic missions in Jerusalem that the Hamas local election victories in Gaza did *not* mean a sudden conversion to armed Intifada and away from the two-state solution. The US embassy in Tel Aviv was told at the end of January by Abusalamia Effrangi, 'a politically savvy and mainstream Fatah member who was involved in developing the Fatah candidate lists', that he and others had seen 'trouble coming'. One problem had been that the candidate lists included local politicians all too well known (and reviled) by the public at large. By contrast only around thirty to thirty-five per cent of the Hamas candidates were active in the faction, while less aligned candidates identified with Hamas's anti-corruption or 'clean government' platform. Fed up with Fatah, both for its corruption and its failure to improve the day-to-day life of Palestinians, voters had gravitated to what Effrangi termed 'anyone but the Fatah candidate'.[3]

Armed with this analysis, Western governments seemed to have drawn exactly the wrong conclusion, namely, that having been motivated less by Hamas's ideology and more with poor governance, they would turn back to Fatah come the higher-stakes parliamentary elections. Few diplomats understood that Palestinian voters might behave similarly when it came to elections for the PLC, which, like the councils, had been run by Fatah with few positive results.

Israel was little help to Fatah, its supposedly preferred faction. Had it not been for what his biographer calls Sharon's 'inexplicable, almost perverse failure to coordinate the Gaza withdrawal with [PA] President Abu Mazen',[4] the outcome might have been different. In particular he offered nothing to reinforce the Palestinian President's championship of peaceful negotiation. As even the US Consul General Jacob Walles would say long after the elections, 'There was no peace process ... [Fatah] had nothing to point to to say "This is how we can achieve it." '[5] Sharon repeatedly cast doubt on whether Israel would allow the freedom of movement necessary for Palestinian parliamentary elections to be held at all, despite the fact that Abbas's promise of the first elections in a decade had helped to define him as an agent of change. It was hard to escape the conclusion that, having long complained about the impossibility of treating Arafat as a 'partner' in potential peace talks, Sharon was equally determined to prove, both to his own public and Israel's Western allies, that the new Palestinian President was no more of one, thus helping further to deflect any domestic or international pressure to begin negotiating with him.

This was more difficult than it had been with Arafat, given that Abbas was not only a strong supporter of a negotiated two-state solution but an unequivocal opponent of armed Intifada. This time, even the US did not buy into Sharon's dismissal of Abbas, instead insisting that the elections go ahead. In particular the administration, freed in its second term from the perceived electoral need to appease the pro-Israel lobby in the US, and backed by leading EU governments including Britain, rejected the repeated demands of Sharon and his ministers that Hamas should not be allowed to contest them. It even insisted that a deeply reluctant Sharon allow voting to take place in what to the Palestinians – and indeed most Western governments – was occupied East Jerusalem, but to Israel's government was part of the 'undivided' capital over which it claimed sovereignty. A refusal to allow Jerusalemites to vote would almost certainly have obliged Abbas to cancel the elections.

In Western minds, the elections were closely tied to Abbas's standing. If Fatah scored a decisive victory over Hamas, it would greatly strengthen his mandate. Indeed, an election which took place without Hamas as the main opposition would be all but pointless, now that the Islamist faction had decided it wanted to take part and not to boycott the poll as it had in 1996. Israel, by contrast, continued to argue that it was a violation of democracy for an armed faction to participate in elections. 'Can you imagine any European country or the United States allowing a terrorist organisation to take part in elections?' said Israel's Foreign Minister Tzipi Livni.[6] The prospect that it might enhance Abbas's authority to beat Hamas in such elections was of less concern to the Israelis, who were anyway arguing that Abbas should not wait for such elections before disarming the militants. The EU/US approach, however, depended on a Fatah victory. As one European diplomat put it: 'We were – more vigorously than the US – saying to the Israelis: you should have the elections [to the PLC in 2006] and let Hamas run so they can be beaten, taken apart. There was no plan B for if they would actually win. Everyone said they would lose.'[7]

The problem was that 'everyone' was wrong. Hamas stunned diplomats, voters and many of its own leaders by winning an overall majority in the 25 January 2006 election with seventy-four seats in the 132-member PLC. Given how severely the people of Gaza would suffer for the choice they made that day, it is worth examining the course, as well as the aftermath, of the election in some detail. For this was a turning point – arguably *the* turning point – in Gaza's fortunes over the next decade.

In time, some would claim the election results reflected a wholesale embrace of Islamic fundamentalism or armed resistance to Israel, or both. The eminent Israeli professor Benny Morris, the pioneer 'new historian' who had moved to the right, asserted that 'only fools and children' thought that Hamas had won the 2006 election because they had an 'uncorrupt image or dispensed food to the poor'. While these were 'factors', he argued that 'the main reasons for the Hamas victory were religious and political: the growing religiosity of the Palestinian masses and their "recognition" that Hamas embodies the "truth" and with Allah's help will lead to final victory over the infidels much as Hamas had achieved, through armed struggle, the withdrawal of the infidels from the Gaza Strip in 2005'.[8]

At the other end of the spectrum, Mahmoud Zahar, the veteran hawk among Hamas political leaders, depicted the faction's victory as 'very indicative ... [that] resistance is more popular than what is called peaceful negotiations with Israel'.[9]

Both overlooked the mundane factors which helped Hamas to victory. For a start, Fatah was hopelessly split. The long-running struggle between the 'insiders', those who had helped to lead the First Intifada on the ground, and the 'outsiders' or 'old guard', who had largely watched it from afar in exile in Tunis with Arafat, came to a head with the internal primaries in late November and early December. In the West Bank, a younger generation came to the fore, with the popular, charismatic – and gaoled – Marwan Barghouti taking ninety per cent of votes in Ramallah. But the old guard struck back, notably in Gaza, rigging votes and allowing their supporters to storm polling stations, lest the same should happen in the Strip, leading Abbas to cancel the primaries, including those already held in the West Bank. Worried about a terminal split in Fatah, Abbas authorised the use of a hybrid electoral system[10] as a compromise. The sixty-six-seat national list of candidates – as distinct from individual constituencies – was a mixture of 'old' and 'new guard'. Barghouti was at its head, but closely followed by two staunch 'old guarders', both Gazans: Intisar al-Wazir, the widow of Abu Jihad (Arafat's close collaborator and fellow founder of Fatah, assassinated by Israel in 1988), and the former PA Foreign Minister Nabil Sha'ath. The compromise angered those on both sides who were left out, with the result that dozens of discontented Fatah would-be candidates chose to run against their officially backed rivals in local constituencies.

As if that wasn't enough, Fatah's campaign was deeply inferior to that of Hamas. A fortnight before polling day, two campaigning experts were dispatched on a fraternal visit to Ramallah by the British Labour Party, then in power under Tony Blair, to see what help they could offer against this unpromising background of disarray. Their 'Strictly Confidential' report after the election was over shows that the pair, Kevin Lee and Scarlett MccGwire, were aghast at what they found. While noting the problem of Fatah candidates standing against each other, they also reported that the campaign was 'very disorganised and lacked strong leadership' with 'no defined command structure' and 'numerous personnel changes'. Good ideas were not 'translated into positive action at press conferences or via materials that impacted upon the voters', and 'there was a lack of research and documented evidence to support the Fatah claims and messages'.[11]

Apart from its attempts to depict Hamas as the Taliban, Fatah's main 'lines' against its opponents, the report observed, were the unconvincing arguments that the faction had refused to take part in the PLC elections in 1996 because it opposed the Oslo agreement and were now doing so when the Road Map offered less hope than Oslo had; and that because the Islamic faction had backed elections going ahead even if Israel did not allow voting in East Jerusalem, Hamas did not care about Jerusalem. 'We came up with about ten lines on Hamas,' the report added, 'which they liked but by this time we were in the final days and only the spokesman was going to use them as we never met any senior candidates.' Nor did the organisers appear to have much idea who and where their supporters were. A phone bank with twenty lines had been installed but 'this was only used to respond to incoming enquiries from voters and not to take a proactive approach'. Much of the senior Fatah figures' energy was consumed by trying to whittle down from 120 the numbers of would-be rival 'unofficial' Fatah candidates – probably, according to one knowledgeable observer, 'less from organisational discipline than by promises of cash, PA positions, and, in Gaza, land recently evacuated by the Israelis'.[12]

After five intensive days with the campaign, the Labour pair's conclusions were overwhelmingly negative. Having met most officials at the heart of the campaign, they noted the reasons for Fatah's defeat: its bad record in government ('They had no good stories to tell that we could find. The ministers whom we met were unimpressive'); the split; and the fact that 'the President is one of the most respected men for his integrity, yet he believed that he should be above party politics and refused to campaign'.

This last point was also made by the head of Shin Bet, Yuval Diskin, who, having made the startling claim that 'no one in the Palestinian leadership receives as complete a picture of what is happening in the territories as [Shin Bet]', said that Abbas's most glaring strategic failure to date was 'that he decided to behave as a Palestinian leader, not as a leader of a political party'.[13] Diskin also described Hamas as a 'serious professional organisation that knows how to think about issues and reach rational conclusions for their own interests ... [and] that the Gaza leadership has the strength to deliver – when they order a halt to terrorist acts, ninety-nine per cent obey'.

On the Fatah campaign, the Lee/MccGwire report concluded, the understanding of the 'people nominally in charge of what would persuade Palestinians to vote for them was considerably poorer than ours' and 'the senior candidates just did their own thing and frankly this seemed to be true all the way down into the little fiefdoms'. It added: 'There was no coordination of events – no plan at all ... no vision ... no real fear that Hamas would win – in spite of all the evidence ...'[14]

Nowhere were these formidable defects more visible than in Gaza, where one young woman Fatah activist, Amani Abu Ramadan, who left her post in the campaign early in despair at how it was being run, recalled driving from the Erez crossing to Rafah with Miguel Moratinos, the former EU Special Representative for the Middle East Peace Process. 'It was complete chaos. The Third Way [the small independent party headed by the able former PA Finance Minister Salam Fayyad and Hanan Ashrawi, a veteran of earlier negotiations] or Change and Reform [Hamas] had someone at reception giving you campaign materials. At Fatah there was basically a bunch of boys sitting at the desk pretending to be a campaign.'[15] All this prompted the disenchanted leader of the Fatah youth movement in Gaza, Abd al-Hakim Awad, to complain after polling day that 'Hamas did not win the elections – Fatah lost them'.[16]

It was hardly surprising that the leading Fatah figure in Gaza, Mohammed Dahlan, a more astute reader of the political runes than many of his colleagues in the West Bank, and a constituency candidate in Khan Yunis, had talked to Yuval Diskin in June 'seeking help from Israel's political leadership in postponing the elections'.[17] Even Abbas was worried enough in the closing stages of the campaign to propose in private (and in vain) that Israel should after all ban voting in Jerusalem – allowing the Palestinian President to postpone the elections while publicly blaming Israel.[18]

In stark contrast to the disarray in Fatah, Hamas, despite its relative inexperience, ran a highly efficient, even professional campaign. Its final decision to participate in the PLC elections, following its success in the municipal elections, had been taken early in 2005, but the principle of electoral participation had been debated within Hamas for about three years. Ostensibly Hamas had boycotted the 1996 elections because they had been prescribed in the Oslo agreement, which it strongly and violently opposed. But, in 1996, it also had little chance of winning against Arafat.[19]

By 2006, however, Hamas's popularity had risen. No doubt this was reinforced among some voters by its contention that it had driven Israeli forces and settlers out of Gaza the previous August – the one Palestinian political dividend Sharon had bequeathed by his unilateral approach to disengagement. In fact its political strength had grown long before disengagement, as the 2005 local elections had shown. But running under the ideology-free banner of 'Change and Reform', as it had in the local elections, the faction left nothing to chance. It employed – among other consultants – Dr Nashat Aqtash, a public relations expert well versed in US campaigning techniques. He had a campaign plan, well-organised local teams to implement it, and a coherent programme of advertising which emphasised candidates were there to 'improve your situation, not because of our interests', which was skilfully targeted through local terrestrial TV stations at the forty per cent of Gazans who could not afford satellite channels.[20]

Ismail Haniyeh, at the more pragmatic end of the Hamas spectrum, was top of the national candidates' list. Significantly, the 'Change and Reform' campaign omitted any mention of the destruction of Israel.

Bassem Naim was in charge of the Hamas campaign in Gaza City. Like many of the faction's senior figures, he was a doctor, a colorectal surgeon, who went on to become Health Minister and later head of Hamas's 'Council of International Relations'. In the summer of 2004, following the targeted killings of Ahmed Yassin and Abdel Aziz Rantissi, Naim recalled, 'most of the leaders were in hiding, and we were called to a meeting with one of them because it was not easy for him to move. All we had was a pen and an empty paper – nothing else. We had no idea about election rules and regulations, nothing. One and a half years later, I was responsible for [the PLC election campaign in] the Gaza [City] governate.'

The planning was meticulous. 'I had about 7,000 people working with me, so we were able to know about each polling station . . . which school was being used, who is responsible for the food supply, arranging the cars . . . who is responsible for legal affairs and problems.' Naim was not surprised by the results. Members of the PA forces, which would be in charge of security on polling day, voted in the run-up to the election; twenty-five per cent cast their ballot for Hamas. That was an indication, Naim said, of what was to come. 'A few days before the election, I'm not saying weeks, I was nearly one hundred per cent sure about how much we will get. We knew exactly house by house who will participate in the election, who will be left and who is still neutral.'[21]

Anyone in Gaza during the week of the election could see Hamas was on a roll. Horn-honking, banner-waving, thirty-vehicle loudspeaker motorcades toured the streets of Gaza City three days before polling day. Fatah belatedly defended itself against Hamas's pitches. At a modestly attended rally outside what had been Arafat's compound, leading Fatah candidate Sami Masherawi declared: 'Fatah apologises for the mistakes of the past. We will not allow a few corrupt figures to damage the Fatah reputation.' Similarly, with little else to counter Hamas's boasts that it had driven Israel out of Gaza, another Fatah activist, Fouad Madi, told the rally: 'It was we who carried the olive branch and the gun. We used force and stones first.' Nearby, a huge banner depicted an armed and masked Fatah militant in combat fatigues proclaiming: 'In Gaza we're victorious and to the West Bank and Jerusalem we are going.'

Later that day I followed Mohammed Dahlan to his home base of Khan Yunis, where an early evening Fatah rally was swollen by ranks of excitable and testosterone-fuelled *shabab*, some firing AK-47s into the air. But here, in the refugee camp of the Gaza Strip's second largest city, doubts about Fatah were still apparent. Samaher Sidha, a twenty-three-year-old mother of four, sitting outside the bullet-riddled home of a neighbour on what had been the front line between the camp and the Jewish settlement of Neve Dekalim until the Israeli withdrawal in August, pointed to the rubble of a house demolished by Israel. She said Dahlan had visited and 'promised he would deal with all this. But we heard this before in the last elections. There were lots of promises but nothing was implemented.' Admitting this was an area where Hamas supplied food and financial help to poor families, including her own, Mrs Sidha said of the PA: 'In ten years they haven't done anything. We want to change them, we have to try something new.' For her, 'corruption and security chaos' were the key issues. Referring to the recent fifty per cent pay rise for PA employees, she added: 'Why did the authority increase the wages of their employees? That was a bribe. We elected Fatah and Dahlan but they haven't done anything about unemployment or started construction work.'

There were similar worries even among enthusiastic Dahlan supporters. Samira Tawfiq, twenty-seven, a PA employee, said she would vote for Fatah and hoped Dahlan would be a future Palestinian President. But she, too, said the lack of internal security and unemployment were key issues. 'We used to see blood when the occupation was here, but we are still seeing it. What we need is a strong leader. Fatah needs to change. But they are not extremists. They will negotiate with Israel.'

A highlight of the campaign's latter stages in Gaza had been a spirited – and unprecedented – TV debate between Dahlan and Mahmoud Zahar, made radioactive by their personal history during Arafat's crackdown on the Islamists in the 1990s. Zahar accused Dahlan of having been behind the 'torture' of himself and other Hamas officials. Dahlan accused Hamas of working to undermine the Palestinian Authority through suicide bombings it perpetrated in 1996 and during more recent years of conflict. Zahar accused Fatah of failing to achieve its goals and said it and the PA were 'sunk in corruption'. But Dahlan derided Hamas's rejection of negotiations, demanding to know how it could look after the future of Palestinians without them. 'How are you going to get workers into Israel?' he asked. 'Via your tunnels or the internet?'

The conduct of the poll by election officials was impressively neutral, despite occasional outbreaks of violence earlier in the campaign. In Shifa hospital in the week before the election, Suleiman Ashabia, a twenty-two-year-old campaigner for the Third Way, was still wincing with pain from the seven bullets he had taken in his hand and legs after being lured to the Maghazi refugee camp by a masked gunman posing as a supporter. 'We are doing a great job in Maghazi,' said Ashabia. 'Whoever it was wanted to stop the hard work.'

On election day, I toured Gaza polling stations from the northern border with Israel to the southern one with Egypt and was struck by how efficiently the Central Elections Commission (CEC) had ensured that representatives of the factions were kept at an unintimidating distance from the entrances. The election was not perfectly smooth: there was a shooting in Khan Yunis, probably tribal in origin. Ten years later, Hamas claimed it only prevented its opponents from ballot rigging by ensuring that its squads of armed men 'protected' the transfer of ballot boxes from polling stations to the CEC's central count.[22] But for the most part in Gaza, guns were kept, if not always out of sight, out of use. The mood among many voters was one of pride, even celebration, that free and fair elections – as international monitors from the Carter Center and the EU judged them to be – were finally taking place. The almost carnival atmosphere was reinforced by the continuous sounding of horns from cars taking electors to the polls and banners – green for Hamas, yellow for Fatah, red for the leftist PFLP – strung across the streets and even attached to children's bicycles.

Most voters were happy to speak about their choices. In Beit Hanoun, opinions differed wildly on the performance of the Hamas council led by Nazeq al-Kafarna, which had now been in office for a year. He had certainly proved a less doctrinaire social conservative than some of his Hamas colleagues. One of only two women Beit Hanoun councillors, Ibtisam al-Za'aneen, elected as an independent, persuaded him to allow her to set up a unit advising eighty women a week, including on the highly sensitive issue of domestic violence. He told her: 'God help you with those sheikhs in the mosque, but go for it.'[23] Hayat al-Masri, twenty-eight, a married student (her family name again undermining the claim that politics were a mere matter of clan loyalty) said that the council had improved roads and was 'excellent'. She added: 'I hope it will improve the economy and security. They are religious and if they can tell people to stop stealing there will be more money for construction.' But Awad Naim, a forty-two-year-old Fatah-supporting accountant, declared: 'Nothing has changed. They have problems with street cleaning, water bills and unemployment, and they are employing Hamas people in municipal jobs.' At the same time, he was scathing about the existing Fatah-dominated Legislative Council. 'It has changed nothing in ten years,' he said.

Hamas was certainly helped by its long-standing network of charitable and social provision for the poor. No doubt, too, some Hamas campaigners had told more persuadable voters that God would be on the side of those who elected candidates strong in Islamic practice.[24] And Hamas emphasised its claim, however dubious, that it had driven Israel out of Gaza. But overall the mood on election day did not feel like that imagined by Benny Morris. For one thing, the detailed results showed that the supposed Hamas landslide was no such thing. In the vote for the national list, for which there was a single Fatah slate, Hamas won twenty-nine seats with forty-four per cent of the vote, while Fatah won twenty-eight seats with forty-one per cent. The collapse of Fatah was due almost entirely to the split caused by rivals fighting each other for votes from the faction's supporters in the constituency section, which accounted for the other half of the 132 seats. With no such internal rivalries, Hamas won forty-five of the sixty-six seats assigned to local constituencies, leaving Fatah with only seventeen. But Hamas candidates won a mere 36.5 per cent of the vote. In other words, sixty-three per cent voted for non-Hamas candidates in the constituency elections. Overall, Hamas won a thumping PLC majority over Fatah of seventy-four seats to forty-five, but secured with just forty-four per cent of the total vote. This hardly suggested a wholesale mass conversion to the idea that Allah would now guide the Palestinians to martial victory over the 'infidel'.

Corruption in the PA had been a real negative. Voters in Gaza saw all too visible signs of lower level corruption or enrichment of those with influence within the PA, from *wasta* (the connections needed to get a government job) to the new Mercedes and beachside villas enjoyed by businessmen favoured by the PA. They knew of persistent reports of ministers and officials receiving kickbacks for land sales or planning decisions, embezzlement, or other backhanders. While apparently uninterested in personal enrichment, Arafat had never lost his habit from the guerrilla days of using external funds to buy loyalty from those under him. When the PA was formed in 1994, the opportunities greatly increased because there was so much more money available.[25]

THE DAY AFTER THE ELECTION, A furious Mohammed Dahlan, who had hung on in Khan Yunis along with one other Fatah colleague, railed against Abbas for allowing the chaos in Fatah to continue in the run-up to the campaign and for appointing the 'incompetent Nabil Sha'ath' as campaign manager.[26] But their failure could not just be attributed to its woeful campaign.

The late Graham Usher, the most astute analyst of Palestinian politics among Western journalists, reached sharply different conclusions from Benny Morris about its causes:

> Overwhelmingly, Palestinians were not voting for political Islam or even armed resistance. There were three reasons for Hamas's success: Palestinian disillusionment that peace or meaningful political negotiations with Israel were anywhere on the horizon, despite a clear majority in favour of such a future; appreciation for Hamas's civic role as service provider, especially during the harsh years of the intifada and for its vanguard position in the armed Palestinian resistance, widely seen among Palestinians as the catalyst for Israel's unilateral withdrawal from Gaza last summer; and, above all, revulsion from a decade of Fatah's misrule of the PA, capped by its failure to bring law, order, economic recovery, and political progress after Israel's Gaza disengagement.[27]

Khalil Shikaki, the most internationally respected Palestinian pollster, was even more emphatic that the result was not a vote for Hamas's 'extremist views', adding: 'Polls I have carried out over the past 13 years show that the Palestinians have never been as moderate as they are today.'[28]

Election day had proved to be another moment of hope in Gaza, because of what Palestinians voters justly felt had been, for all the constraints, an exemplary exercise in democracy. It was already after sunset when Mahdi Hassounia, a forty-year-old car mechanic, left work to thread his way through the noisy crowds of young men waving Hamas and Fatah banners to vote at the Karmel High School in central Gaza City. The crowds had little influence on Hassounia, who determinedly cast his vote for the much smaller leftist Democratic Front for the Liberation of Palestine (DFLP), which helped Fatah to steer the PLO towards a two-state solution as early as 1974. But his pleasure in the election was patriotic rather than partisan. 'It's excellent,' he said. 'We expected there to be more problems, but it has all gone very smoothly. I am very proud that the Palestinian people have sent a good picture, a beautiful picture to the world. Elections like this do not happen everywhere. There have been a few problems, but they could happen anywhere. I hope it will help people to recognise that there should be a Palestinian state.' As Israel and the Western governments reacted to the election over the next few days, however, it became painfully clear that events were not going to work out as Hassounia dared to imagine.

6

'IT'S THE WRONG RESULT': INTERNATIONAL RESPONSE TO HAMAS'S VICTORY, 2006

A HALLMARK OF INTERNATIONAL DIPLOMACY IS the slow pace of collective policy making, even in times of crisis. The decisions of the international Quartet after the Palestinian elections in January 2006 were, by contrast, made with impressive speed. Especially since no prior thought had been given to how to handle the unfolding scenario. In Washington 'no one had even bothered to write a planning paper on "What to do if Hamas Wins" for no one had thought that outcome possible.'[1] The results were reasonably clear on Thursday 26 January, but only officially confirmed by the Central Elections Commission three days later. The next day the US, EU, Russia and the UN, meeting at the urging of Condoleezza Rice on the fringes of a London conference on Afghanistan, signed up to a statement which 'congratulated the Palestinian people on an electoral process that was free, fair and secure' before delivering its punch: the Quartet had 'concluded that it was inevitable' that future assistance to any new government would be 'reviewed by donors against that government's commitment to the principles of non-violence, recognition of Israel and acceptance of previous agreements and obligations'.

The language was suitably diplomatic, but the message could hardly have been clearer. For a Hamas-run Palestinian Authority to qualify for international recognition, let alone aid, it would have to abandon – immediately and in circumstances that would be seen as publicly buckling to external pressure in the aftermath of a stunning election victory – three of its core commitments by renouncing the use of arms once and for all, recognising Israel and ending its decade-long opposition to the Oslo agreement. 'This was a remarkably tough line for the Quartet . . . to take,' an appreciative Elliott Abrams wrote. 'We were delighted.'[2]

These 'principles' – drafted by the US and ratified with remarkable haste by the rest of the Quartet – determined international relations with Hamas for more than a decade. They shaped international, and indeed Israeli, policy on every major event in Gaza, including three wars and a ten-year economic blockade. Regionally, they generated considerable cynicism about the US and Europe's long proclaimed commitment to democracy in the Middle East. And they ruled out what might have been a controlled experiment in whether coexistence was possible with a (relatively) pragmatic Islamist regime desperate for international recognition. The Quartet decision reinforced the destructive split in the Palestinian national movement. Failing either to dislodge or transform Hamas, it instead sharply increased the Islamic faction's dependence on Iran. It was hard, in short, to identify a single gain from what looked in hindsight like a case study in counterproductive Western foreign policy.

Abrams was too modest to say that the 'remarkably tough' 30 January decision was a triumph of pressure applied by Israel and the US, including by himself and Rice. Three days earlier some had expressed doubt about the wisdom of passing such a swift, public and draconian ultimatum without further discussion, especially as Hamas was hardly likely to agree to it. In Brussels, a senior European Commission official cautioned against using aid to the PA as a political lever 'unless absolutely necessary', saying, prophetically:

> One million people in the Palestinian Territories relied directly and indirectly on EU funding. To withdraw it would have dramatic consequences and could lead to violence. The EU was under no obligations to align its position on financial support with that of the US and Israel. The EU had not done so in the past. The wider region was watching the EU response to these elections. If we seemed, by our actions, to be rejecting the results then our claims to promoting democracy would be undermined.[3]

Less explicitly, John Jenkins, the UK's Consul General in Jerusalem, implied in a cable to London that an immediate rush to judgement was unnecessary. 'There is far too much still to be decided by the Palestinians before we are called on to make our own decisions. But we should at least start thinking about what sort of policy and behavioural menu we need to see from Hamas over the coming weeks and months and what the timing needs to be.'[4]

This measured advice was swept aside by the US juggernaut heading to London. The UN's Álvaro de Soto, who was at the envoys' meeting on the Monday morning in advance of the meetings of 'principals', described being 'subjected to a heavy barrage' from Abrams and US Assistant Secretary of State David Welch – including the 'ominous innuendo' that unless UN Secretary General Kofi Annan 'reviewed' its programmes for the Palestinians in light of Hamas's victory, there could be 'repercussions' when Congress was considering grants to the UN.[5]

By now Mahmoud Abbas had made it clear that as the PA President he was ready to open talks with Hamas about forming a government. De Soto suggested the Quartet statement adopt a more positive tone, welcoming the 'movement' Hamas had made by participating in the elections and hoping 'such movement will continue so that the international community can maintain the support it has always provided to the Palestinians'. Before the election, he had proposed – without overt dissent from the Americans, he thought – the Quartet should allow the UN and Russia to open a dialogue with Hamas aimed at accelerating that 'movement'. At the envoys' meeting, however, de Soto got nowhere.

Such a dialogue might have provided, without highly publicised brinkmanship, the chance of drawing out Hamas on whether it would sign up to alternative conditions – including an immediate halt to rocket attacks and the long-term truce it had floated several times before. This could have carried the explicit condition that, if the attacks restarted, the Quartet would break off contact and halt aid to a Hamas-led PA. But it would not have required Hamas to renounce, permanently and as a matter of principle, armed resistance against an occupation deemed in contravention of international law by most of the world. Instead of holding Hamas to an Oslo agreement, which was now arguably moribund, it could – possibly – have coaxed it towards acceptance of the 2002 Arab Peace Initiative, which promised recognition of Israel by Arab states in return for two states on the pre-June 1967 borders, with a state of Palestine comprising the West Bank, Gaza and East Jerusalem. Finally, the diplomatic and financial isolation of Hamas handed it a ready-made excuse if it became unpopular; which was why the internationally respected Salam Fayyad, among others, told European officials that it would be better to put Hamas to the test by allowing it to rule under the same – already quite straitened – budgetary conditions as had its Fatah predecessors.[6]

But it was not to be. By the Monday evening meeting the only remaining dissenter was the Russian Foreign Minister Sergey Lavrov, who argued 'vociferously' with Rice over the implications of the election. Rice, however, played her trump card: the 'peace process' she was now promoting between the new Israeli Prime Minister Ehud Olmert and Abbas would be sabotaged because the Israelis would 'refuse to negotiate if they were forced to accept Hamas as part of the Palestinian political landscape'.[7] Lavrov eventually bowed to this argument.

Hamas's immediate reaction after the election was to call for a coalition with Fatah, though one of its leading figures, Mahmoud Zahar, warned that it was ready to govern alone if one was not agreed. Reluctance within Fatah was also evident from the start when, on the Friday after the election (27 January), 1,000 of its angry activists, including around 100 armed men, burned cars outside the Legislative Council building in Gaza, and chanted slogans demanding the resignation of the Fatah Central Committee, which they held responsible for the defeat, and rejecting a coalition. The reluctance of some of Fatah's most senior figures to join a coalition was also strongly reinforced by Israeli and American opposition.[8] By mid-February US officials, who had already warned that aid would be cut off to any PA that included Hamas, were discussing a strategy by which Abbas would be forced to call a fresh election – with a possibly different result – because the PA would have been 'starved' of funds.[9]

In March, with Abbas remaining as President, Ismail Haniyeh, the first on Hamas's electoral list and now its new Prime Minister, formed a largely Hamas Cabinet, whose writ, as a coalition's would have done, now ran over the West Bank as well as Gaza. Israel halted the payment of the $60m it collected each month on behalf of the PA, mainly in customs revenues, under the Oslo agreement. Washington duly cut off the aid that went direct to the PA, rather than the Palestinian President's Office. And Israel supporters in the US Congress began to prepare legislation (finally passed as the Palestinian Terrorism Act in December 2006) outlawing any recognition or funding of a PA that included Hamas.

But Haniyeh's speech was notably conciliatory towards the international community, to whom it promised 'our government is and [will be] ready for dialogue with the Quartet to explore all avenues to put an end to the state of conflict in the region and bring peace to the region'. Haniyeh went out of his way to praise Abbas for holding the elections, and pledged 'not only our respect for the constitutional relationship with the President, but also our interest in strengthening this relationship'.[10] He even – by implication and within admittedly severe limits – addressed Israel itself; while stressing the suffering inflicted on Palestinians by Israel and the Palestinians' right of resistance, he promised 'necessary contacts with the occupation in all mundane affairs: business trade, health and labour'. (West Bank municipalities controlled by Hamas were already in regular and direct contact with Israel on 'mundane affairs'. This was well known to diplomats representing countries, the UK among them, which were now boycotting Hamas.)

In the assessment of one leading Palestinian expert, the concept of the two-state solution was 'everywhere between the lines in Haniyeh's speech'.[11] On the 2002 Arab Peace Initiative, which offered full recognition of Israel in return for a Palestinian state on 1967 borders, and based on the West Bank, Gaza and East Jerusalem, Haniyeh sought to 'remind the world that the occupation authorities have always ignored the 2002 initiatives. The problem has never been from the Palestinian or the Arab side. Rather, the problem is with the Israeli occupation.'

There was, of course, a question about whether it was sensible for Hamas to rule at all. Omar Shaban recalled a meeting with senior Hamas officials in which he strongly advised them not to try to rule but, rather, use its majority in the PLC to 'monitor' the existing executive, telling them: 'You don't have the experience to be in a government under such a situation and we are under occupation. There are so many obstacles.'[12]

In fact, Hamas was divided over the issue. According to Ahmed Yousef, a Haniyeh ally, the external leadership – i.e. the political bureau including its then Damascus-based chief, Khaled Meshal – were against forming a government, and were mindful of the military coup and civil war which had followed the Islamic Salvation Front's victory in the first round of the

1991 Algerian elections. 'But some people thought "we've been elected by the people to govern, not just watch them from the PLC."'¹³

Ghazi Hamad, another close ally of Haniyeh, thought Hamas should not form the government alone at that time: 'Maybe Fatah did not also help Hamas to establish [a coalition] government, and maybe they were also out to see Hamas sinking and suffering, but I think that Hamas should have opened their eyes and seen from the whole calculation around them it was not suitable to form a government.'¹⁴

With Hamas on proscribed terrorist lists in the US and Europe and facing hostility from several Arab countries – and the PA financially dependent on international donors – Hamad anticipated that Hamas would 'suffer more and more'. But 'unfortunately Hamas did not study such things deeply to see where they can put their feet . . . Maybe some people thought that the international community would change its position and, when they found Hamas in power, they would be pushed to talk to them. But . . . this was not true.'

But Hamad still believed 'it was a big mistake of the EU and the international community to isolate Hamas. And I suppose that if they had helped them from the beginning then the whole political map would be changed.'

This, of course, was the highly partisan view of a Hamas politician. But it was echoed by independent figures in Gaza. Omar Shaban, an economist as well as a consultant to European governments, was scathing about what he saw as the 'stupid decisions' of the international community, for which he blamed 'all the crises in Gaza'. In his view, the Quartet should have offered Hamas a 'package' and given Hamas time to consider it:

> You tell them, 'Look, guys, you cannot expect our international support politically and financially unless you abide with international politics . . . You'll have six months to think about it and if you don't get it, sorry you will be punished.' This would create a dynamic within the Hamas movement. It's like a student – you don't give him an exam on his first day at school . . . Hamas said no because they didn't give them any time to think.

Sami Abdel Shafi, an experienced business consultant who represented the Carter Center in Gaza, characterised the Quartet decision like this:

'Yesterday you supported those elections, today you hear of an outcome and because it's the wrong result you swiftly boycott . . . It is a double standard . . . Europe and the US are talking to political parties that are, to say the least, much less moderate than the guys here.'[15]

Among groups cited by Abdel Shafi whom the West was prepared to talk to was the Lebanese Hezbollah, proscribed by the US as a terrorist organisation. In the case of the UK and the EU, it is the military, and not the political, wing that is proscribed, whereas no such distinction is applied to Hamas. When the British government, apparently with the encouragement of the US, decided in 2009 to resume contacts with Hezbollah's political wing, a Foreign Office official explained to Al Jazeera: 'Hezbollah is a political phenomenon and part and parcel of the national fabric in Lebanon. We have to admit this. I believe such contacts will help push this movement to engage in the political process and achieve peace in the region.'[16] It highlighted the absence of a similar approach to Hamas.

In retrospect, even some of the Quartet 'principals' questioned, indeed regretted, the 30 January decision. One was the British Foreign Secretary Jack Straw who wrote in his memoirs that he was 'uncertain it was right'. Straw cited Tory MP Michael Ancram, who 'believed strongly that simply isolating Hamas made no more sense than refusing to talk to the Provisional IRA while their terrorist campaign was continuing. A key Northern Ireland minister from 1993-7, he'd been at the forefront of the initially secret talks with PIRA while they were still killing and maiming innocents across the UK. Few internal conflicts of this kind have ever been capable of resolution without negotiation with terrorist organisations.'[17]

Straw does not mention it in his book, but three days before the 30 January meeting he had been obliged by his Israeli counterpart Tzipi Livni to defend his assertion of 'respect' for the 'outcome of the election and the democratic wish of the Palestinian people' – even though he had swiftly qualified it by saying that 'we could not accept a political party in power that was still also a terrorist organisation'.[18] According to the official account of the conversation, Livni said that 'the international community did not need to talk about accepting the outcome of the elections'.

Having at the time accepted Livni's sharp rebuke, Straw reflected in his memoirs on a paradox that 'was never to be mentioned in polite company . . . Israeli terrorist groups – Irgun and the Stern Gang – waged a terror campaign against the British in the 1940s to secure their aim of an independent State of Israel.'[19] Livni's own parents had been members of Irgun. Straw added: 'I can . . . understand why so many Jewish people resorted to terrorism in their desperation to establish a Jewish home-land after the unspeakable horrors of the Holocaust. What was the surprise was the way the Israelis had now elevated "not talking to terror-ists" as some kind of issue of principle.'

Straw was not alone in his revisionism. In his book, he recorded that the Americans had agreed with Israel's 'adamant' line against talking to Hamas and, in a reference to the British Prime Minister at the time: 'So, of course, did Tony.' Yet Tony Blair – who backed the American calls for the boycott of Hamas at the time, and applied it, as he was obliged to by US/EU policy, throughout his period as Quartet Envoy from 2007 to 2015 – also changed his mind. In early 2017 – by which time, no longer constrained by office, he had held at least half a dozen meetings in Qatar with the Hamas political bureau chief Khaled Meshal and other senior figures in the faction, including Haniyeh – he said: 'in retrospect I think we should have right at the very beginning tried to pull them into a dialogue and shifted their positions. I think that's where I would be in retrospect. But obviously it was very difficult, the Israelis were very opposed to it. But you know we could have probably worked out a way whereby we did – which in fact we ended up doing anyway informally.'[20]

Blair's Chief of Staff throughout his premiership, Jonathan Powell – a veteran of Northern Ireland peace talks which had concluded the Good Friday Agreement in April 1998 and who, since leaving office, has strongly advocated negotiations with armed groups* – was even more emphatic. In 2017 he said the Quartet approach had been a 'terrible mistake' because there could have been 'an opportunity to unite Palestinians in a way that's been impossible since'. Powell pointed out that negotiations with the Fatah leadership alone – which was, in fact, what Condoleezza Rice would now promote – meant that 'the danger for any Israeli negotiator is you have to make a concession to Fatah, then you have to make a new concession to Hamas afterwards. You want to have one negotiation, not two . . . If you got a united Palestinian team to negotiate with, then life would have been a whole lot easier.'[21]

---

* In 2014, Powell published a book, *Talking to Terrorists: How to End Armed Conflicts*.

In retrospect it's hard to overestimate the impact of the 2006 Quartet decision. Almost every Palestinian civilian wanted unity and to prevent what would soon be the catastrophic split between Hamas and Fatah. It would be understandable for Israelis to take the opposite view. Hamas had been responsible for the deaths of hundreds of Israelis over the past six years. Moreover, Israel's government had at least been consistent; it had opposed Hamas's participation in the elections and could not be accused of changing its mind just because Hamas had won. (The opinion polls suggested that the Israeli public were markedly more dovish about a Fatah–Hamas accord than their leaders. In September 2006, one poll found sixty-seven per cent of Israelis supported negotiations with a Palestinian national unity government that included Hamas.[22])

But the Western governments, having heavily promoted the elections, were not consistent. Despite private doubts in some member states, the EU was equally bound by the Quartet principles that had, to Elliott Abrams' understated satisfaction, assumed 'what may have appeared to be canonical status'.[23]

In April the EU also cut off aid. The impact was widespread, most immediately on the salaries of 140,000 PA employees, including teachers, doctors, nurses, and 70,000 security force personnel. Half of these were paid from the already halted clearance revenues from Israel – money that legally belonged to the Palestinians – and the other half from donors, including the EU. Gazans, especially the poorest, were even more heavily dependent on these PA salaries than Palestinians in the West Bank. By now the joke in Gaza was that PA employees were henceforth going to be paid in dates. But this was not really a laughing matter. Suddenly it looked as though the legacy of the Quartet's stand-off with Hamas was going to be tens of thousands of angry people with no money, and, in the case of the security forces, a lot of weapons.

A dispute over internal security – which finally exploded into an unprecedentedly bloody civil conflict in the summer of 2007 – had its seeds in a tense meeting between the top Hamas and Fatah leaderships shortly after the formation of the new Hamas-dominated Cabinet. Abbas had insisted that, as President, he, not the Hamas Prime Minister Ismail Haniyeh, would maintain control of security forces, which would be answerable to Mohammed Dahlan, now on Abbas's presidential staff. The hawkish Zahar was characteristically abrasive, by his own account telling Abbas: 'We are not here to run an administration through your-self. You are corrupted, and the people punished you.'[24]

A week later Hamas established its own blue-uniformed 'executive force', its first venture in policing, under the command of Jamal Abu Samhadana, a militant leader of the Popular Resistance Committees (PRC), who had been responsible for numerous rocket launches into Israel, and had been associated with the killing of three Americans in Gaza in 2003. 'We appointed 450 policemen and they controlled the streets within a few hours,' said Zahar. In fact, the outcome was compet-ing forces confronting each other with sporadic shoot-outs. The frequently lethal hostilities between rival militias formed an increas-ingly volatile and dangerous background to attempts by Abbas and Haniyeh to establish some form of stable cohabitation.

The attempts nevertheless continued. Abbas launched an untypically flamboyant initiative designed to flush out Hamas's true attitude to negotiations with Israel on a two-state solution to the conflict. A docu-ment jointly signed by Hamas and Fatah prisoners, the latter led by Marwan Barghouti, who was serving multiple sentences in an Israeli prison, represented a striking shift on the part of the Hamas militants. While it did not 'recognise' Israel, it called specifically for a Palestinian state on pre-Six Day War borders; for the PA President to be entrusted by all factions with negotiations; and – for the first time – for 'resistance' to be confined to targets in occupied territory, such as settlements or the troops protecting them, thus ruling out attacks in Israel itself (which would have included rocket attacks from Gaza). The document carried considerable weight as prisoners enjoyed a heroic status among Palestinians. Abbas swiftly endorsed it and announced that Hamas should clarify its official policy by formally backing a Palestinian state in the territories occupied in 1967. Haniyeh and Abbas began negotia-tions aimed at finalising a version of the document both leaders could agree on.

Yet the US and Israel were determined to forestall such an agree-ment. Washington repeatedly warned Abbas and Arab leaders in the region that 'nothing good could come of this effort', that if there was a 'national unity government' the financial boycott would not end, and 'it would end any prospect of negotiations with Israel'.[25]

Ehud Olmert went even further. In an interview on 6 June with Harvey Morris of the *Financial Times* and myself, Olmert made clear that his condition for opening negotiations – that Abbas confront Hamas by military means – was unchanged by the latter's election victory. Moreover, he attributed authorship of this doctrine to the EU and the US.

> Q: In practical terms, what would Abu Mazen [Abbas] actually have to do on the ground in order to qualify in your view for negotiations?
> EO: To carry out the principles in a manner that was defined by the international community.
> Q: Would that mean disarming Hamas, the elected government?
> EO: Of course, of course, of course. This is the principle. This has been defined by you guys, I mean by your governments and I am absolutely ready to subscribe to it.[26]

Events on the ground now rapidly deteriorated. An airstrike in Rafah on a cell which the IDF said was planning an attack on Israel killed Abu Samhadana and three other PRC men. Whether or not Abu Samhadana was deliberately targeted, the calls for revenge were louder because of his new role in the Hamas-led authority. Over the next twenty-four hours rockets were launched into Israel from northern Gaza; Israel mounted artillery attacks in response; seven members of a single family, the Ghalias, were killed in an explosion on a Beit Lahiya beach where they had gone for a Friday afternoon picnic and had started to leave because of shelling a few hundred metres away.

The incident – one of the two worst involving the deaths of Palestinian civilians in 2006 – attracted far more international attention than the killing of Abu Samhadana, partly because of harrowing footage captured by a Palestinian cameraman and broadcast worldwide of ten-year-old Huda Ghalia running distraught across the beach, calling 'father, father, father' and then collapsing beside his dead body. At the scene, blood was caked in the sand, a ripped shoe had a shred of flesh stuck to its upturned sole.[27]

The fragile de facto ceasefire between Hamas and Israel, which had largely held since February the previous year, came under severe strain. The day after the Ghalias' deaths, Hamas's military wing circulated leaflets proclaiming bloodthirsty threats of retaliation. Eyam Ghalia, Ali Ghalia's twenty-year-old son, was the only member of the beach party to have escaped without injury – he had seen his father's intestines hanging from an open wound in his stomach. While he said the calls for revenge were 'understandable from the resistance', he added: 'I think it would be better if the Israelis and Palestinians came to peace and lived together. We have had enough.'

The mood of having 'had enough' was evident a few kilometres away in the Israeli border town of Sderot, target for most of the 200 Qassam rockets that Hamas fired in retaliation. Amir Peretz, the Israeli Defense Minister and leader of Olmert's Labour partners in the coalition, had no need to visit the town to feel the anger of residents over the rocket fire; he had lived there since being brought as a child from Morocco. A former trade union leader and peacenik by instinct, he advocated a two-state solution as a win-win for Israelis and Palestinians; Israel would not only enjoy peace but would be able to switch resources away from the military demands of the occupation to help the poorest Israeli groups, like many residents of Sderot. He found schools closed because of fears for the children's safety and some of his own neighbours on hunger strike in protest over the rockets. One of these, the seventy-two-year-old Moshe Cohen, said: 'I don't want people to think we don't want peace with the Palestinians because of the Qassams. We all want peace. But you see how the world is talking about the Ghalia family when it is not clear we did it. Who pays attention to our problems? Who knows about them?'

Sderot had borne the brunt of rocket fire from Gaza. Looking across the rows of olive trees on the slopes north-east of Beit Hanoun, you can see the town, especially at night, when the houses are lit up. It is only 3.5 miles away. According to Sderot's mayor Eli Moyal, there had been over 1,000 rockets launched at the town since Israeli disengagement from Gaza. It was easy to point out that, unlike in Gaza, there were early warning air raid alerts and shelters – with grim pride, residents liked to describe their town as the 'bomb shelter capital of the world' – and the death toll was a fraction of that on the other side of the border. But, with almost daily rocket fire for long periods, it was not an easy place to live.

For the inhabitants of both Beit Lahiya and Sderot there was now an uneasy lull. But not for long. On 25 June eight Gaza militants carried out a raid via a tunnel on the Israeli military's border post at Kerem Shalom. They killed two Israeli soldiers and lost two of their own number in a shoot-out – and captured a nineteen-year-old conscript, Corporal Gilad Shalit. The militants were a mixed group, from Hamas's military wing, the PRC and the 'Army of Islam', a part jihadist, part semi-criminal group recently formed by Mumtaz Dughmush, a maverick former Fatah activist. The factions claimed the operation was in retaliation for Abu Samhadana's death, but it could also have been designed by hardliners to disrupt the reconciliation efforts by Abbas and Haniyeh.[28]

Haniyeh, presiding over a Cabinet meeting, was apparently caught unawares by the development, suggesting that the military wing did not always consult the Hamas political leadership in Gaza. Hamad said the capture had been a 'big surprise' and that Haniyeh had told him to check with the Qassam Brigades that it was true. '[Haniyeh] asked me to make a press conference, and I did it in English and Hebrew, and said that we would be dealing with him peacefully. We wanted to give some messages to the Israeli side, and to ask [them] not to resort to violence and to start to talk and negotiate.'

Gershon Baskin, an Israeli advocate of coexistence, had contacts with both the Israeli government and the Hamas political bureau. He arranged a phone call between Hamad and Gilad Shalit's father Noam, first to reassure him that the leadership wanted to see his son treated well, but secondly to encourage him to press for a prisoner swap for his son's release.[29] Noam Shalit battled with quiet dignity for five years to secure his son's release. A paler, thinner Shalit finally returned to his home in the northern Galilee in October 2011 in return for the release of more than 1,000 Palestinian prisoners.

But in June 2006 Olmert was not in a negotiating mood. On 27 June Israel launched Operation Summer Rains, which started with an airstrike on Gaza's only power station – a blow that severely reduced electricity for at least 700,000 Gazan consumers, cutting water supplies and depriving people of light, cooking, broadcast news, lifts in apartment blocks and – crucial in scorching summer temperatures – fans and refrigerators. It also further increased Gaza's dependence on Israel – from generator fuel for hospitals to electricity from the Israeli grid, both of which could be turned off and on at will. Although the damage to the power station would eventually be repaired – at a cost of around $5m to international donors – it marked the start of what would be more than a decade of daily power cuts lasting for eight hours or more.

At the same time the Israeli air force destroyed three bridges in central Gaza. The IDF insisted this was to block any attempts by Shalit's captors from moving the soldier from south to north; but motorists simply diverted to a side road and crossed the dried-up Wadi Gaza. Among those inspecting the damage was Zakri al-Ouh, sixty-two, a construction worker who had helped to build the bridge. 'When it rains, maybe in September, then it will be impossible to use the road, but at the moment I can't see how this can help the soldier,' he said. 'At first I was in favour of handing back the soldier as quickly as possible. We have to consider the power of Israel against our own weakness. But now they have done this I think there should be an exchange of prisoners before he is handed back.'

His views were echoed by others. An opinion poll taken in early July found that seventy per cent of Palestinians in both Gaza and the West Bank approved of the factions' refusal to release Shalit without a prisoner exchange.[30] To many in Israel, not least the parents of serving soldiers, Shalit's capture was their worst nightmare, an unforgiveable exploitation of a young man at the start of his adult life. For Palestinians it was totally different. Around 10,000 of their own prisoners were languishing in Israeli gaols. Some were detained without charge; some were serving long sentences dating to before the Oslo Accords, and Palestinians regarded almost all of them as POWs. In this context, Shalit's incarceration seemed to many Palestinians a reasonable *quid pro quo* – even in the face of the adverse consequences for Gaza over the next six months.

Two days after Shalit's capture, Haniyeh and Abbas announced a reconciliation agreement based on a revised version of the Prisoners' Document. The main importance of this agreement – scarcely noticed at the time in the furore over the soldier's abduction – was that it would remain for the next decade and beyond the basis for Hamas's claim to political legitimacy in the eyes of the world.

Meanwhile, Olmert faced deeper trouble on another front. Three weeks after the capture of Shalit, three Israeli soldiers were killed and another two abducted by Hezbollah militants on Israel's northern border. Once again, Olmert's response was not to negotiate but to launch a military offensive, triggering a thirty-four-day war that left around 1,000 Lebanese, 121 IDF soldiers and forty-four Israeli civilians dead. The inconclusive outcome and the impact of constant Hezbollah fire on northern Israel badly dented Olmert's popularity.

In Gaza, while Israel continued the military pressure on the Palestinians, the impact of the economic boycott of the Hamas-led PA was deepening. In Gaza City's long-established gold and jewellery souk that summer, something unusual was happening: the dealers were doing all the buying, and the customers all the selling. Zarifa Abdel Khadr, a seventy-eight-year-old grandmother, had come to sell for about £150 two gold rings she had owned for half a century to help her four daughters and five sons, three of whom were PA employees in their third month without a salary. She hadn't told her family what she had done. 'They wouldn't allow me to do this if they knew,' she said. 'I'll buy flour, the basics and give it to them. I'll tell them God sent it to me. Of course the rings are dear to me, but my children and grandchildren have to eat.'

The PA had been in serious financial trouble before Hamas took over. In 2005, it had been running a deficit of more than $60m a month, some sixty per cent more than it was receiving in external aid.[31] Several of the main European donor countries had stopped paying into a World Bank trust fund precisely because of the PA's inflated payroll and – for senior public servants – high salaries. Thanks to a combination of Israel withholding clearance revenues which provided sixty per cent of PA income, the drying up of donor funding, and tough US regulations aimed at preventing banks from handling funds for the PA, the Authority had been unable to meet its wage bill since March 2006. The result was that seventy-one per cent of those lucky enough to have a government job were now below a poverty line defined as an income of less than $460 a month for a family of six, compared with thirty-five per cent a year earlier.[32] The PA had also cut social security payments for the very poorest families.

In June 2006, the EU finally persuaded the international Quartet to sanction the Temporary International Mechanism (TIM), which was intended to provide aid – including salaries in health and education – while bypassing the Hamas-led authority. But the process, which was delivering around $132m per quarter by the end of the year, was a cumbersome and inefficient way of 'paying more to help less of the Palestinian population'.[33] The TIM, precluded from dealing directly with the Ministry of Health, was, for example, having trouble making up acute drug shortages. At Shifa hospital, Intisar al-Saqqa was waiting for Taxotere, a drug needed to treat her breast cancer that had metastasised to a lung and her liver. 'I don't blame anybody,' she said. 'I just want all this to end.' And even if patients could secure the vital permit for treatment in Israel or the West Bank, the PA – according to the Hamas-run Ministry of Health – was running out of money to pay for it.

In March 2006, Israel stopped the last few Palestinians leaving through Erez to work in Israel (between the 1960s and the start of the Second Intifada in 2000, some 26,000 Gazans had worked in Israel every day). The lifeblood of Gaza's private sector exports was already beginning to suffer. The main cargo crossing at Karni was frequently closed during 2006, although it did not permanently close until the following summer. There had been a single plot to attack it by the maverick quasi-warlord Mumtaz Dughmush, which had actually been foiled by PA security forces. Moreover, during 2004 when there was a much higher level of violence, the crossing had been closed for only twenty per cent of the time, as opposed to fifty per cent now. But there was little serious international agitation to try to revive an agreement that had started to disintegrate even before Hamas was elected. James Wolfensohn – who had already vainly warned a US Senate Committee that ceasing to pay PA employees would have dangerous consequences, including 'radicalisation', in Gaza – offered President Bush his view in August 2006 after stepping down as Quartet representative four months earlier. 'I told him that there would be no peace between Israel and the Palestinians unless we went back to the November plan agreed by Secretary Rice, the Israelis and the Palestinians in my presence . . . [Without it] Hamas would become stronger and more radical and a frustrated and angry youth would give their lives against a dominant Israel.'

Wolfensohn recalled leaving with the President's thanks 'ringing in my ears'; but he did not think that Bush or Elliott Abrams, also present, 'gave any weight to my views'. If anything that was an understatement.[34]

By the end of 2006, the cumulative effect of these factors was pervasive. Adeeb Zarouk's story was fairly typical. Married with seven children, the forty-four-year-old was a capable, hardworking and cheerful man, a good Hebrew speaker who had become used to decent wages – and the 4 a.m. starts to get out through Erez – in Israel over twenty years as a freelance welder and electrician, and then another five employed by an Israeli company in the now flattened Erez industrial zone. We met one morning in December as his wife Majda was preparing a breakfast of beans, falafel and a few tomatoes which, she volunteered, had cost three shekels (36p at 2006 prices). After three months on an UNRWA temporary employment programme at £120 a month, Zarouk was trying to make a living repairing TV satellite dishes or doing other jobs. But the work wasn't coming. Over breakfast, Zarouk started to say: 'When your son asks you for a half a shekel, and you don't have it . . .' He broke off, embarrassed because he had started to cry; he got up to rinse his face in the sink. Recovered, he said he had voted Fatah in the election. But, he said sarcastically, 'I blame democracy. The whole world wanted us to have democracy and said how fair had been our election. The problem is they didn't like our results.'

Often as not, it was the women who led their families' struggle for survival. In September in Shujaia, Itidal al-Nazli, thirty-five, had shown me the sparse contents of her refrigerator. Despite the daily and lengthy interruptions to the electricity supply since the Israelis had bombed Gaza's only power station in late June, it was where she still stored the more perishable food for her family of ten children – including quadruplets. It contained six shrivelled peppers, a bag of coffee, three olives in a bowl, a bag of charcoal and three bags containing crusts of bread. Coming from an originally Gazan family, she was ineligible for the UN food coupons handed out to refugees. Once or twice a year, she said, some refugee friends passed on a sack of flour and oil, beans and lentils. She had paid neither her £37-per-month rent nor £18 per month in water and electricity charges for the past six months. Her husband Sami, thirty-eight, had done odd jobs for a few days a month, but work had dried up. 'We don't have anything. The children eat the same food as I do – lentils and beans. Meat? We never see it,' she said.

Her two-room apartment had bare breeze-block walls and concrete floors. The living room was furnished with one single bed; most of the children slept on a blanket on the floor. Yet there seemed something irrepressibly cheerful about Mrs al-Nazli, who, despite coming from a poor family, took a two-year qualification in teaching Arabic only to find, like so many other Gaza graduates, there were no jobs. If she had a job, she might have had fewer children, she said, while adding quickly with a radiant smile that 'they are a gift from God'.

A few doors down on the same street, however, Souad al-Quraya, who was thirty-three, couldn't stop crying as she described the rudimentary breakfast of a single shekel's worth of bread and beans she had eaten with her five children. Her much older husband, Samir, had lost his job two years earlier when he was diagnosed with cancer and was in hospital in Egypt. She had scraped by with the help of savings and the £32-a-month PA social security – until that had stopped after Hamas's election victory. She had to borrow £48 every month to make the rent on the family's home and keep at bay a landlord who 'comes to the door and won't leave till he gets it,' she said. Neighbours helped when they could, she said, but, unusually, her father, 'God forgive him,' had stopped visiting. 'He said my husband's brothers should help me now. But they have done nothing and it is hard to ask them because I have my dignity.'³⁵

HOSTILITIES BETWEEN ISRAEL AND HAMAS CONTINUED well into November 2006 when the IDF launched a fresh incursion into the much-battered Beit Hanoun, where depleted orange groves were a favoured site for Hamas rocket launchers. Among the dead were eighteen members of the Athamneh family, including six children under sixteen; another died later from his injuries. It was the most harrowing of all the incidents in Gaza that year. All the victims were civilians, and the family were Fatah supporters. An internal IDF investigation found a defective microchip in the artillery battery's guidance system had misdirected an attack on a 'launching space' in nearby orange groves. Amid an international outcry, there was considerable criticism in Israel, including from Alex Fishman, *Yedhioth Ahronoth*'s military analyst, who asked why the shelling went on for around fifteen minutes. 'Why wasn't the falling of each shell monitored by human means?'³⁶ The anguish of the surviving members of the family was total. Two days afterwards, eleven-year-old Mustafa Athamneh, whose mother, Nihad, was killed in the alley outside the house as they tried to escape, could not stop crying. 'I was with my mother when she fell down,' he said. 'I ran away.'³⁷

Among the subsequent rocket attacks, one launched at Sderot killed fifty-seven-year-old Fa'ina Slotzker, the ninth Israeli to be killed by a Qassam from Gaza since 2000; another severely injured a bodyguard of Amir Peretz. In a nervous Sderot, opinions varied. Mayor Moyal insisted that tougher military measures were needed to stop the rocket fire, and a resident whose window had been blown out in a rocket attack said: 'The army should go into Beit Hanoun and demolish all the houses so there are no areas to shoot from. That is the only possible solution.' But student Orly Saroussi, twenty-six, wanted a ceasefire. 'We can't go on like this,' she said. 'This is just a chain of destruction.' While acknowledging that many of her neighbours took a tougher line, she said: 'Children are being killed. Children are hurting. We can't live like this.' By 26 November, Abbas had persuaded the factions to stop rocket attacks and tunnel digging in return for a halt to Israeli attacks on Gaza. It was, at least, a short respite. Since the beginning of July, in the immediate aftermath of Shalit's abduction, 317 Palestinians had been killed by Israeli security forces, of whom two-thirds according to the Israeli human rights organisation B'Tselem were 'not involved in hostilities'.[38] As well as the two Israeli soldiers killed during Shalit's capture, two more soldiers had died and two civilians in Sderot.

Meanwhile, Hamas had found new sources of funding – even if, in the absence of cooperation from the banks, it had to resort to unconventional means of transporting it. Israel prevented Haniyeh from bringing suitcases stuffed with $35m in cash across the Rafah border in December. But Mahmoud Zahar had brought $20m in nine suitcases across the same border in June and, by his own account, repeated the action 'several times'. Iran had announced a £250m subvention to Hamas. Although relations between the two had been cordial since the 1990s,[39] they now reached a zenith that lasted until Hamas annoyed the Iranians by criticising Syria's President Bashar al-Assad for the Iranian-supported war against his own people. Hamas insisted Iran's largesse was funding essential services like health and education in Gaza, although Iranian cash was also used to buy weapons. Israel and some of its Western allies understandably excoriated Hamas's links with Iran. But to a large extent, the West had driven Hamas into the arms of Iran – not a natural fit for a Sunni organisation born out of the Muslim Brotherhood – by denying funding to the government it was trying to run. Omar Suleiman, head of Egyptian intelligence, close interlocutor of Israel and no friend of Hamas, had warned the international community back in February: if the West cuts off Hamas, 'Iran will give them the money'.[40]

The money started to flow to Fatah, too. By the end of 2006, Abbas had suggested a fresh election, an idea opposed by Hamas. Israel released direct to the Palestinian presidency $100m of the $400m in clearance revenues it owed the PA. And the US was awaiting Congressional approval for $86m for training and 'non-lethal' equipment for Abbas's presidential guard, and another $42m for promoting 'alternatives' to Hamas.[41] These moves reflected hope that Abbas would at last be ready to confront Hamas and relief that he seemed to have abandoned efforts to form a unity government with the Islamic faction. Those attempts had foundered on the difficulties of forming a new Cabinet, US and Israeli warnings that a deal would jeopardise the chances of peace negotiations, and the mounting death toll in violence between Fatah and Hamas – which now included the three small children of a prominent Fatah intelligence colonel, Bahaa Balousha, shot dead as they were being driven to school.

While Abbas and Haniyeh had tried to reach an accommodation, they had had no encouragement from the international community. The more aggressive elements in both factions had been strengthened. And now Hamas and Fatah had the funds – and arms – to equip themselves for the conflict ahead.

There was not much light relief amid the misery and bloodshed in December 2006, though a local band hired to entertain the spectators at a Hamas rally, of all places, tried to provide some. The Gaza City rally had featured the usual martial displays: military wing members abseiling down a building overlooking the stadium and unfurling a twenty-foot portrait of a seventy-year-old female suicide bomber who had blown herself up the previous month. Prime Minister Haniyeh, fresh from an attack on his convoy earlier in the week which had killed a bodyguard, and for which Hamas blamed Fatah, was driven into the rally in a Mercedes under heavy armed escort, before promising he would not agree to fresh elections. But then the highly professional and identically beige-suited five-man vocal group launched into a humorous – and surprisingly even-handed – counterpoint Arabic rock operetta. Two of its members, each representing one of the main factions, performed a raucous duet about the impact of the international boycott. 'Hamas waters our olive trees,' sang one. 'Can't you recognise Israel just a little bit?' intoned the other. 'We are not getting salaries. You are making us beggars.' Then the 'Hamas' and 'Fatah' singers came together in a chorus to Palestinian 'unity'. The audience was appreciative. But unity was not what 2007 had in store for the Palestinian people.

7

'SO MANY HARD TIMES AHEAD': CIVIL WAR, 2007

'I<small>T NEVER CEASES TO AMAZE ME</small> how the people continually put up with all the crap in Gaza,' Miriam Faris mused in her diary in January 2007. 'The *belad*?* You could cut it with a knife. The way the politics are going, everyone expects the worst.'

The power shortages had already started to appear in the daily entries she had been writing since the previous September from her vantage point running Rosy, a gym, hair and beauty salon in Gaza City, with her husband Mohammed. 'Electricity getting worse not better. Khan Yunis and Rafah are getting [power] from Egypt now but not us, it's really a catastrophe.' 'Generator completely broke.' 'No fish in Gaza due to Israeli closures. Many things missing: school things, fruit, hair colours. Chocs. Rafah closed.'

Also recorded was the repeated fighting between Fatah and Hamas militias. 'Testosterone all over the place. Soldiers upstairs and shooting . . . really big guns . . . Mohammed came back from Rosy walking, he left the car there so it didn't get shot again. A girl in the building next door got shot dead just sitting in her room. She was about to wed next week. As usual Mohammed doesn't know what to do with himself so I gave him a job to cook for the soldiers upstairs, poor sods didn't have provisions. Most of the staff got sent home early.'

---

* Arabic word meaning 'land' or 'country'.

When Miriam Clarke was growing up in the 1960s, the youngest of nine children, in the south-west Cumbrian coastal town of Millom, she never dreamed she would have two sons named Awny and Samir, teach herself fluent Arabic and spend over half her adult life in the Gaza Strip. But then, she didn't expect to fall in love with Mohammed Faris when they met by chance on holiday, let alone that their marriage would still be going strong after more than thirty-five years. Back then, by Miriam's account, he was an extrovert 'Jack the lad who could have any girl he wanted'. And she was a sassy, no-nonsense twenty-two-year-old whom Mohammed remembered as 'so quick and intelligent, with this repartee'.

The couple married in El Arish in the northern Sinai in 1980. They had planned to get married in Gaza, but the imam they went to disapproved of Mohammed marrying a foreigner, possibly because he had seven daughters of his own and didn't want an upstart like Miriam taking one of Gaza's more eligible men. The newlyweds went to live in Cumbria – 'I liked the Lake District but I couldn't believe you couldn't get garlic,' said Mohammed – and then London. A good English speaker, Mohammed worked for a while as a deputy pub manager but, although highly regarded by his employers and earmarked for promotion, he missed Gaza and his family. 'Every day in England it was "your country this" and "your country that",' Miriam said. 'So when he wanted to come here I said, well that will shut him up.' Turning to Mohammed she added, laughing, 'And now you can get it about *your* country.'

Mohammed, his father and his brothers built up a family company. By the mid-1990s it was one of Gaza's leading importers of consumer goods – televisions, refrigerators, washing machines – and water pumps and industrial machinery. The company had a million-dollar turnover; Mohammed met Yasser Arafat to discuss economic issues. He had the money to establish Rosy in 1999 for Miriam to have 'something to do' now their sons were growing up; but soon repeated interruptions to imports took their toll; the firm went bust and suddenly what had been conceived almost as a hobby became the couple's only livelihood. It was never easy, but as the economy began to slump in 2006, and Rosy's services became an unaffordable luxury for an increasing number of Gazan women, it grew to be more of a struggle.

Then Miriam started the highly personal diary she called 'Life in the Muddle East', peppered with words in transliterated Arabic and full of wry reflections on the sheer difficulties of day-to-day life in Gaza: her and Mohammed's struggle to run a going concern with mounting debts; the impact of political events on family, staff and friends; friction with business partners and creditors. 'Mohammed tried to reason with Ramsy and Senna to no avail,' ran one entry on the latter. 'Qatar trying to reason with Hamas and Abu Mazen with slightly more success.'

By 23 January 2007, the last of several ceasefires had broken down. A wave of shoot-outs, lethal mutual attacks on Fatah and Hamas strong-holds and hostage-taking led to a staggering seventy-four Palestinian deaths in just two weeks, many of innocent bystanders. The anger in civil society was impossible to ignore. A furious Raji Sourani of the Palestinian Centre for Human Rights, who remained in Gaza through-out the worst of the Israeli–Palestinian conflict, thumped his fist on his desk and said: 'If this [violence] will continue, you will not find me here. Not because I'm afraid but because I cannot tolerate it. It's breaking my heart. It's the new *nakba*.' Sourani, who blamed both Fatah and Hamas, added that each faction needed to realise the other would 'continue to exist'.

Among those watching the carnage unfold on Arab satellite TV – the coverage on Al Jazeera more favourable to Hamas, that on Al Arabiya leaning towards Fatah – was King Abdullah of Saudi Arabia, who now summoned Abbas, Khaled Meshal and Haniyeh to Mecca in an effort to prevent a full-scale civil war, promising $1bn to Gaza if the two sides could form a stable coalition. 'No work cos the *belad* is bracing itself for the Mecca talks,' wrote Miriam on 5 February. 'My girls in the salon are debating whether to come to work or not on Wednesday cos there may be shooting if the talks go sour.' But then on 8 February: 'Work in the beautician mainly, but still not enough to get us out of the quagmire we are in. Fatah and Hamas agreed to make one government. People shoot-ing in the streets from joy this time . . .'

Palestinians follow political developments addictively for the simple reason that they affect their everyday lives. And the joy was understand-able since the agreement seemed to herald an end to the inter-factional fighting. A coalition government was formed in less than a month, with Haniyeh as Prime Minister and Azzam Ahmad of Fatah as Deputy Prime Minister. In addition the Cabinet contained three credible figures from outside either faction, including the former International Monetary Fund official Salam Fayyad as Finance Minister. Under the agreement Hamas accepted that, as President, Abbas had the right to negotiate with Israel. And two of the harder-line Hamas politicians, Mahmoud Zahar and the previous Interior Minister Said Siyam, were excluded from the Cabinet.

The day before the official formation of the unity government on 13 March, Miriam had tersely recorded in her diary an event that underlined the prevailing lawlessness in Gaza at the time. 'They've kidnapped Alan Johnston, poor sod. He's so friendly with the people.' Just sixteen days before the end of his three-year tour of duty as the BBC's correspondent in Gaza, Johnston was seized about a hundred metres from his office. Another car slewed in front of his; he was bundled in at gunpoint by two men who shoved a hood over his face and forced him to lie on the back seat. So began the worst sixteen weeks of his life.

Johnston, the only foreign journalist resident in Gaza, had covered previous – and mercifully much shorter – kidnappings of foreigners, including Kate Burton and her parents, and two Fox News journalists the previous year. He had recently moved to a new beachfront complex, thought to be safer. The previous year he had mused on the subject in an edition of BBC Radio 4's *From Our Own Correspondent*, saying, 'if my turn comes I will be terrified'. At a party in Jerusalem in early 2007 he had discussed with me the fears of kidnap we all had as reporters covering Gaza at the time.

Since 2004, Johnston had reported its relentlessly turbulent story, up to and including the descent into anarchy of which he himself was now a victim, with distinction. He was 'a friend of the Palestinian people', as his father Graham put it in one of his judicious broadcasts during his son's captivity, but also a stickler for facts. He learned a modest amount of Arabic, which was an undoubted help – possibly even a life-saver – during his captivity.

Recalling his life-changing experience ten years later, he pointed out that he was not tortured, and contrasted his own kidnapping with what he saw as the incomparably greater – and inescapable – 'ocean of suffering' by other civilians in conflicts around the world, including Gaza itself. Nevertheless his kidnapping was extremely dangerous, for Johnston himself and for Gaza. If it ended badly, it would confirm that the Strip was facing 'Somali-isation' – prey to any freelance group or clan with guns and determination, and with agendas alien to the vast majority in Gaza. In the meantime it afforded him a unique, if wholly unwelcome, close-up of a group more extreme and unpredictable than Hamas.

For most Palestinians, for whom hospitality is so deeply embedded a characteristic, the kidnapping became a powerful symbol of the bloodletting and disorder into which the Strip had fallen, which left an estimated ninety Palestinians dead and 336 injured in 2006. Palestinian journalists held a three-day strike in support of Johnston, clashing with PA security forces. They were not acting only from professional respect for Johnston. 'I feel so bad and angry,' Raji Sourani said a fortnight after Johnston was seized. 'Not just because I know Alan as a human being, a first-class professional journalist and a friend. This is not in our political culture, or in our social culture. We are shooting ourselves in the head with acts like this. We are deforming our image.' At a meeting in Khan Yunis to protest the kidnapping, everyone present had 'spoken up' for Johnston, 'from the mayor to the smallest grassroots groups'. Sourani added that 'everyone', including the PA security services, 'knows who Alan's kidnappers are, but we have no accountability to the rule of law'.

Without naming names, Sourani was talking about members of the Dughmush clan; they were the ones who had kidnapped the Fox News employees the previous year, releasing them after two weeks, and they typified the less benign aspects of kinship in the Strip. Historically clans were a powerful force in Gaza society, with a tendency to pursue their own collective interests; many had been co-opted by Yasser Arafat, who in return for their loyalty allowed the clans to interweave themselves with PA institutions, including the security services, to maintain their dominance of certain commercial markets – tyres, in the case of the Dughmush – and to settle their own internal or inter-tribal disputes.[1] After Arafat's death, however, and in the vacuum left by Israel's destruction of the PA's infrastructure, the clans began to assert their independence, acquiring many of the weapons left by the disintegrating security services of which they had been a part, and sometimes pursuing their own vendettas. Such blood feuds could last a lifetime. There's a typical Gaza joke about a man who takes revenge on his enemy a full fifty years after the original slight: 'Why the hurry?' comes the riposte.

Part of this tribally driven breakdown of law and order arose because the clan elders and *mukhtars* whom Arafat had courted began to lose their authority over the younger, more headstrong members. One of these was thirty-year-old Mumtaz Dughmush, who in 2006 established a militia of clan members with a radical jihadist flavour. During the 1990s he had been a member of the PA Preventative Security Organisation headed by Mohammed Dahlan, but during the Intifada he joined Jamal Abu Samhadana to form the militant Popular Resistance Committees. After the 2006 elections, Dughmush, whose militia was now operating autonomously with the title *Jaish al-Islam*, or 'Army of Islam', joined with the PRC and Hamas's Qassam Brigades to capture Gilad Shalit. But then his armed group broke with Hamas, abandoned its role in the custody of Shalit, and defied the Islamic faction's authority as the elected government by kidnapping the two Fox News journalists, and subsequently was said to have offered the services of several hundred armed men to Fatah.

By now Hamas had indicated it wanted to curb the power of the clans, and relations with some of their leaders were beginning to deteriorate. But *Jaish al-Islam* appeared beyond the control of the Dughmush elders, who would later say publicly they opposed the kidnapping, but without effect. Johnston was held for at least part of his incarceration in the Dughmush family territory in the Sabra neighbourhood of Gaza city, where his abductors could rely on a lack of interference or betrayal by the neighbours and kinsmen. The last room he was brought to (in the third move of his kidnap) was certainly in the Dughmush compound. Johnston's incarceration was, of course, vastly shorter than Gilad Shalit's – not to mention that of Palestinian prisoners, some of whom have been confined in Israeli gaols for more than a quarter of a century. But the Israeli soldier was at least being held by armed groups nominally answerable to an elected authority in Gaza, to which international interlocutors had access. Conventional wisdom in Gaza at the time was that the agenda of Johnston's kidnappers was criminal, even if dressed up as fundamentalist jihad. Certainly the kidnappers were essentially outlaws – part of why his abduction was so dangerous for Johnston.

But while *Jaish al-Islam* leaders may have been using the kidnapping as a weapon in their power struggle with Hamas, Johnston would recall a decade later that the people holding him were 'the real jihadi deal':

I never had any doubt that the people who were . . . conducting the kidnapping were of a genuinely jihadi persuasion. I felt that I had been rounded up by these more rabid individuals, but then once I was in their hands . . . I felt from the first moments to the last that this was a jihadi cell of some kind.[2]

Johnston was lying on his thin mattress on the first night when a figure in a white robe, his face masked by a red chequered headdress, entered the room and told him in English: 'Alan Johnston, we know everything.' As Johnston would write later that year, the man's voice was calm, even kindly; he said that the hostage would not be killed, be treated well, in accordance with Islamic custom, and that he would in time write a book and get married.

> They wanted prisoners to be released . . . I said that Britain will never release any [prisoners] . . . and he stopped me and said "Britain will be forced to listen". It was definitely in the classic jihadi [anti-]crusader type. For example they asked me, what was I? I said I was a Christian, and he said, was I a crusader like George Bush? I knew enough about Gaza to know that you would never dream of not saying that you were the people of the book.

Johnston said that his main memories were of his 'mental battle', once he realised he might be held for years, with no certainty about how it would end; it was a 'vast project, a huge continual effort' to keep his mind 'in the right place . . . not letting myself get frustrated or angry'. In a breakthrough after more than a month, the hostage finally persuaded his guards to let him have a radio, on which he could hear the BBC World Service, 'which I'd worked on for most of my career, and everybody on it I know' – and which was by then doing a daily 'Alan Johnston slot'. On the night he was given it, he wrapped the radio in a blanket and pressed the speaker against his ear 'because they would not want me listening to English with neighbours hearing it, everything had to be thought through . . . It was the day of the Grand National and just the idea that you were suddenly listening to all that mad British fun while locked up in Gaza . . . It was just too much to believe and made you desperately homesick but also glad to be hearing it. But then the first bulletin that evening said that I had been killed. Just incredible, the surrealism . . . to hear people that I knew from my own place back home telling me in that place that I had been put to death and then thinking about what that meant for my folks. Probably the bleakest night of your life really, where in those dark moments you're thinking that maybe the PR department is only slightly ahead of the executive branch of the operation and then you sit there all night listening to every movement in the flat and a car came in the street and I thought: "So is this them? Is this the people who've come to do this thing?"'

It wasn't. But nor was it the last of the 'three or four moments' when Johnston thought that possibly 'it was more likely that I would die than that I would live'.

Johnston's most constant guard was Khamis, a moody man in his twenties who spoke no English, was wanted by Israel, but almost certainly also by his enemies in Hamas and Fatah. Johnston gradually gleaned that Khamis belonged, like the majority of Palestinians in Gaza, to a family of 1948 refugees from what is now Israel, and like a large minority had been gaoled at some point by the Israelis. He was capable of sudden rages. Having lost ten kilograms and 'always a bit hungry', Johnston one day thought to roast an onion and picked up a ladle. 'So I put the onion in it and just put it over the gas ring, and it had the effect I wanted on the onion, but it made a pig's ear of the back of the ladle. And he went berserk about that, furious. He was very house proud. He was really angry about the state of that ladle.' But he was a 'complex individual' capable of occasional decency as well:

> Scotland was playing France in football on the telly, and he called me through and let me watch that. There was a time when my folks appeared at a news conference and he called me through to watch that, and . . . I saw my folks walking by the loch in front of the house and it was just incredible you know, snow on the rocks just by the edge of the sea, you know, you're just in this jihadi hideout watching your folks walking down the beach down from the house.

> You glanced around the room, there was nothing there, maybe just three or four Kalashnikovs and I'm pretty sure there was a hand grenade on the shelf under the TV . . . and there was an M16 [rifle].

One factor that sharply differentiated his kidnappers from Hamas, which has always limited its goals to the Holy Land, was their demands for the release of prisoners who had no direct connection with the Israeli–Palestinian conflict, including Palestinian-born Jordanian citizen Abu Qatada, with close past associations with Al Qaeda, then in detention in the UK, and the Iraqi national Sajida al-Rishawi, facing execution after conviction in Jordan for her failed role in the Al Qaeda-organised suicide bombings that killed sixty people in Amman in November 2005.

At one point Johnston heard Khamis having an argument before coming in to chain him up for the first time. Khamis said that Johnston's captors, apparently furious at reports speculating that al-Rishawi was about to be executed (this did not in fact happen until 2015), would decide the next day 'whether I would be executed and he said that if we do it it'll be with a blade . . . and he seemed to enjoy telling me that'.

> On the other hand, there was a bizarre thing: he told me 'I don't like this chaining you up. If they are going to make me chain you up, I've told them I'm going to leave'; but then I was in a difficult position because it's much better to be chained up by a bloke who doesn't want to chain you up. So I had this kind of odd conversation, where here's this guy who's my keeper, my guard, and is at that point chaining me up, but I'm saying 'No, no, I don't want you to go, there's no need for that.' I was thinking even at the time that I've got to persuade him that he should stay on and that it's okay. You don't want a guy to come who is very pro-chaining up. So that was a difficult period, and it was only one night that I was chained up, but it stays with you all your life, that. The thing that you don't realise until you get chained up is that as bad as the sense of constriction is the noise – every single smallest movement is accompanied by a chinking of the links. To wake up in chains is something extraordinary. After that they took them away, perhaps Khamis won his argument or their anger subsided or they realised that Sajida wasn't going to be killed or whatever, but that period of tension dissipated.

There would soon be others, however. In the meantime, the less turbulent periods taxed Johnston's undoubted mental strength. He would constantly compare his plight with those of others he saw as much worse off, writing a few months later, 'I felt I wouldn't be able to pick up a book again about the Holocaust if I were somehow to break down mentally under the very, very much easier circumstances of my captivity.'[3]

After he got a radio, he discovered for the first time that there was a worldwide campaign for his release – which included many Palestinians. He could hear the personal World Service messages to him from Terry Waite and Brian Keenan, the latter saying: 'The mind and body are stronger than you think.' All this was hugely heartening. But it could not eliminate his low moments, however hard he was focused on containing them:

> One day I sat down with Khamis – this was the closest we'd ever come to any real conversation – and I said I'm tired of this, when do you think this might end; do you think they're going to release those prisoners? And I needed to get it into their heads that that was never going to happen. They needed to know that this wasn't going to end with three prisoners walking out of somewhere, least of all Abu Qatada. So Khamis said, 'Will they let Abu Qatada go?' and I said '*abadan*' – never – and they said 'then for you *abadan*'. The one time I remember just getting so frustrated was when they said again on the radio that they wanted Abu Qatada, and this was the thing I knew was never going to happen and it just would go on and on and on, they still wanted that bloke.[4]

By June both Johnston and his kidnappers were becoming increasingly preoccupied with events nearer home, as Gaza descended into factional fighting once again. The Mecca deal had been a shotgun marriage which had not really resolved the all-important question of who was going to run internal security – at a time when factional infighting and widespread lawlessness had made it the most urgent priority. Moreover, for all the Saudi king's authority, the coalition badly needed wider international support if it was to survive, let alone function as a service provider. Abbas and Fayyad had asked both for Western aid and for Israel to release the remaining $300m it owed the PA in customs revenues. The requests were in vain; Israel was implacably hostile to the new government, while a more relaxed Bush suggested to Ehud Olmert that he 'did not think this unity government could last'.[5] Bush was right; but it was something of a self-fulfilling prophecy.

The compromise candidate as Interior Minister had been Hani Qawasmi, a little-known Gazan academic with no experience of security issues, and with little influence over either of the main factions.

Qawasmi wanted to merge the Hamas executive force with the Fatah-dominated PA security forces, but this was sternly opposed by Fatah. In May Qawasmi resigned; Israel allowed a contingent of newly US-trained Fatah forces to enter Gaza through Rafah, and Hamas gunmen attacked a convoy that it claimed was carrying arms to Fatah, setting the scene for bloody confrontations in the second half of May and the first half of June, with both sides claiming the other was preparing a 'coup'.

The resumed fighting between Fatah and Hamas was exacerbated by the continued Israeli attacks on Hamas positions, reciprocated and sometimes triggered by rocket fire. There were times when the internal fighting would be briefly interrupted by repeated ceasefires – seven in all during the month and often lasting no more than a few hours – only for the cross-border conflict to flare up again.

Late on the night of 15–16 May, Ghazi Hamad was in a convoy on the way to police headquarters for negotiations on just such a ceasefire when it was stopped and surrounded by a twenty-strong Fatah security unit. According to Hamad, 'I heard a walkie-talkie and they were saying "Ghazi Hamad is in the car." They told me that I had to get out, and they were pointing the Kalashnikovs on the windows everywhere. So I put my hand on the handle of the door to open it, but the driver screamed at me "please keep the door closed, don't open it," so I closed it again. The armed people stood back half a metre and started to shoot more than 100 bullets. The bullets penetrated the wheels. The driver was in a panic. I put my head between my legs, and I asked him "please go, don't stop."' Luckily for Hamad and his driver but unknown to him until that point, the car, lent to the delegation by the PA security apparatus, was armoured. When a senior Egyptian diplomat, travelling in the car behind raised his hand, he took a bullet in his finger.[6]

The incident was only one of dozens, many with fatal consequences, being perpetrated almost every day by adherents of both Hamas and Fatah. The entries in Miriam Faris's diary conveyed the almost surreal effort of uninvolved Gazans trying to live normally amid the factional fighting:

> *Belad* going crazy, loads of robberies and beatings between gangs; 3 shot outside Rosy. I'm so tired. There's no respite from all this crap.
>
> Our part of town was quiet partly cos of presidential guards all over the place. Shati camp had shooting and Naser area early in the

morning, About 01.30 a car threw a guy out who was bound and then they shot him outside Rosy. People gathered round and the body was taken away and after fifteen minutes the street was normal again.

Poor Rose was still in Rosy at 03.00, her husband came for her but too much shooting to get out. As we came home earlier than usual I tattooed my eyebrows while Mohammed cooked an Italian meal cos it's our wedding anniversary.

Shooting . . . all night. My eyebrows were still swollen . . . Hamas fired many Katyushas into Israel.

Israel continue their bombardment towards Hamas . . . more casualties today. It's really weird how it's this beautiful sunny day and now Qassams (rockets) are flying all over the place.

But much worse was yet to come. The decisive battle began on 11 June; with Mohammed Dahlan, the most prominent Fatah figure in Gaza, absent abroad, apparently for medical treatment, and many of the senior figures in both factions in hiding, Hamas militants began to sweep through the Strip, seizing or destroying Fatah installations and killing many of those inside. By 15 June, the presidential compound, the Preventative Security Force headquarters, and the main Saraya* security and prison compound had all fallen to Hamas. Perhaps civil wars are always among the most brutal; if so, the forces of both sides in this one were no exception. A total of 350 Palestinian lives were lost in the factional infighting, including non-combatants, some of them children. A cook working for the presidential guard and a passenger abducted from a Khan Yunis taxi were two of the victims hurled – respectively by Hamas and Fatah militias – blindfolded and handcuffed from the roofs of high-rise buildings. Prisoners were summarily executed. When hundreds of non-combatants marched through Gaza City demanding an end to the killing, two of the demonstrators were shot dead – it was not clear by whom.

In the end, however, despite their numerical superiority, many in the Fatah militias surrendered, deserted or prepared to escape from Gaza through Erez, Rafah or by boat. For surrender was no guarantee of safety. When the Preventative Security Force headquarters fell to Hamas

---

* The forbidding British-built fortress-like compound subsequently used in turn as a security headquarters and gaol by Egypt, Israel, the PA and Hamas.

on 14 June, according to a National Security Force member who took part in the defence: 'most of us surrendered; only some kept shooting. We were about twenty-five in all. They put us all against the wall and told us to come forward and shot at us, especially aiming at the legs but as people fell they were hit in other parts of the body . . . it was a massacre . . . I heard that seventeen of my colleagues died and the others were all injured.'[7]

Hamas was now in total internal control of Gaza. One Hamas account suggests that this happened more by luck than design: a popular imam had been killed by Fatah militants, provoking the Hamas forces. They then stormed the presidential compound in retaliation and, much to their surprise, the Fatah defenders of the Saraya capitulated fast, their commanding officer telling Hamas: 'You don't have to fire and attack the place, come and we'll give you the keys.'[8] On the other hand, Hamas's al-Aqsa radio had earlier forecast that Hamas forces would push north from Khan Yunis, taking the presidential compound and then the security headquarters in Gaza City, which suggests some advance planning, at least in the last stages of the short and bloody civil war, on the part of the Hamas fighters.[9] There is little evidence that either Haniyeh or Abbas envisaged seizing total control in Gaza at the expense of the other. But there were those in each faction who had opposed the coalition from the outset; and the hawks on each side had grounds for fighting to frustrate what they saw as the ambitions of those on the other.

Either way there were some gruesome reprisals against Fatah leaders who did not leave in time. A leading Fatah militant in northern Gaza and a close ally of Mohammed Dahlan, Samih Madhoun, had proudly announced in a radio interview that he had killed Hamas members. He fled his own home on 14 June, seeking the safety of the presidential compound. According to his brother, Hamas militiamen opened fire on him as he approached one of their checkpoints and he fired back, killing one of the Hamas gunmen. The Hamas operatives grabbed him and took him to the parents of the man he had shot dead, and urged the parents to kill the captive Madhoun in revenge. When the grieving parents refused, the Hamas gunmen killed him themselves and mutilated the body; a video of the execution was put on YouTube.[10]

Had Hamas pre-empted a US-backed coup to dislodge it by military means? In March 2008, the journalist David Rose published an article in *Vanity Fair* pointing to a 'covert initiative approved by Bush and

implemented by Secretary of State Condoleezza Rice and Deputy
National Security Adviser Elliott Abrams to provoke a Palestinian civil
war'.[11] The report, not explicitly denied by Rice, quoted a telling remark
by David Wurmser, who had resigned as Vice-President Dick Cheney's
chief Middle East adviser a month after the Hamas takeover: 'It looks to
me that what happened wasn't so much a coup by Hamas but an
attempted coup by Fatah that was pre-empted before it could happen.'
Rose also relied on a State Department document which envisaged an
ambitious plan to support the forces loyal to Abbas, putting the total
cost for salaries, training and 'the needed security equipment, lethal
and non-lethal,' at $1.27bn over five years.

Certainly the PA/Fatah forces that fought Hamas had help and were
getting active encouragement from the Western powers[12] – notably the
US and, on a smaller scale, Britain. Although he would be absent from
Gaza when the fighting peaked, Dahlan had been supported by a hand-
picked 'special force' trained with Western assistance under the aegis of
General Keith Dayton, the Bush-appointed US security coordinator in
the Middle East. With similar help, Abbas's presidential guard was
augmented by 700 new recruits,[13] along with training and equipping of
National Security Force personnel in which the UK had been involved
since at least 2005.[14] Indeed this help, even if 'non-lethal', cast some
doubt on the EU's cautious public welcome for the Mecca agreement; it
was clear that if Mecca broke down – as it did – EU members would be
rooting for Fatah. It also became clear from the 'Palestine Papers', leaked
to Al Jazeera in 2011, that Dayton was presiding over a regular 'quadri-
partite security meeting' in which the US, Israel, the PA and Egypt were
discussing at the top level ways of containing Hamas; the fullest set of
leaked minutes, from April 2007, focused in particular on trying to stop
Hamas smuggling arms. Nor, as Rose pointed out, was it a secret that
500 smartly turned out members of a National Security Force unit, with
new weapons and vehicles and answerable to the absent Dahlan, had
come across the border in May after forty-five days' training in Egypt.
Dayton's staff were also on the phone to Fatah leaders in the closing
stages of the battle, attempting to stiffen resistance.[15]

But if the Americans thought they could lever Hamas out of power
by helping Fatah forces in the summer of 2007 it was a fantasy, even if
they did not realise it at the time. This does not detract from the argument that Hamas *thought* a coup was being planned against them and

that they acted accordingly. Moreover, in his book, published in 2013, Abrams acknowledges that 'in theory had the Dayton programme continued year after year while Hamas forces grew no stronger, we might have reached the point where PA forces could defeat Hamas'. But the publicly announced decision on more finance for the Fatah forces at the end of 2006 – let alone whatever more far-reaching plans had been hatched in Washington – was very slow in bearing fruit, partly because Congress delayed its approval of the funding and then reduced it by about $30m. Abrams' own account, while consistent with the aspiration reflected in the leaked material, is really a complaint that *not enough* was being done to strengthen Fatah forces for a showdown with Hamas militants who were more disciplined, organised and motivated:

> Ward [Dayton's predecessor] and Dayton had faced the great frustration of having to achieve a task, professionalisation of the PA forces, without any resources to work with; they were forced to be all talk until the fall of 2007, months after the Hamas action, when the first funds arrived.[16]

Interviewed much later by Abrams himself, Jake Walles, who had been US Consul General in Jerusalem at the time, said: 'I think that Hamas really did think that we were conspiring with Dahlan to bring them down. I don't think we were *in the sense that they believed we were*, but . . . I think [Hamas] felt there was a risk that this "conspiracy" would topple them – this non-existent conspiracy. So rather than wait for it to happen, they just pulled the plug' (my italics).[17]

But whether or not the 'conspiracy' was as 'non-existent' as Abrams and Walles would claim in hindsight, it's clear that Israel was not inclined to join it. Its security experts were far more doubtful than their US interlocutors about the ability – and even the desirability – of investing in and arming Fatah forces to take on Hamas. The head of Shin Bet, Yuval Diskin, who had a lively sense of the respective organisational skills of Hamas and Fatah, made his marked lack of faith in the latter clear in a briefing to journalists.[18]

In late May the US ambassador Richard Jones met the new Director General of Israel's Defense Ministry, Pinchas Buchris, to ask for permission to bring in small arms for Fatah. The Israeli official prevaricated, telling Jones that his 'concern was whether the equipment would end up in the right hands or not. We do not want the equipment to go to Hamas so that it can be used against us.' In reply Jones said a little plaintively that 'if Fatah did not receive help Hamas would gain total control of Gaza'.[19] That the provision of such 'help' to Fatah might actually provoke a Hamas takeover of Gaza, rather than prevent it, seemed not to have occurred to Jones.

MEANWHILE, ALAN JOHNSTON HAD BEEN INCARCERATED for almost three months. Without knowing that his fate would be determined by the outcome, he had been all too aware of the civil war erupting round the building where he was being held in a locked and shuttered three-room apartment – the second hideout he was moved to and the one in which he spent the longest. 'You know you're having the worst possible day when your kidnapper comes in to tell you to stay away from the windows on account of the civil war that's raging so close to the flat. So there was a whole new form of danger . . . I remember thinking even if these people were ever to be persuaded or want to give me up, we're looking at a Somalia-type situation where I'll never get more than four blocks without somebody else getting me.'

Once Hamas had secured its victory on 14 June, however, Johnston heard Abu Obeida, spokesman for Hamas's military wing, 'saying on the radio that this journalist kidnapping thing had to end'. His release had become a *sine qua non* for showing that, once in unchallenged control of Gaza, Hamas could now restore order. Hamas's military wing, the Qassam Brigades, 'had threatened the people who took Alan Johnston', Miriam Faris wrote in her diary the following day. 'So maybe something good will come of all this. It's a relief to me that I'm not afraid to be kidnapped now but the future has so many hard times ahead.'

In fact the radio announcement was scant comfort for Johnston; if anything, the opposite. It was deeply alarming for his abductors, who feared Hamas might close in any day. Johnston was ordered to put on a suicide vest for a video recording, in which his captors threatened to detonate the vest if he was taken by force. The video went out on 26 June, coincidentally on the same day as one from Gilad Shalit – also heavily scripted, in his case by Hamas – 'regretting' the Israeli military's 'lack of interest in me' and urging Israel to meet Hamas's demand for negotiations on Palestinian prisoner release in exchange for Shalit's freedom.

For the first time, Johnston's lead gaoler Khamis appeared in military fatigues. Johnston was moved to another apartment for one night, and then back to the building in Dughmush territory where he had first been taken. By now Hamas had detained three *Jaish al-Islam* members and his abductors, Khamis told Johnston, had set up a military position in the flat below. 'You just worried that they might fight it out . . . that the place would need to be stormed rather than me being given up . . . that that would be done in an incredibly violent way, so the idea that I would be the one who wouldn't be killed seemed a bit remote.'

By now in Gaza, I visited Ahmed Yousef, then a close aide to Ismail Haniyeh. He said only 'the safety of Alan' had deterred Hamas from using force to release him, but that while he recognised that the British government did not want it to do so, 'we cannot hold the whole Gaza strip hostage to this situation. We have to deal with this situation one way or the other.' When I asked him about the possibility that Johnston would be harmed or even killed if Hamas militants stormed the Dughmush compound in Sabra where he was now known to be held, Yousef replied with chilling bluntness: 'He will be a martyr to the Palestinian cause.'

Hamas seemed to mean it. In the early evening the following day, the faction's blue-uniformed executive force members were guarding street corners and patrolling the roofs of high buildings round the neighbourhood. Members of the Qassam Brigades, their faces masked by black balaclavas, clustered in side streets and on wasteland within Dughmush territory. Hamas cut off electricity and water to several Dughmush streets and questioned members of the clan seeking to get out of the area to safety. Accepting the *mukhtar*'s word that only a minority of clan members approved the kidnapping, the police allowed those not suspected of being connected with it to leave.

In the end, the show of force was just enough to persuade the now furious and deeply reluctant *Jaish al-Islam* to surrender their hostage in return for their survival. But for Johnston, unaware of that, the danger was far from over. In the middle of the night, a hood was put over his head and he was frogmarched down the stairs of the building, struck and banged against the walls as he descended, before being thrown in

the back seat of a car. On either side of him were Khamis and a second
guard, Issa – by now 'two of the most angry people I felt like I'd ever
been in the company of'.

> They had to drive through Hamas lines . . . us three unhappy people in
> the back of this thing, me hooded and everything, and Issa . . . scream-
> ing at me, just heaping rage really, they were screaming at the driver, at
> me, at people outside the car and there was a moment when we must
> have been stopped, and through the wool of the mask I could see the
> barrel of [Issa's] AK-47. It was just very close to my eye and he was
> screaming and I was sure that in my appalling Arabic I heard the word
> 'brain' and I imagined I was hearing bullet and brain, and you can see
> the line of argument there.

Suddenly Khamis struck Johnston's face with his elbow; the BBC man
could taste the blood in his mouth. Khamis then flung open the door
and he was out in the street with his Kalashnikov.

> I could see that through the wool of the mask and you could see him
> screaming and pointing his gun around and you didn't know why the
> whole car wasn't being filled with bullets. It couldn't be more fraught,
> they couldn't be handling it in a less calm way . . . That bit with the
> bloke Issa and the Kalashnikov very close to your eye, all your life
> you're never going to forget that and it was a sense that this was beyond
> threatening. In retrospect a lot of these things have sort of a faintly
> darkish humour. They seemed to be shouting at the driver – and it was
> possible to believe that one was shouting 'go' and the other was shout-
> ing 'stop'. And when it did finally end and I was sort of dragged out . . .
> and the hood came off, and just sort of chucked in the street and they
> just sort of drove off, then you look around and you can see that there
> are about eight – ten – twelve armed men in the street and at that point,
> you don't know who they are really, and they just stepped forward and
> they took me by my arm and led me and began to walk with me with-
> out speaking.

For a second, Johnston thought he might have been handed to another
gang of kidnappers. But the men were from Hamas. The walk of around
thirty metres took him round a corner and into a garden where he saw

his friend and colleague Fayed Abu Shamalla of the BBC Arabic service. He knew, finally, that it was over.

The release of Johnston was a decisive moment in Hamas's consolidation of control in Gaza. It would not be the last time it would confront sporadic attempts by clans to assert their autonomy – including the Dughmush – but it was the last such attempt to have had any serious chance of succeeding. Four days later it recaptured a lioness kidnapped from Gaza zoo two years earlier by members of the notoriously tough Abu Hasanein family. Besides charging the public for photo-ops with the creature, clan members, widely believed to be involved in drug-running, had reportedly been in the habit of bringing the lioness along to meetings to settle disputes with their adversaries. Trivial compared with the release of Johnston, the recapture of the animal was nevertheless demonstrative: clan power in Gaza, like the lioness, was back in its cage.

But any hopes Hamas had that its success in freeing Johnston would provide a fresh opportunity for some sort of rapprochement, if not with the US, then with the Europeans, or at least the British, were mistaken. Sensibly the UK government had agreed to waive the bar on contacts with the Islamic faction in order to press for Johnston's release. To discuss Johnston – and only for that purpose, as he assured reporters in Gaza – Richard Makepeace, the British Consul General in Jerusalem, had twice met Ismail Haniyeh, whose 'crucial role' in securing the hostage's freedom was acknowledged by Foreign Secretary David Miliband.[20]

During the kidnapping the resident MI6 man in Jerusalem had met Khaled Meshal, the Hamas political bureau chief, in Damascus. Besides offering reassurance that Hamas would do everything it could in the Johnston case, Meshal used this rare opportunity confidently to predict that sooner or later the Western powers would hold much wider political talks with Hamas. Why not do so sooner, he asked, rather than wait for years of more agony, deaths and hopelessness in the Middle East?[21]

By now the voices being raised in favour of that course were gradually becoming more formidable. A few months later a group of eleven leading Israeli writers – including the three most internationally famous, Amos Oz, A. B. Yehoshua and David Grossman – proposed that Israel should open talks with Hamas on a ceasefire to end the Israeli incursions and strikes on Gaza and the Qassam attacks on neighbouring

Israeli communities along the border, which had continued unabated during the summer months.

Former Israeli intelligence chiefs such as Efraim Halevy, the ex-director of Mossad, and Shlomo Gazit, who had been Israel's first – and long-standing – military co-ordinator in the Occupied Territories after 1967, both called for a wider dialogue with Hamas. Halevy had first suggested this as early as 2003, scorning the expectation that Abbas would start a civil war by conducting the military crackdown on Hamas demanded of him by Israel and the US. This was not because Halevy had the remotest 'sympathy' with Hamas – 'I think they are a ghastly crowd' – but because 'the danger is that they will not be defeated, that they will become more despairing . . . and they will no longer feel constrained by anything, because there is nothing left for them to hope for'.[22]

Halevy made another point, thrown into sharp relief by a statement from Osama Bin Laden's deputy in December 2006, angrily condemning Hamas for participating in elections that 'will not liberate a grain of sand in Palestine'. Negotiating with Hamas was necessary to stop Al Qaeda's more radical ideology attracting Palestinian adherents. Halevy argued, 'We're dealing in issues which are existential to free society. When you look around for potential allies in this war, sometimes you have to settle for strange bedfellows.'

He was now joined by Colin Powell, George W. Bush's immediate past Secretary of State, who said in a National Public Radio interview after Hamas's military victory over Fatah that the Middle East Quartet needed to 'engage' with the faction:

> I don't think you can just cast them into outer darkness and try to find a solution to the problems of the region without taking in to account the standing that Hamas has in the Palestinian community. Hamas, which controls Gaza, is not going away and enjoys considerable support among the Palestinian people. They won an election that we insisted upon having. And so, as unpleasant a group they may be and as distasteful as I find some of their positions, I think through some means Hamas has to be engaged.[23]

That was the opposite conclusion, however, to the one drawn by the recently elected Olmert government – and, in turn, by the Middle East Quartet, which the Bush administration heavily dominated. As the fighting between Hamas and Fatah was reaching its bloody climax in mid-June, the US ambassador Richard Jones had met Amos Yadlin, the influential head of Israeli Military Intelligence (IDI), in Tel Aviv. When the ambassador said that if Fatah was defeated there would be calls – he did not say by whom, but presumably had his own superiors in mind – for Mahmoud Abbas to establish a 'separate regime' in the West Bank, Yadlin commented 'that such a development would please Israel since it would enable the IDF to treat Gaza as a hostile country rather than having to deal with Hamas as a non-state actor'. He added that Israel could work with a Fatah regime in the West Bank.[24]

By the time Johnston was released, events had already inexorably unfolded exactly as the Yadlin–Jones meeting had anticipated. Immediately after the defeat of his forces in Gaza, Abbas, in Ramallah where he had been throughout the factional fighting, dismissed Ismail Haniyeh as the PA's Prime Minister and swiftly appointed a new Cabinet, with Salam Fayyad as Prime Minister. The US (which had already announced its plans for a peace conference later in the year, to which Olmert and Abbas would be invited but not Hamas) and the EU resumed funding for the PA. This allowed the PA once again to pay its tens of thousands of employees in Gaza but on the unorthodox proviso that they stay at home and not work for the Hamas authority, a system still in force nine years later.

In September, Israel's Cabinet, echoing Yadlin's prediction, formally declared Gaza a 'hostile entity', underpinning and intensifying the blockade it imposed after Hamas had taken control in June. Once again there was no shortage of advice about what this would mean for Gaza, where eighty per cent of the population, according to the Israeli human rights agency Gisha, was now dependent on humanitarian aid, which was about all that Israel was allowing to flow into Gaza.

Three weeks after Hamas seized control, seventy-five per cent of factories in the Strip were unable to function normally because of the halt to imports – and exports – through the main cargo crossing at Karni. Some 30,000 industrial workers – ten per cent of the labour force – were likely to lose their jobs, with an immediate effect on 210,000 dependants. Karni had been closed by Israel because the PA employees in Fatah who had operated it on the Palestinian side had fled after the fighting, and Israel refused to deal with Hamas. This was just the start. But while Hamas proposed either that the Fatah employees came back, or that a Turkish company be hired to operate the Gaza side of crossing, Abbas showed little interest in such a solution; nor was he pushed to seek one by his Western paymasters. Instead he showed every sign of relief that he could turn his back on Gaza and concentrate on running the West Bank.[25]

If anything there were more tensions within Hamas than in either the PA or the Western powers about a catastrophic division for the Palestinians, which would last for at least nine years. Ghazi Hamad, one of Haniyeh's closest advisers and strategists, who had been against Hamas going into government in the first place, was strongly opposed to the Islamic faction's decision to set up a rival administration in Gaza after Abbas's dismissal of the Hamas Prime Minister, not least because he correctly anticipated the reaction from Israel and the West. If one of Israel's goals had been to complete the separation of Gaza and the West Bank, the division left by the brief but bloody civil war played into its hands. Fatah activists had swiftly reacted to the defeat in Gaza by ransacking and burning Hamas-affiliated institutions in the West Bank, which Ghazi Hamad believed had hardened Hamas's determination to run Gaza on its own. Hamad nevertheless resigned as Haniyeh's spokesman in protest at the takeover, saying much later that he thought it was 'a big disaster, because I knew that after this Hamas would suffer more and more isolation in Gaza'.[26] Having resigned his post as government spokesman, a few months later Hamad would be put in charge of the crossings – not exactly a power station in Siberia, but away from the centre of political power in Gaza.*

For the civilian population, whatever their political allegiance, the seemingly unchallenged control now exercised in Gaza by Hamas had one unmistakable benefit: order, if not exactly law, had returned. It was safe once again to walk the streets, even at night. At many points in the previous months it had been impossible to do so without risking crossfire from the little knots of armed men of each faction staring each other down from street corners.

Nor did foreigners seem any more at risk of being kidnapped. In the immediate aftermath of Johnston's abduction – when it was assumed it would end, like all the others, in a matter of days – foreign journalists had continued to travel throughout Gaza. But the combination of

---

* Hamad was appointed Hamas Deputy Foreign Minister in 2012.

mysterious acts of lawless violence against secular or Christian targets, armed gangs on the loose, the determination of Johnston's abductors, and rumours of gunmen arriving at one downtown media office saying they were looking for more foreigners to kidnap had turned Gaza into what the Foreign Press Association had called, by April, 'effectively a no go area' for foreign reporters.

I had made one journey that April of 2007 to the Strip, hitching a ride from Erez into the centre of Gaza City with a UN convoy, along with a dedicated young Briton, Lauren Aarons, who had taken Kate Burton's job with the Al Mezan human rights agency when Burton left after being briefly kidnapped with her parents. Now Lauren was sadly collecting her belongings because she, too, had been advised to leave Gaza in the wake of Johnston's kidnapping. Once in the city, and for the first and last time in all my trips to Gaza, an (uninvited) PA police car accompanied us for protection. It was a sunny spring day; the city, as busy as usual, could not have seemed more normal.

Yet an hour earlier someone had used explosives in broad daylight to blow up a Honda belonging to Muna al-Ghalayini, the part-owner of the popular Roots restaurant. Maybe this was an act of revenge by a young man who had been refused admission on one of the restaurant's family-only nights a few days earlier; or maybe it had a more sinister purpose, like that of the extreme Salafists who were probably behind the fire that had the previous week consumed the computer and 5,000-book library of the al-Atta social centre in Beit Hanoun. A similar, if unknown, group had planted a bomb that wrecked the entrance and frontage of the Christian Bible Society the following Sunday. The 'Salafist' label is misleading in that, although Salafism is a fundamentalist, ultra-conservative branch of Islam, who regard the *Salaf*, the earliest generation of the Prophet's disciples, as their role models, only a minority of its adherents are jihadis, prone to the use of violence.

In time, this violent minority would prove a challenge to Hamas's authority in Gaza. But that April it was still the rivalry between Fatah and Hamas itself that was threatening the fragile coalition formed after the Mecca summit and which was still being denied Western funding. On the way in from Erez, David Shearer, the thoughtful New Zealander who headed the UN's Office of Co-ordination and Humanitarian Affairs, had mused on the unity government – at whose birth the Saudi king had been midwife, and which was then just three weeks old. It would need money to 'perform', he suggested, but if it did there would be a chance of stability. But if it fell apart 'there would be an increase in violence, including factional violence', in which many people would be killed.

This had been prophetic, precisely borne out by the Fatah–Hamas battles of June just two months after Shearer had spoken. For the exceptional savagery of that conflict the factions and their leaders had only themselves to blame. And maybe it would have happened anyway even had the Western powers given the unity government a chance to succeed. The Israeli intelligence perception, as relayed to Ambassador Jones by Amos Yadlin on 12 June, was that Abbas and Haniyeh had managed to form a close working relationship but that neither were in control of their military wings, and that Hamas's Qassam Brigades had been acting on its own initiative, with the 'tacit consent' of the Damascus-based Hamas political bureau chief Khaled Meshal. But Yadlin* made another perceptive point in his meeting with Ambassador Jones back in June: he did not believe that Hamas's attacks on Fatah had been part of a 'premeditated effort to wipe out' their rivals. Instead Hamas had been able to take over Gaza any time it wanted to and that this had been the situation 'for the past year'.

If the US did foster a covert coup against Hamas, then it (unlike Israel) woefully underestimated Hamas's military superiority. But if it did not, at the very least it did nothing to restrain its favourites in Fatah from setting themselves a trap into which they then walked. Either way, both the US and, by their acquiescence, however reluctant, the Europeans, bore some responsibility for the outcome: Hamas's unchallenged internal control of Gaza.

While that control restored a greater sense of security on Gaza's streets than its public had known for the previous eighteen months, it came at a heavy price for the opponents of Hamas, which launched a severe crackdown against many of the Fatah activists who had not already fled Gaza. True, this mirrored similar treatment of its own adherents by Fatah-dominated security forces in the West Bank. Amnesty International

---

* After a distinguished military career since flying as a pilot in the 1973 Yom Kippur War, and having retired from heading Military Intelligence, Yadlin became head of the Tel Aviv University's Institute of National Strategic Studies.

noted in October that each faction had detained – and sometimes tortured – more than a thousand supposed political opponents in the previous four months, 'compounding and exacerbating the human rights and humanitarian crisis caused by Israeli military campaigns and block-ades'.[27] Amnesty pointed out that Abbas's PA – now solidly backed by the Western powers – had failed to hold to account Fatah gunmen who had abducted, attacked or killed alleged Hamas supporters in the West Bank, or burned down houses, businesses and charities suspected of links to Hamas 'sometimes in full view of security forces'.

But it did not spare criticism of the Hamas authorities in Gaza. While acknowledging 'the marked improvement' in public security, it said that previous lawlessness had been replaced by 'internal repression', with Hamas mounting targeted attacks on individual Fatah members or security force personnel, breaking up demonstrations and weddings at which Fatah slogans had been chanted, and attacking Palestinian jour-nalists covering such episodes. Detainees held by the Hamas executive force and its military wing reported being tortured, ill treated or 'routinely' subjected to severe beatings. At least two detainees, Walid Abu Dalfa, forty-five, and Fadhel Dahmash, thirty-one, had died while in executive force custody during July.

Yet these telling criticisms had little effect, to judge by the bloody end to a demonstration in Gaza City that November. Fatah organised – with Hamas's permission – a rally at the al-Qatiba grounds in central Gaza City to mark the third anniversary of Arafat's death. The crowd was unexpectedly large – maybe 100,000 – and when I arrived I found hundreds of demonstrators were already escaping amid the sounds of sporadic gunfire. Through the crowd I could see a group of young men carrying the body of another, draped in a blood-stained black and white chequered scarf, one of six Fatah demonstrators shot dead during the protest. A frightened woman stood by a wall clutching a small boy by the hand, pleading with a taxi driver to give her a lift. The woman said that she had gone to look for her older son, who had wanted to see the rally. 'I will have to go home and wait for him,' she said. 'I have no other option. I blame Hamas for this. Why did they have to be there? They should have left it alone.' At al-Quds hospi-tal, its corridors crowded with the relatives of forty injured people, nearly all with bullet wounds, Taher Nasser, twenty, was lying on a stretcher while a friend held a drip for him. 'We were shouting "Abu

Ammar, Abu Ammar''' he said. 'And Hamas started throwing sound grenades.* Then I got shot in the back.'

Hamas claimed that Fatah gunmen had started the shooting. But the ever-vigilant Palestinian Centre for Human Rights, with a valiant record of documenting abuses by Israel and both the main Palestinian factions, laid the primary blame on Hamas. At 11.30 a.m., its report said, a jeep carrying armed plainclothes Hamas security men had driven 'provocatively' towards hundreds of demonstrators, who then threw rocks at the police, who in turn responded with indiscriminate gunfire. Having found no evidence of shooting from among the Fatah crowd, PCHR was sceptical of Hamas's claims. But in any case 'the duty of the police and security personnel is to protect participants. And in the case of coming under gunfire, as claimed by governmental sources in Gaza, indiscriminate, excessive, and lethal firing by the police at civilian gatherings is not justified.'[28]

The next morning I went to a mourning tent in Beit Hanoun for Ibrahim Ahmad, a devout and sporty thirteen-year-old, the youngest victim among the demonstrators. It was a scene all too reminiscent of funerals of children killed by Israeli airstrikes or tank fire. Ibrahim had gone to dawn prayers, his brother Amjad, twenty-three, explained, before taking a taxi with himself and two other older brothers to neighbouring Beit Lahiya, where they joined the rapidly growing procession to the Arafat commemoration. Later they'd become separated but Amjad had thought little of it, because the rally had initially had a happy, almost carnival, atmosphere. By the afternoon, Ibrahim's body was in the Shifa hospital morgue; he had been shot in the neck and side.

As the mourners sat with the Ahmads, a staunchly Fatah family, on a long row of plastic chairs in the alley next to Ibrahim's home, his father, who had lost his job when Israel closed the Karni crossing five months earlier, was too distraught to join in the increasingly political family discussion raging round him about the meaning of Monday's events. 'He's a kid. He had no weapons or anything else. I blame the security forces. They're the ones supposed to be in charge of security.' His brother-in-law Jihad Awda added bleakly: 'Even the Israelis do not do this.'

---

* A non-lethal explosive device used to disorient by emitting a temporaily blinding light and a very loud noise. Used by the British SAS when they lifted the 1980 Iranian Embassy siege in London.

The shootings marked a low point in the faction's suppression of dissent – and the day carried a double-edged message. On the one hand, the huge showing at the Arafat rally demonstrated still lively support for an alternative to Hamas, the Fatah faction that Arafat had founded and Hamas had defeated in Gaza five months earlier. On the other, it proved that any idea cherished by Israel's Western allies that Gaza's civilian population, increasingly suffering from Israel's draconian blockade, might somehow rise up against Hamas was a fantasy. Israel, having successfully separated Gaza from the West Bank, was fully in control of Gaza's borders, airspace and territorial waters. But it was Hamas that had, and would continue to have, control inside the Strip.

A fortnight after the Arafat demonstration, the summit which Condoleezza Rice had long been trying to arrange finally took place at the naval academy in Annapolis, Maryland, attended by Olmert, Abbas and Arab leaders. The object was to kick-start negotiations between Israel and the Palestinians on a 'West Bank first' peace agreement. Hamas was not invited, of course; Gaza was barely discussed. But as Miriam Faris wrote perceptively in her diary: 'The peace talks have begun and it's like everyone in Gaza is attending as all are awaiting the result. OK nobody has any hope they say, but they have really. That's what has kept the whole Palestinian nation going for 50 years.' In Gaza at least, those hopes would lead only too swiftly – yet again – to bitter disappointment.

8

THE GAZA DIET: SIEGE, 2008–9

IN THE GOOD YEARS YOU COULD hardly hear yourself speak for the din of sewing machines and Arab music blaring incessantly as a hundred employees, men and women, cut and stitched the jeans at Abed Rabbo Aziz's factory at the edge of the Jabalya refugee camp, where his family had been making clothes for nearly four decades.

But when we first met in September 2007, it was not a normal time, even by Gaza standards. Abed Rabbo confessed that this was the first day in three months he had steeled himself to go upstairs to the eerily quiet first floor, where rolls of brightly coloured thread hung on the walls beside idle machines. Picking up at random a paper trouser pattern sent from his main customer, a clothing company in Tel Aviv, he uncovered a colony of tiny ants on the workbench underneath, busy in the heavy heat of a late summer Gaza afternoon. 'You see what happens when we aren't working?' he asked wearily.

The Aziz brothers' factory, like hundreds of others, had been closed since mid-June. Israel had responded to Hamas's victory over Fatah by shutting the main commercial crossing at Karni, halting the two-way cargo traffic – inward of raw materials, outward of finished goods – on which Aziz, like hundreds of other manufacturers in the Strip, had depended. Since then, the modern machines from Japan and the US, worth £125,000, had been silent. Four thousand pairs of trousers, packed in plastic bags, were piled near the door, each labelled with the Israeli firms they were destined for. In his warehouse across the street some thirty rolls of cloth were gathering dust. Abed Rabbo, thirty-nine, had no way of shipping out finished garments and therefore of generating the cash he needed to pay his skilled – now laid-off – workforce, many of whom were now driven by economic circumstances onto the Hamas payroll. At first he made modest loans to some of his desperate long-standing employees. Now he could not afford that. Sitting over coffee at the ominously tidy desk in his small ground-floor office, he said quietly to no one in particular: 'I'm so tired of this.'

The factory was fairly typical of the garment sector, the biggest in Gaza's manufacturing industry with nearly a thousand firms. After taking the factory over from his father, Abed Rabbo used his businessman's permit to travel frequently to Israel, drumming up business. Restrictions on imports and exports had started after the Oslo Accords, but the company continued making jeans for the Israeli market throughout the Second Intifada and beyond. Despite regular Israeli military incursions, some uncomfortably close to the factory, and even through electricity blackouts which frequently followed Israel's bombing of Gaza's power station after the abduction of Israeli soldier Gilad Shalit, the fragile commercial lifeline between Gaza and Israel endured.

By the late 1980s over eighty per cent of Israeli clothing companies had become, because of global competition, dependent on cheap Palestinian labour in Gaza. One alternative, China, was not ideal for the young fashion market in Tel Aviv where trends changed almost monthly and goods shipped from the Far East might well be out of date by the time they arrived. In time several of the Israeli businesses switched to Jordan and the West Bank, but Gaza was competitive on price and, as important, quality. In the summer of 2007, the main worry for Aziz, conscious of the fickleness of the market he was serving, was that the neatly packed finished jeans would be out of fashion by the time he could ship them out. Like most other Gazans, he could hardly have imagined that the blockade would still be in force a decade later.

Aziz, who had been paying his employees between £5 and £10 per day depending on their skill, said the jeans he made for his main customer, Tel Aviv clothier Yehuda Shoshani, would retail in Israel for four times as much as he would be paid for them. But Aziz, who understood very clearly the difference between the two economies, was not complaining. 'He is excellent, the best there is,' he said of Shoshani. 'There is one hundred per cent trust between us.' The feeling was mutual.

The Karni closure had already cost Shoshani £500,000 and forced him to lay off eighteen workers for lack of finished garments from Gaza. But when I telephoned him in Tel Aviv, he said without hesitation of Aziz: 'He has been here many times. We eat together, we drink together; it's like he's part of the family.' And the workmanship of Aziz's firm? 'They can compete on quality with anywhere in the world.' It was not just Gaza's economy, but hundreds of similar relationships across the border, based on mutual respect and regular contact between a Palestinian and an Israeli, that were broken by what every Gazan knew simply as 'the siege'.

Aziz's father had started the firm in 1969, two decades after he was brought to Gaza at the age of ten by his refugee parents. They had fled from Simsim, a now obliterated Palestinian farming village, a mere fourteen kilometres across the border from where the factory now stood, whose residents had resisted Israeli fighters in 1948. Some of the stubbornness of his Simsim forebears seemed to have rubbed off on Aziz; on more than half a dozen visits to the factory over the following decade, I never saw him stint in his efforts to overcome the formidable obstacles to the trade that had sustained the family for so long.

If Abed Rabbo Aziz had thought, in September 2007, that things couldn't get any worse, he was quickly disabused. A fortnight after we first met, Israel's Cabinet passed the resolution that, for the first time, defined Gaza as 'hostile territory', and promised that 'additional sanctions will be placed on the Hamas regime in order to restrict the passage of various goods from Israel to the Gaza Strip and reduce the supply of fuel and electricity'.[1] The move began a draconian ban on imports of all but the most basic supplies judged necessary by Israel for 'humanitarian' purposes, while leaving thirty-five per cent of the population in 'deep poverty' and rising. Without food aid, the World Bank added, the figure would be sixty-seven per cent.

The effectiveness of the Israel-imposed blockade was remarkable. In 2007 alone garment production, dependent on exports to Israel and the West Bank, lost potential sales of $24m. The World Bank summary of what happened to Gaza's two biggest manufacturing industries was succinct: 'In June 2007, about 6,500 worked in the furniture sector and 25,000 in the garment sector. As of June 2008, those numbers dropped to 75 and zero, respectively.' The Bank did not need to spell out the multiplier effects on dependants of Gazan employees, fifty-three per cent of whom had worked in the private sector before the siege. But it did point out that the 'erosion of whatever private sector backbone remained in the economy' would be 'progressively more difficult to reverse'.[2]

Northern Gaza's famously high-quality strawberry crop was just one example that November. Five months earlier Beit Lahiya farmer Jamil Abu Hmaideh had lost his non-combatant twenty-one-year-old son to crossfire in the Hamas–Fatah fighting. Now he was about to go bankrupt. His crop of luscious low-insecticide, high-quality strawberries should have fetched him £3–£4 a kilo in exports to Europe, allowing him at least to break even after borrowing £13,000 in plantation costs. Now he would make 25p a kilo at most in a saturated and impoverished local market. Most of the crop would anyway rot; the closure of Karni meant he could not import the plastic sheeting needed to protect his crop from the winter rains and frosts. 'I am not Fatah, I am not Hamas,' said Hmaideh. 'I am a farmer. We built this market with our blood. How are we going to get these markets back if the Dutch and other Europeans are left waiting for our products?'

In fact the Dutch government had urged Israel to allow the crops through, guaranteeing the security of their passage through Israel. But Israel refused, with what was beginning to look suspiciously like the backing of the (EU-supported) PA government in Ramallah. Was the PA – whose President Mahmoud Abbas was now calling openly for an end to the Hamas regime – really pressing as it claimed for the reopening of Karni? 'They keep telling us it is a very high priority for them and they are continually raising it,' said one European diplomat involved in discussions on the crossings at the time. 'But there seems to be some discrepancy with what happens.'

For Israel, and perhaps increasingly the PA, all was now subordinated to ensuring that Palestinians in Gaza learned that life under Hamas control would bring nothing but misery. Yet the siege would hurt the Gazan public far more than Hamas itself. And the price the population would be paying by the end of the year would be greater than anyone yet imagined.

Meanwhile, Gaza's weekly donkey market was a good place to test the impact of fuel cuts in the winter of 2007. Gazans had been buying and selling donkeys since biblical times. But now, on a stretch of rough ground in Shejaia, two kilometres from the Israeli border, they were selling their cars and buying donkeys instead. Such was the demand that the creatures were sixty per cent more expensive than they had been six months earlier.

Understandably, customers were inspecting the donkeys closely before test-driving them hitched to carts. 'You need to make sure it doesn't kick people with its back legs, that it's strong and that the colour of the coat is all right,' explained Saber Dabour, twenty-five. Like tens of thousands of Palestinians in Gaza, he had recently lost his job, and had bought a donkey for 410 Jordanian dinars, or just under £290, to sell vegetables door to door from a cart. 'There are no jobs here, so I am going to create my own work,' he said. 'A donkey doesn't need tyres, it doesn't need spare parts, and it doesn't need gasoline.'

Cart-maker Ashraf Kishko, forty, was also cashing in. 'We are going back to the period of the Turks!' he remarked. This was no doubt an exaggeration; but you could see what he meant as brand new Toyotas and Mitsubishi SUVs cruised along smooth roads on the other side of the nearby border.

The sudden new demand for donkeys was an easily intelligible example of what economists – in particular Sara Roy, the leading foreign expert on the political economy of Gaza – called 'de-development'. It also exposed something that Roy had been charting since the 1980s: the utter dependence of Gaza's economy on Israel's. Since the Six Day War, Gaza had been obliged to rely on Israel for work, whether inside or outside the Strip, for consumer goods, and for essential utilities, including water and electricity. If Israel chose to cut any or all of this off, Gaza was left bereft. It was that process, whether by cutting the lifeline to businesses like Aziz's, effectively sub-contractors to Israeli companies, or the steady degradation of electricity and water supplies, which was now under way and would continue for the next decade.

The event which first illustrated the impact of the blockade (as well as showing how fast Gazans adapted to sudden change) came in January 2008. Hamas militants temporarily relieved the mounting pressure by laying seventeen explosive charges to blow huge gaps in the barrier along Gaza's southern border with Egypt. Within hours, what had been before disengagement a 200-mile-wide Israeli-patrolled corridor at the Rafah border became a giant shoppers' car park as cars, vans, donkey carts and cattle trucks packed with thousands of Palestinians hurtled south along the main road to fill their empty jerrycans with Egyptian petrol, or bring back from northern Sinai everything from olive oil to mattresses, from cement to computers, medicine, flour, cooking gas, tobacco, chocolates, ovens – even $1,000 Chinese-made motorcycles. All were either unavailable or, since the closure, vastly more expensive in Gaza. 'We are going to heaven,' one ecstatic teenager speeding south had shouted from the back of a pickup truck towards Rafah.

Mohammed al-Sheikh, a thirty-year-old butcher from Deir el Balah, where the price of beef had almost doubled to £7.50 a kilo, had taken an Egyptian taxi to the north Sinai village of Sheikh Zayed and walked back to the border leading a frisky black and white cow he had bought for 4,000 Egyptian pounds, or £360. The haul of Marwan Talah, a twenty-five-year-old farmer from Gaza City, included six brown shaggy-haired sheep and two bags of Egyptian cement, which nearly every Gazan seemed to have bought that day. The long absence of cement imports through the closed Karni cargo crossing had not only halted construction throughout Gaza, but meant that its families could no longer cover the graves of their dead.

The reprieve exposed a pent-up demand which helped to convince many shrewd southern Gaza entrepreneurs to dig the commercial – as opposed to weapons-smuggling – tunnels under the border, which soon became the dangerous but lucrative mainstay of the Strip's economy. After eleven days Egypt closed the border again.

Since the Annapolis summit convened the previous November, Olmert had pursued two separate tracks with White House backing. The first was to try and reach a West Bank-only peace agreement with Mahmoud Abbas on a future Palestinian state. The second was to bear down on Gaza economically and militarily with even more vigour than before. In December, Olmert had rebuffed an offer relayed to him by Ismail Haniyeh for a ceasefire in return for Israel lifting the siege. Predictably the cycle of violence had begun again.

By now the closure had thrown 80,000 private sector employees out of work, with the result that the Hamas payroll,[3] from civil servants to militants in the Qassam Brigades, was increasing in size. It was hard to see how the Israeli Cabinet's decision in September 2007 to tighten the blockade further – and what it came to call 'economic warfare'[4] – would help to stop rocket fire. Indeed, it gave Hamas a *casus belli*, or at least every reason to prove to other factions and the wider population that they were 'resisting' Israel's measures.

As the violence continued on both sides, Olmert, ostensibly in response to rocket attacks, cut supplies not only of electricity from the Israeli grid but of fuel, including industrial diesel for Gaza's only power station, meaning long periods of darkness and bitter cold for much of Gaza. Businessman Abed al-Aseli was forced to recruit a rota of sons, daughters, nephews and nieces to operate a manual hand pump in place of an electric respirator to keep his bedridden twelve-year-old son Maher, paralysed seven years earlier in a car crash, breathing during the long power cuts. In his apartment, lit only by a single lamp powered by cooking gas, al-Aseli responded sharply to the suggestion that this was a price Palestinians in Gaza were paying for the Qassam rocket fire. 'Are all the people in Gaza firing Qassams? Perhaps there are a hundred or two hundred people firing Qassams. And there are one and a half million people in Gaza. We are not all launching Qassams. Is Maher launching Qassams?'[5]

The first few months of 2008 were punctuated by funerals on both sides of the border. Israel launched Operation Hot Winter, an incursion into northern Gaza, after another spate of deadly attacks and counterattacks. On 2 March, thousands of Gazans streamed on foot through streets to and from near-continuous burials in Beit Lahiya and Gaza City's Sheikh Radwan cemetery after fifty-four Palestinians were killed in what was then the most lethal single day of violence since the beginning of the Second Intifada eight years earlier.

Four days later, a lone Palestinian walked into the library of the Mercaz HaRav yeshiva in Jerusalem and shot dead eight of its Jewish rabbinical students, aged between fifteen and twenty-six, before he himself was killed. It was the worst attack on Israeli civilians in two years. Although the killer's sister claimed he had been affected by the recent deaths in Gaza, he came from a suburb in East Jerusalem. But angry and grieving students demonstrated outside the college, chanting, 'Let the army go into Gaza.' In an emotional speech at the funeral the next day, the head of the yeshiva, Rabbi Abraham Shapira, denounced the government's 'weakness in the face of terror in Gaza'. This could only reinforce Olmert's rejection of Egyptian efforts to broker a Gaza ceasefire between Israel and Hamas.

The costs of not agreeing such a ceasefire were severe on both sides. Five Israeli civilians and nine Israeli soldiers were killed in the first six months of 2008 by rockets, mortars or gunfire from Gaza. This had instilled fear in southern Israel – in an area widening because of Hamas's use of longer range rockets reaching as far as Ashkelon, the closest big Israeli city to the Gaza Strip, fifteen kilometres from Beit Hanoun. But these attacks had not closed the gap between Israeli and Palestinian deaths. Three hundred and ninety Palestinians were killed in Gaza during the same period, of whom 155 appear to have been civilians.[6]

Amid these bleak developments it was all too easy to forget that Gaza was not just a battlefield, but a territory in which many hundreds of thousands of people were striving not only to live a normal life but in many cases to pursue their dreams. Ex-PA policeman Nader al-Masri's ambition that 2008 spring was to run the 5,000 metres in the upcoming Beijing Olympics, just four months away. He had already won two successive half-marathons in Gaza on a course which ran along the coast road from Deir el Balah to Gaza City. When we first met he had been waiting since January for an Israeli permit to be let out of Gaza to Qatar to train for Beijing. Al-Masri had already made the Palestinian team under an IOC system which gave places for ninety athletes from nations which would otherwise not compete. But he was determined to break through the thirteen-minute barrier for 5,000 metres and qualify in his own right.

It was hard to think of any athlete facing the obstacles he had already encountered. He had saved just enough from his £260 per month Ramallah-paid salary to buy new trainers, but the embargo meant there were none in Gaza. The Qataris had sent him a pair of Olympic-authorised spiked running shoes, 'But they would be ruined in a moment if I had worn them in Gaza.' So he relied on his old Adidas trainers, torn and holed round the instep from overuse at the dilapidated and unfinished Yarmouk stadium in Gaza City and on the dusty, cratered roads and rubble-strewn open spaces near his home.

As the northernmost border town, Beit Hanoun had been among the most war damaged since the beginning of the Second Intifada. Yet al-Masri had not stopped running – he normally did around 120 kilometres a week – other than during the very worst of the Fatah–Hamas fighting the previous year. Even during the lethal feud that erupted three years earlier between the al-Masri clan and the Kafarnas, keeping most uninvolved members of both confined in their houses for safety, al-Masri kept fit by endlessly running up and down a narrow 200-metre alley outside his home. 'With the Israeli forces, you know where they are and you just run in a different direction,' he explained, recalling that period. 'But something like this, you never know when someone may shoot.'

By comparison with Gaza, Qatar's purpose-built running tracks were an athlete's paradise. 'They have all the capabilities,' he said. 'Sports fields, psychological relaxation, good food – and it is open to the world. And they have good relations with the Palestinians.' With the Rafah crossing shut, in February the Israeli authorities had told al-Masri that he did not fit the 'humanitarian' grounds for permits to cross through Erez. However, thanks to concerted pressure from the Israeli human rights agency Gisha he eventually got his permit to travel to Qatar in the first week of April. It was too late to complete the training he needed to make the 5,000 metre qualifying time, but he went to Beijing all the same, proudly carrying the Palestinian flag at the opening ceremony, his appetite now sharpened to try for London in 2012.

But then, overcoming adversity had long been a Gaza characteristic; even the fuel shortages acted as a spur to improvisation. Swapping a car for a donkey was one answer. But there might be another. One morning in June 2008 an unremarkable looking white Peugeot 205 eased into Omar al-Mukhtar Street in Gaza City, much less busy than normal because of the fuel shortage, then at its most acute. At the wheel was Fayez Annan, forty-two, the former Gaza head of the pro-PLO Palestine TV, which had been shut down in the Strip when Hamas seized control of the territory a year earlier. I was on the back seat. Taking advantage of the lack of traffic, Annan accelerated close to forty miles an hour, a little faster than is safe in the city centre. But he had something to prove, namely that the car was no milk float. For the vehicle was powered by electricity, and was the creation of Annan and Wasseem al-Khazendar, forty-eight, the owner of a well-known Gaza company selling electrical motors, tools and switchgear.

There was nothing new, of course, about electric-powered vehicles, which had been first developed in Europe in the nineteenth century. Indeed, al-Khazendar had closely followed the saga of General Motors' EV1 electric car programme, prompted by low emissions legislation in California but cancelled in 2003 partly because of pressure from major oil companies. But this was the first year that the US Tesla all-electric Roadster had been available to consumers, and a year before Mitsubishi entered the same market. So Annan and al-Khazendar's pioneering conversion of the French saloon into Gaza's first electric car – six months in the making, powered by an AC induction motor and thirty-eight twelve-volt batteries – felt like a modest engineering triumph in a city starved of almost every commodity, including spare parts. It was a dramatic improvement on the smelly, heavily polluting and motor-corroding substitution of cooking oil for diesel that increasing numbers of desperate drivers were opting for that summer. And the tiny, flat Gaza Strip was ideal territory for an electric car.

At the end of the trip, al-Khazendar said he had wanted 'to make a car which was environment-friendly. Even if you aren't adding cooking oil, diesel is bad for the environment, and an electric car is much cheaper to run.' Especially in Gaza, where desperately scarce petrol cost about £1 per litre – and more than three times that on the black market. Essentially, he said, 'the idea is very simple – take out the mechanical motor and put in an electrical motor'. A simple mains plug would charge the batteries. 'It is like charging your mobile. You can do it anywhere – even while you are shopping.' Unsurprisingly, around 400 Gaza motorists had already registered interest in converting their cars at an average estimated cost of $2,500.

For now, however, the would-be customers would have to wait. And wait. To serve even this limited demand, Annan and al-Khazendar needed a supply of new electrical motors, instead of the used industrial motor in the prototype, and higher-powered, lighter batteries which placed less strain on a car's axles. That would be impossible as long as the economic blockade lasted. Nor was the constantly interrupted electricity supply optimal for running a chargeable car. But, Annan was not too modest to say, his experiment demonstrated how people in Gaza 'have the brains and capability but [not] the materials'. For many Gaza Palestinians, the converted Peugeot became a symbol of local ingenuity. So did he see the electric car not only as a way of rising to the challenge of a blockade, but also as a kind of resistance? 'Let's not call it that,' he replied. 'Let's call it "finding solutions"'.

The two friends were frustrated that their creation could not be developed beyond the prototype. They could have no inkling that by the end of the year they would be confronting far worse trials than a shortage of fuel and electric motors. Just over a week after that test drive, Gaza had what seemed like the first good news since Hamas's enforced takeover a year earlier. Olmert finally agreed to an Egyptian-brokered six-month ceasefire with Hamas. Continued pressure from Cairo had been one factor, but another was the intervention of ex-US President Jimmy Carter.* In March 2008, Carter, along with a senior adviser, the late Robert Pastor, a professor at Washington's American University and a former diplomat, had visited Damascus to discuss a ceasefire with the Hamas political bureau chief Khaled Meshal. Pastor's record of his own preliminary – and wide-ranging – private meeting with Meshal, reported here for the first time, sheds an interesting incidental light on the Hamas leader's attitudes during this period, including his willingness to see a Palestinian state on 1949–67 borders along, Pastor reported, with a twenty-year *hudna*, or truce.

Meshal made it clear he was 'not talking about' recognition of Israel: 'Arafat recognised Israel, but he did not achieve peace or independence . . . Why is it so important for Israel to be recognised? They already have a state.' On the other hand, referring to the Arab Peace Initiative, framed in Beirut and again endorsed by the Arab League in 2007, he added that 'King Abdullah of Saudi Arabia has promised recognition since 2002 if Israel would just accept the 1967 borders. He asked me if I objected to his proposal, and I said "no". Two months later, the Israelis rejected the offer. Was Hamas an obstacle to that initiative? No.'

While stressing the faction's readiness for a ceasefire, in the shorter term Meshal rejected the Israeli demand that Hamas should halt the smuggling of weapons into Gaza: 'Hamas will continue to try to bring in arms until the occupation ends.' Depicting this as necessary for defensive purposes, he claimed that Abbas had recently disarmed some militant Fatah leaders in the West Bank city of Nablus in return for a promise of immunity from Israeli attack, but that the militants had been subsequently killed by Israel. 'This was an attack against Fatah – not Hamas. If they treat Fatah like that, how can we expect them to honour an agreement with us?'

But when Pastor asked him what his wishes were for five years' time Meshal replied: 'Five years from now, I would wish that the Palestinian people could achieve freedom from occupation and establish a Palestinian state with real sovereignty on the 1967 borders and that

---

* Carter, the architect of the 1979 Begin–Sadat Treaty, had never abandoned his efforts to solve the Israeli–Palestinian conflict. They were among the many activities for which he had been awarded the Nobel Peace Prize in 2002.

there would be no more bloodshed.'[7] Had the international Quartet been prepared to talk to Hamas this might have been the basis of a fruitful dialogue. But the ban on such contacts remained total.

With Olmert under heavy pressure from Egypt's President Hosni Mubarak to agree a ceasefire, one was finally struck on 19 June. Carter's contribution had been first to persuade Hamas to shelve its insistence on an immediate extension of the ceasefire to the West Bank, and secondly to improve the climate by persuading Hamas to allow and then deliver, through the Carter Center, the first letter from the imprisoned soldier Gilad Shalit to his family. It was agreed that military operations would cease on both sides and Israel would 'lift the siege of Gaza'.[8] It came as a widespread relief to Gazans and to many in the Israeli communities along the Gaza border that had endured 4,000 rocket attacks over the past year.

The military impact was dramatic. Just eleven rockets were fired over the next four months, mainly by smaller non-Hamas factions, and there were no Israeli casualties (and no incursions on Israel's part). When it came to the blockade, however, the June agreement was much less effective – a defect which would loom large during the rapid deterioration at the end of the year. Although the daily truckloads of goods entering Gaza doubled to 200, they were still just over a quarter of what they had been in January 2007, when Israel had already started to impose restrictions; the bar on exports remained in force. The limits by both Egypt and Israel on the movement of people remained draconian. Ten people a day – mainly very critical medical patients – were leaving through Erez compared with 270 in the first half of 2007.[9]

But in any case the ceasefire did not last. On 4 November 2008, the day of the US presidential election, Israel discovered a tunnel entrance 250 metres inside Gaza which it said could be used for launching kidnapping operations against soldiers like the capture of Gilad Shalit more than two years earlier. Israeli forces moved into the Gaza Strip, killing five Hamas militants. Predictably, the rocket fire started once again; an Israeli in Sderot was injured. Israel's initial response was confined to closing the crossings but gradually Gaza was descending into warfare once again; on 12 November the IDF shot dead another four Hamas militants. On 24 December, ten days after Hamas had declared the end of the six-month truce and fired some eighty rockets and mortar shells into Israel, the Israeli Cabinet took the fateful decision – one that would remain secret for the next seventy-two hours – to launch an unprecedented offensive in Gaza. This was called Operation Cast Lead.

There were several political factors contributing to the decision and its timing. One for Olmert especially – and to some extent for the IDF – was to exorcise what many in Israel saw as the failure of the assault on Lebanon in 2006. Another was the government's own disarray. Olmert had come under mounting pressure over a series of corruption allegations and was facing a challenge from Livni for the leadership of Kadima, the breakaway party from Likud they had helped Ariel Sharon to found. In September, he had announced his resignation in the (eventually vain) hope of clearing his name as a private citizen. But Livni was unable to assemble a coalition and Olmert remained as caretaker Prime Minister until elections scheduled for February 2009, with Livni as Foreign Minister and Barak as Defense Minister.

Livni, like Olmert, had made the ideological journey from a belief in 'greater Israel' stretching from the Jordan river to the Mediterranean. She now believed in partition – and indeed in negotiations with Abbas to secure it. But she was, and would remain, a hawk on Hamas. And the whole government, weakened by Olmert's travails, was under pressure from Likud opposition leader Benjamin Netanyahu, who repeatedly accused ministers of failing to clamp down vigorously on Hamas.

Officially, the Israeli government would repeatedly explain its decision as 'crucial' to the country's 'security interests' and a response to the rocket fire.[10] But it had been Israeli forces who by killing the five Hamas militants in November 'effectively ended the ceasefire' in the view, among many others, of an independent Israeli research organisation with close links to the intelligence community.[11] And what went unnoticed at the time was that the rocket fire could have been stopped in return for a lifting, or significant easing, of the siege.

As conditions worsened significantly in December, the Carter team became active again. Pastor described to the historian Avi Shlaim how he had visited Khaled Meshal in Damascus in mid-December to be told that Hamas would agree to renewing the ceasefire on the same terms as in June, which Hamas now put in writing. Pastor then took the document to the Israeli Defense Ministry's top official, Amos Gilad, telling him that 'if Israel accepted and agreed to implement the proposal, which it had previously agreed to but did not implement, the rockets would stop being fired from Gaza into Israel'. Gilad said he would show the document to Barak and return with an answer within twenty-four hours. But Pastor received no response, despite persistent calls to Gilad's office.[12]

Recalling these events in 2009, Pastor wrote that he had assured the Defense Ministry official that 'Hamas would renew the ceasefire if Israel . . . agreed to open the crossings to allow legitimate produce to go into and leave Gaza'. Not only Israel, but its US and European allies would repeatedly justify the coming offensive by reasserting Israel's 'right to defend itself' against rocket fire. But Pastor challenged this:

> The conclusion seems inescapable. Israel had another option to defend itself. Hamas had demonstrated its capacity to stop the rockets between July and November, but after the Israeli incursion of 4 November and without an opening, Hamas decided to renew rocket fire. Israel had the option to open the crossings, and if it had done so, the rockets would have stopped, and there would have been no need to invade Gaza.[13]

That view was publicly supported by Brigadier General Shmuel Zakai, in charge of the IDF's Gaza Division until 2004, who complained on Israel's Army Radio that Hamas had not been offered 'the carrot' of economic improvements in the Strip. 'You cannot just land blows, leave the Palestinians in Gaza in the economic distress they're in, and . . . expect that Hamas will just sit around and do nothing. That's something that's simply unrealistic.'

Nor was the message Pastor brought back from Damascus confined to a single unofficial back channel. On 16 December the US Consul General in Jerusalem reported back to Washington that his highly respectable Gaza contacts – who were in regular touch with Hamas even if privately hostile to it – were making almost identical points to Pastor's. For example, Ryad al-Khodary, the former President of the Fatah/PLO-linked al-Azhar University, told the US consulate's Gregory Marchese by telephone that 'Hamas wants the ceasefire to continue according to the original Egyptian-brokered understanding, as Hamas's leaders know they will not gain from continuing closures and fighting', and that, 'Hamas's brutality and political missteps have hurt its popular standing, and it needs the crossings open to govern effectively.' Gaza's citizens, he noted, 'suffer terribly under the closure, and blame Israel and the international community, not Hamas, for their predicament'.[14]

Al-Khodary was not exaggerating. A confidential Red Cross report was circulated to diplomatic missions in November which drew a grim picture of an increasingly impoverished and indebted lower-income population: selling assets, slashing the quality and quantity of meals, cutting back on clothing and children's education, scavenging for discarded materials to sell, and depending on dwindling loans and handouts from slightly better-off relatives. 'Chronic malnutrition is on a steadily rising trend,' the ICRC said, 'and micronutrient deficiencies are of great concern.' It seemed as if the goal attributed to Dov Weisglass of putting Gaza on a 'diet'* with the blockade had been fulfilled.[15]

Under the leaky asbestos roof of a three-room house in Gaza City, Rabbia Farahad, fifty-nine, his wife Najah and their ten children were eating fruit once a month and vegetables once a week. 'If we have apples I give out half of one to each,' Najah said. 'This is the worst Eid we have ever been through,' said Rabbia, who had previously been a farmworker in Israel. 'Before, people used to help us but now no one has any money.' For his sixteen-year-old daughter, Tahani, Israel was not the only culprit; the split between Fatah and Hamas was another. 'First I blame the Israeli occupation [for the blockade],' she said, before adding sarcastically: 'Then I blame our two beloved governments. They are the reason for this.'

Tahani Farahad's remark illustrated why Hamas, worried about its declining popularity, was eager to ease the blockade in return for renewing the ceasefire. This raised an uncomfortable question for the international community. For the Middle East Quartet had called for a 'new approach' to Gaza on 2 May 2008 and on 24 June had defined quite specific objectives for improving conditions in the Strip.[16] These included, most notably, 'increased humanitarian and commercial flows through the Gaza crossings under the management of the Palestinian Authority, consistent with the November 2005 Agreement on Movement and Access' (AMA). So the Western powers had a position, if not on the war, at least on the siege. A desire to see it lifted was not some maverick goal by Hamas but, at least in theory, that of the whole international community. The UN and international aid agencies had repeatedly

---

* Weisglass denied that he had said this.

contended that Israel was violating its obligations under the Geneva Convention to those living in occupied territory.

Israel was consistent in refusing Hamas's demand that it return to and implement the terms of the June ceasefire; the siege remained central to its strategy of 'economic warfare'. But the international community was not consistent. Behind the scenes, Blair – as the Dutch had the previous year – asked Israel to allow strawberry and carnation growers to ship their seasonal crops worth over $6m to European markets, and he pushed Barak 'forcefully' to allow $250m in cash needed to pay PA employees in advance of Eid to be sent to Gaza banks, only to be told 'there were plenty of shekels in Gaza'.[17] But there was no attempt at public or inter-governmental level to link the two highly desirable objectives of a ceasefire and an easing of the siege.

Indeed, just as Gaza was sliding to war in this diplomatic vacuum, the EU, whose Slovenian presidency formally condemned the 'collective punishment' inflicted on Gaza, decided unanimously on 8 December to formalise an agreement reached shortly before the June ceasefire for a significant upgrade in EU–Israel relations, providing for 'increased diplomatic cooperation; Israel's participation in European plans and agencies; and examination of possible Israeli integration into the European single market'.[18] The agreement, won in the face of counter-lobbying by Egypt and other Arab states, had been a diplomatic victory for Livni and reinforced the EU's policy of 'decoupling' its trade and diplomatic relations with Israel from events in the Israeli–Palestinian conflict.*

The EU governments essentially accepted Israel's narrative that its military operations in Gaza, past, present and future, were legitimate acts of self-defence against rocket fire – without any reference to the possibility of an agreement that might end that rocket fire in return for easing the siege. In doing so they were closely following the approach of the Bush administration in the US, which by now was correctly expecting a much wider and deeper Israeli military operation in Gaza.

---

* As it happened, given the deterioration in Gaza, this was too much for the European parliament, whose foreign affairs committee postponed a ratification vote. But it was only in July 2009, *after* Operation Cast Lead and Netanyahu's election, that European governments deferred their plans for an overall upgrade, although Israel continued to benefit from many earlier agreements, including those exempting it from tariffs on goods imported from non-EU countries.

Within six days of the US Consulate General in Jerusalem relaying the possibility of a ceasefire with Hamas, Washington was hearing a much starker secret message from James Cunningham, Bush's ambassador in Tel Aviv. Anticipating an imminent war on Gaza, Cunningham suggested that the State Department should have a plan for when it was under way. The ambassador unhesitatingly recommended that the administration should: 'start with putting the blame on Hamas for the illegitimacy of its rule in Gaza, its policy of firing or allowing other factions to fire rockets and mortars at Israeli civilian targets, and its decision to end the '*tahdiya*' [calming] period; and support for Israel's right to defend itself, while also emphasising our concern for the welfare of innocent Palestinian civilians and US readiness to provide emergency humanitarian relief'.[19]

The Tel Aviv embassy was reflecting not only Israeli but US policy, which was not to try and prevent a large-scale military assault by Israel on Gaza, but to do everything to justify it once it happened.

9

'NOT A HAIR WILL FALL OF A SOLDIER OF MINE': OPERATION CAST LEAD, 2008–9

IT'S A SAFE BET THAT NO one set out to kill Wafer Shaker al-Daghmeh that afternoon, least of all in front of her three young children. This was May 2008, and men from the IDF's Givati Brigade were going house to house on a search and arrest operation in New Abasan, a village east of Khan Yunis and close to the Israeli border, when they arrived at the thirty-four-year-old UNRWA elementary schoolteacher's home between 4.15 and 4.30 p.m. It was a period of high tension, particularly in border areas; the military's incursion into the area that day, which ended with the killing of one militant and injuries to twenty-three other people, came after a week in which more than a hundred Palestinians had been arrested or held for questioning up and down the Gaza Strip.[1] The Israeli soldiers knocked at Mrs al-Daghmeh's house; receiving no immediate answer, they detonated an explosive charge just as she was going to open the wooden door, blowing most of her head from her body. Samira, thirteen, her four-year-old sister Roba and two-year-old brother Qusay ran into another room, where they stayed, with a soldier guarding the door, for another five hours or more.

Four days later, the tiles above a washbasin opposite the front door of the house were still heavily spattered with dried blood. A portrait of Arafat on the wall testified to the family having voted not for Hamas but for Fatah, which had indeed arranged the funeral. There was a pile of splintered wooden planks from the destroyed door on the floor where

Mrs al-Daghmeh's body had lain after the troops commandeered the house. As her husband Majdi, who had been away from the house at the time, described what his children had told him about that fateful afternoon, we could hear the noise of gunfire from Israeli military vehicles, uncomfortably close, from another incursion under way. His wife, aware of the operation in the area, had been putting on a headscarf when the troops arrived. The children had said a 'tank' (more likely an APC) had parked outside. 'Samira heard a very loud explosion and there was a lot of smoke. She looked for her mother but couldn't see her.'

Samira said: 'There was one soldier at the door of the room. I asked him, "Where is my mother?" He was speaking in Hebrew and I didn't understand him.' She said that when the soldiers finally left in darkness at around 9.30 p.m. she crawled with her siblings to another room. 'There were still tanks outside and if I had gone out they would have seen me. I tried to call my father on my mother's Jawwal* but there was no signal. I lifted the carpet and saw a bit of my mother's clothes. She was not moving. I did not see her head.' When the units finally left the area at around 11 p.m., Samira ran to the house of a neighbour who called an ambulance to take her mother's body away.

I might have half forgotten this episode, one of so many, had it not been for the recollection of a staff sergeant who had been serving in the Givati Brigade at the time. 'There was an operation in the company next to mine where they told me that a woman was blown up by a fox,† her limbs were smeared on the wall, but it wasn't on purpose. They knocked and knocked on the door and there was no answer, so they decided to open it wet [using live fire]. He put down a fox and just at that moment the woman decided to open the door. And then her kids came over and saw her. I heard about it during dinner after the operation, someone said it was funny, and everyone cracked up, that the kids saw their mother smeared on the wall.'[2]

The staff sergeant's account had been given to Breaking the Silence, an organisation of veteran combatants who had served in the IDF since the beginning of the Second Intifada. By 2006 Breaking the Silence had taken more than a thousand testimonies from soldiers about their

---

* The name of the leading Palestinian phone company is also customarily used by Palestinians to describe any mobile handset.
† Israeli military slang for an explosive charge.

service in the West Bank and Gaza, in the face of increasingly virulent attacks from the Israeli far right and, in latter years, from the Netanyahu government – as well as expressions of strong support from some former military and intelligence chiefs.[3] Yet the organisation's objectives remained what it had always been. Its founders had 'taken it upon themselves to expose the Israeli public to the reality of everyday life in the Occupied Territories . . . and to stimulate public debate about the price paid for a reality in which young soldiers face a civilian popula-tion on a daily basis, and are engaged in the control of that population's everyday life'.[4]

As a second-hand story without dates or names, it can't be proved that the soldiers mentioned in the staff sergeant's testimony were recounting the death of Mrs al-Daghmeh. But, given the similarities, it's overwhelmingly probable that they were. You have to hope that the young conscripts' semi-hysterical laughter was a nervous reaction, a manifestation of delayed shock. They had, after all, had the presence of mind to cover Mrs al-Daghmeh's mutilated body with a carpet, and to keep the children away from the body at least for the five hours the soldiers had remained in the house. The incident had been out of the ordinary – perhaps even traumatic – enough for the soldiers to describe it over the evening meal; but there was no sense that the death by explo-sives of an innocent mother in front of her three children somehow violated the prevailing norms laid down by their superior officers. It's impossible to know either the reason for, or the length of, the delay before Mrs al-Daghmeh got to the door; maybe she was a little longer than usual putting on her headscarf, a normal action of women at home in Gaza when strangers, especially men, are coming to the door; maybe the soldiers, despite the claims that they 'knocked and knocked', simply didn't give her enough time.

It's impossible to know because the requests by the UN for a military investigation went unanswered. Three days after the incident, the general counsel for UNRWA, Lex Takkenberg, wrote to named officials of the Israeli Foreign Ministry, the Ministry of Defense and the IDF's civil affairs division COGAT seeking an investigation. The letter said that UNRWA's own investigation had indicated that there were no mili-tants in the vicinity at the time, that the house next door had been occu-pied by troops, and that 'Mrs al-Daghmeh's house was not a target of the operation but an operational post'.

In August, more than three months after his first letter, Takkenberg wrote again – this time in somewhat sharper terms – pointing out that he had had no reply and that no effort had been made to contact Mrs al-Daghmeh's family. He continued that the UN's own enquiries had 'raised concerns whether the force used was proportionate to the military objective sought or that appropriate precautionary measures were taken'. He added: 'The absence of any indication that an impartial investigation is under way would not appear consistent with a commitment to prioritising accountability for IDF actions.' That letter, too, went unanswered.[5]

The incident passed virtually unnoticed outside Gaza at the time. By the start of the next year, 2009, it was wholly overshadowed by the thousands killed or injured in Operation Cast Lead, then the most lethal military operation conducted within Israel–Palestinian borders since the Six Day War in 1967. But Takkenberg's second letter raised an issue that would become even more relevant during that very onslaught: were the IDF's actions 'proportionate' to whatever military objective Israel was pursuing, were 'appropriate precautionary measures' taken to protect innocent civilian life, and how 'accountable' were the IDF's forces?

Because of what has happened since, it is easy to underestimate the impact of Cast Lead. Once it was under way, Hamas rocket and mortar attacks targeted communities in southern Israel, including Askelon and Beersheeba, killing three Israeli civilians and one member of the Israeli security forces, and wounding dozens more. Nine soldiers were killed inside Gaza, more than a hundred wounded, one critically and twenty moderately to seriously. Hamas also summarily executed at least two dozen alleged Palestinian collaborators, informers and political opponents during the war. During the three-week operation 1,391 Palestinians were killed by Israeli forces, 759 of them, according to B'Tselem, 'not taking part in hostilities'; 15,300 Palestinians were wounded, 350 of them seriously to critically.[6] The Palestinian casualties were unprecedented in scale. And the war was significant for a clear shift in the unwritten rules of engagement governing its conduct by the IDF. As such it was a turning point for Israeli military operations in Gaza.

Operation Cast Lead began on 27 December 2008 with heavy aerial, naval and artillery bombardment. A week later four IDF brigades – some 10,000 troops – began a ground operation which left widespread destruction in their wake. The war ended with a ceasefire on 18 January; President-elect Barack Obama was inaugurated two days later.

While the offensive caused growing unease among some Western governments, particularly in Europe, it also demonstrated that when an Israeli Prime Minister has the support of a US President – even one at the end of his term of office – he can be confident of acting without serious international or domestic restraint. Even Arab countries were slow to take limited diplomatic action until after the ground invasion was under way. They finally called for a ceasefire resolution at the UN Security Council on 8 January. Condoleezza Rice, worried about US and her own standing in the region, was inclined to support the resolution, whereas George Bush would have vetoed it. They compromised: the US abstained. And the war continued for another ten days.

It was impossible to ascribe 'victory' to either side. Memorably, Foreign Minister Tzipi Livni said: 'We have proven to Hamas that we have changed the equation. Israel is . . . a country that when you fire on its citizens it responds by going wild – and this is a good thing.'[7] But the bellicose pre-war talk of 'crushing' or 'removing' Hamas proved to be no more than that; Hamas lived to fight another day.

At least as hollow, though, was Ismail Haniyeh's claim of victory. Hamas did not get the siege lifted, and a joke doing the rounds among middle-class Palestinians was that, with many more victories like that, soon there would be no more Gaza. For Mustafa al-Nahabin, sixty-one, who had voted for Hamas in 2006, and whose house had been first occupied by Israeli troops and then bulldozed, his political affiliation would now be determined by which faction delivered reconstruction. 'We voted for Change and Reform in the election,' he said drily. 'We got change, but we didn't get reform.'

Al-Nahabin's was one of 3,500 homes destroyed. With widespread damage caused to farming and utilities, including water and sewage, and at least 258 factories and warehouses, the war cost Gaza an estimated $2bn in total assets. As Amr Hamad, the executive manager of the Palestinian Federation of Industries (and later the US consulate's representative in Gaza), said: 'What they were not able to reach by the blockade, they have reached with their bulldozers.'

Much of the destruction of factories and infrastructure came later in the war. At its start, despite frequent threats, no one had been prepared for the aerial bombardment on the morning of Saturday 27 December

– some one hundred strikes across the Strip, including one which killed ninety-nine Hamas police cadets at a passing-out parade and nine passers-by in central Gaza City. 'Woke up at around eleven to the sound of bombs flying all around us,' Miriam Faris, the British owner of Rosy's beauty salon, who, with her husband and son, had been up until the early hours chatting with dinner guests, wrote in her diary. 'We didn't know which window to go to for all the bombs being hit on all Hamas places . . . So far 155 dead and 250 injured.' Later that day, she added: 'Gaza hospitals overflowing . . . Rosy closed of course, so is all of Gaza. 6pm: over 200 dead, 400 wounded and both rising.'

By the end of the day, the death toll was 230. As the bombs struck the police parade, journalist Mohammed Dawwas saw from the window of his nearby seventh-floor flat his terrified nine-year-old son Ibrahim rushing home from school. The following day, he recorded in a diary for the *Independent on Sunday*: 'Ibrahim is too frightened to go out with his brothers to play. He had been doing an exam when the bombing started yesterday and I was stuck in the lift because of yet another power cut. He arrived back, shaking and crying. When I went to get some food he said, "please *baba* [father], don't go out."'[8] The emotional scars left by the bombing that Saturday morning ensured that Ibrahim would henceforth yearn to leave Gaza, a desire he still harboured eight years later, at the age of seventeen.

Israel did not permit foreign journalists entry to Gaza during the war – and Egypt only started to do so at the very end (although the Egyptian-American Ayman Mohyeldin, whose daily reports riveted Al Jazeera viewers, was already there when the war started). Consequently, the foreign media was dependent on courageous reporting by Palestinians inside Gaza, whose stake in the outcome was much higher. They included Taghreed el- Khodary of the *New York Times*, the *Guardian*'s Hazem Balousha and a brave and thoughtful young journalist called Fares Akram, then a freelance, but later El-Khodary's successor and later still the correspondent of Associated Press. For all of them, but particularly Akram, the war was very much more than just another story.

In a dispatch for the *Independent*, Akram described how, on 3 January, at the outset of the ground invasion, a week after the airborne operation had begun, his forty-eight-year-old father had been killed on the family farm by an F16 bomb. Akram's father was an experienced

Israeli settlers escorted from Neve Dekalim by troops, Gaza, August 2005. Ariel Sharon's evacuation of Gaza's Jewish settlements generated outrage and grief among the departing residents but not the full-scale violence many had predicted.

Abed Rabbo Aziz in his idle factory, September 2007. He had made jeans for the Tel Aviv fashion market, but the closure of Gaza after Hamas seized control forced him to halt production.

The Gaza City coastline at its wintriest in February 2007, the day before the short-lived Mecca agreement between Fatah and Hamas that would soon disintegrate into civil war, and a month before the kidnapping of the BBC's Alan Johnston.

A playground in the ravaged Jabalya district after Operation Cast Lead, November 2009. More than 3,500 homes were destroyed in the 2008–9 war and more than 20,000 people made homeless, many of them becoming refugees for the second time.

After a six-year business cycle that had gone from 'excellent to good to bad to unbelievable', Abdel Salem al-Shobaki's concrete works were just being kept afloat thanks to imports of cement through the smuggling tunnels in 2009.

In the 1990s travel agent Nabil Shurafa was awarded a regional 'Top Ten' certificate by British Airways for 'outstanding sales achievement'. By July 2010 he was struggling to keep his business going in a territory where most people were now forbidden to travel.

Long-distance runner Nader al-Masri leads in the first Gaza marathon, 2011, as a schoolgirl runs in front of the competitors.

Mousa Sweidan walks through his father's damaged home in the Sha'af neighbourhood of Gaza City. When Israeli tanks entered the area the family of fifteen fled and took shelter in a UN school.

Wreckage of an Israeli home in Beersheba hit by rocket fire from Gaza during Operation Protective Edge. Five Israeli civilians and one foreign national, as well as 66 Israeli soldiers, were killed during the 51-day operation.

An Israel Defense Force artillery unit near the Gaza border during Operation Protective Edge, July 2014. Of the Palestinians killed by Israeli forces in OPE, 1,391 'did not take part in hostilties', 765 were participating militants and 46 were status unknown (source: B'Tselem).

A Hamas poster at the Erez crossing warns against collaboration. Israeli intelligence officer (right): 'What do you think of working with us?' Palestinian (left): 'The Palestinian never betrays.'

At a Gaza rally, Hamas fighters stage a mock rescue of a Palestinian prisoner before a replica of a recently blown-up Israeli bus, April 2016.

Hopes of a Gaza generation: outstanding Edward Said Conservatory graduate Sara Akel (top) practised on a virtual piano for years because of a shortage of instruments in Gaza; Yasmin Dawwas (below left), ambitious to become a heart surgeon, graduates in medicine at Al-Azhar University, 2016; her sister, Mariam (below right), a budding writer and graduate in English and French, stands in a strawberry field at Beit Lahiya.

judge in the old Palestinian Authority, a passionate opponent of violence who hated what Hamas had done to Gaza's legal system, and had resigned when the faction took over to care for the farm – 'our beloved place' – north-west of Beit Lahiya, close to the Israeli border, with its lemon groves, olive and apricot trees and, latterly, sixty dairy cows. The white, red-roofed, two-storey house was pulverised by the strike. Akram's father's body was reduced to little more than what his uncle had described 'with brutal honesty' as 'just a pile of flesh'. The following day, Akram wrote:

> Like most Gazans, my mother, my sisters and my wife – who is nine months' pregnant – and I have spent the past week of the Israeli onslaught trapped inside our flat in the city. My father had decided to stay up at the farm; he knew it would be impossible to get back to tend the livestock if the expected troop invasion began. But he called us every day.
>
> The last time I saw him was on Thursday when he brought cash and a bag of flour. We talked about the imminent birth of my first child and how we would get my wife, Alaa, to hospital amid the bombing and chaos. Of course, on Saturday evening there was no hope of getting an ambulance up to the farm because the roads were cut off by the Israelis. So my uncle and brother drove the 8km and the rest of us sat, in shock, shivering in the dark apartment, the sound of non-stop tank shelling around us. Deep down we all knew Dad was dead.
>
> The men arrived to find a smoking pile of rubble. Mahmoud, a teenage relative, was with my father when the Israeli bomb smashed into the house. The force of the airstrike threw him 300 metres ... The Israelis may say there were militants in the area of our farm, but I'll never believe it. The most advanced point for rocket-launchers is 6km south. Up at the border, it is just open farmland with nowhere to hide.[9]

Akram concluded:

> My grief carries no desire for revenge, which I know to be always in vain. But, in truth, as a grieving son, I am finding it hard to distinguish between what the Israelis call terrorists and the Israeli pilots and tank crews who are invading Gaza. What is the difference between the pilot who blew my father to pieces and the militant who fires a small rocket?

I have no answers but, just as I am to become a father, I have lost my father.

Somehow Akram found the emotional energy to cover the bombing which killed twenty-one members of the Samouni family who had been sheltering in a building owned by Wael Samouni in the Zeiton neigh-bourhood of Gaza City. What had helped Akram and others to start piecing the story together was a remarkably precise account given to B'Tselem three days after the episode by Maysaa Samouni.[10]

The Samounis, mostly smallholding farmers, lived on a twelve-acre stretch of land consisting of fig and olive trees and chicken coops, along a semi-rural lane which ran west from the main Saladin road in the southern Gaza City suburb of Zeitoun. The Samounis' lives changed forever when troops from the Givati brigade arrived before dawn on 4 January, as the ground invasion that had started that night pushed west towards the coast. The bombing of Wael Samouni's building was only one among many incidents contributing to the Palestinian death toll; fifty-one others were referred by the Military Advocate General (MAG) to the military police for investigation when the war was over. But it was one of the worst single incidents and raised a number of questions about the conduct of the war by Israeli forces.

Maysaa Samouni testified that fourteen members of the family had been sheltering in the house of her father-in-law, Rashed. Troops with blackened faces and wearing body armour knocked on the door and ordered them at gunpoint to go next door to the house of Talal Samouni, Rashed's brother, where another twenty-one members of the extended family had gathered for safety. Here, too, soldiers had arrived earlier in the day.

Talal Samouni, a fluent Hebrew speaker who had worked as a mechanic in Israel for thirty-five years, introduced members of the family to the Givati troops one by one. Maysaa explained that a little later the soldiers had directed all thirty-five family members to an unfinished building owned by Wael Samouni and used for storing fruit and vegetables. Already there were about the same number again in the building; and by the evening there were around a hundred people inside. Although they could hear repeated firing, they felt secure know-ing the Israeli soldiers were aware of their presence, and that the group included women, elderly people and small children.

Around six o'clock the following morning, the area was quiet, and one family member, Adnan, proposed fetching his uncle and family from their house so they could join them. As Adnan stood at the entrance of the building with three other Samouni men, a missile, probably from a drone, was fired at them. It killed one of the men, Mohammed, outright, and injured the others, including Talal Samouni's son Salah, thirty. Maysaa's husband, twenty-one-year-old Tawfiq, was among those who rushed to help. Another shell or missile crashed into the roof, filling it with smoke and dust. Maysaa threw herself over her nine month-old-daughter Jumana. As the smoke started to clear, she saw that at least twenty people were dead, including her husband, her parents-in-law and five-year-old Mohammed, 'whose whole brain', as Maysaa reported, 'was outside his body'. The injured were on the ground, screaming. Maysaa used a handkerchief to staunch the blood pumping from her daughter's left hand; Jumana had lost a thumb, and her second and third finger.

Shortly afterwards, her brother-in-law Musa, an accountancy student at al-Azhar University who, like Maysaa, had suffered only minor injuries, suggested they make a run for the nearby house of his uncle, Assad Samouni. When they and Musa's young sisters, Islam, five, and Isra, two, arrived they found the house filled with soldiers and around thirty Palestinians – about a third of them men, who had been blindfolded. One of the soldiers gave Jumana first aid, bandaging her hand. The troops released everyone except Musa and his uncle Imad – now also blindfolded and handcuffed – 'in case Hamas came', apparently, in other words, as potential human shields. The rest walked along the main Saladin road towards the city centre; after about 500 metres, Maysaa found an ambulance which took her and Jumana to Shifa hospital.

Four days later when the Israeli military temporarily waived its ban on paramedics reaching the scene, ICRC and Palestinian Red Cross staff – on foot – had been able to evacuate the wounded. Among twenty survivors were four small children in one house, too weak to stand, beside their dead mothers. They found another two wounded children as well as fifteen corpses. But, given the time they were allotted by the IDF, they were unable to drag out all the bodies from the mound of rubble and broken concrete until the first day of the ceasefire on 18 January.

The scene at the Samounis' compound the following day was grim. The two houses – Rashed's and his brother Talal's – had been occupied by troops from the Givati Brigade. The buildings were still standing, unlike a dozen others and the small local mosque, whose minaret was lying in the sand. But the houses had been ransacked. Furniture and electrical appliances appeared to have been tossed out of the window, gaping holes had been made in the wall for firing positions, furniture smashed, clothes piled on the floor, pages of family Qur'ans torn out and the remains of soldiers' rations littered through the rooms. Graffiti in Hebrew and English proclaiming 'Arabs need 2 die', 'No Arabs in the State of Israel' and 'One down and 999,999 to go' had been scrawled on the internal walls along with Stars of David. A drawing of a gravestone bore the inscription 'Arabs 1948–2009'.

A later painstaking investigation by Amira Hass of *Haaretz*, including interviews with soldiers who were in the area and had testified to Breaking the Silence, concluded that the decision to attack the men outside the Wael Samouni building (probably with a drone missile) and then the building itself was based on a misreading of a photographic image from an IDF surveillance drone showing the group collecting firewood outside the house. The survivors then hurried into the building, only for it to be struck by another two or three missiles. The assumption made from the photograph was that this was a militant squad carrying weapons, probably a rocket-propelled grenade. So the strike did have a military objective, albeit a fatally misguided one.

But this was not the whole story. The question further arose of whether the Brigade Commander, Colonel Ilan Malka, knew there were a hundred or so civilians in the building at which he directed fire (and if he didn't, given that at least some soldiers on the ground from his own brigade were well aware of the fact, why not?). During the investigation two other *Haaretz* journalists, including its military analyst Amos Harel, reported being told by 'security sources' that the investigation was considering allegations that Malka had been warned there could be civilians in the area. He told military investigators he had not been aware of such warnings, but, rather than deploying 'gravity bombs', he used missiles of lesser force which he regarded as proportionate to the 'threat' to his troops at the time.

In May 2012, more than three years after the episode, the Military Advocate General, Avichai Mandelblit, produced his findings – or the 800-word summary he was prepared to share with the public – closing the file on the military police's criminal investigation into the episode.

For anyone without knowledge of the details of the investigation – i.e. everyone outside the relevant sections of the IDF – the report is bewildering. The only point of fact on which it differed from the unanimous Samouni testimonies was in contending that there were no grounds for 'the allegation that IDF forces directed civilians to gather in the house which was later struck'. But even if the Samounis' testimony – about which they were still adamant eight years later – is discounted, the report did not challenge the assertion that soldiers were present when Maysaa Samouni and her family entered the Wael building and therefore knew they had taken refuge there.

Mandelblit, later appointed by Benjamin Netanyahu first as Cabinet Secretary and then as a somewhat controversial Attorney General, ruled there were 'no grounds for employing criminal or disciplinary measures against any of those involved in the Incident'. On the other hand, he acknowledged that 'a number' of the Brigade Commander's decisions had been 'deficient'. Because of the 'professional shortcomings' of the Brigade Commander's conduct during the episode, the IDF Chief of Staff now banned him from 'future promotion to a command in an operational environment'. Mandelblit said 'lessons needed to be drawn in order to prevent the reoccurrence of similar incidents in the future'.[11]

Quite what 'shortcomings' fell between the 'deficient' conduct expected of a Brigade Commander, and that deserving 'criminal or disciplinary' measures, were not spelled out. But the MAG said the criminal investigation had 'comprehensively' refuted allegations that the strikes had been 'intentionally' directed at civilians or carried out in a 'reckless manner'.

The most high profile of those allegations were contained in the comprehensive April 2009 report of the UN Fact Finding Commission chaired by the eminent Jewish South African judge Richard Goldstone, which infuriated Israel's government by declaring that Cast Lead was 'a deliberately disproportionate attack designed to punish, humiliate and terrorise a civilian population'.[12] In 2011, however, Judge Goldstone bitterly disappointed many pro-Palestinian activists and commentators by 'recanting' the finding. Explaining why he no longer thought that civilians were 'targeted as a matter of policy', Goldstone cited the Samouni case, referring to the likelihood that the attack was based on a misreading of a drone image, and went further, writing – a month before the MAG reported – that 'an appropriate process is under way, and I am confident that if the officer is found to have been negligent, Israel will respond accordingly'.[13]

Among those who attacked Goldstone over his apparent reversal was the US academic Norman Finkelstein, a passionate critic of Israeli policy, who excoriated the judge's focus on 'intentionality'.[14] Goldstone had asserted: 'That . . . the crimes allegedly committed by Hamas were intentional goes without saying – its rockets were purposefully and indiscriminately aimed at civilian targets.' Indeed, all the main human rights agencies, including Human Rights Watch and Amnesty International, repeatedly asserted that Hamas was guilty of war crimes by targeting civilian communities in Israel. Rocket launches may cause fewer deaths than suicide bombings but they are no less violations of international human rights law.

At least implicitly, Goldstone contrasted this 'intentionality' on the part of Hamas with its absence in Israel's case. But Finkelstein accused Goldstone of ignoring in relation to the IDF a cardinal principle in the law of armed conflict, enunciated by the (Israeli) world authority on the subject, Yoram Dinstein – namely that 'there is no genuine difference between a premeditated attack against civilians [or civilian objects] and a reckless disregard of the principle of distinction [between civilian and military targets]: they are equally forbidden'.[15]

Whether or not Goldstone had ignored the principle enunciated by Dinstein, the MAG did not. By saying that the attacks on Wael Samouni's building were neither intentionally aimed at civilians nor 'carried out in a reckless manner . . . with respect to the possibility that such civilians may be harmed', the Advocate General showed he understood it very well. But there was nothing in his report to back up his assertion that the airstrikes on the Wael Samouni building were not 'carried out in a reckless manner', especially as even the MAG thought several of the Brigade Commander's decisions had been 'deficient'. Instead, the report made a very general reference to the 'complex operational circumstances of the Gaza Operation, which took place mostly in a heavily populated urban environment', and 'the fact that prior to the incident, RPG fire was directed towards the IDF ground forces in the area'. (It does not say how long prior, and indeed there was no evidence of militant activity in the area at the time of the attack.)

The reason this argument matters is that there is another way of seeing the IDF's approach, not only to the Samouni incidents but to the whole Gaza operation – that the commanders were not 'targeting' the civilian population so much as subordinating the protection of civilian life to that of their own soldiers.

Within six months of Cast Lead, Breaking the Silence collected about thirty testimonies from Israeli combatants which covered, among much else: the killing of at least two civilians; the vandalism, looting and wholesale destruction of Palestinian houses; the commandeering of Palestinian 'human shields'; the first widespread use by the IDF in Gaza of notoriously imprecise mortar fire and white phosphorus ammunition, and what another battalion commander was quoted as describing to his troops as 'insane firepower with artillery and air force'. But even more striking was the number of cases in which soldiers were made aware of a new determination to prioritise their own lives over those of Palestinian civilians that would give them considerable leeway. One testified that his battalion commander had pledged: 'Not a hair will fall of a soldier of mine. I am not willing to allow a soldier of mine to risk himself by hesitating. If you are not sure, shoot.'[16]

Another recalled that his battalion commander had said the operation was not 'a limited confrontation such as in Hebron, and not to hesitate if we suspected someone nor feel bad about destruction because it is all done for the safety of our own soldiers . . . if we see something suspect and shoot, better hit an innocent than hesitate to target an enemy'.

The leeway was partly based on a widespread assumption that if residents had been warned by leaflets that strikes or the arrival of ground forces were imminent, then anyone left was a possible target – 'no one should be there'. But as Human Rights Watch put it after weeks of postwar fieldwork: 'The warnings were too vague, often addressed generally to the "inhabitants of the area". The leaflets dropped from high altitudes scattered over wide areas; many Gaza residents told Human Rights Watch that they disregarded the leaflets because they were so common, widely dispersed, and imprecise. In addition, the warnings did not instruct civilians where to find safety after fleeing their homes. At the beginning of the ground offensive on 3 January the IDF warned residents to "move to city centres", but then some city centres came under attack, including United Nations schools in urban areas where civilians had sought shelter.' But in any case, HRW argued, leafleting did not absolve military forces from an army's obligations under international humanitarian law. 'Attacking forces may not assume that all persons remaining in an area after a warning has been issued are legitimate.'[17]

A few months later in Jerusalem I met one of the soldiers, who said the now prevailing policy had 'taken the targeted killing idea and turned it on its head'. Instead of using intelligence to identify a terrorist, he said, 'here you do the opposite: first you take him down, then you look into it'. As he explained it, the approach 'doesn't mean that you need to disrespect the lives of Palestinians but our first priority is the lives of our soldiers. That's not something you're going to compromise on. In all my years in the military, I never heard that.'

The IDF was quick to pour scorn on the Breaking the Silence report, making much of the fact that the soldiers were not named and that the organisation was not prepared to hand over the testimonies for investigation by the military. There were good reasons for this; to have their names published would risk disciplinary action or even criminal proceedings over their involvement in events they described. Beside adverse consequences for the soldier, that would bolster a tendency for which the IDF had already been criticised by Israeli human rights agencies, namely to focus a (very limited) number of prosecutions for human rights breaches on low-ranking soldiers rather than their senior officers. Yehuda Shaul, a former combat soldier who had served in Hebron, and a founder of Breaking the Silence, pointed out that not only had the testimonies been checked and cross-checked, but had been taped, and all the names were known to the organisation – and in at least one case to the IDF itself.

But what was more surprising about the IDF's fierce rebuttal was that the new doctrine of prioritising soldiers' over civilian lives highlighted in the Breaking the Silence testimonies had been officially – and publicly – articulated more than three years earlier. In 2005 an authoritative redefinition of what was expected of IDF combatants in their treatment of civilians in warfare, overturned a crucial and long established assumption which had underpinned the military's own code of ethics. The 'purity of arms' section of the ethics code, entitled *The Spirit of the IDF* and given to every new recruit – says that 'IDF soldiers will not use their weapons and force to harm human beings who are not combatants or prisoners of war, and will do all in their power to avoid causing harm to their lives, bodies, dignity and property'.[18]

The Israeli philosopher Moshe Halbertal, who helped to draw up the code in 2000 (and incidentally became a fierce critic of Goldstone's original report), would explain much later that efforts to prevent civilian harm 'surely must include the expectation that soldiers assume some risk to their own lives in order to avoid causing the deaths of civilians'. This was not demanded by international law, Halbertal suggested, 'but it is demanded in Israel's military code, and this has always been its tradition'.[19]

But in an article in the 2005 *Journal of Military Ethics*, two key Israeli figures, Asa Kasher, a professor of philosophy at Hebrew University, and Amos Yadlin, Commander of the IDF Defense College, and the former head of Military Intelligence, insisted that while such a doctrine applied to conventional wars – those between armies – it should not apply to the new warfare against 'terrorism'. In simple terms, the code had implicitly embodied a kind of hierarchy of protection of human life in war: in order of priority, this had run: 'our' civilians; 'their' (or 'enemy') civilians; our soldiers; their soldiers. Kasher and Yadlin now explicitly created a new hierarchy for the 'new warfare': 1. our civilians; 2. those 'not involved in terror' who are not 'ours' but are under 'effective control' of our state; 3. our soldiers; 4. those 'not involved in terror' when '*they are not under the effective control of* [our] *state*' (my italics). To this descending order of priorities Kasher and Yadlin added two more categories: persons 'indirectly' (5) and 'directly' (6) 'involved in terror activities'.[20]

Kasher and Yadlin did not mention specific theatres of warfare; indeed, they argued that their doctrine should apply universally to 'counter-terrorism' operations; but locally it was easy to see that, while it might not mean a change in the treatment of Palestinian civilians in, say, East Jerusalem, where they were 'under control of the state' (Israel), or perhaps even in parts of the West Bank, it would apply to Gaza. Without discussing the complex issue of what constitutes 'control', the article offered a green light for non-combatant lives in Gaza to be set at a lower priority than those of Israeli soldiers.

The doctrine was to say the least debatable. It was not clear morally why non-combatants in Gaza should be treated differently from other 'enemy' civilians simply because the militias there – over which the civilians did not exercise control – are classified as 'terrorist'. Avishai Margalit, an eminent Israeli philosopher with an international reputation, and the American political theorist Michael Walzer, an expert in just war theory, challenged the Yadlin/Kasher argument head-on as 'wrong and dangerous'.[21] Their rebuttal was comprehensive but in summary observed that the argument 'erodes the distinction between combatants and non-combatants, which is critical to the theory of justice in war (*jus in bello*)', adding that Yadlin and Kasher had given 'no good reasons' for the erosion. Just war theory, Margalit and Walzer argued, requires that 'the two nations, the two peoples, must be functioning communities at the war's end. The war cannot be a war of extermination or ethnic cleansing. And what is true for states is also true for state-like political bodies such as Hamas and Hezbollah, whether they practise terrorism or not. The people they represent or claim to represent are a people like any other.'

Perhaps because the controversy was conducted at an academic level, the radical change outlined by Yadlin and Kasher was noticed less than it might have been. Officially, moreover, the article did not supersede the IDF's code of ethics. But it was written under the aegis of the IDF National College of Defense and assumed high importance in Israel's strategic circles. Amos Harel of *Haaretz* reported in February 2009 that the massive firepower in Cast Lead had indeed been deployed in accordance with the Yadlin/Kasher doctrine and quoted Kasher, 'who has strong, long standing ties with the Army', as saying that their ideas had been 'adopted' by Moshe Yaalon, who was IDF Chief of Staff when they were first drafted, and his successors.[22]

Israel was wholly entitled to point out that the widespread principle that an army should protect civilian lives, even at some risk to its own soldiers, had been violated elsewhere often enough, for example during the US–British operation in Iraq from 2003. What Israel had pioneered, however, was a new principle, which relieved its army – and perhaps in time, as Kasher has himself suggested, those of other countries – of much of their obligation to protect civilians in military operations. Cast Lead saw the first conscious application of this principle, but not the last.

When the ground invasion was under way, Miriam Faris kept a daily tally of the death toll in her diary, along with her own observations on the conduct of all the parties:

4 January: No goods in the shops even if you have money to buy. Fatah [the PA] is a disgrace watching what's going on, people's whole lives disappear before their eyes not to mention their loved ones . . . Hamas

people came trying to use one of Abu Ala's flats but he and Mohammed went out and told them that they couldn't cos all of us would have to leave the building, in the end they went. I was so pissed off about it after all this going on and they want to sling themselves amongst us.

6 January: Egypt is taking some of the injured but it's only a trickle compared with the amount of hurt and dying. Doctors from other countries are waiting to be allowed in at Rafah border with Egypt but so far have not had permission.

7 January: Mohammed went to the supermarket and found flour, M+Ms, Twix, biscuits, honey. We're rich! Israel Cabinet will meet today to study the 3rd phase, will they nuke us and finish off with the Palestinian problem? . . .

8 January: 7 a.m. We were all excited at the thought we may have electric by 4 p.m. but Red Cross guy and electric men went to fix lines and they got shot at by Israeli troops. The driver of the lorry of supplies for UN got killed. At last human rights have started moving their arses and all the NGOs all over the world.

Miriam's 4 January entry touched on a frequent Israeli justification for civilian casualties – the tendency of Hamas militants to operate from civilian areas. Yadlin and Kasher had argued that 'jeopardising ["our"] combatants rather than bystanders' would mean shouldering responsibility for the 'mixed nature of the vicinity' for 'no reason'. (Projected onto the situation described by Miriam, this seemed to mean that if the Hamas men had refused to leave, Israel had no duty to try and minimise the risk to her and her husband.) But Margalit and Walzer rejected this, arguing that the terrorists' responsibility for the 'mixed nature of the vicinity' did not absolve soldiers from trying to minimise the risk to non-combatants. If it did, what was to stop the soldiers themselves using such civilians as human shields, a practice officially condemned by the IDF? And were Israeli residents who were (in their case voluntarily) neighbours of the military HQ in residential Tel Aviv not entitled to protection?[23]

Many of the cases referred for investigation by the MAG did not anyway involve self-protection of soldiers. In the same week as the Samounis buried their dead, I drove out to Juhr al-Dik, a rural village whose green and fertile fields stretched right up to the Israeli border. When Israeli troops moved into central Gaza, some of its houses had been commandeered as military posts. The tracks of tanks as they swept west, bisecting the Strip between the border and the sea, were still visible. They had left their mark: more than a hundred houses had been reduced to rubble; olive groves, citrus orchards had been razed and sheep pastures had been churned up by armoured vehicles. This scene greeted the village's 2,500 residents when they returned from the temporary haven in the Bureij refugee camp to which they had fled; only about half still had homes.

Yet not all of those who had tried to escape Juhr al-Dik had made it out, even when they were obediently fleeing because of Israeli warnings. At around 6.15 a.m. on 4 January, the first full day of the ground offensive, a tank shell landed at the house of the civilian Abu Hajaj family, the shrapnel injuring twelve-year-old Manar. Palestinian Red Crescent and Red Cross ambulances could not get through because of the troops' presence. Badly scared, the family of fifteen fled down the lane and took shelter in a basement occupied by a neighbour, Mohammed al-Safadi, and ten members of his family, about 250 metres to the east. The whole group included seventeen children under the age of twelve.

Al-Safadi, fifty-nine, a carpenter, explained that the Israeli military broke into a radio broadcast to announce those in border areas should leave their homes, holding white flags. His son Ahmed, twenty-three, and Majda Abu Hajaj, thirty-five, tied white scarves to broomsticks and led the group out. The Abu Hajaj family were also anxious to get medical treatment for Manar. As they passed the Abu Hajaj home, they were fired on from waiting tanks. Al-Safadi was carrying his infant son, Mohammed, and walking close to Majda's sixty-five-year-old mother, Raya. Majda fell dead, apparently shot in the back, and as the group ran back the way it had come Raya was also shot. Al-Safadi grabbed the wounded woman and they ran for the cover of the Abu Hajaj house. 'She was saying, "My hand, my hand", and then she lost her breath and died,' he said.

The rest of the group made it back to al-Safadi's house despite continued fire – and some shelling on the surrounding open land – from the tanks. After a night in the house, al-Safadi said the group decided 'that it was better to be shot while we are walking than shelled in our home'. They used the cover of trees to make their way back to the centre of the village, and on to the relative safety of the Bureij camp. The bodies of

Majda – crushed and mutilated by a tank, the family said – and Raya were not recovered until the ceasefire nineteen days later.

Of fifty-two Cast Lead incidents known to have been referred by the MAG to the Military Police – most involving deaths of unprotected civilians in airstrikes, artillery or mortar attacks, and tank fire or naval shelling – all but four closed without any prosecution. One soldier was sentenced to fifteen months for stealing a Palestinian's credit card; two others were gaoled for three months and demoted 'from staff sergeant to sergeant' for using a nine-year-old boy as a human shield to open a bag wrongly suspected of being booby-trapped. The fourth originally arose out of the Abu Hajaj deaths; a soldier was convicted of 'use of an unlawful weapon' and 'inappropriate conduct' – but, puzzlingly, after admitting killing not the two women but another, unspecified, person twenty-four hours later.[24]

The IDF also used white phosphorus shells, a practice it abandoned after the war. Although it was certainly not a main cause of casualties, one set alight the Abu Halima family's house in the northern Gaza Atatra area during the ground invasion on 4 January. Mahmoud Abu Halima, twenty, described seeing the corpse of his forty-five-year-old tenant farmer father Sadallah 'stuck together' with the still smouldering bodies of Mahmoud's three younger brothers, seemingly having hugged them to him in his last seconds. Like other residents, the family had stayed in their home despite leafleted IDF warnings to leave, believing, on the basis of past experience of incursions, that they would be safe.

But eleven days later, in a much higher-profile case – for which the IDF eventually apologised – white phosphorus shells hit the UNRWA headquarters in Gaza, burning down a warehouse storing medical supplies, food, clothing and blankets for Gaza's (then) 950,000 refugees, and leaving wedges of white phosphorus. The compound had opened its gates to 600 Palestinians living in a nearby twelve-storey apartment block, which UNRWA had been warned was going to be hit. It also contained a depot storing 149,000 litres of fuel, with another 49,000 litres in trucks parked within the precincts.

A much greater catastrophe was only averted because of the prompt and courageous action of two UNWRA field officers, Jodie Clark and Scott Anderson. The pair risked their lives by clambering under a fuel truck to retrieve a wedge of explosive phosphorus. Clark explained:

We were talking to the IDF, we were telling them that they were shelling the UNRWA compound, and . . . the warehouses where they knew
that we had all the food and medicine. And particularly they had
communicated every single day of the war to assist us to get those
goods in, so I was saying to them why did you assist us to get it in if
you're blowing it up now, you're burning it to the ground . . . If you hit
the fuel station, UNRWA will be history . . . Initially [they were] denying that they were hitting our building – 'no, we're not hitting your
building, we're targeting somewhere'. [I said] 'You are hitting [it] my
dear! I am standing in my building, it is collapsing around me, there is
a huge fire, you are hitting the UN compound.' And it took us two
hours to convince them that they were actually hitting the UN
compound . . . We had about seven vehicles that were well alight . . .
and white phosphorus was still burning on the ground. And we fought
the fire hand on hand for four hours before the fire trucks arrived, and
it was massive, the fire was like running water . . . And then the fire
extinguishers finished, we had nothing . . . [25]

The argument that the IDF was not deliberately targeting civilian Gaza
(as opposed to subordinating civilian lives to those of its own soldiers)
was harder to sustain in relation to the wholesale destruction of
Palestinian buildings, workplaces and infrastructure, much of it in the
closing stages of Cast Lead. Indeed, the level of destruction suggested
that the IDF had carried over from Lebanon in 2006 to Gaza in 2008–9
at least elements of the 'Dahiya doctrine'* – prescribing (for future wars
in Lebanon against Hezbollah) what the Israeli analyst Gabi Siboni
described as 'force that is disproportionate to the enemy's actions and
the threat it poses. Such a response aims at inflicting damage and meting
out punishment to an extent that will demand long and expensive
reconstruction processes.'[26]
    There was no shortage of examples especially in the industrial sector
along the eastern Gaza Strip's north–south road, less than a kilometre
from the Israeli border. Dr Yaser Alweyda, owner of one of Gaza's
biggest food-processing plants, stood beside the burned-out ruins of his
factory, warehouses and incinerated refrigeration vans, worth in total
about $22.5m. As the sole Gaza agent for the leading Israeli dairy

---

* So called after the southern suburb of Beirut devastated in the 2006 Lebanon war.

company Tnuva, Alweyda, who had kept production going right up to the war, was proud of his long connections with Israeli business. Now he thought Israel wanted 'to destroy the weak Palestinian economy . . . and ensure that we will never have a state in Palestine'.

When the war was over, many somehow managed to pick themselves up, but resilience came harder for others. The bombing of Wael Samouni's building had been especially hard for Hilmi Samouni. As the smoke had started to clear, Hilmi had seen beside him the bodies of his father Talal and his mother Rahme, his wife Maha, aged twenty, and their six-month-old son Mohammed. It bothered Hilmi that he had no pictures of any of them; they had disappeared in the heat of the invasion.

A year after the war, Hilmi Samouni was spending most of his time pottering round the house, helping to look after his seemingly self-possessed eleven-year-old sister Mona. She showed me her artwork, inspired by her memories of the morning of 5 January 2009 and encouraged by a psychologist treating her for PTSD. 'This is me cleaning the face of my mother who is dead. This is my father who was hit in the head and his brains came out. This is my dead sister-in-law. This is my sister taking the son from my sister-in-law . . .'

That November in 2009 you could see how traumatised the family still were. The widowed Zeinat Samouni could not stop crying as she described how they left the house – and the body of her husband – with her older son Faraj, carrying four-year-old Ahmad, shot and heavily bleeding, to the house of another relative. As evening came, she gave Ahmad, his face now yellowing, bread dipped in water. 'It was like feeding a bird,' she recalled. The family called an ambulance but were told that it was too dangerous for it to approach the area. Ahmad died in the early hours of the next morning. 'If we'd been able to get an ambulance, I think he would be alive now,' she said. Zeinat's daughter, ten-year-old Amal, carried in her pocket two worn photographs of her dead father and brother. 'I want to look at them all the time,' she said. 'My house is not beautiful without them.' The psychological trauma for Amal had been compounded by the fact that she ran off before her mother and siblings left the house after the shooting. Dehydrated and in shock, she was one of the injured children the Red Cross rescued three days later.

Yet seven years later Amal had matured into a tall, polite and seemingly composed sixteen-year-old in the eleventh grade at school. Having at the age of nine said that she wanted to be a doctor when she grew up, she now said: 'I want to study journalism so I can write about the crimes of the occupation.' Mona Samouni, now eighteen, was in the midst of her final *tawjihi* exams and doing well, said her brother Hilmi, who had a job serving coffee to civil servants in a Gaza ministry. 'It took her four years to recover.' But Faraj Samouni doubted that the family would ever fully recover. 'Are you able ever to forget seeing your father shot dead and your brother bleeding to death? I don't think so.'

Maysaa was perhaps the most robust, living, she said, by the mantra 'what doesn't break you, makes you stronger. More strong. More brave.' Seven years after the bombing that widowed her at the age of nineteen, this seemed more than a cliché.

Since her husband was killed, Maysaa had married again, had a second daughter, Jenan, who was nearly two, and had finished a degree in IT education. She would have liked to work but because of a lack of funding there were no vacancies for teachers. Jumana, now eight, arrived back from school and went to play in the sunshine. If you didn't know you might not notice the three missing fingers on her left hand, a permanent reminder of a catastrophe she cannot remember.

But her mother recalls 'every detail from the first moment to the last. When I tell the story to anybody it's like a picture in front of my eyes.'

10

'THEY'RE PUNISHING THE WRONG PEOPLE': SIEGE, 2008–12

CRAWLING SOUTH ALONG THE DANK METRE-HIGH passage, I glanced up at the crude wooden supports, all that was preventing the thick layers of clay and sand above my head from crashing down and burying me alive. Anyone who had been in a narrow-seam coal mine could relate to the mild sense of claustrophobia, but here it was compounded by knowing that a dozen people had been killed in tunnels like this in the previous month. Getting in meant lowering yourself down the shaft like an ungainly monkey, groping for narrow ledges embedded in its wooden walls. Given the awkward access and the cramped conditions, it was a surprise to see the tunnel lit up when you reached your destination. This was October 2008 in the subterranean smugglers' world below Gaza's border with Egypt.

Above ground was a tent city, at first sight like some sprawling Bedouin encampment stretching along the old Philadelphia Corridor which, until 2005, had been the Israeli-controlled no man's land between Egypt and Gaza. Overlooked by the watchtowers of Egyptian security on the south side and the apartment blocks raddled by years of Israeli shelling on the Palestinian side, the tents protected entrances to between 400 and 500 smuggling tunnels from the weather.

In the glow of bulbs running off long cables from Rafah's municipal power supply, 'Felix', a cheerful twenty-seven-year-old Palestinian, was using his intercom phone to talk to his Egyptian counterpart at the other end of the tunnel a kilometre away. Beside him, long steel cables were hauling canisters of Egyptian-made cooking gas into Gaza. Two hundred had arrived that morning alone. 'I spent two years doing a diploma in decoration,' Felix explained. 'But I have five children to support and this is the only work I can find.'

Every merchant who bought one of the prized blue canisters paid a $40 premium for the difficult and dangerous transportation, said Ahmed, his boss. But in Gaza, where cooking gas had been virtually unobtainable for months, the merchants easily recouped that by selling them on for $100 or more – along with almost anything from diesel fuel, clothing, chocolate, cigarettes and potato chips to live cattle and the inevitable motorcycles.

A few hundred metres away, Karim and Eyad were supervising the digging of a new, and deeper, stone and cement shaft. The men, both aged thirty-five, had paid the Hamas-controlled Rafah municipality 10,000 shekels (£1,665 at 2008 prices) for a permit to dig the tunnel, under new regulations. As a lean dun horse hauled away buckets of mud, Eyad explained the difficulties of routing tunnels to escape the attention of Egyptian forces, who had pledged to destroy them. 'We use Google Earth to plan the tunnel,' he said. 'We have to find a hidden place, a deserted house or something like that.' In constant phone contact with an Egyptian worker – well paid for risking a prison sentence if discovered – and using a long pole that could protrude above the ground, 'we make a sign of where we've got to. Then he tells us, "yes that's the right place" or "move to the left or right" or "go another 50 metres"'.

Karim, once a building worker in Israel who later began training to be a doctor until his money ran out, said the cost of building the tunnel was about $70,000. 'I sold my car, my wife's gold, everything to pay for it.' He was conscious of the risks. 'I could be digging my own grave,' he reflected, looking down the shaft. But he hoped to make between $10,000 and $50,000 a month once it was operating twenty-four hours a day, seven days a week, out of which he would pay the twenty workers he planned to employ. None of the tunnellers – then or later – gave their full names. While the tunnels were operating openly on the Palestinian side, sanctioned – and indeed taxed – by Hamas, it was very different on the Egyptian side of the border. 'If we want to go to Egypt, we could be arrested,' Karim explained.

The tunnels had already proved to be Gaza's only safety valve in the face of what was, by now, more than a year of the Strip being treated as a 'hostile entity'. Much of the adverse publicity over the embargo concerned the bizarrely capricious list of goods Israel had banned, which included nutmeg, industrial margarine, musical instruments, A4 paper, newspapers, baby chickens, crayons, crockery, toys and books (other than those imported by the UN), hummus with pine nuts (but not hummus without pine nuts) and even pasta until an infuriated John Kerry, then chairman of the US foreign relations committee, protested at its inclusion. One of the criteria adopted by the military was nutritionally precise: the number of trucks arriving with food supply each day was based on a carefully calculated minimum need of 2,279 calories per person, which experts decided could be provided by 1,836 grams of food.[1]

More serious for hospitals and other public services was the highly restrictive list of 'dual use' goods which were also banned on the grounds that they or their components could be turned to military use by Hamas. The list included X-ray machines, items with chemical content, such as disinfectants, and UPS (uninterrupted power supply) units used to ensure the functioning of life-saving equipment in the face of regular and lengthy power cuts. While the tunnels went some way to making up for dire shortages of all but the most basic 'humanitarian' supplies allowed in by Israel, the transport costs meant that the smuggled supplies in the first three years after Hamas's takeover usually came at a price many Gazans could not afford.

The speed, scale and ingenuity of the tunnel growth was a tribute to Gazan enterprise and adaptability. Yet it also helped to illustrate how the siege, far from hurting Hamas (as opposed to the civilian population), actually benefited it for the six years between 2007 and 2013, during which the commercial smuggling tunnels flourished. The tunnels created a substantial black economy and a cluster of powerful entrepreneurs, often with close ties with Hamas, at the expense of conventional businessmen, many of whom had fostered close and long-standing links with Israeli customers and suppliers. The Hamas government – or more properly 'de facto' government since it was no longer officially recognised as such by even the PA – levied taxes worth, at the peak of the tunnel smuggling, an estimated £1m a day[2] both in fees paid by the tunnellers and taxes raised on smuggled goods.

Something was happening which was more dangerous than the mystery of why coriander was banned by Israel and cinnamon was not: the steady dismantling of what had once been a functioning – and legit-imate – economy. Not only did the smuggling enterprise fail to improve the lives of the eighty per cent of families in Gaza dependent on some form of aid, or fifty-two per cent of households who were food insecure in 2010,[3] but the tunnels did next to nothing to rescue the stricken manufacturing and agricultural sectors which had traditionally been the motor of Gaza's economy and which had been heavily dependent on exports out of Gaza. The fact that the smuggling industry rapidly became the largest private sector employer in the Strip underlined Gaza's disastrous level of unemployment – at around forty-five per cent in 2010, one of the highest in the world. Indeed, between 2006 and 2010 employment in manufacturing fell, largely through the double ban on exports and raw material imports, by eighty per cent, from 33,150 to 6,546.[4] This in turn enlarged the pool of potential young recruits to the Hamas payroll – including the Qassam Brigades and its security forces.

As the tunnels industry flourished, providing at its peak wages of up to $75 a day for labourers, an astronomically high figure for Gaza, some families were facing the winter in tents because of the desperately slow pace of reconstruction after Operation Cast Lead. The wreckage even generated its own micro-economy. At 6.30 each morning, Saber Abu Freih and his sixty-year-old mother Ghazala arrived at what was once their house, partly to sift through the rubble to find jewellery they had left behind eleven months before and partly to load a donkey cart with blasted masonry needed to make new breeze-blocks for small-scale construction. 'We are clearing the land, collecting stones that will be used for building,' he said cheerfully. 'We may only get ten shekels [£1.60] a cartload. But what can we do?'

At the nearby al-Shobaki concrete works, their loads were ground down and made into building blocks. Owner Abdel Salem al-Shobaki succinctly described the business spiral of his company since the works opened at the height of the Intifada in 2003: 'Excellent to good to bad to unbelievable.' The 'bad to unbelievable' period had begun after the Hamas takeover of Gaza and the tightening of the siege, which left al-Shobaki short of a crucial commodity that he used to import from Israel. Since June 2007, he said, he'd had 'four thousand tons of gravel but no cement'. Then, in late 2009, almost a year after Operation Cast

Lead, al-Shobaki was finally able to procure enough cement through the tunnels to start up the works again. (Gazans were often sceptical about the quality of Egyptian cement; a joke doing the rounds was that a new Hamas-affiliated mosque on Gaza City's beach road remained incomplete because the imams were holding out for Israeli cement.) But the problem was the price. Al-Shobaki paid 1,400 shekels (£220 at 2009 prices) a ton for smuggled Egyptian cement, compared to the 380 shekels (£60) or so he paid when it came from Israel. 'First I'd like to see reconciliation between Fatah and Hamas,' he said, 'and then I'd like to see the crossings open. Anyone who says that the Israeli economy and Gaza's are not connected is stupid. They are one economy.' Nevertheless, the tunnels had allowed him to restart production, although at next to no profit.

But the constant commercial traffic through the tunnels could not disguise the scale and impact of Gaza's de-development. Jawdat al-Khodary, one of Gaza's most prominent businessmen, coined a term for another aspect of Gaza's isolation – the 'mental siege'. We met in late 2009 on the eve of the Eid in his beachfront restaurant, part of an elegant complex containing a hotel and the well-designed archaeological museum he had built the previous year to house a small proportion of his collection of Gaza antiquities from the early Bronze Age to the Ottoman Empire: heavy stone anchors from Roman times; ancient Egyptian alabaster plates; clay wine jars and Corinthian columns from the Byzantine period; oil, water and perfume pots; a clay wheel from a (now reconstructed) toy cart from the Philistine period, between 1600 BCE and 1200 BCE; glass bottles from the Hellenistic age and miniature sculptures in ivory. And a special source of pride: a clay coffin lid in the form of a man's head from the eleventh century BCE.

Yet today the restraurant and museum were empty. 'Why do you think there's no one here?' al-Khodary asked. 'Because most people are fasting before the Eid. Twenty years ago, only one per cent would have done that. Now it's about ninety per cent.' Although Hamas had issued no edicts on this, al-Khodary believed the phenomenon was the result of messages handed down from the mosques since Hamas came to power. He saw this, and the similar turnaround in those going to the mosque to pray regularly, as evidence of the Islamic Hamas's 'credibility in the street'. The greatest internal pressure on Hamas came not from Fatah, which had been effectively repressed in Gaza, but from more extreme Islamist groups. Why, al-Khodary asked, was Israel fostering a climate which risked nurturing groups more extreme than Hamas and 'worse than the Taliban'? 'Israel is so stupid,' he said. 'They are punishing the wrong people.'

The punishment was severe, the steady deterioration of Gaza's water supply being just one example. Only five to ten per cent of Gazans had access to safe drinking water through taps.[5] A large majority depended on tanker operators selling water filtered by commercial mini-desalination plants; according to local and international NGOs some forty-five per cent of such plants produce water that has some biological contamination.[6] Although the World Health Organization had not reported any cases of cholera, which can be a consequence of contaminated water supply, a quarter of illnesses in Gaza were estimated to be water-related.[7] Water bought from carriers was also up to five times more expensive than mains network water,[8] meaning that before long some families would be spending as much as a third of their income on it.[9]

The water crisis was largely man-made, and it was impossible to separate this particular supply issue from that facing the Palestinians as a whole. After the 1967 war Israel took control of all water sources in the Occupied Palestinian Territories, boosting the ability of the water utility Mekorot to supply Israeli consumers including those in the settlements in the West Bank – and until 2005 – Gaza. By 2009, each Israeli – including settlers – enjoyed over four times the access to water afforded Palestinians; for agricultural irrigation the gap was a multiple of five.[10] Over-pumping by Palestinians of the underground Coastal Aquifer, part of which flows from Israel, and by now Gaza's only natural water source, began before 1967, under the Egyptians.[11] But since then Gaza's water supply has also been caught in a vicious circle of depletion and contamination. The Wadi Gaza, the stream, also starting in Israel, which had historically been the Strip's main source of surface water, had long been diverted to Israeli use. So, more recently, had the aquifer.[12] According to one Palestinian account the Gaza Strip enjoys only a quarter of the total extractions from the Coastal Aquifer.[13] In any case, by 2012 the aquifer was seriously contaminated by seawater – seeping in because it is pumped so much faster than it fills up – and by some 90,000 cubic centimetres of untreated or partly treated sewage, which was entering the ground or the Mediterranean every day.[14] An already degraded sewage infrastructure had further deteriorated because of

2008–9 war damage, the difficulty of importing spare parts under the siege and the impact of electricity outages on pumping stations.

But the impact of Gaza's isolation was also psychological. The Gaza Community Mental Health Programme (GCMHP) was founded by the late Eyad Sarraj, one of the leading figures in Gazan civil society for many years. A psychiatrist trained in Britain, Sarraj was secular in his outlook, with a balanced, humane view of current events. An outspoken advocate of Palestinians against the Israeli occupation, he nevertheless criticised abuses by the Palestinian factions, whether secular or Islamist. He had been arrested three times by Arafat's PA in 1995, mistreated and beaten by men, some of whom had been prisoners in Israeli gaols and whom he subsequently treated.

Sarraj understood that the gap between mental illness and medical provision in Gaza was among the widest anywhere in the world, made even more so by being an almost taboo subject. He made sure GCMHP had the best available staff.

Hasan Zeyada, a senior psychologist, was one of these, a thoughtful English and Hebrew speaker who had trained in psychology at Tel Aviv University (at a time when it was possible for Gazan students to do post-graduate work in Israel). After the war, he treated, among many others, patients in rehab for addiction to the painkiller Tramadol (smuggled in from Egypt through the tunnels). It was a form of drug abuse which reached – and has since remained at – a near-epidemic scale in Gaza.

Abu Ahmed, an unemployed forty-five-year-old father of ten children who had lost a good job as a truck driver after the blockade started in 2007, explained how he lived through the war – including a ground incursion in his neighbourhood during which Israeli forces had fired white phosphorus shells – in a daze. By then he had been taking 800mg a day of the synthetic opioid, smuggled through the tunnels, almost three times the prescribed upper limit of 300mg. 'Of course you care about the children,' he insisted, 'but you feel less frightened.'

Tramadol was wrecking his life. 'I had a headache, pain in every part of my body. I had to go the bathroom every ten minutes. I was sweating. Then you take one pill and you feel better of course.' On a friend's advice, Abu Ahmed turned to the GCMHP where he was treated with a mixture of talking therapy and alternative medication to wean him off the drug. He was understandably grateful.

While women were especially vulnerable to depression as they felt they only existed to serve their husbands and children, Zeyada said the men often felt powerless and emasculated because of their inability to protect their children in war or provide for them in relative peace. Abu Ahmed agreed. 'If you have children and you can't find work to give them what they need, then you can't sleep.'

Zeyada mused more widely about the conflict. Fusing his expertise in psychology with his understanding of the Holocaust, he said that it sometimes seemed to him that Israel was exhibiting the classic syndrome of an abused child abusing others in return.

More surprisingly, as an experienced psychologist in Gaza, Zeyada was sure another factor in mental ill health was the deep split between Fatah and Hamas. Not only did it divide individual families, but for many Gazans, he suggested, it compromised their proud Palestinian national identity with a divisive factional one which makes them especially sensitive to criticism and hostility from political opponents. There were even cases, he said, from school playgrounds of conflict breaking out between children favouring (for non-political reasons) a particular colour T-shirt: yellow (Fatah), green (Hamas).

Yet as always there was another side to Gaza, even in the aftermath of Operation Cast Lead and as the Israeli blockade continued to tighten. Despite – and in some cases even because of – the ravages of war and economic blockade, culture and social life and even sport continued with an obstinate brio.

The artist Maha al-Daya and her husband Ayman Eissa, also a painter, lived in a prematurely ageing apartment block overlooking a desolate stretch of wasteland on the edge of Jabalya in northern Gaza. The climb up the grimy stairs to their fourth-floor apartment wound around a lift shaft with no lift. It was as if the developers had created the building round the shaft in the hope of better times, when a lift might actually be affordable . . . the incurable optimism of Gaza. It was a shock to find inside the flat elegant furniture and decoration that were a stunning exhibition of the couple's visual tastes and work. The walls were covered with their paintings: a haunting portrait of a naked child with a large, almost triangular head by Ayman; Maha's own vibrant land- and seascapes, chronicling an ever-changing city and its coast. The table on which she served coffee was covered with a red and black cloth she had hand-stitched in the pattern of a chess board. The chairs were scattered with cushions decorated with kaleido-scopic embroidery.

One of the couple's friends, the young Gazan painter Sharif Sarhan, had photographed scenes of the destruction and later turned them into a series of war paintings. Neither artist would take commissions from the armed factions. Sharif said he wasn't 'angry' with artists who did such work. 'I found a job, but maybe they had no other option,' he said. 'But I won't do it. I'm not Hamas nor Fatah. I'm Sharif.' But Maha differed even from Sharif in her refusal to be a war artist. During Operation Cast Lead, she could see the white phosphorus used in the bombing of nearby Atatra. 'We saw the ball of fire, like an octopus.' But though this powerful image testified to her painter's eye, she did not commit it to canvas. 'I couldn't draw anything,' she explained. 'I was living in a depression during and after the war. I was very afraid and very worried.' To make matters worse her husband had been stranded at his Egyptian university, forced to watch on television what his family were going through every day of the war. When she finally picked up a brush again two months after the 2008–9 war, her first painting was of recovery, the repair of one of her characteristic fishing boats on the Gaza City beach.

MEANWHILE, THE BLOCKADE SUDDENLY BECAME THE focus of global attention. On 31 May 2010 Israeli commandos shot dead eight Turks and one Turkish-American aboard the *Mavi Marmara*, the flagship of a flotilla that had set sail for Gaza with the blessing of Turkey's then Prime Minister Recep Tayyip Erdoğan in a deliberately high-profile attempt to break the blockade with 6,000 tonnes of humanitarian supplies. Israel defended the episode on the grounds that the vessel had defied warnings to turn back, that seven of its soldiers were injured by Turkish activists resorting to using iron bars and other weapons when the commandos boarded the ship, and that the flotilla had been organised by IHH, a Turkish charity sympathetic to Hamas. But Israel's lethal violence put its diplomatic relations with Turkey into deep freeze for six years; mean-while, a prominent Turkish-funded memorial honouring the fallen Turks was erected at Gaza's dilapidated and non-functioning port.

The worldwide news coverage of the incident made it much harder for Western governments to ignore the dire effects of the blockade. In London, for example, an internal Foreign Office paper prepared for

Foreign Secretary William Hague ahead of the 21 June meeting of the Middle East Quartet stated that the 'unacceptable and counterproductive [blockade] hurts the people of Gaza, holds their future hostage and undermines work to drive reconstruction, development and economic empowerment. At the same time the blockade empowers Hamas through the tunnel economy and damages Israel's long-term security through the corrosive impact on a generation of young Palestinians . . . This is the moment for the international community to act.'[15]

Hague urged Tony Blair, as the Quartet envoy, to press Israel to implement an action plan calling for immediate entry of materials needed for UN reconstruction; a shift from the 'far too restrictive' list of eighty-one items allowed into Gaza to a simple blacklist which banned specific goods and assumed everything else was permitted; dealing with 'dual use' items, including cement pipes and steel, not by banning them but by 'robust' monitoring once they were inside Gaza to ensure they did not fall into the hands of Hamas; and perhaps most importantly to reopen land crossings, beginning with the main cargo crossing at Karni 'to enable trade to flow to and from [i.e. exports] kickstarting economic recovery'.

The lengthy negotiations which Blair then indeed undertook with Israel's government, now headed by Benjamin Netanyahu, produced some results but fell far short of the 'transformative solution' to Gaza's plight envisaged in the FCO paper. To have achieved it would have required a level of international unanimity and determination, especially on the part of the US, that was simply not forthcoming.

The blacklist was substituted for the infamous 'white list'. The range of consumer goods and some commercial raw materials imported from or through Israel was expanded. These brought down prices for competing smuggled goods – and most Palestinians who could afford them preferred Israeli goods to Egyptian ones. But the admission of potential 'dual use' goods for closely monitored international projects was still painfully slow. By contrast, the private sector – and Hamas – continued to rely on ever-increasing quantities of cement from the tunnels.

Indeed, the private sector construction boom fuelled by the import of cement and building materials meant that, from late 2010, in Gaza City at least there seemed to be a building site on every street. It had also had the temporary effect of reducing unemployment from about forty-five to about thirty-three per cent. The boom was profitable both for Hamas – which started to levy ten shekels (£1.65) on every ton of aggregate, twenty on cement and fifty on steel – and for Gaza's new rich business class, evidenced by the handsome villas the tunnel operators were building themselves outside Rafah.

For these businessmen, who often had close ties to Hamas, the paradoxical combination of tunnel smuggling and Israel's easing of restrictions on imports of consumer goods made retail especially attractive as they looked around for investment opportunities. In the summer of 2010, a new shopping mall opened in Gaza, electrifying Israel's conservative bloggers, who seethed with assertions that it made a mockery of claims that Gaza was seriously impoverished by the blockade. The air-conditioned mall had eight stores over two floors, branded carrier bags, separate prayer rooms for men and women, and sixty sales assistants employed directly by the newly formed Gaza Shopping Centre Company. The mall even had its own website offering home delivery.

By November 2010, however, only seven per cent of UNRWA projects had been approved for materials imports.[16] Karni remained closed to trade in and out of Gaza, but for a single conveyor belt used for importing gravel. In 2011 even the conveyor belt was stopped. For as long as the tunnels lasted Hamas would have all the cement it needed. The UN, precluded by policy from using the tunnels, was desperately short of it. The exports on which Gaza's economy had long relied were still banned.

Nor did the post-*Mavi Marmara* negotiations yield any improvement on free movement of people. For the runner Nader al-Masri, leaving, if even only for a short time, was the only way he would be able to qualify for the 2012 London Olympics. I met him again in August 2011. It was Ramadan, blisteringly hot, and the athlete had neither eaten nor drunk since before dawn and would not do so until dusk, still a couple of hours away. By then he would have completed twenty-five circuits of the stadium in his straight-backed, graceful running style. It had also been a day of fierce Israeli bombardment of Gaza and militant rocket attacks out of it. But al-Masri's focus was intense. He was on a mission to achieve the qualifying time for the 5,000m for London 2012. 'If he can leave Gaza now to train he has a chance of doing it,' said his forty-seven-year-old coach, Majed Abu Marahil, another Gazan ex-Olympian. The stadium, next to the municipality's rubbish dump, had been spruced up by the Hamas authorities, but with football in mind. Turf had been laid on the previously grassless pitch; but the running track was still sand, instead of the kind of synthetic all-weather track on which his potential competitors elsewhere would be training.

Once again al-Masri had been hoping to train in Qatar. To illustrate its importance he said that in 2006 he had comfortably beaten a Korean rival at the Asian Games. 'I came back to Gaza after the games, and he went to training camp. A year later he defeated me.' Fellow competitors told him they trained at camps for six months before events.

But al-Masri did not make it to Qatar, and had not been able to qualify. It was easy to blame Israel, of course, but neither the highly intelligent but apolitical al-Masri nor coach Abu Marahil felt it was so simple this time. Indeed, it was beginning to look like politics of another kind – the all too familiar 'forgotten Gaza' syndrome among Palestinian authorities in the West Bank.

The PA's long-established 'Mr Sport' was Jibril Rajoub, the former head of the feared Preventative Security Organisation and then Arafat's 'security adviser'. Like Mohammed Dahlan, his arch-rival in Fatah, he had been accused of torturing Hamas detainees in the 1990s. Now Rajoub had a combined role as head of the Ramallah-based Football Association and chairman of the Palestinian Olympic Committee. Abu Marahil thought that al-Masri's difficulties in getting out of Gaza to train were because Rajoub had not found the funds to get him to Qatar. Rajoub told me 'the occupation' – in other words Israel – was to blame for refusing the necessary permits. Yet the Israel Olympics Committee said it had had no request for help in al-Masri's case, as it normally would for Palestinian Olympians seeking a permit. And al-Masri could have left through Rafah, which at that time was open fairly regularly, had an exit permit been the only problem. Either way al-Masri's dream of qualifying for London 2012 was stillborn.

A perverse effect of the movement restrictions was to make Gazans a mystery, even to other Palestinians. In 2012, Iqbal Qishta, an elegant hairdresser and beautician, happily (though unusually for Gaza) unmarried at the age of thirty-seven, was refused a permit to attend a hairdressers' convention in the West Bank town of Tulkarm; although, as a veteran of such events in better times, she was hardly a security risk. She was half irritated and half amused that visitors from Gaza were now such a rarity that West Bankers regarded them as ingenues at best and barbarians at worst. 'Do you all live in asbestos shacks?' she remembered being asked at a similar convention in Jericho. 'They wouldn't believe we were from Gaza . . . It's because of the media. They just show bombardments, or they go to the Beach [refugee] camp and show kids playing in some sewage puddle, people wearing bad clothes and graffiti. They don't go to the Mövenpick [now the al-Mashtal hotel, but still known by the name of the Swiss company that built it] or the Lighthouse Restaurant or the Deira.'

Iqbal Qishta had a point; for all Gaza's imprisonment, the construction boom was not the only (temporary) relief. Even after five years of siege, Gaza retained its paradoxical status as at once the most stricken and the most metropolitan and sophisticated of Palestinian conurbations, in which at one extreme narrow alleys separated the overcrowded, zinc-roofed, breeze-block slums of the refugee camps, and at the other fashionable young women, some daringly without headscarves, smoked *narghila* under a new moon on the beachside terrace of the stylish, Arabesque Deira hotel, overlooking the same Mediterranean as forty miles north in Tel Aviv.

But neither the temporary construction boom nor the sudden sprouting of service industries could disguise the hole where Gaza's core economy had once been. For Gaza's once thriving and now stricken manufacturing industry, the expansion of consumer imports was either of no help or an actual setback. A case in point was the Gaza Juice Factory, which as a going concern in 2010 was a distinct rarity in Gaza. Forklift truck drivers were loading lorries with juice for dispatch to Gaza supermarkets. The shop floor had been kept scrupulously clean and well maintained; machinery gleamed; bottling machine handlers wore surgical masks and hair covering to maintain hygiene standards.

It's hard to think of a business which more graphically illustrated the economic history of the Strip over the previous twenty years than the Gaza Juice Factory. It was opened with considerable fanfare by Yasser Arafat, just three days after his triumphant return to Gaza from Tunis on 1 July 1994. This was a mere coincidence, but Arafat made the most of it, arriving in a convoy of ten military trucks and two stretched Mercedes with armed security men hanging out of the windows.[17] The factory, he announced, symbolised the 'reconstruction and development' that impoverished Gaza so badly needed.

The Gaza Juice Factory's opening was more than symbolic. It was originally conceived in 1988 by Rashed Shawa, a former mayor of Gaza City. His concern had been to find a way of exploiting a major surplus of oranges from the groves of Gaza, and his idea was to produce concentrate to export.

Gaza's orange groves, traditionally abundant, had long provided its most crucial export and by the mid-twentieth century were a vital economic lifeline. After 1967, however, citrus – and particularly oranges – gradually became another victim of the 'de-development' of Gaza. In the mid-1970s, Israel halted exports to Europe and Singapore via its own Citrus Marketing Board, and instead encouraged Gazans to concentrate on markets in the Muslim world.[18] By 2007, when Ayed Abu Ramadan, an urbane Egyptian-trained engineer from a well-known Gaza family, took over the factory, it was in deep trouble. The economic siege was tightening and the surplus of oranges the factory had been founded to exploit had turned into a shortage. The difficulties of exporting, the temptation of many farmers to abandon their fruit trees for jobs in Israel, efforts by Israel to persuade Gazan farmers to switch to strawberries for which Israeli demand outstripped supply, and the appropriation of land for Israeli settlements in Gaza were among many reasons for that decline.

Another reason that citrus was now in short supply was the large-scale bulldozing by the Israeli military of agricultural land, which, for example, virtually eliminated the orange groves of Beit Hanoun, where local farmers used to boast the sweetest fruit in the Middle East. According to Union of Agricultural Workers figures, 136,217 citrus trees were among the agricultural resources damaged or destroyed by the Israeli military in the 300-metre 'buffer zone' inside the border between 2005 and 2011.[19] According to the IDF, groves provided cover for the firing of rockets.

By 2007 the factory could no longer depend on local oranges, even if it had been possible to export the concentrate. It was now operating less than six months of the year. The factory was transferred to the Palestine Investment Fund, an offshoot of the Palestinian Authority run as a private company, and Abu Ramadan was appointed its CEO. He immediately saw 'strong points for us' in the siege due to the non-availability of most consumer goods from Israel, and began diversifying into products – jam, tomato ketchup, frozen vegetables and candied fruits – no longer easily obtainable in Gaza. And when he could source the fruit, either locally, from Israel when possible, or imported through the tunnels from Egypt, he manufactured juice or squash for the local market. None of this was easy. The 'subway tolls' – as Abu Ramadan delicately described payments made to tunnel operators and taxes levied by Hamas on imports like plastic bottles, machinery, spare parts, flavourings and fruit – were high.

Gazan ingenuity helped. Ibrahim Suweiti, the factory's highly skilled maintenance manager and chief production engineer for twenty years, and Mazen Qunduq, its resourceful mechanic, bought a second-hand bottling machine from Egypt which they shipped through the tunnels in pieces and assembled at the factory. But often they would visit equivalent Egyptian factories, taking cameras to photograph machines costing $20,000 to $30,000. 'And then I was creating the machines in Gaza for $5,000 or $6,000,' said Qunduq.

Then came the winter of 2008–9 and the concerted bombardment during Operation Cast Lead of selected factories lining the eastern road running parallel to the Israeli border. In the case of the Juice Factory, which ceased operating during the war, Israeli shells hit the evaporator – along with a huge eleven-compartment freezer, with a 2,000-ton capacity. Once again, the standard explanation of the Israeli military for the destruction of factories was that they had been used as rocket-firing bases by Hamas militants. But, said Abu Ramadan, 'everything was okay until two days before the end of the war when Israel started systematically destroying factories in the east. If there had been rockets [the militants] would have fired them early in the war and [Israel] would have destroyed the factories early in the war. All the destruction happened towards the end of the war.'[20]

But there was now another problem. The post-*Mavi Marmara* deal struck by Blair and Netanyahu, which had allowed a significant widening of the range of consumer goods brought in from Israel, had a perverse consequence for the Juice Factory. In 2007, Abu Ramadan's rationale had been to turn the blockade into an opportunity by manufacturing processed drink and foods unavailable in Gaza. Now juice was allowed in from Israel and the West Bank, which posed a direct competitive threat to the Juice Factory's lines. Abu Ramadan reduced the retail price of his flagship product, Tropika, to compete with imported juice. But this meant narrowing his margins even further. As

Abu Ramadan put it: 'This is like tying someone's hands up and telling him to get into the boxing ring.'

In early 2011, Hamas took over the factory from the Palestinian Investment Fund – or 'seized' it, in the PIF's words – installing a new board of directors answerable to its own economic ministry. The new owners wanted Abu Ramadan to stay, but he decided to resign after ensuring the factory was handed over 'in good order' and with all its existing workforce. The factory, and its workforce were intact. Its troubles were far from over. But for now it was still in business.

The takeover of the juice factory by the Hamas de facto government was another sign of its tightened grip on Gaza. Some of this was social; cafés or hotels allowing women to smoke shisha would find themselves visited by police, youth clubs would be told to stop programmes which included mixed dancing even by young children. An old 1936 law from the British Mandate was expanded to prohibit all sex outside marriage.[21] Sometimes a new dress code would mysteriously emerge, only to vanish again under protest. Schools in Gaza City, for example, would insist that female pupils wear *abayas* instead of the standard smock and jeans, apparently because of a government edict which the Hamas Education Ministry then denied had ever been issued.

Similarly, the de facto government denied any responsibility for – and indeed condemned – an attack in June 2010 by militants on the venue for the hugely oversubscribed summer games run for 250,000 children organised by UNRWA, and with which Hamas competed with its own quasi-military games. After the attack, John Ging, UNRWA's redoubtable Director of Operations, was visited by three fifteen-year-old girls pleading with him not to stop the games, in which children enjoyed supervised activities including the *dabka* (traditional Palestinian dancing), swimming, sandcastle building, bouncy castles, volleyball, football, painting and origami. The previous year the children had entered the *Guinness Book of Records* for flying the largest number of kites simultaneously. And, indeed, the 2010 games went ahead and were once again highly successful.

That said, the 2.30 a.m. attack, in which around twenty-five masked and armed men systematically vandalised the temporary site on the beach south of Gaza City after handcuffing and hitting the security guard, Ibrahim Eleiwa, had depressing overtones. As the vandals left, they tucked an envelope into Eleiwa's jacket containing three bullets and a letter in Arabic apparently intended as an ominous message for Ging: 'We were shocked when we heard about establishing beach locations for girls at the age of puberty and adolescence aiming to attack Muslims' honour and morality. You have to know that we will give away our blood and life but we won't let this happen and will not let you malicious people beat us. So you either leave your plans or wait for your destiny.' Eleiwa told the police he thought they were from Hamas; either way, Hamas security personnel, who in that period were mounting checkpoints across the Strip at night, did not prevent their free passage to the camp.

Whether or not Hamas adherents were responsible, such incidents were not calculated to endear the more secular-minded Palestinians to the regime. It was not the Taliban, or anything like it; women were educated in Gaza in large numbers, and the Strip did not feel like a police state; many Gazans remained openly critical, at least in conversation, of their government, often blaming Hamas for the dire economic conditions. But they were an added vexation for a people that had faced one catastrophic war and three years of siege and isolation.

Some of that vexation was expressed in late 2010 and early 2011 in a brief, peaceable revolt from Gaza's youth against the corrosive split between Hamas and Fatah. It was a popular cause. Many Palestinians blamed both factions for pursuing their own interests rather than those of Gaza's beleaguered civilian public. In December 2010, a group of young artists and professionals published a 'manifesto for Gaza's youth' which condemned the 'nightmare within the nightmare', as they termed a schism which they saw, with some justification, as severely undermining the Palestinian national cause.

Spurred by the Arab Spring, a demonstration for 15 March was organised through social media; instead of the slogan which had galvanised anti-Mubarak demonstrators in Cairo, 'the people wish to end the regime', they substituted another in Gaza: 'the people wish an end to disunity'. It was one of the biggest demonstrations since Hamas's takeover, bringing thousands of young people – some Fatah, but some non-aligned – onto the streets. The demonstration ended in clashes between protesters and Hamas supporters. One of the demonstrators' leaders was Assad Saftawi, a blogger, playwright and 'artivist', who claimed he had tried to stop protesters leaving the square because 'The Hamas youth had a plan . . . they were throwing stones and moving back, and we were going forward, so they were trying to lure the people. And they catch many people with this move. We tried to stop our people moving out of the square. The police arrested them and hit them. They had electric truncheons. They hit me maybe four or five times.'[22]

Hamas denied being behind the violence, saying on its website with carefully judged ambiguity that the demonstration had broken up after 'clashes between different youth groups'. The protest did not lead to the longed-for reconciliation between Fatah and Hamas.

Easily the most highly publicised event of 2011, both in Israel and in Gaza, was the prisoner swap that secured the release of Gilad Shalit on 18 October, after more than five years in captivity, in return for that of 1,027 Palestinian prisoners. Among the long-standing militants released in return for Hamas giving up Shalit were two involved in the abduction and murder of two Israeli soldiers in 1989,[23] and Yahya Sinwar, a founder of Hamas's military wing who in early 2017 was elected as leader of Hamas in Gaza, replacing Haniyeh. But the agreed list did not include Marwan Barghouti, who had led the Fatah militants during the Second Intifada and was seen by many as the ideal successor to Mahmoud Abbas. By suggesting that capturing a soldier was a more bankable means of securing prisoner releases than negotiation, the releases underlined Israel's tendency to make concessions to the Palestinians only under pressure, from whatever source. Faced with an irresistible public clamour for the release of Shalit, Netanyahu was agreeing to what his predecessors, Sharon and Olmert, had consistently refused to in negotiations with the anti-violence Mahmoud Abbas, and free prisoners with 'blood on their hands', including ones whose incarceration dated back to before the Oslo Accords. And by excluding Barghouti he was continuing to incarcerate the one figure who had the best chance of uniting the Palestinians and delivering a two-state solution to end the conflict, and who was seen even by some mainstream Israeli politicians as the 'best partner' for peace negotiations.[24]

There was widespread hope in Gaza that the deal might benefit the legitimate private sector through a major relaxation of the siege, particularly of exports. Both Netanyahu and his predecessor, Ehud Olmert, had linked the blockade's continuation with Shalit's captivity. The lifting of some import restrictions in 2010 had allowed the most determined manufacturers to start bringing in the raw materials they needed to function. In theory, the ban on exports was no longer supposed to be total, but in practice this had meant a handful of isolated – and pains-takingly negotiated – consignments bound for Europe, or in one case Saudi Arabia. But there was no permission for Gazan business to resup-ply what had long been its biggest markets, Israel and the West Bank. This did not change with Shalit's release. In the first five months of 2007, when trade had already slowed in the aftermath of Hamas's election victory, 4,769 loaded trucks left the Strip. In the same period of 2013, the number was eighty-one.

One of those who bucked the trend was veteran clothing manufac-turer Kamal Ashour, whose small family firm became the first in Gaza to export garments in five years. Ashour's Gaza City factory opened onto Izzedine al-Qassam Street, named, like Hamas's military wing, in honour of the Islamist *mujahid* who led the anti-Zionist, anti-Mandate Black Hand organisation and was shot dead by British police in 1935. In May 2012, he had just dispatched, after months of diplomatic traffic between Israel, the UK and the Middle East Quartet, 2,000 acrylic cardigans and polo sweaters to the British firm of JD Williams.

Ashour, a spry septuagenarian, was pleased to have secured the order. But he had no illusions it was going to be the first of many. In any case, what he really wanted to do was to start selling again to Israel, for decades the destination of eighty per cent of his produce. 'The Jews understand me very good. For business, Tel Aviv is better for me than London or New York,' he said, breaking into English with some passion. After Shalit's release in 2011, he used his coveted businessman's permit to visit his longest-standing Israeli customer's premises and drink tea with him. One of the Israeli's sons told his father: 'Look, Shalit's out. The crossings must open now. Kamal could produce ten thousand pieces for us.' At which point the clothier thrust a wad of 14,000 shekels (around £2,300) in banknotes into Ashour's hand as a down payment for just such an order. Through no fault of either businessman the order was never delivered.

This was all the more frustrating for Ashour because the easing of import restrictions after the *Mavi Marmara* episode had allowed him to bring in from Turkey the acrylic cloth to make his sweaters for export. It had also allowed the Gaza Music School to bring in instruments to replace those destroyed or damaged when the school was hit early in Operation Cast Lead. The Music School was another utterly unexpected Gaza asset. I visited it in January 2012, shortly after it had been designated one of the Edward Said network of conservatories. Inevitably there was a power cut on an afternoon already chilly and darkening. One student, Sara Akel, played on the piano two études by the Austrian composer Carl Czerny and a Bach Polonaise with such concentration and confidence it was hard to believe she was only twelve. Afterwards she said how much she loved the school and its teachers, several of whom were émigrés from the former Soviet Union who had married Palestinians. She wanted, she said, to become a professional musician. In Gaza? 'Why not?'

That unaffected 'why not?' felt like a rebuke to the underlying assumption that Gaza, with all its problems, was a cultural wasteland. As indeed was the school itself, a centre of artistic excellence to which fifty-two boys and seventy-three girls came three times a week after their normal school days for two sessions: one learning an instrument and another in musical theory. That afternoon we could hear from another room twenty or so young voices softening to near inaudibility before rising to a crescendo as they ran through their scales. Ibrahim Najar, the Conservatory's director, a music graduate of Cairo University and a maestro of the *qanun*, was at the piano coaxing his *solfège* class to extend their vocal range.

To get into the school, the students didn't need to have played an instrument before, but had to pass a highly competitive test in ear and rhythm. Then they could choose to learn a Western instrument, or, as many did, an Arabic one like the *oud* or the *qanun*. Eleven-year-old Adnan al-Ghalban explained succinctly why he had dropped the piano for the *qanun*. 'It talks better than the piano.' Another pupil, Feras Adas, a café owner's son who dreamed of becoming a famous guitarist, was optimistic that the attack which had damaged the school in the first wave of bombing in December 2008 would not be repeated. He had his own nine-year-old's view of the power of music to transcend enmities. 'I think it will not be hit,' he said cheerfully. 'The Jews like this kind of thing.'

Whether thanks to luck or judgement, Feras was right. The school survived the next war intact.

NOT MANY PEOPLE OUTSIDE ISRAEL OR the Occupied Territories would have noticed a limited escalation in the first half of November of the relatively low-level cross-border violence which had continued off and on since the end of Operation Cast Lead.[25] But on 14 November a missile fired from an Israeli drone killed the Qassam Brigades commander Ahmed Jabari as he drove through a quiet residential street in Gaza City. The assassination marked the beginning of Operation Pillar of Defense, the biggest aerial bombing campaign since Operation Cast Lead which was met by a barrage of retaliatory rocket and mortar fire from Gaza.

The reasons for Jabari's assassination were disputed. Whether authorised or not, negotiations were under way to end the escalation of the past few weeks when Israel launched its offensive. If this had borne fruit, Jabari would have signed off on it for Hamas. Indeed, Gershon Baskin, the Israeli peace activist in contact with Hamas's Ghazi Hamad over a putative prisoner swap for Gilad Shalit, claimed that Jabari had, twenty-four hours before his death, received the draft of a ceasefire agreement with Israel which Baskin had written with a Hamas interlocutor and which Israeli officials were waiting to examine. Either way the following week militants fired around 1,500 missiles, killing six Israelis. A few rockets, including Iranian Fajrs with a range of seventy-five kilometres, reached further than before including to Tel Aviv and the Jerusalem area; on the other hand, this was the first successful tryout for Israel's US-financed Iron Dome anti-missile system, which Israel said neutralised 421 rockets fired from Gaza. While casualty estimates varied, they all put the total Palestinian death toll during the eight days of Pillar of Defense at more than 150.

Defense Minister Ehud Barak said the operation was intended to establish 'deterrence' and deal a 'painful blow' to Hamas. Israel no doubt also wanted to dent Hamas's confidence that its star was rising, thanks to a potential ally in Egypt's new Muslim Brotherhood President Mohammed Morsi. Aluf Benn, editor-in-chief of *Haaretz* and an astute Israeli observer of the regional diplomatic/security scene, suggested yet a third motive. Declaring at the end of the war that since Israel, by choosing Jabari as a target, had killed its 'subcontractor in charge of maintaining Israel's security in Gaza', it was likely there was, not for the first time, an internal political reason for the operation; it would 'go down in history as another showy military action initiated by an outgoing government on the eve of an election'[26] – one called by Netanyahu for January 2013.

During the period of Pillar of Defense, Egypt was cooperating quite closely with the Obama administration in Washington. The Morsi government brokered a ceasefire which, on paper at least, was as good as Hamas could expect. The terms provided for a halt to targeted assassinations and Palestinian attacks, relaxation of restrictions on movement and trade and an opening of the crossings. No explicit mention was made of a requirement on Hamas to end arms smuggling, although the US announced its commitment to curbing weapons imports by Hamas, presumably with the cooperation of Egypt. Hamas's claims of a 'victory' were, if exaggerated, more plausible than after Cast Lead; the decline in its popularity in Gaza, where the ceasefire was met with celebrations, was probably arrested for the moment.

To the extent that the siege had been intended to dislodge, or even undermine, Hamas, it had been an abject failure. But it had been notably effective in depressing conditions for the rest of the population. In the words of UNRWA chief Filippo Grandi, the siege had 'completely obliterated' Gaza's economy.[27] The temporary tunnels/construction boom did not alter an unemployment rate among youth – the sector most susceptible to the recruitment overtures of the armed factions – by then running at 48.9 per cent.[28] The Strip had been, in the memorable summary of the World Bank, 'starkly transformed from a potential trade route to a walled hub of humanitarian donations'.[29]

11

'WELCOME TO THE BIGGEST PRISON IN THE WORLD'

FOUR ELEGANT, FAINTLY ART DECO MIRRORS painted by a local artist and depicting the Eiffel Tower, Big Ben, the Leaning Tower of Pisa and the Statue of Liberty, along with a large relief map of the world, decorated the walls of the Shurafa Travel and Tourist Company office in Gaza City. They were poignant reminders of the two busiest eras of Gaza's best-known travel agency: from 1952, when the late Hashem Shurafa founded it, to the Six Day War in 1967; and the tantalisingly hopeful post-Oslo years, from 1993 until the Second Intifada of 2000. That his mild-mannered son Nabil had managed to keep it open when Gaza was, as he put it, 'the big prison', was a triumph, if not of hope over experience, at least of Palestinian steadfastness.

We first met in July 2010, after Shurafa's first, modest break for more than three years. In the aftermath of the Israeli commando raid on the Turkish flotilla in late May, Egypt opened the Rafah crossing each day to avoid stigma attaching to its own involvement in sealing Gaza's borders. Shurafa broke off explaining the difficulties of being a travel agent in a territory where most people were forbidden to travel in order to take a call from one of his few customers, a bank employee booked on a Cairo–Damascus Egyptair flight at 2.30 a.m. the following day. 'You'll get the bus from Rafah at eleven,' he told him. 'Be sure to tell the [Egyptian] soldier that you have to be at the airport by 1 a.m. at the latest. The flight goes from terminal three.'

The man was one of about 150 Palestinians then managing to get to Egypt each day. When the deposed Hosni Mubarak was finally replaced as Egyptian President in 2012 by the more Hamas-friendly Muslim Brotherhood Mohammed Morsi, conditions at Rafah improved further, with passages through the crossing in each direction reaching around 40,000 a month, or 1,300 per day. But the impact of Morsi's fall after just a year was dramatic. In 2015, the first full year of Abdel Fattah el-Sisi's presidency, Rafah was open for just thirty-two days, with average monthly passages falling to 2,396.[1] By the summer of 2016, because there was so little certainty that a passenger would be let through, Shurafa had to wait for a phone call saying his customer was actually on the road to Cairo before confirming the flight.[2]

There was probably no better way of understanding the see-sawing impact of Gaza's turbulent history on its inhabitants' freedom of movement since the middle of the twentieth century than through the prism of this once flourishing family business. In the 1950s and early 1960s, with oil production rapidly expanding in the Gulf, the demand for well-trained Palestinian teachers as well as technicians increased. The agency became one of only two outlets in Gaza accredited by the International Air Transport Authority, and the only sales agent in the Strip for the old British Overseas Airways Corporation (BOAC). 'In those days, if a Palestinian bought a ticket directly at Cairo airport, the airline still sent the commission to us,' said Shurafa wistfully. 'They protected their agents. They don't do that now.' For around five years, after the Six Day War and the Israeli occupation of Gaza, the business slowed to a near-standstill. His father nevertheless kept it going, on a care-and-maintenance basis (a decision the son clearly regarded as a model for his own desperately lean period over the decade since Hamas took control of Gaza). After a blanket closure of Gaza was lifted by Israel in 1972, travel became possible again. Palestinians were able to go abroad, this time through the Erez crossing via Israel. Business started to pick up.

Although Israel gradually reimposed and tightened restrictions on Palestinians entering Israel from the early 1990s – requiring them for the first time to apply for individual permits – overseas travel abroad, especially by businessmen and Palestinian expatriate professionals, picked up in the wake of Oslo and the return of Yasser Arafat to Gaza. Shurafa Travel was awarded a 'Top Ten' certificate by British Airways for 'outstanding sales achievement' in 1996–7. Most thrilling of all was the opening of Gaza's short-lived Yasser Arafat International Airport in 1998, when US President Bill Clinton flew in to join Arafat at the ceremony. Shurafa was on the inaugural Palestine Airways two-hour Fokker 50 flight to Istanbul. 'An American reporter asked me what I felt before the flight left,' he recalled, 'and I said: "To you this may seem like a small airport but to me it seems bigger than JFK."' Although the airport stopped operating after the beginning of the Second Intifada and Israel bombed its runway in 2001, the PA manned the modern Arabesque terminal building for another five years, a prematurely ghostly relic of better days. Through the Second Intifada staff would even switch on muzak and signs announcing flights to Casablanca or Cairo for curious visitors.[3] But the terminal building was bombed by Israeli forces after the capture of Gilad Shalit in 2006, and Palestinian scavengers finished the job, leaving it little more than a pile of rubble.

The Second Intifada brought more closures, but it was after Hamas's enforced seizure of full control of the Strip in June 2007, and the subsequent near-total closure of both the main border crossings, Rafah and Erez, that the Shurafa family business was threatened with going under. Somehow Shurafa kept it going, and by 2016 he still stood by his earlier mantra: 'If I only thought about economics I would have closed down a long time ago. This is my country and this is a family business and this has helped us to resist the siege.'

That summer of 2016 you only had to go to Rafah on one of the rare days the crossing was open to see the pent-up demand for travel out of Gaza, and how far the occasional openings of the border were from meeting it. One hot June afternoon, when the Egyptians had opened the crossing for four days as a 'goodwill' gesture ahead of Ramadan, scores of families, children wedged among the piles of heavy suitcases, were packed into the main transit building outside the gates of the Rafah crossing, hoping to hear they had made it to the crucial first stage, a bus ride to the Palestinian terminal.

Most of those waiting that afternoon had arrived at or before dawn despite not being on the day's list of those to be admitted. Given that tens of thousands had registered their applications to leave Gaza – this was only the seventh day the border had been open since January – and that only a few hundred were likely to be allowed to cross, their chances were slim, to say the least. But they were determined to wait until closing time around 4 p.m., with little to distract them except for the nut and *tourmos* sellers who arrived wherever crowds gathered in Gaza, and the occasional loudspeaker announcement barking through the hubbub for named individuals to go inside to the counters.

In theory those allowed through were named on a list drawn up by the Hamas authorities from among the 30,000 registered applicants, with exit permits limited to medical patients, students and those with foreign residency or passports. In practice it was rather different. The previous day, six buses, each carrying between eighty and ninety passengers, had been turned back at the Egyptian terminal with promises that they would be admitted 'tomorrow'. But of 339 passengers who did get through, 149 were in a category called 'Egyptian coordination' – which meant, in the telling euphemism of Gisha, they were 'from a list that is not consistent with the priorities of the Palestinian Crossings Authority'.[4] In other words, they either had *wasta* (connections) with Egyptian officials or the money to bribe them. Egyptian immigration officers had the final say on who got through.

Mohammed Salah, forty-three, a Palestinian with an Egyptian passport, had been told by the Hamas authorities at the Khan Yunis stadium, where those trying to leave were first processed, that he would get through but his wife, Wissam, forty-one, and six children wouldn't. Yet the whole point of the trip was a farewell family visit to Wissam's father, who was dying in Cairo. 'I am the only one of his children not there,' she said. 'I haven't seen him for five years.' They had arrived at the stadium at 3.45 a.m. and, despite being told it was pointless, left in a taxi for Rafah at 9 a.m., and walked with all their baggage the mile from the checkpoint where the taxis stop to the crossing. Wissam's statelessness – she has no passport – had its origins deep in Gaza's pre-1967 history. Whereas Jordan, in control of the West Bank from 1948 until the Six Day War, offered its own passports to Palestinians, Egypt supplied Gaza residents only with an 'Egyptian travel document'. Wissam had begun to apply for a Palestinian ID, the first step to a Palestinian Authority passport, in 2008, but the process had been halted because of the war. Mohammed said: 'Both sides say it's the other's problem.' Now it seemed that Wissam's father would never see his daughter and Gazan grandchildren again. Had Mohammed, a former member of the PA presidential guard in Gaza, considered a bribe? 'No,' he said firmly. 'That would violate the rights of others.'

Not everyone was so scrupulous. Sitting on a row of chairs inside the immigration hall, the floor strewn with empty food packaging and plastic water bottles, a 26-year-old graduate student had paid a broker $2,000 to bribe Egyptian officials to put him on their list, an illegal but frequent practice. The student had been waiting for a year and a half to start his master's degree in law in Colombo, Sri Lanka. 'The problem is that whenever I have a visa for Sri Lanka, the crossing has been closed,' he said. 'This is the first time that Rafah has been open while I have a current visa. The visa runs out in thirty days.' The payment, from which the broker would take a commission, would only be made if he got through.

Rafah was such a focus of Gazan anxiety because of the extreme difficulty of getting out via Israel. Residents in the small minority with an Israeli permit first approached 4/4, the Hamas checkpoint, once a single container, now a fully manned border terminal with separate offices for Hamas's own *mukhabarat* (intelligence service) and interior ministry officials. They could not fail to notice two large graphic posters, anticipating an interrogation that might lie ahead: 'Be careful. Don't respect Jewish intelligence. If you are crossing the border for medical reasons they will say that if you help them they will help you. But trust in God will look after you and give your health, not the Israelis.' The second, overlooking the passport/ID check-in counter and vividly depicting a hyper-anxious Palestinian, one hand holding a telephone to his ear, the other rubbing his eyes with his fingers, as if regretting what he might have done, read: 'Beware of accepting an offer! Take care of your priorities: your livelihood, your treatment by God and your national honour. The future of your family and reputation is a priority over collaborating with the occupation.'

If cleared for travel, they took a Hamas-approved taxi the single kilometre to '*hamsa-hamsa*' (5/5), the much older terminal operated by employees of the Ramallah PA (because they alone could coordinate with their Israeli counterparts by telephone). They walked – or, if sick or lucky, took a tuk-tuk* or Turkish government-provided golf cart – another kilometre along a caged walkway to the border. To the right was the town of Beit Hanoun, to the left a desolate wasteland, worthy of a

---

* A motorised rickshaw of the kind brought into Gaza in large numbers through the tunnels from Egypt from the spring of 2010.

Paul Nash war landscape, all that was left of the old and once bustling Erez industrial zone. For several years after it had been levelled by Israeli armoured bulldozers to stop it being used as a rocket launching site, Palestinians with donkey carts had scavenged here for scrap metal and gravel while watching for birds flying out of the watchtowers on the nine-metre-high concrete barrier the traveller could now see ahead. The birds were a sure sign that a soldier had mounted the watchtower to shoot if the scavengers had come too close. Now there was nothing left to scavenge.

Finally, monitored by CCTV cameras, the travellers reached automatically operated steel doors, and then the turnstiles through which they had to squeeze with their baggage, marking their arrival in Israel's hangar-like 375,000-square-foot Erez terminal. Israel built it in 2005 at a cost of around $60m, just when it was disengaging from Gaza. A kind of monument to an unattainable future, it had all the hallmarks of an international border crossing capable of processing a theoretical 45,000 travellers instead of the tiny fraction of that number who were now allowed to pass through each day. Those who were allowed through came into minimal contact with Israeli border officials, who watched from behind armoured glass from a first-floor observation point, occasionally barking instructions through speakers. The automated steel doors and remotely operated conveyor belts for trundling luggage through X-ray equipment had a capacity way beyond what was needed. So, too, did the electrically operated high-tech revolving body scanners. Once through the final turnstiles and awaiting – sometimes for hours – an ID/passport check the traveller might or might not be taken for a Shin Bet interview.

By the spring of 2017, the numbers leaving through Erez had dropped to their lowest level for three years. True, after the fatal shooting of the Qassam Brigades commander Mazen Fukha in late March, Hamas itself stopped everyone leaving Gaza for ten days – while continuing after that to forbid Palestinians going to Erez for the special 'security interviews' Israel was increasingly demanding as a preliminary to the granting of permits. Gazans were, as they described it, 'caught between the two *mukhabarats*'. But this merely reinforced a steady downward trend imposed by Israel. Before the Second Intifada there were 500,000 passages through Erez per month; in February 2017 the number was 7,301. In 2016 the Israeli authorities had explained, 'Hamas has repeatedly tried to exploit travellers, including medical patients, and build up its terror infrastructure in Israel and the West Bank. Israel has no choice but to prevent the entry into Israel of Palestinians who are liable to harm state security and to endanger the security of its citizens.'[5]

It was hard to assail the logic of Israel, as an occupying power, in using its checkpoint to prevent those thought liable to carry out attacks from entering the country. But this explanation hardly did justice to such a spectacular reduction in permits. Indeed, Israel's own officials had long before suggested a broader reason: Eitan Dangot, then the military Co-ordinator of Government Activities in the Territories (COGAT), told a government meeting in 2012, for example, that a ban on families from Gaza visiting relatives held in Israeli gaols, introduced after the capture of Gilad Shalit, had been part of a government policy to 'separate' Gaza from the West Bank in order to pressure Hamas and support the Palestinian Authority.[6] By then Shalit had been freed and Dangot was responding to arguments by other Israeli officials that the problem of hunger strikes by gaoled Palestinian prisoners would be relieved by ending the ban.

Security was obviously one factor, though only one. Indeed, those likely to be refused permits included victims of Israeli military operations[7] – as well as businessmen who had had their factories destroyed[8] – on the grounds that they might be tempted to take revenge against Israelis. Bilal Abu Daher, a Gazan student, was disabled by being badly wounded during Operation Cast Lead, but he did not admit to this when applying for an exit permit for fear that it would ruin his chances of securing one.[9] Then a teenager, Abu Daher, from Juhr al-Dik, the central Gaza village closest to the Israeli border, fell from the third floor of his family's home when it was hit directly by tank shells. The resulting serious head injury left him unable to walk without a stick, his balance and speech badly impaired and with a tremor which made it impossible for him to write without help or drink without a straw. In December 2015 he was referred to the Makassed hospital in East Jerusalem for further rehabilitative treatment unavailable in Gaza, and was allowed through Erez without difficulty. A German volunteer doctor at the Jerusalem hospital examined him and scheduled neurosurgery for 14 March 2016. Then his problems began.

When he arrived again at Erez, travelling for the operation, he said, a woman officer told him he could not go to Jerusalem because the 'situation is not very good right now'. He said he had argued with her and she said: 'Go back to Gaza. Make Hamas treat you. Your relatives are Hamas and you are a terrorist.' He applied twice more for permits to go to the Makassed hospital and each time was rejected by the standard text message sent out by the Gaza office of the PA Civil Affairs Department (Israel refused to deal with Hamas officials). 'Dear Citizen, your request result. Bilal Abu Daher: your request has been rejected.'

Armed with his written referral from the Shifa hospital – 'severe head injuries since 2009 due to falling down from high. Right-brain stemmed contusion which leads to deep paraparesis left more than right. Difficulty of speech and other skills' – Bilal applied for another permit. He was told he would now need a 'security interview' by the Israelis. His fairly routine interview illustrated how Palestinian civilians seeking to leave Gaza found themselves embroiled in a war of nerves waged by both Israel and Hamas. Because Israeli intelligence officers ordered inter-viewees to hand over their mobile phones, so they could be checked for contacts and any information they might hold, Hamas security men routinely told them to hand their phones over to *them* to be returned later – a practice naturally well known to Israeli intelligence.

Abu Daher said he was 'interrogated' by Hamas at 4/4 by a man call-ing himself Abu Jalal, told to give up his mobile phone and warned only to give essential information to get him through the interview. Sure enough the Shin Bet man 'asked me for my phone. I said "I don't have a phone." He said "You've started to lie." I said I meant I don't have the phone with me. Hamas security have it.' It's hard to know whether Abu Daher's interrogator genuinely suspected that he was linked to the armed factions. Abu Daher said the Israeli then asked him to name 'all the prisoners you know who were released in return for Gilad Shalit'. 'I said: "I only know one person."' He was asked how many brothers he had. 'Five sisters, two brothers.' 'Leave the girls. Let's talk about the brothers, the terrorists. Which faction do they belong to?' 'None of them belong to the factions.'

When he was allowed to return to the Palestinian side, his ordeal was still not over. A Hamas internal security man grilled him about what information he had given. Abu Daher 'told him all the questions in the interview. But the man from the [Hamas] *mukhabarat* got angry and said he thought I was lying.' Eventually he was allowed to return home; by mid-2017 he had still not been allowed to cross.

In many cases it was hard to divine any 'security' motive.[10] After Hamas won the elections, Israel tried to exclude Gazan Palestinians from the West Bank. In 2009 Nisrin Jilo, a poor single mother of two children, aged four and twelve, who had moved from Gaza to the West Bank city of Qalqilya with her parents twelve years earlier, was living there happily until she was summarily deported in 2007 with her mother and younger sister after an Israeli soldier inspected their Gaza IDs at a checkpoint. Her own children and younger siblings remained in the West Bank with the extended Jilo family. Two years later, having moved from house to house to lodge with various relatives in Gaza, she was desperately missing her children, whom she could only afford to telephone twice a week. 'They only know me from the phone,' said Nisrin. 'They don't know my face, only my voice.' Just as distraught was her forty-five-year-old mother Kawkab, who cried as she described how her eleven-year-old daughter, Nisrin's sister Sabrin, who had made good progress at school before, had now flunked her year-end exams. 'She told me "don't be angry. I failed. I always think of you. When you get back I will pass."'

But there was also another motive for the movement restrictions – the recruitment of potential informers. Samir Abu Yusef left Gaza in 1994. After spending three years at an industrial training centre in Jericho, he settled in Qalqilya, where he married a local woman, Kawther, had four children, and established a carpentry business and a home. On his way back from a job in Israel he was ordered by border police to produce his ID card. A few hours later he was in the back of a military jeep speeding to the Erez crossing into Gaza. He said that at the crossing he had been told by a Shin Bet officer that if he collaborated with Israeli security forces he could rejoin his family. 'He said: "I don't want big things, just little ones like who's thieving and so on." But I knew this would only be the beginning. I refused.' Two years later he had still not seen his family.

The Erez crossing continued to prove an ideal place for attempts to recruit (or coerce) collaborators to undertake the dangerous task of spying on the militant factions. A typical case was that of twenty-eight-year-old journalist Bassam al-Wahidi. He described in a sworn affidavit how he was interrogated in late August 2007 over six hours, missing his surgical appointment at St John's hospital in East Jerusalem to save his right eye from retina damage, a procedure unavailable in Gaza. After arriving on the Israeli side, he was led to an interrogation room where a man speaking perfect Arabic introduced himself as Moshe and told al-Wahidi that if he did him a 'favour' Moshe would tell 'the big leaders in the Israel Defense Forces that al-Wahidi "was a good guy" and should be helped'.

The 'favour' Moshe asked of al-Wahidi was that he use his profession as a journalist to find out who was launching rockets and where, and to attend press conferences of factional military wings. He would be given an Israeli mobile phone chip to call a number with information. If he proved himself over ten days, he would be allowed to go through Erez 'with no permit' for treatment at the world-renowned Ichilov hospital in Tel Aviv. Moshe also hinted that al-Wahidi would get financial and other help. Al-Wahidi said that he would not cooperate and that he would go to human rights organisations, the Red Cross and the press. He said Moshe laughed, saying: 'What you are talking about does not exist in the dictionary of the IDF.' Al-Wahidi said that when he invited Moshe to arrest him or allow him out for medical treatment, he replied: 'I will send you back to Gaza and let you live the rest of your life blind because you are stupid.' Al-Wahidi was indeed sent back to Gaza and lost the sight in his right eye. By the time he was able to get out through Rafah to an Egyptian hospital he was told it was too late to save it.

More than nine years later, al-Wahidi, a Fatah activist, explained that because of the consequent strain on his left eye as well as incipient retinal problems, he now only had sixty per cent vision in his left eye. Moreover, he had started to develop serious muscle and bone pain – diagnosed as probable osteoporosis – caused by treatment of his eye with cortisone. Oddly, he had found no problem in recent years getting Israeli permits – eight in all covering a total period of eight months – to travel to Ramallah in connection with his work as a member of the PA President's social development team in Gaza. Then suddenly the permits stopped again, just when he most needed one. Because of his bone disorder he was referred to the West Bank An-Najah University hospital in Nablus. He was given three appointments, in January, March and Aril 2017 and each time was refused, as usual without a reason. Al-Wahidi, now married with two children, said that, looking back, he did not regret what had been a 'hard decision' to refuse Moshe. Conscious that his case was not extreme he said it might be much harder for others – for example, for the parent of a sick child.

The fear of confrontations with Israeli intelligence heightened the tension felt by almost all Palestinians seeking to leave through Erez. When Mariam Dawwas, a strong-willed modern languages graduate, was invited to join a 'Seeds of Peace' programme in New York, involving dialogue between young Palestinians and Israelis in January 2013, she was obliged to go to Erez for a security interview in order to get her US visa at the American consulate in Jerusalem. It would be hard to imagine a Gazan less likely to generate suspicion; but when she got to the Israeli side of Erez a soldier insisted she strip to her underwear and have a metal detector pass over her body, 'including the sensitive parts'.[11] She was taken out of the terminal complex through an underground passage decorated with portraits of Palestinian leaders, including Arafat and Ahmed Yassin, with big Xs stamped on them and abusive terms like *sharmuta* (whore) and 'fuck you' in Arabic and English. She was then left in a dark room for half an hour, which she took to be a form of psychological intimidation. She was photographed holding a card with an ID number like a 'prisoner' before being taken into another room for questioning.

Mariam was most afraid of being asked by her Shin Bet interrogator to become a collaborator 'and if I refused, I was afraid that they would force me to do so'. Her fears may have been exaggerated but they were not irrational. There was none of the threatening tone in the interview there had been in the al-Wahidi or the Abu Daher cases; indeed, if anything, the interrogation afforded a glimpse of the 'softly-softly' approach that Shin Bet adopted with such applicants. Consistently polite, the intelligence officer offered her coffee and food (which Mariam refused), told her she had done 'nothing wrong' and they had nothing 'on her'. He asked about her local mosque, whether she knew people in Hamas and Fatah, and whether she had dealings with the Islamic student society at al-Azhar University, where she was studying. To all of this she replied that she took no part in politics. The Shin Bet man hinted he could help her to study for an MA degree abroad and she could return to work in an 'international organisation', cooperating with Israel in the meantime. Mariam refused, telling him: 'You see what I'm going through to, just to go to Jerusalem. It's not possible to continue this way. Something will blow up or explode.'

She was kept waiting for another two hours, so that it was too late to get to the US consulate before it shut. By the standards of many interrogations, Mariam's experience was among the mildest. Once allowed out, she acquired her US visa with ease. She had not compromised, yet she still regarded the day as 'the worst of my life' and elected to make the actual trip to the US through Rafah, then relatively easy with Morsi still in power, rather than risk a repeat performance at Erez.

Understanding Gaza's history, she pointed out that things had been different in the years after the Six Day War, long before she was born. Moshe Dayan had said 'something really important. He told the people, the Israelis, don't make Palestinians feel like they are occupied. He said open the borders, let them work, let them get money, okay, don't let them feel that they are occupied. What's happening now is the opposite, you know, the hate for it is growing. You know, as long as separation is still here and the borders are closed, and you keep on killing the Palestinians in Gaza and you're making their life impossible, then no one will ever accept the Israelis or the Jews.'

Mariam was right to point out that the draconian controls on Palestinian movement to and from Gaza meant conditions were as different from Dayan's 'invisible occupation' as possible, not least in severing so many of the contacts that once existed between its residents and Israelis (not to mention with Palestinians in the West Bank, which the Oslo Accords reaffirmed was part of the same entity as Gaza).

The prohibition which had been imposed since then on students doing postgraduate work (let alone their first degrees) in Israel or the West Bank (the latter ban drawing a joint protest from four leading Israeli universities to their government) made study abroad all the more attractive. This, too, became much more difficult once Hamas controlled Gaza. The waits, including for students with visas and often scholarships from the host countries, could be long, even indefinite. The environmental studies graduate Wissam Abujwa had won a place at Israel's Arava University to do his MA in 2000, only to be prevented from taking it up when the Second Intifada broke out in September. Eight years later he finally got an Israeli permit to leave for an alternative place at Nottingham University's world-class school of chemical and environmental engineering, and only because there had been a high-profile British campaign spearheaded by students at his university. The smile on his face as he finally had the permit in his hand at Erez was as striking as the dignified, almost formal way in which he marked the occasion. 'I am glad that the UK Government and Mr Kim [the then

Foreign Office Middle East Minister, Kim Howells] intervened, and I am happy the Israelis responded to that,' he said. He also thanked Tony Blair, the Middle East envoy; Gisha; the Nottingham vice-chancellor; and the *Independent* newspaper for highlighting his case. But he added: 'There are perhaps seven hundred students in there still waiting who didn't have the British government working for them, who aren't getting any help as I did.' A perverse aspect of Israel's draconian closure was that in a way it suited some in Hamas; by contributing to what the businessman Jawdat al-Khodary had called the 'mental siege', it kept to a bare minimum the exposure of young people to the kind of foreign secular influences which might lead them to challenge Hamas's social and political attitudes.

For the young people themselves, it felt relentlessly oppressive. This being Gaza, when in 2016 Israel facilitated a highly publicised operation to rescue an ailing lion and other animals from the bankrupt Khan Yunis zoo, there was a blizzard of social media comment of the 'lucky lion' variety. A few months earlier, Fr Mario da Silva, Brazilian parish priest for Gaza's tiny Latin [Roman Catholic] community of Palestinians, had breathed new spiritual life into the most common metaphor Gazans use about the Strip. Welcoming from the pulpit of the Holy Family church a delegation of visiting bishops from Britain and elsewhere, he remarked that Pope Francis had designated 2016 as 'the year of mercy'. Observing that prison visiting was one of the Church's seven 'corporal acts of mercy' Fr Mario added: 'I thank you for visiting the biggest prison in the world.'

As in a conventional prison, some of the inmates decide to break out. It was hardly surprising when a survey in 2016 found that forty-six per cent of Gazans wanted to emigrate for good, compared with less than a quarter in the West Bank.[12] There had been a surprising number of Gazans – perhaps as many as 200 – among the desperate 500 refugees who drowned off the coast of Malta in September 2014 when their overcrowded fishing boat was rammed by a bigger one. They had made the fateful Italy-bound voyage from Damietta in Egypt after being smuggled through the tunnels under Rafah.[13] Then there were the fence jumpers, who reached record numbers in 2015, when Israeli security forces arrested 249 Palestinians who had climbed over or through the heavily patrolled perimeter fence into Israel, compared to only nineteen the year before. Alex Fishman, military analyst of the Israeli daily

Yedhioth Ahronoth, wrote: 'Most infiltrators captured in 2015 are job seekers, people willing to risk their lives just to make a living.'[14]

Faris Sanaa, had twice – in April and August 2012 – clambered over the fence near his home in the Bureij refugee camp at around 4 a.m. with three friends. The first time, he said, 'we started to run. We had no idea what direction to go in.' By about 7 a.m. they found themselves near what seemed to be an army base. After questioning, they were returned by Israeli troops to Erez. The second time, the group at least took the precaution of consulting Google Earth, but they were still spotted a few metres from the fence by soldiers in a jeep. This time they were transferred after questioning to the gaol at Beersheba. At Sanaa's trial, he was sentenced to eleven months. Gaol had its problems, but overall the food was good and he earned between 200 and 300 shekels a month working in the factory, packing cleaning towels, sheets and floor mops, which he spent on cigarettes and food in the canteen shop. The PA also paid 400 shekels a month to the families of Palestinian prisoners in Israeli gaols. Life, he felt, was 'better' in prison than in Gaza – 'everything is available there'.

It will probably never be clear whether similar motives played any part in another break-out, one that briefly became a cause célèbre in Gaza at the end of 2015. The Hassan family had, like tens of thousands of other Palestinians, watched with mounting horror pictures on the Hamas-run al-Aqsa TV of Egyptian soldiers shooting dead an unarmed Palestinian in the sea at Rafah on the evening of 24 December 2015.[15] The sequence showed a naked man first walking purposefully, with just a momentary glance towards land, south through the surf into Egyptian waters then, as shooting began, plunging headlong into the knee-high shallows, floundering, before being buffeted, apparently lifeless, by the waves. Throughout this episode, lasting about a minute, you could see the little white splashes thrown up by at least twenty-eight bullets. The camera showed a bearded and anorak-clad Hamas border policeman on the beach, gesticulating to the Egyptian troops who appeared to be firing from their concrete watchtower just inside the border. At one point the Hamas man twirls his hands by the side of his head to indicate the supposed craziness of the victim. In another segment, three Egyptian soldiers unceremoniously carry the corpse up the beach, its nakedness a powerful reminder that the victim had posed zero threat.

What did not occur to Khalil and Amna Hassan was that the man they had been watching was their own twenty-eight-year-old son, Ishaq. He had not come home as usual after his English class and hadn't answered his mobile, but his family assumed that he had been at a local wedding party or staying with friends or another sibling. It was only when he had still not returned home in the early hours and they had called the local police and the hospital that the shocking truth emerged.[16]

The Hamas policeman who had tried to signal to the trigger-happy Egyptians, Bilal al-Amar, explained that Ishaq had been among a group of people watching an Egyptian team a couple of hundred metres down the coast filling tanks to flood the smuggling tunnels as President Sisi had ordered. It was then that Ishaq had taken off his shirt and walked into the sea; then, once in the water, he removed his trousers and pants.

Ishaq was unemployed, though he often helped out in the small shop run by one of his brothers. In 2007 he had been wounded in crossfire as he walked home one night, just as the Fatah–Hamas violence was reaching its bloody climax, an injury that caused him frequent pain. His mother said: 'He was depressed, but not to the extent that I ever thought he would do something like that.'

The day before his death Ishaq had stayed overnight in Rafah with his much-loved married thirty-four-year-old sister Nadia Khatila and her children. The following morning she thought he was going back to Gaza City. He kissed the children goodbye and told them he would bring them some sweets next time.

This was a very Gazan tragedy. At the desolate stretch of beach where it happened, the very south-east corner of the Mediterranean, you could see jutting into the sea a disused, rusting metal grid erected by the Israelis long before disengagement; Ishaq had easily walked through it into Egyptian waters. Al-Amar said he had shouted to Ishaq to come back but he ignored him. And then in a few seconds the shooting had started, shooting that would have had al-Amar in its sights had he tried to manhandle Ishaq out of the water.[17] As the policeman described what had happened, we were watched by curious and grinning Egyptian soldiers through the very turrets in the watchtower from which Ishaq had been shot.

Whatever the underlying cause for Ishaq's behaviour nothing could obscure the brutality with which Egyptian soldiers repeatedly shot a defenceless Palestinian, and with apparent impunity. He could surely have been arrested rather than shot, never mind shot as many times as he was. The episode starkly demonstrated that Egypt was capable of enforcing Gaza's incarceration as ruthlessly as Israel. For many appalled Palestinians his death briefly became a symbol of the thwarted desire for freedom harboured by a generation isolated from the rest of the world by Gaza's heavily patrolled and walled-in borders.

12

'LET'S NOT DIE TOGETHER': OPERATION PROTECTIVE EDGE, 2014

IT WAS POSSIBLE THAT ELEVEN-YEAR-OLD MOHAMMED al-Rifi's temperament – headstrong, boisterous, mischievious – would help him through his lifelong ordeal. He lay on his side in al-Wafa hospital paralysed from the neck down – in the opinion of his doctors permanently – and dependent on a ventilator for breathing. It was almost two years after an Israeli aerial missile attack during Operation Protective Edge had smashed his spine and killed his father, his twin brother Omar and four cousins.

Extraordinarily, Mohammed's intelligence and personality remained what they were before his world was overturned in a second. When he was referred to al-Wafa, Gaza's only hospital for medical rehabilitation, in November 2014, his 'cranial abilities', in the clinical language of an official report, 'were normal and there were no signs of cranial nerve affection; almost normal swallowing and he was receiving a regular oral diet. He communicated both verbally (laboured speech, short responses of two words max. at once) and by facial and head gestures.' By 2016, speech still wasn't easy for him but that did not affect his willingness to chat. His favourite subject was maths, he said, but complained that his English teacher only came once a week. 'I would like to learn more English. I know words related to the hospital like hypobaric oxygen and pulse oximeter.'[1] He said he hoped one day to be a doctor, and had enjoyed a recent visit to the beach with other patients. Asked what he remembered about that terrible day, he was matter-of-fact: 'I don't remember anything before or after. My aunt didn't tell me for two months that my father and brother had been killed. There were nine of us and seven died.' How did he react when his aunt told him the truth? 'I cried.'

His uncle Tareq's memory was clearer. Less than a week before the end of Operation Protective Edge, nine members of the al-Rifi family had set out in a tuk-tuk for the four-minute ride to the 150-square-metre patch of land they owned in the al-Nafaq area of Gaza City, to irrigate their fruit trees. The neighbourhood was quiet, no different from during the previous day's ceasefire, and two of the three brothers on the trip, Nasser, thirty-seven, and Tareq, forty-one, brought their boys along for the outing. Once there, the children ate some fruit in the shade of a fig tree. Tareq remembered hearing a drone in the sky; then two missiles struck. 'After the bombing everything seemed so calm . . . No one knew we were there.' He tried to reach his phone to call for help. 'I tried to crawl but it was so hard. I saw my brothers were badly injured, and the children too. I thought I was going to die. I just gave up and started saying the *Shahada*.* I don't know how long I was there. I thought about death, and then there was someone searching [local residents hearing the explosion had come to the scene]. I tried to say the *Shahada* more loudly so they would hear me.'[2]

Tareq's injuries included damage to his liver and intestines, a badly fractured left elbow and permanently impaired hearing and vision. But the news he heard by degrees as he slowly began to recover in his bed at Shifa hospital was far worse. Two of his sons, Ahmed, three, and Maram, seven, had been killed instantly, along with his brothers, Nasser (Mohammed's father) and Mohammed (his uncle). Then, as the war ended, his two remaining sons, Abdullah, six, and Ziad, ten, died from their injuries, leaving his daughter Dina, then a year old, as his sole surviving child.

Two years later, he was still trying to make sense of what happened. 'I can't find an explanation. Later I heard that there had been a place near the land where people had been firing rockets. During the war we'd

---

* The central declaration of Muslim faith: 'There is no god except God, and Muhammad is the Messenger of God.' Many Muslims believe a dying person who says it will enter paradise.

been going back and forth and nothing had happened. If I had thought it wasn't safe, we wouldn't have taken the children.' Nor was this unusual; while no civilian would sensibly go too close to the border or near a rocket landing site, people did travel around the city during the war. Moreover, according to PCHR, residents of other areas who had been given Israeli warnings to leave their homes had been advised that the al-Nafaq area was safe. Tareq added: 'We are Muslims. We have faith. We believe in God. We believe when a person is born it's all written. This is a test from God that we can't argue with. We can make efforts to do things but what is written is going to happen. I lost four children. I cannot question God "why did you do this?" He does everything for a reason.'

Mohammed's mother, Heba – now widowed with four young children – heard the explosion from her apartment on the fateful morning, but thought nothing of it 'because we have nothing to do with Fatah or Hamas or any of the factions'. Her sister-in-law Ragda had been washing dishes when a friend phoned. 'She knew, but she didn't know how to break the news.' The friend casually asked how Ragda's brothers were. 'I said "they're on our land", and she said: "are you sure they're OK?" Then, after a few minutes, the friend called back again and said: "are you sure your brothers are OK?"' Ragda now understood 'there was something she didn't want to tell me'. So she ran to the land to discover her brothers and nephews had been hit.

Hundreds of conversations like this, with people uncertain how to tell their friends, neighbours and relatives that they had been bereaved, had happened, in one form or another, for the forty-six days the war had already been going on. The deaths of the al-Rifi family attracted little publicity; it was just another lethal incident after scores of others, many involving much larger numbers of casualties. Estimates varied slightly, but at least 2,202 Palestinians were killed during the fifty-one days of war, 1,391 of them non-combatants according to B'Tselem.[3] Mohammed was only one of more than 350 children the UN said were permanently disabled. Ten times as many were physically injured, and the number psychologically traumatised incalculable.

Partly because Hamas was militarily better prepared, casualties among Israeli soldiers were much higher than in Operation Cast Lead: sixty-six. Five Israeli civilians were also killed. An operation in which the IDF launched more than 6,000 airstrikes and fired more than 14,500

tank shells and 19,000 explosive artillery shells resulted in 8,000 housing units and seventy-two medical facilities, along with water mains
and power lines, wholly or partly destroyed, and many ambulances
damaged. At its peak 500,000 people had to flee their homes, a large
proportion taking shelter in UN schools,[4] as it was impossible to escape
altogether; 53,000 people had been unable to return to their homes two
years after the end of the war.[5] The economic impact was judged by
Gaza's prominent economist Omar Shaban to be three times that of
Operation Cast Lead, including at least 350 factories destroyed.[6] As
with Cast Lead, the operation started with heavy aerial bombardment
on 8 July 2014, followed by a ground invasion which began on 16 July.
Most Israeli ground forces left Gaza on 3 August, but, despite a series of
short-lived ceasefires, broken by one side or the other, the conflict did
not end until a final Egyptian-brokered ceasefire on 26 August.

The 2014 war might have been avoided partly thanks to an unusually
positive development in Palestinian politics. On 2 June 2014 Fatah and
Hamas formed a new 'consensus' government of independent 'techno-
crats'. In April when the two factions had announced their intentions,
Benjamin Netanyahu swiftly accused the moderate anti-violence Abbas
of aligning himself with 'terrorists' and tried to persuade Israel's Western
allies to fall into line. Instead the EU and even the US, who had originally criticised the agreement, cautiously welcomed it while deciding to
'wait and see' how it played out in practice. The pact was more favourable
to Fatah than Hamas, a reflection of the latter's severely weakened position. First it had been alienated from Iran and obliged to leave Damascus
in 2012 after coming down against Bashar Assad's murderous suppression of Syrian rebels. Then, in 2013, Egypt's Muslim Brotherhood
President Mohammed Morsi fell, to be replaced by Abdel Fattah el-Sisi,
who was even more hostile to Hamas than Mubarak had been. In Gaza,
where the agreement that had ended the eight-day 2012 bombardment
had not fulfilled hopes of easing the siege, conditions were made even
harder by Egypt's closure of Rafah, and systematic flooding and destruction of the smuggling tunnels. One of Hamas's primary hopes out of a
new deal with Abbas was that the PA would pay the salaries of its own
public employees in Gaza; as a *quid pro quo* it was prepared to see PA
forces return to Gaza – for example at the crossings – under the auspices
of a cabinet which, while nominally independent, leaned much more to
Fatah than Hamas. This might have been an opportunity for Abbas to

begin reasserting control in Gaza by an agreement with a weakened Hamas. It also made yet another Gaza war less inevitable. But it would have militated against Netanyahu's systematic separation of Gaza from the West Bank and undermined one of the arguments on the Israeli right against negotiating on a Palestinian state with Abbas, namely that there was no point as long as Hamas ran Gaza and Abbas did not represent the Palestinians as a whole. Instead Netanyahu refused to allow the transfer of PA funds to pay the Hamas employees, until he had a change of heart in October 2014, two months after the war had ended. Before the war his aides told a US diplomat that Abbas's willingness to strike a deal with Hamas meant there was 'no difference between him and the terrorists' – the reason Netanyahu now used to resist pressure from US Secretary of State John Kerry to get back into talks.

But an unexpected event horrified Israel less than a fortnight after the Hamas–Fatah pact was concluded: the kidnap and murder of three Israeli teenagers, Naftali Fraenkel, Eyal Yifrah and Gilad Shaar, as they were hitch-hiking in the West Bank. Having located the car in which the teenagers had been picked up by two Palestinians, the security services had evidence, including bullets from the car, which strongly suggested the boys had been killed soon after their abduction. But they refrained from making it public until the boys' bodies were found over a fortnight later. Netanyahu ordered a comprehensive sweep of the West Bank and the arrest of hundreds of Hamas activists, including fifty-eight of the ex-prisoners who had been released in the swap for Gilad Shalit in 2011, a measure Hamas believed violated the terms of the agreement after the 2012 Operation Pillar of Defense. Netanyahu was also at pains to say that 'sadly' the abduction – for which he repeatedly blamed the Hamas leadership – 'illustrates what we have been saying for months, that the alliance with Hamas has extremely grave consequences', as if the reconciliation deal had somehow caused the murder.[7] In fact the PA had cooperated closely with Israel's hunt for the perpetrators. The arrests did not help to locate the dead teenagers; indeed, while a Hamas-affiliated cell in Hebron was almost certainly responsible, the view of both the police and Shin Bet was that the abduction had been a local freelance operation and that the Hamas leader Khaled Meshal was telling the truth when he said that it had not been ordered by the leadership.[8] But the crisis in the West Bank escalated when three Israelis kidnapped a sixteen-year-old Palestinian boy, Mohammed Abu Khdeir, from a street in East Jerusalem where he lived, ostensibly in retaliation for the kidnapping of the Israeli teenagers, and later murdered him by burning him alive. Inflamed by the killing, and also by the earlier cooperation given by Abbas's PA security forces to their Israeli counterparts, angry Palestinians took to the streets in demonstrations across the West Bank; in solidarity, factions other than Hamas fired rockets into Israel from Gaza. And after 6 July, when an Israeli bombing raid killed seven militants, Hamas began firing rockets of its own; on 8 July, Israel launched Operation Protective Edge.

By now faced with its own political weakness and an ever tightening siege, Hamas apparently saw the war as its only chance to escape from its predicament – and just possibly secure an easing of the blockade – after the failure of the unity government to deliver. The Israeli State Comptroller's report on the war, published on 28 February 2017, devoted much space to the lack of information given to ministers about the threat from Hamas tunnels. But the more important section was his finding that this had been a disaster waiting to happen. The independent Comptroller, whose job it is to review aspects of government policy, made clear that the Cassandra in the story was Eitan Dangot, the head of COGAT, who as early as April 2013 had warned a Cabinet meeting that Gaza's economic and humanitarian crisis could explode within two years. Yet there was no ministerial meeting to discuss just that between Dangot's warning and the war breaking out. The Comptroller, Joseph Shapira, also complained that there was no attempt to resolve the mounting crisis by diplomatic means. And, most breathtakingly of all, he quoted – *three* times in case anyone missed it – the then Defense Minister Moshe Yaalon musing at a meeting in his office two days *after* the war broke out – and had another forty-eight days to run: 'If Hamas's distress had been addressed a few months ago, Hamas might have avoided the current escalation.'[9] It was hard not to conclude that if Netanyahu and Yaalon had not wanted the war – for example, as a means of sabotaging the Hamas–Fatah reconciliation deal – they had sleepwalked into it.

Gaza has had an extraordinary capacity to generate massive newspaper and global TV coverage during Israel's periodic large-scale military operations. The summer of 2014 was no exception, even though the ground invasion, after more than a week of aerial bombardment, immediately followed the downing over Ukraine of the Malaysian airliner MH17 by a Russian-made missile which killed all 253 passengers on board.[10] But equally striking is the speed with which Gaza drops from the headlines once the warfare is over. This belies the lasting importance of the 2014 offensive.

As Harvard's Gaza expert Sara Roy has said, the war 'profoundly changed the way people think. Perhaps most significant is the sense of collective dread and desperation that permeates the Strip, more keenly felt than ever before.' The reason, she observed, was not so much the war itself but the 'inhuman conditions' in Gaza, which remained unchanged after it.[11] Instead of the war ending with a bankable agreement that would guarantee an easing of the blockade, it left those conditions if anything worse than before. And Operation Protective Edge created yet another cohort of Gaza's overwhelmingly youthful population whose formative childhood memory – and only knowledge of Israelis – would be a terrifying fifty-one-day onslaught by their neighbour's tanks, artillery, drones and F16s.

As with Cast Lead, it was hard to see a winner. Hamas declared the 'victory of the resistance';[12] Netanyahu hailed the operation as a military and diplomatic success which had inflicted on Hamas 'the greatest blow since it was founded'[13] and revelled in goals which Hamas had failed to achieve in the ceasefire agreement that ended the war: an airport, a seaport, the release of the Hamas prisoners freed in the 2012 agreement and rearrested after the abduction of the three murdered teenagers. Yet Hamas had failed to end the siege and Israel had failed to extinguish Hamas as a military and political force. True, the post-Protective Edge ceasefire, strongly enforced inside Gaza by Hamas, showed a record low number of rockets fired in the subsequent two years – a mere thirty-five, and those mainly by Salafist groups. Israel can claim this was a deterrent effect of the operation; indeed, that is one hawkish view of how it goes in Gaza: every few years, in the phrase used by the cheerleaders of Israeli force, it is necessary to 'mow the grass' to ensure relative calm. Until the next time.

For the operation did little to destroy the faction's defensive – and offensive – capacity that could not be reversed. Tunnels are a case in point. Underground passages, like the one from which Gilad Shalit's abductors emerged in 2006, had long been used for operations by Gaza militants. The destruction of thirty-two tunnels that extended into Israel was proclaimed as a central achievement of the 2014 war. Such tunnels understandably strike deep into the Israeli psyche, conjuring the prospect, however unrealistic, of large numbers of heavily armed militants charging freely into southern Israel, and were probably the biggest single factor to guarantee overwhelming public support for the war among Israelis, which averaged at ninety-five per cent according to polls by the Israeli Democracy Institute.[14]

Yet afterwards Hamas quickly set about rebuilding the tunnels (at the incidental cost of the lives of at least a dozen or more young Palestinians recruited by the Qassam Brigades to dig them, when they periodically collapsed while under construction). Indeed, in 2017 the Israeli military began work on a massive underground barrier to forestall their use.[15] In addition, an extensive network of tunnels under Gaza itself enhanced Hamas's guerrilla capabilities to retreat and surprise, and helped deter Israeli ground forces from penetrating the urban Gaza Strip as far as they had done in 2008–9. And despite Egypt's concerted operation against the separate smuggling tunnels under the Rafah border, Hamas retained enough of them to continue importing weaponry through the northern Sinai – including longer range rockets, which in 2014 were capable of reaching Israel's largest cities. This calls into question whether, even judged narrowly by Israel's own interests, the cost to the grieving families of civilians killed in communities along the Gaza border and sixty-six soldiers was worth it. Or the monetary price it paid in billions of shekels spent on a war that, without a political solution, showed every sign of being repeated in the future.

Thirdly, and perhaps even more sharply than Cast Lead, it exposed the uneasy silence of the international community as it watched the steady undermining of its own policy on the Israeli–Palestinian conflict. Indeed, that silence, or at least the refusal to condemn the mounting civilian death toll at the hands of one of its allies, provoked the UK's Conservative Foreign Office minister Baroness Sayeeda Warsi into resigning her post. The Obama administration would probably have backed a ceasefire on the 2012 terms,[16] yet in public it, and its European allies, were mainly reduced to parroting the mantra that 'Israel has a right to defend itself' against Hamas. That disjunction was illustrated by an ironic off-camera remark by US Secretary of State John Kerry on 20 July, after the most severe of the incursions into Gaza City, in the eastern neighbourhood of Shujaia. The IDF, after encountering serious Hamas resistance that resulted in the deaths of thirteen soldiers, unleashed a massive barrage of artillery and mortar fire which, according to UN figures, killed fifty-five civilians in six hours. 'That's a hell of a pinpoint operation,' Kerry told an aide who reported the episode to him.[17] While Kerry used his best efforts to bring an early end to the war, his ability to do so was, as usual, severely hampered by the bar on all US/EU contacts with Hamas. Mediation was left to the Sisi government in Egypt, which was as anxious as Israel not to see Hamas accrue any political advantage from the war. Back in Shujaia itself meanwhile, on the first day of the normally joyful festival of Eid al-Fitr – 29 July, in 2014 – still-dazed residents returned to the scene of the battle, stumbling across mountains of rubble that had been their homes to retrieve what possessions they could find, a blanket here, an unopened bag of nappies there.

Generally the IDF's rules of engagement followed those of Cast Lead, though Protective Edge was far longer and caused many more casualties. But one difference was the number of residential buildings struck while their inhabitants were in them, often asleep. B'Tselem examined seventy strikes on Gaza and pointed out this was a *prima facie* violation of humanitarian law, which requires that, to qualify as a military target, a building 'must make an effective contribution to military action, and harming it must give the attacking party a clear military advantage'.[18] Nor was it enough that a member of an armed faction lived there to exempt the party from an obligation to protect civilian life, B'Tselem argued. Early in the war, the IDF defended some such bombings by explaining that they were the houses of militants; while rarely explaining specific cases, it more latterly described them as 'control and command' centres for the armed factions, or serving some other military role.

It seems unlikely that the home of fifty-one-year-old Mahmoud Lufti al-Haj in the Khan Yunis refugee camp was playing such a role when it was one of the first inhabited homes to be flattened at around 1.20 a.m. on 10 July, apparently by two F16 bombs, which killed al-Haj, his wife, and six of their children, aged between fourteen and twenty-nine. Al-Haj's son Nasser, twenty-five, survived only because he was walking back after chatting with friends about 500 metres away, having been warned by a neighbour to get home because of the drone humming like a giant electronic mosquito in the sky above. One of his brothers, Omar, was later identified by a research agency with close links to Israeli intelligence as a member of the Qassam Brigades.[19] Assuming this is correct, at twenty he is unlikely to have been a senior figure. The other family members were civilians. Three weeks later, as Israel's bombardment and ground invasion continued, the melancholy debris of the al-Hajs' domestic life was still scattered amid the mountain of rubble to which their home had been reduced: tomatoes by now rotting in the sun, a sandal, a cheese grater. In an exercise book decorated with roses, twenty-year-old Asmaa al-Haj, a biology major at Gaza's al-Azhar University, who had been killed in the strike along with her parents and five siblings, had written in neatly legible English: 'An empirical formula is a mathematical equation which predicts observed results but is derived from experiment or conjecture and not directly from first principles.'

One afternoon two-thirds of the way through the war, when young Mohammed al-Rifi still had two weeks of normal life ahead of him, I went to the surgical ward of the Shifa hospital to meet injured children. Most had just been in the wrong place at the wrong time. Many of them had been operated on by Ghassan Abu Sitta, a senior consultant surgeon at the American University of Beirut Medical Center. Abu Sitta had personal reasons for coming to Gaza: in 1948, his Palestinian family had fled from Beersheba to Khan Yunis. At the Shifa that day he said that some of the injured children needed up to five operations before rehabilitative therapy could begin, mainly to clean their wounds of the debris – masonry, sand, pieces of wood – embedded in their bodies.

One of the most seriously injured children was eight-year-old Mohammed Badran, blinded and terribly disfigured when his house was bombed. He had been going to fetch some marbles from his bedroom, to play with children from next door, when the bomb struck. Not understanding that he had lost his sight, he asked the nurses when he arrived at the Shifa: 'Why have you switched the lights out?' His mother Taghreed, forty, only her eyes showing through her *niqab*, was at his bedside comforting him and helping nurses to clear mucus which was building up in a breathing tube from his trachea. Lying in the next bed was his seventeen-year-old sister Eman, grimacing with pain from two serious leg injuries. Mohammed needed complex surgery unavailable in Gaza, which is why his mother was agitating to get him transferred abroad. At one point, Mohammed, unseeing, simply held out his arms, seeking only a hug. Taghreed immediately bent down, enfolded him in her arms and clutched him to her cheek.

Two days later, I drove to Nusseirat after reports that three men had been killed in an F16 bombing of the refugee camp's biggest mosque, al-Qassam, in the early hours. The devastation was spectacular. The mosque had been flattened; only its minaret, one of the tallest in the Gaza Strip, still standing. A large crowd gathered to watch a bulldozer search for bodies in the rubble. (This was a frequent sight in August 2014; the diggers were often needed to lift the slabs of concrete, sometimes entire floors, below which the dead and occasionally the still living might have been trapped after a bombing.) There had been a dramatic warning to the neighbouring apartment building, but not to the mosque itself. Yahya al-Tawil explained he had been asleep when the phone rang. 'A man's voice said in Arabic, using my name: "Yahya. This is Mousa from the Israeli *mukhabarat*. I want to warn you that you have five minutes to leave the house because we are going to hit the mosque."' He and his brother had frantically woken the entire family group of thirty-five, including nineteen children, leading them from their beds out of the building. The frontage of their building was destroyed in the bombardment.

One of the dead men, it rapidly emerged, was Nidal Badran, the father of Mohammed, the eight-year-old lying blinded in Shifa hospital. What had the forty-four-year-old policeman with twenty years' service under both the PA and Hamas regimes been doing in the mosque just after 3 a.m.? At the family's home later that day, Kemal Badran, Nidal's English-speaking brother, who worked for UNRWA's information office, said Nidal was a religious man who frequently went to the mosque before dawn prayers to wash and read the Qur'an. 'Maybe [the Israelis] did not know that there would be anyone at the mosque at this time,' he suggested. In fact the Israelis knew there were men in the mosque and exactly who they were. As well as being a policeman, Badran was also a communications officer, probably a senior one, for the Qassam Brigades. He had been holding a meeting with two fellow Hamas operatives.[20]

Hundreds of civilians, children and adults, were killed in 2014 without having any conection to the armed factions. Yet the apparently 'hard case' of Mohammed Badran underlined an unmistakable truth. Hamas, like Fatah, had a base in Palestinian society; as Raji Sourani, certainly not a supporter, put it during the war, Hamas was 'part of the Palestinian DNA'.[21] Activists in all the factions, including Hamas, had homes, brothers, sisters, wives, children and parents. Someone could agree or strongly, even violently, disagree with a faction while related to someone who belonged to it. For example, Khalil Shikaki, the renowned

Rafah-born but Ramallah-based Palestinian pollster, senior fellow at Brandeis University, former visiting fellow at the Brookings Institute, regular interlocutor with Western diplomats and Israelis, was the brother of Fathi Shikaki, founding leader of Islamic Jihad, architect of suicide bombings, shot dead by Mossad in Malta in 1995 after visiting a supportive Colonel Muammar Gaddafi in Libya, and whose portrait still adorned lampposts across the Gaza Strip twenty years later. But did this connection justify the killing of entire families because one of their members was a militant – any more than it would have done to assassinate Khalil Shikaki? And children could hardly be accountable for the political choice of a parent. Indeed, this was implicitly recognised by Israel when it granted a permit for Mohammed Badran to travel abroad for treatment, first in Jordan and then in Spain.

Unfortunately, there was little doctors could do to restore his sight. When he returned to Gaza, he moved to al-Nour, UNRWA's rehabilitative school for the blind. Mohammed, aged ten when we met again, said the school was fine 'but the other one was better. I miss my friends and I miss writing.' (He was being taught Braille.) He seemed calm as we talked; but his uncle said a few days earlier 'his brother and sister were watching TV and he started screaming and crashed everything around him. He said, "they are watching TV, what can I do now? I can't see anything."'

For Hasan Zeyada, the senior psychologist at the Gaza Community Mental Health Programme, the war meant that personal trauma had come home. He remembered all too vividly the night of 29 July, which saw the most intense bombing in Gaza City, around the apartment he shared with his wife and four children: Ali, three; Hala, eleven; Zaina, six; and Ahmed, four. He felt for himself the powerlessness of a parent struggling to insulate his children against their fear:

> The whole city was lighting up. It was terrible. It was very painful for us as fathers and mothers. We had the feeling we can't do anything. You can't escape. We think we're naked; there is great danger but what can we do? And your children are so scared . . . the feeling of helplessness in war and specifically on that night . . . I cannot support or reassure them.

A week earlier, the family house in the Bureij refugee camp had been destroyed in an airstrike that killed Zeyada's seventy-year-old mother, three of his brothers, his sister-in-law and his thirteen-year-old nephew Shaban.

Towards the end of the war the Israeli air force began to destroy entire Gaza City tower blocks, rather than pinpoint-targeting militants suspected to be hiding in them as before. Zeyada and his wife prepared bags of essential belongings – papers, clothes, money – in case they were forced to evacuate as residents of other blocks had been. Zeyada explained to the children what was happening:

> My daughter Zaina told me 'Dad, what will happen with my toys?' And so I told her: 'Zaina, don't worry. We will be fine and we will refurnish another apartment and we will survive.' And she tried to say 'no.' 'Zaina, say ya Allah [dear God].' And she said 'no, I will not say ya Allah. He is a weak one. He can't do anything . . . I asked him to protect my beloved people, my grandmother, my uncles and he didn't, so I will not say ya Allah.' I will not forget her reaction, her tone, her anger, the tears in her eyes that night.

Hundreds, perhaps thousands, of children had reacted similarly all over Gaza; but not in most cases watched by a parent as steeped in the observation and treatment of trauma as Zeyada.

Zeyada declined to discuss why the Bureij house might have been targeted, on the grounds that nothing could justify what he saw as a wholly unjustifiable act. It does seem that a militant with the family name of al-Maqadmeh was in the house at the time, whether uninvited or not. In August 2016 the IDF claimed the house had been used as an 'active command and control' centre, and that 'findings indicated' that the casualties included 'three military operatives in the Hamas and Palestinian Islamic Jihad terror organisations who were members of the [Zeyada] family'. In 2017, however, a Dutch lawyer opened proceedings in Holland on behalf of the family intended to test the moral, legal and factual justification of the bombing.

This followed an unexpected coda to the bombing. The other surviving Zeyada brother, Ismail, an economist, was married to a Dutch woman, whose elderly great uncle Henk Zanoli had been active in the wartime resistance. In 1943 Zanoli had hidden an eleven-year-old orthodox Jewish boy called Elkhanan Pinto, saving him from the Holocaust in which all the immediate Pinto family perished. Learning of the bombing in the Bureij camp, the ninety-one-year-old Zanoli protested by returning a medal from Yad Vashem, the Jerusalem Holocaust museum, honouring him as a 'Righteous Among the Nations' for risking his life to save Pinto seventy-two years earlier.

Henk Zanoli declared: 'I gave back my medal because I didn't agree with what the state of Israel is doing to my family and to the Palestinians on the whole.'[22]

Returning from Gaza in late July, the *Channel 4 News* presenter Jon Snow editorialised about the deaths of children in a YouTube video that featured a young Palestinian girl with a fractured skull she had suffered after being thrown in the air, her family said, by a missile. Pointing out that Gaza had an 'unbelievably young' population Snow added: 'If you know ten-year-olds, five-year-olds, four-year-olds, and think you can control your children, that they won't be somewhere where they can be hit . . . In a densely packed urban area if you're going to throw missiles, shells and the rest you are undoubtedly going to kill children. And that's what they are doing.'[23]

Snow was right. Four days after most of Israel's ground forces had started to pull out of Gaza, Zuheir Dawaswa described how his son Ibrahim had been killed that morning on the way to Friday noon prayers at the local mosque. Dawaswa and his three sons had finished washing at home before prayers, and Ibrahim had run to the mosque ahead of the rest. 'I heard an explosion and I walked out of the house to see what it was. My son had been going to the mosque. I had no idea I was going to find him dead.' Shrapnel had sheared through Ibrahim's head; four friends had been injured.

Standing at a street corner with his other two sons, Zuheir Dawaswa asked how the boys were expected to cope after seeing the body of their brother. With his hand on seven-year-old Mohammed's head, Dawaswa added: 'He is a very young boy who has lived through three wars. He should be playing and doing other things than mourning his brother. You can imagine that now the boys will grow up wanting revenge and to get Israel out of here.'

A much higher-profile example unfolded on the beach in front of international journalists at the Deira hotel earlier in the war, before the ground invasion: a missile attack that killed four children, all members of the extended Bakr family, and injured several others, on 16 July. Two years later Mohammed Bakr, a fisherman from the Beach refugee camp, and the father of the youngest of the dead children, nine-year-old Ismail, recalled the children wanted to play football indoors but he had a headache. 'So I asked them "go away don't play here". There was no empty land in front of the area because the street is very narrow. It was hot and they went to another place, playing football, but it was hot there as well, so they said "let's go to the beach to play." So they went there, and what happened, happened.'[24]

One of the journalists watching from the Deira's terrace was the *Guardian*'s Peter Beaumont, who later administered first aid to the injured:

> The first projectile hit the sea wall of Gaza City's little harbour just after four o'clock. As the smoke from the explosion thinned, four figures could be seen running, ragged silhouettes, legs pumping furiously along the wall. Even from a distance of 200 metres, it was obvious that three of them were children. Jumping off the harbour wall, they turned on to the beach, attempting to cross the short distance to the safety of the Deira hotel . . . They waved and shouted at the watching journalists as they passed a little collection of brightly coloured beach tents, used by bathers in peacetime. It was there that the second shell hit the beach, those firing apparently adjusting their fire to target the fleeing survivors. As it exploded, journalists standing by the terrace wall shouted: 'They are only children.' In the space of forty seconds, four boys who had been playing hide and seek among fishermen's shacks on the wall were dead.[25]

Mohammed Bakr described in 2016 hearing about the attack:

> I was at home, and I heard my brother's wife screaming 'Where are your kids?' to my wife. So I said 'What happened? My kids are here.' She says: 'No, there was a massacre happened on the beach, and they are saying they are from Bakr.' I went straight to the hospital, and to the morgue. It was full of mess, I couldn't recognise anyone, I was in shock. Some bodies had the brain outside, some lost their arms or legs. I recognised Ismail and Mohammed, his cousin, in the morgue. And they told me that there were another four in the ICU in a very critical condition.

Unsurprisingly, several NGOs submitted formal complaints about the boys' deaths to Israel's Military Advocate General who concluded that the 'tragic incident' arose because the boys had been mistaken for Hamas naval commandos, but that misidentification did not violate international law. His report explained that the first strike had targeted a military compound 'used exclusively by Hamas's Naval Police' which 'spans the length of the breakwater of the Gaza City seashore, closed off by a fence and clearly separated from the beach serving the civilian population'; that a container within the compound holding military equipment had been attacked the previous day by the IDF; that 'an intelligence assessment' had indicated that Hamas naval personnel were planning to enter the compound to prepare an operation against the IDF; and that figures entering the compound 'at a running pace' were therefore – wrongly as it turned out – identified as naval militants. It stressed that at no point, including at the time of the second strike when the figures were running along the beach, had it been realised they were children.[26]

There is no reason to doubt this was indeed a case of mistaken identity, although as with the Samouni case in Operation Cast Lead the outcome cast serious doubt on the usefulness of the IDF's visual surveillance. Nor was it clear that the military had taken 'all feasible precautions', which the ICRC says are required by international law to determine if a potential target is a civilian.[27] There also appeared to be discrepancies between the MAG's description of the site originally targeted and that of journalists at the scene. Beaumont, like other journalists present, was not interviewed during the MAG's 'thorough and extensive' investigation. But he wrote after publication of the report that when he and colleagues visited the structure where the boys had been playing immediately after the incident, they found 'a small and dilapidated fisherman's hut containing a few tools' and that the supposedly closed site was in full view of international hotels housing journalists, none of whom had reported seeing militants in the area. The breakwater, he added, 'was on a busy public beach, accessible from a side lane not only to the fishermen who use it, but to local Palestinians who come to sunbathe and swim within feet of it'.[28] The building did not seem to have been quite the unmistakable military bunker the IDF had depicted.

In many other cases the damage was 'collateral', often inflicted by mortars, tank shells and especially artillery, which are notoriously imprecise forms of ammunition. The use of such ammunition carried enormous and well-known dangers, especially, but not only, in densely packed urban areas. In such circumstances, it was hard to locate the dividing line between the 'deliberate' targeting of civilians and operating in such a way that many civilian deaths – including those of children – were inevitable. A case in point were the seventy houses identified by B'Tselem where at least three, and often many more, family members were killed whether they contained militants or not.

The night of 29–30 July saw probably the most intense bombing of the war. Israeli fighter jets, tanks, artillery and naval ships launched 150 separate strikes across Gaza, killing some thirty Palestinians and hitting houses and public buildings, including its only power station, in the centre of the Strip. From the cavernous al-Quds hotel, the sky was lit up to near-daylight levels as targets along the city's coastal road, like Ismail Haniyeh's house in Beach Camp a few hundred metres away and the nearby old sea port, were struck. Anxious that glass in the hotel windows might be shattered, I left my room and wandered downstairs to find a group of teenage boys evacuated from Shujaia. We drank tea and, surreally, watched the scenes we could see from the building being played back to us live by Al Jazeera on the hotel lounge's TV. I remember wondering, as the ground shook, what it must have been like for small children across the city to experience such an aerial onslaught. At daybreak, the air was cloudy with smoke and black dust from what had been several hours of continuous bombardment.

Later that morning we learned that four 155mm HE (High Explosive) artillery shells had hit the Jabalya Girls A&B elementary school, where some 3,000 Palestinians were sheltering in desperately cramped conditions; around thirty families in each classroom. Twenty people had been killed, including three children and an UNRWA employee. As we drove to the school, bystanders were staring anxiously at the sky as at least one drone hovered noisily overhead and shelling continued to rumble in the distance. Outside the gate were the corpses of perhaps half a dozen donkeys, felled by shrapnel from one of the shells. There was a huge hole in the front wall of classroom one. Outside it, amid the rubble, a mattress and a pillowcase were soaked in blood.

The IDF said that day it had responded after being fired at 'from the direction' of the school. Artillery shells are not precisely accurate, so they are frequently fired in rounds or barrages. Because of the destruction they cause, normal battlefield procedure requires the enemy to be at least 250 metres from the army's own troops to ensure the latter's safety – if they are under cover, or 350 metres if they are not. Either the shelling was an error, or the IDF applied a significantly greater safety margin to its own troops than it did to Palestinian civilians who in this case, as UNRWA had warned the IDF at least seventeen times, most recently on the evening before the attack, were sheltering in the school.

Later that day in the Shifa hospital morgue, Yassin Suleiman, forty-five, came to collect the body of one of the victims, his cousin Ibrahim Suleiman, a strawberry farmer. It was laid out on a steel table, the blood still showing through the bandages around the two stumps of his legs, amputated by the surgeons in a desperate but vain effort to save his life. Suleiman explained that after Ibrahim's house in Beit Lahiya had been hit by a shell, he came with his wife, their seven children and other close relatives to the Jabalya school. But with grim prescience, after thirteen Palestinians had been killed six days earlier at a similar refuge in a UN school at Beit Hanoun, Ibrahim had decided to split the extended family group into four and send most of them to three other school shelters in Jabalya. 'He told them: "Let's not die together", his cousin said. That morning's shelling had been a bleak vindication of Ibrahim Suleiman's decision.

As a quietly angry Yassin Suleiman prepared to remove Ibrahim's body from the morgue for his funeral, he considered that the world seemed to regard the lives of Palestinians at a different, lower 'level'. He said: 'My message is that if this was happening in Europe, the world would not be silent. We are not the world's enemy but the world is standing by Israel. If they continue to stand by Israel they will regret it.'

Yet, remarkably, the attack on the Jabalya school was not the last such tragedy. Less than a week later, on 3 August, twelve Palestinians, including several children, were killed in a mid-morning attack, apparently by a drone-fired missile at the entrance to another internally displaced person (IDP) shelter at the UNRWA Rafah Preparatory A Boys' school. Again, the UN said it had given the school's coordinates to the IDF no less than thirty-three times over a seventeen-day period (UNRWA emailed the Israeli military's civil affairs division COGAT with the full coordinates twice a day).

Less than an hour later you could still see pools of blood outside the gate where the missile had been fired at three men on a passing motorbike, who were subsequently said by the IDF to have been Islamic Jihad militants. But most of the dead had been among some 2,700 refugees taking shelter in the school. Young Palestinians from the school were outside the gate, some buying ice creams, lollies and sweets from street vendors. (Though apparently unconnected, the strike came two days after 'Black Friday' when a young IDF officer, Hadar Goldin, went missing during a firefight at a tunnel entrance discovered by troops in Rafah. Invoking the 'Hannibal doctrine', normally understood to mean that it is better that a soldier should be killed than captured, the military unleashed what a detailed Amnesty International report – disputed by Israel – claimed were 2,000 missiles and shells, including one-ton bombs, into densely populated areas, killing between 100 and 135 civilians over four days, but most on 1 August, when the IDF was seeking to close off tunnel openings, intersections and a Rafah hospital to prevent the militants from escaping with the abducted soldier. On 2 August 2014 parts of Lt Goldin's uniform were discovered and he was pronounced dead. Over three years later Hamas were refusing to release his remains without a significant release of Palestinian prisoners.)

More generally, Israel repeatedly argued in its defence that Hamas not only hid among its own civilians but targeted Israeli civilians, while Israeli forces not only exclusively pursued military targets but took 'every precaution' to preserve civilian life. But leaving aside the massive asymmetry between Palestinian and Israeli civilian deaths – a ratio of 200–1 in Operation Protective Edge at the most conservative estimates – two wrongs, in the age-old cliché, did not make a right.

Israel was fond of saying that no developed democratic country would accept indiscriminate attacks on its citizens of the sort perpetrated by Hamas. While this was true, it wasn't clear that many other developed democratic countries would have used tank, artillery or aerial bombardment to destroy houses, killing large numbers of its inhabitants, including children, because a member of the group perpetrating such attacks was living in or even operating out of them.

And as during Cast Lead, Israel contrasted Hamas's *intention* to harm or kill civilians with what it claimed was its own attempts to avoid civilian casualties. But in an article on the aerial bombing of 2014 the late David Landau, the Israeli former editor of *Haaretz* and the biographer of Ariel Sharon, refuted this. For Landau the Halakha Jewish prohibition of *psik reyshey* (Hebrew: 'actions with inevitable consequences') nullifies the claim 'to moral superiority because its pilots and artillerymen did not intend to bomb or shell children or other civilians' (whereas Hamas's rocket launchers absolutely did). 'There is no defence of no-intent when the unintended offense is inevitable. The record shows the death and wounding of non-combatants as virtually inevitable in the bombing of the crowded Gaza Strip . . . dangerous consequences that were clearly foreseeable and inevitable.'[29]

The carnage in Gaza City's Beach Camp on 29 July in which eight children were killed as they played in the street was certainly caused by a misfired Palestinian rocket, probably by Islamic Jihad.[30] But in the overwhelming majority of cases, the deaths and destruction inside Gaza were wrought by Israeli forces. As in Operation Cast Lead, there was widespread razing of agricultural land and industry – including 360 factories, or ten per cent of the total – according to the Palestinian Federation of Industries.

One of those was the Gaza Juice Factory; it did not survive the war. One November afternoon in 2015 I went back to see what was left of it. The structure itself was still mostly standing, but the interior was a mass of twisted, broken pipes, mangled girders and cylinders leaning at crazy angles, the shards of rusting metal on a floor scorched by the fire that had burned for days. It was as if some Luddite giant had run amok in the factory with an axe and a flamethrower. It seemed eerie, standing by a ripped hoarding flapping in the breeze with the words – in English – 'Gaza Juice Factory' still just legible, to think that the weed-ridden wasteland in front of the building had been the garden of shrubs, trees and well-mown grass that had so impressed visitors five years earlier. A security guard agreed to call a former employee who lived nearby. The man, who gave his name only as Said, had worked at the factory since 1995 and remembered Abu Ramadan, the factory's CEO until 2007, as 'a good man. He knew what he was doing. No one could replace him.' He did not think much of the Hamas-appointed management who had taken over from his former boss. But, he added, 'at least we had a salary. Now there is nothing.'

PART TWO

13

'FROM THE MIDDLE AGES TO THE NINETEENTH CENTURY': HAMAS SHIFTS ITS GROUND

HAMAS'S STAGING WAS NOTHING IF NOT elaborate. In front of a huge image of the Dome of the Rock was an eerily convincing life-size mock-up of the green No. 12 Egged bus blown up in the holy city by a Palestinian suicide bomber ten days earlier. Its shredded wheels, wrecked cab, burned-out roof and smashed windows, celebrating the explosion which had injured twenty passengers, formed the backdrop of an event that was less a rally than a show.

The April 2016 spectacle began with a deafening recreation of the bus bombing, complete with smoke pouring from its roof and heavily amplified songs glorifying the 'Jerusalem Intifada' – the wave of (mainly stabbing, but also car ramming and shooting) attacks on Israelis through the previous winter, which from October 2015 to the end of the year resulted in the deaths of thirty-five Israelis, and 149 Palestinians, mainly shot, as they carried out or attempted such attacks.[1] Hamas also supplied less martial diversions, such as a group of women in traditionally embroidered dresses dancing the *dabka*, while a camera drone from Hamas al-Aqsa TV buzzed overhead. There was plenty for the drone to film, including a staging by Qassam militants, in camouflage fatigues and balaclavas, of the capture of an Israeli soldier and a playlet depicting a caged Palestinian prisoner on hunger strike being rescued by Qassam fighters.

In his speech Ismail Haniyeh, still then Hamas's political leader in Gaza, praised 'heroic' Abd al-Hamid Abu Srur, who had planted the bomb on the Egged bus, becoming the first suicide bomber for nearly a decade. But, in an odd mix of the standard glorification of martyrdom and a relatively nuanced political message, Haniyeh was apparently trying to reassure the Fatah leadership, ever watchful of the prospect of a Hamas-run state beyond its reach. Restating demands for an airport and seaport in Gaza, Haniyeh added: 'This doesn't mean that Gaza will turn into a separate state from our Palestinian territories.'

This was characteristic of Hamas, in which a belief in armed resistance co-exists with a heavy dose of practical politics, core militant ideology with the challenges of governing more than 1.8 million people and trying to open up to the outside world. For that reason it's often hard to detect whether one stream is dominant within the movement at any time, and, indeed, whether Hamas simply thrives, if that's the word, by maintaining a controlled ambivalence between the two.

Nowhere were these tensions more on display than in the launch in Qatar in early May 2017 of Hamas's long awaited new document of 'principles', which significantly moderated (though did not actually replace) the language of its notorious 1988 Charter. The document read as if it had been written by a committee, which essentially it was, the product of four years of drafting before a consensus could be found among the movement's top leadership. Yet the drive for reform, however limited, was primarily the work of the outgoing head of Hamas's political bureau Khaled Meshal, the veteran Doha-based 'outside' leader of Hamas, against whom Netanyahu had ordered a botched assassination attempt during his first premiership in 1997. If nothing else, the length of time he took to get it agreed demonstrated a wide range of opinion within the faction.

The document did not offer recognition of Israel, it did not renounce its claim to the whole of historic Palestine* and, during the no doubt tortuous textual wrangles, it dropped a sentence from an earlier draft which, explaining that Arabs were not to blame for the European

---

* Likud, the party of Benjamin Netanyahu, has also never renounced its original 1977 party platform proclaiming that 'the right of the Jewish people to the land of Israel is eternal and indisputable . . . and . . . between the Sea and the Jordan there will only be Israeli sovereignty'.

persecution of the Jews, said: 'Anti-Semitism was a basic reason for the appearance of the Zionist movement.'[2]

But it sought to shed the anti-Semitism of the 1988 Charter by declaring: 'Hamas does not wage a struggle against the Jews because they are Jewish but wages a struggle against the Zionists who occupy Palestine.'[3] In a clear attempt to move closer to the Egypt of President Sisi and to reinforce its status as an autonomous Palestinian organisation, it avoided any reference to its origins in the Muslim Brotherhood, Sisi's bête noire. And, most noticeable of all, it indicated its acceptance of a future Palestinian state on 1967 borders. This was not new, since it had been said at various times by Hamas leaders, but it had not been issued in such a public document before. The critical interpretation was that such a state in Hamas's long-term view would be only an interim stage towards replacing Israel, while the more optimistic one held that in practice Hamas now understood that a Palestinian state from the Jordan river to the Mediterranean would not happen.

Officially Israel was predictably quick to dismiss the document out of hand. Netanyahu called it 'a smokescreen' and dramatised his disdain by posting a Facebook video of himself tearing it up and throwing it in a wastebasket. But other prominent Israelis were not so negative. While saying he did not know whether the shift was 'tactical' or reflected 'a big change in official policy', Giora Eiland of the National Security Council under Ariel Sharon and Ehud Olmert described it as a 'positive' move,[4] putting it partially down to Hamas's realisation that 'in order to please the world they have to speak in much more moderate terms to persuade more and more players that they are a pragmatic player that can be a partner for dialogue'.

That job of persuasion now passed from Meshal to Ismail Haniyeh, his successor as head of the political bureau. Haniyeh had been seen as belonging to the (relatively) pragmatic end of the Hamas spectrum. At the outset of its rise to office, he was one of its more personally popular figures, with humble origins in the Beach refugee camp, a richly modulated voice reciting the Qur'an when preaching in Gaza's mosques, an impressive use of the Arabic language, and even a reputation as a good midfielder in the Islamic Association football team in his youth. All this helped to make him the most acceptable face of the movement in the 2006 elections as number one on the national Hamas list, and therefore Prime Minister after the faction's unexpected victory.

At the Islamic University, where he studied Arabic literature in the 1980s, he headed the students' council on a Muslim Brotherhood ticket. The quadriplegic Sheikh Ahmed Yassin, who founded Hamas in 1988, took him under his wing. So began his political ascent, rising to be his mentor's bureau chief. But while Haniyeh was fully part of the collective leadership which sanctioned suicide bombing from the 1990s, he advocated the ballot box alongside the explosive vest. He had been among a minority who wanted Hamas to fight the elections that validated Yasser Arafat's leadership in 1996 but lost out to those arguing that this would be an endorsement of the Oslo Accords, which had provided for the elections.[5] It took another decade for his group to get their way.

It was Haniyeh who in December 2014 signed off on a carefully measured letter to Tony Blair, then envoy of the international Middle East Quartet, which already contained elements of the May 2017 document. The 'Your Excellency Tony Blair ... Sincerely, the Islamic Resistance Movement-Hamas' letter,[6] sent in English four months after the 2014 war, began with a declaration hard to refute: 'The situation in Palestine is obviously in its worst phase throughout the history of the Palestinian struggle for freedom.'[7]

But the real meat was in sub-points that followed to describe the Islamic movement's 'vision': 'Hamas will not oppose a Palestinian state in the 1967 borders with Jerusalem as its capital and with keeping the right of return for the Palestinians' and 'Hamas is committed to the national reconciliation document signed by the Palestinian factions in 2006, which determined the common national position regarding all issues.' (This was the Prisoners' Document of 2007.*)

Haniyeh's victory in internal elections to succeed Meshal indicated that the centre of Hamas's political gravity had shifted back to Gaza, where Yahya Sinwar had been chosen to succeed him as leader of Hamas in Gaza, and deputy head of the political bureau. Sinwar's background was different. Closely associated with Hamas's military wing, thought to have backed him for the leadership, he had been in an Israeli gaol for twenty-two years, released under the prisoner swap for Gilad Shalit. It would remain to be seen whether Sinwar would necessarily fulfil predictions of a hard-line militarist stance or whether he would emerge as a

---

*   See Chapter 6.

politician capable of using his credibility to unite the military wing behind a more pragmatic course – seeking to bring the movement closer to Egypt than Iran, for example.

Hamas is disciplined, usually reaching a common stance after, as over the document of 'principles', sometimes prolonged internal debates. But it has also thrown up distinctive personalities – and tensions between them. It was reported, for example, that the hawkish Mahmoud Zahar was voted off Hamas's overall – as opposed to the Gaza – political bureau in 2013 although he refused to confirm it.

When I visited Zahar in 2016, a bodyguard emerged from a security post outside his house and guided me into his elegant garden, of which Zahar – an Egyptian-trained thyroid surgeon – was clearly proud. Clad in a cream *jalabiya*, he rose from his desk in the shade, where he had been writing. The demeanour of a benevolent if slightly austere grand-father, courteous to his visitors, was enhanced by his being accompanied, throughout the conversation, by his four-year-old grandson Mohammed, who at one point asked Zahar to comb his hair. The man long regarded in Israel as near the top of the list of its public enemies, duly obliged. On previous occasions when I had interviewed him his car would, unconventionally, be parked for security reasons inside the arched reception room where he entertained visitors; now it was hidden under a grey awning outside the house.

A certain flintiness in his manner was hardly surprising; two of his sons, Khaled and Hassam, were killed by Israelis and his home had been hit by airstrikes four times. He was a prominent founder, first of the Islamist Mujamma, offshoot of the Muslim Brotherhood in 1973, and then of Hamas during the First Intifada in 1988. Several of his co-founders were dead, all assassinated by Israel.

His approach to the two-state solution, at least rhetorically, remained more uncompromising than Haniyeh's had been. One condition imposed by the Quartet after the 2006 elections was that it recognise Israel. A month later, Haniyeh had then explained why that had been rejected: 'We say: Let Israel recognise the legitimate rights of the Palestinians first and then we will have a position regarding this. Which Israel should we recognise? . . . the Israel of 1948; the Israel of 1956; or the Israel of 1967? Which borders and which Israel? Israel has to recognise first the Palestinian state and its borders and then we will know what we are talking about.'[8]

Zahar's language, by contrast, suggested that, while Hamas might accept a Palestinian state on 1967 borders as a sub-optimal advance, the refusal to recognise Israel was more fundamental:

> The people are going to be part of this state and the administration will represent the people as we do here. But the essential point is: are we ready to recognise Israel? That means are we ready to renounce our right in the area occupied in [19]48? This is the essential point.

Zahar nevertheless sought to shrug off the Hamas 1988 founding Charter, which he said dismissively had been written by 'one of the very old men in Hamas' at the time of its foundation and no longer represented 'our vision and philosophy'.

Rejecting charges of anti-Semitism (rather than 'anti-Zionism') against Hamas, Zahar insisted: 'We are here not against the Israelis because they are Jews, [but] because they are occupiers.'[9] He insisted Hamas had treated the captive Israeli soldier Gilad Shalit well: 'We treated him very kindly, we provided him with a comfortable life.'

But some of Zahar's sentiments are rebarbative to Western opinion, whether religious or humanist. He has no trouble attributing Israel's creation to the outcome of long-standing European persecution and expulsion of Jews. He does not deny 'what is called the Holocaust'. Instead he claims Hitler treated the Jews 'very badly', because their leaders 'cooperated with enemies of Hitler . . . It was a political stand from the German government against the leaders of the Jews there, who played every dirty game as anti-German.' (But, no, he didn't think Jews as a whole had been 'collaborators' any more than Palestinians were because their President Mahmoud Abbas was.)

Even if this bizarrely shocking claim were correct (and as I posed the question I had the sense of being drawn against my better judgement onto Planet Zahar), how would that conceivably justify killing six million people, an act of genocide unparalleled in history? 'I am not justifying, I'm against killing a single body because he is Christian for his Christianity, or a Jew because he is a Jew, or a Muslim because he is Muslim.' It was no more correct, he said, to talk of the 'Jewish' – rather than Israeli – occupation than it would have been to describe the British Mandate as the 'Christian occupation'. 'The only people in the world respecting human beings is Islam, regardless of their political attitude.

Look [referring to himself], who is the man in the very best relations with Christians here?'

There was something at least in this last point. More than ten years earlier, during the furore over anti-Islamic cartoons published in a Danish newspaper, I had happened on a meeting at the Holy Family School, run by the tiny 'Latin' – or Roman Catholic Christian – community, to be greeted by the unaccustomed sight of Zahar sitting in a classroom in front of a nervous group of a dozen nuns convened by the local priest, Fr Manuel Musallam, because the Holy Family Church had received a threatening fax. Zahar reassured them: 'You are our sisters who live side by side with us along with the foreigners who come to serve this community.' He insisted Hamas's armed wing would keep the nuns safe until the still unformed Hamas government could ensure their official protection.

Zahar defended past suicide bombing, on the familiar grounds that, lacking the sophisticated First World weaponry of Israel, Hamas fell back on a military tactic which 'costs us one remarkable man in each event'. Indeed, he defended random attacks on innocent Israeli civilians by asserting that there were no innocent Israeli civilians. 'Every Israeli male and female' either was, had been, or would be, a soldier, in contrast to 'the Palestinian side' where men volunteer for military service, a strange argument since conscripts could just as easily be argued to be more 'innocent' than volunteers. Since he strongly objected to the term 'terrorists', what term would he use for ISIS? 'Criminals' he said, his voice rising, who are 'killing innocent people'.

Zahar was also one of the most forceful exponents of Hamas's social conservatism. Although, like most in Hamas, he was in favour of the education of women – his daughters went to university and his wife (he has only one, unlike some Palestinians in Gaza) was a teacher – he condemned relations between men and women outside marriage. 'You are corrupted, and look what happened in your society: the number of crimes, the number of corruptions and illegal sex, and thousands and thousands have no father, he is not sure [if he is the] father because the mother practised sex with thousands and thousands. This is not our style. We consider you as corrupted people.'

So what about polygamy? 'It is our religion. We should change it for your West? You are not our god and you are not our prophet, and we only accept the doctrines of our god and of our prophet.'

Hamas's similarly forbidding attitude to 'illegal' homosexual acts formed part of the case for executing, in February 2016, Mahmoud Eshtewi, a prominent Qassam Brigades commander in the Zeitoun district of Gaza City. Originally the rumour – subsequently rejected by senior Hamas figures – was that Eshtewi had tipped off Israeli intelligence about the hideout of military leader Mohammed Deif before an attempt to assassinate him. But then on 7 February 2016 the Brigades issued a terse statement announcing Eshtewi had been executed 'for behavioural and moral violations to which he confessed'. This, it emerged, had included, but was not confined to, the 'accusation' that he was gay. In the view of human rights groups, the incident illustrated Hamas's summary approach to punishment. Human Rights Watch, along with local agencies Al Mezan and the Independent Commission of Human Rights, condemned both the lack of proper civilian court proceedings to try Eshtewi and the use of capital punishment.

There was nothing new in that. After both Operation Cast Lead and Operation Protective Edge, Hamas executed Palestinians accused of collaboration – in the latter case, twenty-five people in seventy-two hours. On 22 August eighteen people were summarily shot dead. Eleven, including two women, were executed in a deserted park in Gaza City, and seven in front of a large crowd after being lined up against the wall of the ancient al-Omari mosque by black-clad, hooded gunmen. Neither Hamas nor its armed wing officially claimed responsibility, although a Hamas-affiliated website said seven had been convicted after 'revolutionary military trials' under the 1979 'Revolutionary Penal Code' formulated by the then Arafat-led PLO. As Human Rights Watch pointed out, Gazan military courts had previously convicted defendants of collaboration and sentenced them to death after 'unfair trials' based on confessions that lawyers and family members said were coerced.

The 2014 executions followed a pattern set after Operation Cast Lead. In the January 2009 aftermath of that war, Fawzi Barhoum, one of Hamas's official spokesmen, acknowledged to me at the time that 'spies' had been killed by 'the resistance'. He said it was impossible for Israel to have assassinated the Hamas Interior Minister Said Siyam without information from such 'spies' because he had been constantly moving 'from place to place' during the offensive.

This aggression extended beyond collaborators to political dissidents during – and immediately after – Operation Cast Lead. On crutches and with a heavily bandaged left leg, Eyad Obeid, a young Fatah activist, described to me in January 2009 how he had been in a shop near his home when four masked men carrying AK-47s pulled up in a 4x4 and bundled him into the vehicle. Once on the road his abductors repeatedly questioned him about his previous job in the PA-run Preventative Security Organisation. The ordeal ended with him being shot below the knee – a classic 'punishment shooting' of the sort used by the IRA during the Northern Ireland Troubles, and one of dozens claimed by Fatah to have been inflicted by Hamas during this period.

Such shooting attacks on mere political dissidents – as opposed to suspected collaborators – abated over the next few years, but Hamas officialdom could still be highly sensitive to criticism, including that of a jocular nature. The detention of Ayman Aloul, a forty-four-year-old journalist with a droll wit, was a mixture of Keystone Cops and vague but unmistakable menace. Aloul was the well-known Gaza correspondent for Iraqi TV and the editor of Arab Now, a popular local news website. Although a straight reporter of facts, he also had a satirical turn of mind, evident from his posts on Facebook, which had 80,000 followers. Under the hashtag #GiveUsOurBorderBack he urged Hamas to allow PA forces to man the Rafah crossing to get Egypt to reopen the frontier. His large following helped to make the hashtag near-viral. He also criticised the high level of taxes imposed by Hamas, and the quality of healthcare; and he had – bizarrely – incurred a lawsuit from the Deputy Minister of Education Ziad Thabet for describing how at one government school Hamas teachers sat in one room and those not in Hamas in another.

On 3 January, three unmarked cars belonging to the de facto government's internal security force arrived at his home. According to Aloul's account, laced with sardonic humour, 'it went exactly like this: "Hello, we are from the interior security, we want to arrest you and search your house, and please give us your mobile now." '[10] He was taken to the Ansar Security compound and relieved of all personal belongings, 'including my shoe laces – in case I hung myself,' he laughed. He was shown to a 2.1 by 1 metre cell and kept overnight. The following morning Aloul was interrogated for three hours, either with a plastic bag over his head or forced to wear specially darkened glasses through which it was impossible to see. A man calling himself Abu Ramiz asked him: 'Who is sponsoring you: the CIA? Egyptian intelligence? Jordanian

intelligence? Abbas? The Israelis?' Twice Aloul was struck by the interrogator, which he found 'not painful but humiliating'. And he was questioned about baseless allegations of personal misdemeanours, involving
women and drugs. 'They asked me, "who brings you weed?" They asked,
"the women . . . who are they? What are their names?" I laughed . . . and
I said, "You didn't catch me when I was with them, and you want me to
confess now? You should've caught me."'

He was taken to a section of the gaol called The Bus. 'I was very
excited – I thought I was being taken on a nice trip,' he joked. The Bus
is a series of small rooms, visible to a guard behind wire fencing, in
which prisoners are forced to sit in child-size chairs – 'very uncomfortable' – while blindfolded. After a week of interrogations and physical
abuse, Aloul was released and announced he would stop his political
posts. Goaded by the Al Arabiya TV satellite channel, which asked him:
'so Hamas were able to shut you up?' Aloul replied: 'Yes, I am not as
powerful as they are.' But, ever the humourist, he satirically reinforced
the point by borrowing the popular 'Be Like Bill' meme on Facebook.
'Ayman is watching the Barcelona game,' he wrote. 'Ayman is commenting on the match. Ayman doesn't talk politics. Be like Ayman.' The posts
were replicated in different forms and reposted by his followers. In one
act of defiance, he did not delete his original Facebook posts. 'I paid for
these posts [by being detained], didn't I? I'm not going to remove them.'

A few days after we spoke, I bumped into Aloul at a journalism
awards ceremony in Gaza City. He told me he was planning to leave
Gaza for a TV job elsewhere in the region if he could, not least because
his sense was that, despite Arab Now being the third most popular news
site in Gaza, big advertisers were shying away from it in order not to
offend Hamas. Sure enough, when the Rafah crossing briefly opened a
few weeks later, Aloul somehow managed to get to the front of the
queue to leave. It was a decision which suited him, and probably the
Hamas authorities as well.

After his first long sleepless night in The Bus, Aloul's guard had
sought to cheer him up by telling him some prisoners had not been
allowed to sleep for several nights. One, said the guard, 'is ISIS, and he
is with us [for] two weeks now, and didn't get any sleep'. For Hamas had
also been robust in cracking down on extreme Salafists. Some of these
ultra-militants regarded ISIS as a model, criticised Hamas for being
insufficiently fundamentalist, were behind attacks on Christians in

Gaza, and in some cases fired rockets into Israel even when Hamas was enforcing a ceasefire. In confronting them, Hamas was prepared to risk dissent among armed militants, including some of its own members, to consolidate its control. Its most famous clash with militant Salafists was in August 2009, when a Salafist sheikh, Abdellatif Musa, called his supporters to Friday prayers at a mosque in Rafah where he was expected to launch a ferocious verbal attack on Haniyeh. Armed Hamas militants arrived at the mosque initially seeking to negotiate with the sheikh to avoid a confrontation, but after a Qassam Brigades officer was killed by a sniper, the Hamas fighters stormed the mosque. Musa and another Salafist leader died when they detonated suicide belts.[11]

In April 2011, in perhaps the worst atrocity committed in Gaza against a Westerner, the 'Group of the Companion Mohammed Bin Maslamah'[12] kidnapped a popular pro-Palestinian Italian activist, Vittorio Arrigoni, apparently in a bid to free the leader of the Salafist Unity and Jihad faction Hisham Saidani, who had been detained by Hamas after he issued a fatwah against Christians in Gaza. By the time Hamas forces found the house in northern Gaza, west of Jabalya, where Arrigoni had been held, he was dead, having been brutally beaten then strangled by his captors. A member of the International Solidarity Movement, Arrigoni was the grandson of partisans who fought the Nazis in Italy during the Second World War, to which he attributed his commitment to justice and human rights.[13] Hamas reacted to his murder fiercely, killing two of the group's activists and later securing the conviction of four others. While the killing was an undoubted blow to Hamas's reputation for law and order in Gaza, there was no repeat of the episode over the next five years, although presumed Salafists would be responsible for sporadic rocket attacks during the de facto ceasefire of 2016.

Hamas had long been diligent in enforcing ceasefires, when it had agreed them, for example running motorcycle patrols along the border to seek out potential rocket launchers and would-be attackers of Israel – a fact visible to Israeli intelligence and freely acknowledged in private by senior IDF officers. A few months before Arrigoni's murder, I met a militant who had been arrested by Hamas for trying to lead what he would only call an 'operation' against Israel. Wearing Western clothes, and not obviously a Salafist, he would not say what faction he belonged to, let alone his name. Our encounter was somewhat melodramatic;

given the registration number of our taxi, parked by arrangement at a busy junction on the edge of the Jabalya refugee camp, he seemed to emerge from nowhere, and slipped into the vehicle saying, 'Let's get out of here. There are eyes everywhere.' In the secluded garden of a city centre hotel, where he stopped speaking whenever a waiter drew near, he insisted that although he was on Israel's wanted list it was Hamas's internal security force that made him nervous. Describing his arrest, he said he had been beaten with fists and rifle butts:

> They said to me: 'You're trying to make an operation. This is forbidden. There is a *hudna* [truce]. We have no resistance here. Gaza has been liberated. If you want to do an operation, do it in the West Bank, or in 1948 territory [Israel].' They are always in border areas, telling people don't get close to the border. They used to be with the resistance, but once you get into authority you change. They want to protect their authority and they fear that there is going to be a war.

Six hours' detention is not a long sentence. But Hamas had prevented the mysterious anti-Israel operation the man intended to lead. And he was extremely wary of being caught again.

Hamas was united in enforcing ceasefires when it chose to, as it did in the three years after the 2014 war. But you don't have to spend much time with Ghazi Hamad and Ahmed Yousef, two of Haniyeh's advisers over the years, to detect a marked difference from Zahar's more hawkish approach. For Zahar, the PA are 'spies', Abbas is a 'collaborator' and Fatah is a self-interested opponent driven by antagonism to Hamas. Conversely, although highly critical of some of Fatah's positions over the years, Hamad and Yousef had been among the most ardent advocates for reconciliation between the Palestinian factions – though Yousef vigorously condemned Abbas's attempts to pressure Hamas in the spring of 2017 by cutting the salaries of his own PA employees in Gaza and cutting payments for electricity from Israel.

After retiring as Deputy Foreign Minister, Yousef presided over a think tank named *Bayt al-Hikma*, the 'House of Wisdom', which he has fostered as a bastion of pluralism. Based on the eleventh floor of a highrise in central Gaza City, its leather armchairs and ample conference table resembled a cross between an English gentlemen's club and a merchant bank with an Islamic twist. While Yousef was hardly a laissez-faire liberal towards overt dissent, he was proud that *Bayt al-Hikma* covers the Palestinian political spectrum. A prolific author, he was writing what in Hamas terms was bound to be a startlingly revisionist biography of Yasser Arafat, whom he regarded as a 'great man'. Instead of the ritual Hamas denunciations of Oslo, he argued there might have been more 'justification for why [Arafat] took that risk than the Islamists have traditionally allowed him' and that he had 'good intentions' in striking the deal with Rabin. More remarkably still, he argued that it might have succeeded had it not been for the suicide bombings that Hamas orchestrated in the 1990s. 'Some of the military operations practised by the resistance in the mid-90s gave the Israelis justification to escape from the Oslo requirements,' he said. Indeed, Yousef's approach to the subject of suicide bombing was notably different from Zahar's: 'When I was in the USA, I wrote to them and said that this is destroying the image of the Palestinian struggle. The Israelis have the best PR machine, and they can easily use this against us. This kind of operation damages the ultimate goal, so many of us inside the movement, especially those of us living in the West and seeing how it affected the minds in the West, we were writing letters and saying that it was damaging.'[14]

Yousef also hosted a short visit by Salam Fayyad, the independent former Prime Minister of the PA, frequently reviled first by Hamas and subsequently by Fatah, but regarded in the West as a highly capable administrator and a reasoned, though also passionate, advocate of the Palestinian cause. Yousef urged Fayyad to spend more time in Gaza and build a political base in the Strip.

Of Mohammed Dahlan, Zahar's bitter Fatah opponent dating back to the 1990s, Yousef was surprisingly sanguine. While freely acknowledging the accusations of corruption against Dahlan and the fact that he was 'hated' by many Hamas activists, he noted his backing by governments in the region and his popularity, especially, but not only, among younger Fatah activists in Gaza. Contrasting him with 'the very arrogant' Palestinian President Abbas – by 2016 Dahlan's sworn enemy – he said that 'people know him, he's the man from the [Khan Yunis refugee] camp, that's why he's so popular.'

Hamad, a fluent Hebrew speaker and therefore relatively frequent (telephone) interviewee by the Israeli media, was born in 1964 in the Yibna refugee camp in Rafah, long seen as a militant stronghold. Editor of the Hamas weekly newspaper *Al-Risala*, he was gaoled by Arafat's security services for his acerbic criticism of the repressive tendencies of that regime. Since Hamas took control, he had repeatedly used his journalistic skills for collective self-criticism aimed at both Hamas and other factions. Back in 2006, when Hamas was observing a ceasefire with Israel but infighting between all the factions was costing civilian Gazans dear, he used a column in the Palestinian newspaper *Al-Ayyam* to address armed militias – while he was Haniyeh's spokesman – in terms few Hamas officials would use in public:

> Please have mercy on Gaza . . . It is strange that when a big effort is taken to reopen Rafah crossing to ease the suffering of the people, you see others who go to shell rockets toward the crossing. I'm not interested in discussing the ugliness and brutality of the occupation because it is not a secret . . . I prefer self-criticism and self-evaluation. We're used to blaming our mistakes on others.[15]

He wrote several other articles, including a remarkable one in 2016, by which time he was again a de facto minister, pointedly praising Tunisia's Islamist leader Rached Ghannouchi for agreeing to share power and Islamists in Morocco for cooperating with the monarchy. It was hardly surprising that he had been one of the first figures openly to emphasise Hamas's willingness to contemplate a Palestinian state on June 1967 borders, and reconciliation with Fatah.

By 2017 the chances of reconciliation between Mahmoud Abbas and Hamas could hardly have been more distant as the eighty-one-year-old Palestinian President took punitive steps in the spring and summer 2017 against Gaza, ostensibly with the aim of forcing Hamas to surrender control of the Strip to the PA. Ironically, in its hour of need Hamas turned to the Fatah figure it had once demonised above all others. Ahmed Yousef's relative warmth towards Dahlan turned out to be less eccentric than it had seemed. Dahlan was given much of the credit for brokering a deal with the Egyptians for supplying fuel for Gaza's only power station when Israel further cut the meagre electricity supply at the behest of Abbas. This followed a remarkable meeting, facilitated by Egyptian intelligence, between Dahlan and Yahya Sinwar, which reportedly began with both men reminiscing about their childhood at the same school in the Khan Younis refugee camp.[16]

To avert a crippling electricity crisis, Sinwar was happy to apply the principle of 'my enemy's enemy'. Once Abbas's close Fatah ally, Dahlan had long fallen out with the President, who saw him as a threat as well as a would-be successor. Since 2007, when Hamas had defeated Fatah and overrun the absent Dahlan's home, Dahlan had been banished from Gaza. Then he was exiled from the West Bank, amid claims and counter-claims between Dahlan and Abbas of corruption, including unsubstantiated accusations by Abbas's Fatah allies that Dahlan had been complicit in Arafat's death; Dahlan had been convicted *in absentia* in Ramallah on other Abbas-instigated corruption charges in 2016. For Dahlan, his engagement with Hamas the following year offered the chance of increasing his influence at least in Gaza, reinforcing the already substantial charitable payments that he had been channelling to the Strip. These were largely financed by the United Arab Emirates, where Dahlan now lived, and brought into Gaza by his wife Jahlia. If and when Dahlan returned from exile it looked as if his first destination might be Gaza rather than the West Bank.

A rapidly shifting regional dynamic would also prove a test for Hamas's new leadership. Khaled Meshal had left Damascus in February 2012, after Hamas infuriated the Assad regime by declaring its support for the Syrian opposition, and settled in Qatar. This threatened the close relationship with Assad's ally Iran, which significantly reduced its financial aid to Hamas. Qatar proved a hospitable host, but in 2017 Saudi Arabia, along with Gulf allies and with at least initial encouragement from Donald Trump, began its concerted effort to isolate Qatar unless it agreed to a series of demands including cutting its support for Hamas.

The still open question in the summer of 2017 was whether all these developments would lead to a lasting if qualified rapprochement with Egypt. One hope was that Egypt would significantly ease the siege of Gaza by lifting restrictions at the Rafah crossing, in return for Hamas's commitment to help Egypt against Islamists operating in northern Sinai, possibly including the extradition of seventeen men in Gaza who were wanted by Cairo.

For all the enmity turned on it by the Saudis, and the UAE, Qatar had probably been a force for stability in Gaza. It had certainly become a serious player in the Strip, not least through its aid, including the highly efficient reconstruction of war-destroyed homes. Qatar's 'ambassador' to Gaza, a fast-talking, heavy smoking, traditionally robed and moustachioed businessman, Mohammed El-Emadi, was an increasing presence in the Strip. True to Qatar's enigmatic regional status (at once severely criticised by the US for 'terrorist financing' of Islamist groups, including in Syria, while as a Western ally still host to the main American operational base in the Gulf), El-Emadi boasted excellent relations not only with Hamas but with Yoav 'Poly' Mordechai, head of the Israeli military's civil affairs division COGAT, the main address for granting permission for importing building materials.[17] He now had a team working from smart new offices in Gaza's Meshtal hotel. The branding extended even to its local internet network, named ThankyouQatar.

Qatar may also have given greater support to the more pragmatic approach by Meshal than Damascus would have done. Either way, if Dahlan was a surprising interlocutor for Hamas, Tony Blair was perhaps even more so. It was in Qatar that Tony Blair, by now heading his own 'Middle East Initiative', had chosen to engage with the Hamas political bureau leader over the two years since receiving the Hamas letter of December 2014. It's hard to escape the irony; the invasion of Iraq cost Blair his reputation with a large swathe of the British public; his prolonged support of Israel's much criticised war in Lebanon against Hezbollah in 2006 probably cost him his job as support ebbed from him among MPs in his own party. Yet he had held at least half a dozen meetings – at least one of which was with Haniyeh as well – with the leaders of an organisation widely proscribed as terrorist. The meetings took place at Meshal's home in Doha, partly to pursue the possibility of a long-term truce with Israel in return for a major easing of the siege. One issue concerned radioactive semantics. In saying that it would accept a Palestinian state on pre-1967 borders, was it prepared to agree to use the term 'two states' – an inching towards the recognition of Israel which Hamas had long refused? Another was whether, rather than disarming, Hamas was at least prepared to 'freeze' its imports of weaponry through the tunnels. There was no evidence the second happened when Meshal stood down; and the first was still too controversial within Hamas to surface in the May 2017 principles document.

But Blair had not been alone in his efforts. Qatar especially was involved. El-Emadi wouldn't discuss the mediation project in 2016 beyond acknowledging that it was on his radar while implying that he and Blair might have complementary roles: 'He can't talk to the Qassam Brigades. I can.' Successful or not, Blair's unofficial diplomacy was still a turnaround. As British Prime Minister in 2006–7, he had backed the international boycott of Hamas demanded by the US and Israel, one which helped to seal Gaza's isolation and impoverishment and which, ten years later, still bound the governments represented in the international Quartet. Now he had joined an admittedly lengthening list of apostates, Israeli and foreign, who believed that, as part of the problem, Hamas would have to be part of the solution. As Prime Minister, moreover, Blair had been a supporter of the 'West Bank first' approach to peace-making that characterised the failed Annapolis initiative and sought to bypass Hamas. Now he held that 'any peace process which ignores Gaza is a process doomed to fail'.[18] It was hard not to wish he had come to this realisation while still a head of government.

Hamas could not escape criticism for violating human rights. Indeed, in May 2017 Human Rights Watch strongly condemned its military wing for holding incommunicado two Israelis with a history of serious mental illness, a Jew of Ethiopian descent, Avera Mangistu, and a Bedouin, Hisham al-Sayed, who managed to cross the border into Gaza during their wanderings in 2014 and 2015 respectively. Though having no connection with the military themselves, they were presumably being held hostage in the hope of securing the release of more Palestinian prisoners, although Hamas would not officially discuss their cases or say where they were being held.

Weeks before the new 'principles' document was unveiled, a Hamas commander, Mazen Fukha, was mysteriously shot dead in the Tel el Hawa district of Gaza City. Blaming Israel for the killing – which, after a period of official silence, its Defense Minister Avigdor Lieberman denied – Hamas's reaction was harsh: it made dozens of arrests, set up roadblocks and checkpoints across the Strip, commandeered CCTV security film from business and private householders, shut down the port – a favourite spot for Gazans to take their families for relaxation – and for ten days prevented fishermen from going to sea, apparently to stop the gunman or his collaborators from escaping the Strip. In late May the summary execution of three men it had accused of carrying out the killing on Israel's orders were broadcast live by Hamas – and condemned by international rights groups.

So Hamas had often been repressive, sometimes brutally so, towards active dissidents, among others – as had Mahmoud Abbas's PA, frequently at times in the West Bank – not to mention most of the

Palestinians' Arab neighbours. But politicians in Israel and the West also frequently depicted Hamas as a simple extension of worldwide militant fundamentalism, of which it showed no sign. Benjamin Netanyahu's claim that 'Hamas is ISIS and ISIS is Hamas'[19] did not hold up. Hamas had been condemned by both ISIS,[20] which accused it of being insufficiently Islamic and threatened to overrun it in Gaza, and by Al Qaeda, for embracing the 'infidel religion of democracy'.[21] With its acceptance of women in education and the workplace and its benign attitude to the tiny Christian minority, it was also far from being a Palestinian Taliban. Even if it had tactically cooperated with ISIS adherents channelling weapons to it from the northern Sinai – as Egypt insisted, and Hamas denied – its goal was a specifically Palestinian one, without designs for global jihad. Neither in its methods or its goals was it aligned with ISIS, whose would-be adherents in Gaza it had devoted considerable force and energy to suppressing, ironically in Israel's own security interests as well as its own.

While Hamas had other serious differences with Fatah – including its criticism of the PA security forces' cooperation with their Israeli counterparts – its most fundamental ideological dispute had long been over its adherence to the goal of a Palestinian – indeed Islamic – state on the whole of what it regarded as Palestine, in other words eliminating Israel. Yet Hamas would never have commanded the support that installed it in power in 2006 if a serious peace process had been under way between Israel and the Fatah-dominated PA. A decade later, its espousal, however provisional, of a state on 1967 borders looked like a tentative attempt to edge it nearer to the centre ground of Palestinian politics. 'Hamas has dragged itself from the middle ages to the nineteenth century,' joked one experienced Palestinian Hamas-watcher and critic in Gaza. For Hamas publicly to endorse the 2002 Arab Peace Initiative, which promised recognition of Israel by the Arab states – other than Egypt and Jordan, which already recognised it – would have been a much more decisive step. There was no certainty; but by using Hamas's new document as a reason for – at last – engaging with Hamas, the Europeans, among others, might just have coaxed the faction's new leadership into taking that twenty-first-century step.

14

'THEY WILL ALWAYS MISS HOME'

LETTER FROM GAZA IS A WORK of fiction by the celebrated Palestinian writer Ghassan Kanafani,[1] the PFLP spokesman killed at the age of thirty-six with his young niece by an Israeli-planted car bomb in Beirut in 1972. It's written as a letter by a Palestinian from a refugee family in Shujaia in response to a call from his oldest friend Mustafa to join him in Sacramento, California, so they can realise the dreams they had as children of making their way in the world: 'We used to shout "we'll get rich."' But the letter breaks the news that, despite the offer of a place in UCLA's Department of Civil Engineering, the writer will not, after all, leave Gaza for ' "the land where there is greenery, water and lovely faces" as you wrote'.

Instead it ends with a passionate plea to Mustafa to come home. The writer explains that he recently returned to Gaza for a holiday from his job in Kuwait and has learned that his thirteen-year-old niece is in hospital, badly wounded in an Israeli bombing raid. Visiting her, he tries to comfort her by telling her that he has brought the red trousers she asked him to buy in Kuwait:

> Nadia trembled as though she had an electric shock and lowered her head in a terrible silence. I felt her tears wetting the back of my hand. 'Say something, Nadia! Don't you want the red trousers?' . . . I heard her voice again, coming from faraway. 'Uncle!' She stretched out her hand, lifted the white coverlet with her fingers and pointed to her leg, amputated from the top of the thigh.

For Nadia's uncle, it is a moment of shattering insight. He hears later that his niece had thrown herself over her younger siblings to protect them from the bombs. He urges Mustafa to return to Gaza to 'learn from Nadia's leg' what existence is worth.

The dilemma at the heart of the story was familiar to many Palestinians in Gaza. Kanafani's story spoke to many who had considered joining the diaspora: on the one hand, the chronic lack of opportunity, the fears of relentless conflict, the claustrophobic sense of imprisonment; on the other, abandoning friends and families to their fate, the agonies of watching their dangers and hardships from exile, and a deep homesickness. Indeed, the only difference between the twenty-first century and when Kanafani had been writing in the sixties was the difficulty of actually getting out.

FOR SOME PALESTINIANS IN GAZA, THE choice was clear – one way or the other. Hasan Zeyada, the Gaza Community Mental Health Programme psychologist, whose loss of his mother, brothers and nephew in the 2014 war could hardly have been more traumatic, was determined to stay: 'I'm not wasting my energy trying to think about leaving Gaza. My children have the right to decide and make their own plans. I have discussed the issue with my wife and I would not leave. I cannot guarantee I will have a better life. I have a job, I have a home and family and I put my energy in my small family and my large family and try to help my people here as a professional.'

By contrast Jehad Saftawi, an excellent photo-journalist, and his wife Lara, also an accomplished artist – both in their twenties – were not only determined to leave to start a new life but finally, after endless bureaucratic wrangles and attempts to cross through both Rafah and Erez, made it out in 2016. Over dinner of stuffed courgettes she had cooked in the couple's flat a few months before they left, Lara said the 2014 war, during which the twelve-storey apartment block next to theirs had been destroyed by an Israeli airstrike, had finally led them to decide to leave when they could. While both had seen more than enough dead bodies and ruined buildings when out observing and reporting during all three wars, the last one had seemed much closer to home. 'In 2014 we felt like it's coming,' said Jehad. 'Lara was hiding herself under the table a few nights when we were in our apartment.'[2] Like Hasan Zeyada, they had vivid memories of the heavy bombing on the night of 29 July – Jehad had posted a scarily vivid video of it on YouTube ironically titled 'Welcome to my apartment balcony in Al Zafer (1) Tower at the 11th floor of Gaza City'. The devastation inflicted by the wars and Israel's siege, he said, had damaged 'people's mentality . . . We're doing harsh things to each other, like it's an impossible place to live. People now are [committing] suicide – every day you hear about a story.'

Jehad had been born into the elite of Palestinian nationalism. Like his 'artivist' cousin Assad, he was the grandson of the famous Assad Saftawi, a 1948 refugee from what is now Ashkelon, a co-founder of Fatah, and a devout Muslim but an opponent of Hamas, who was mysteriously murdered in Gaza in 1993, the year before Arafat's return. Jehad's father Emad – Saftawi's son – had been an Islamic Jihad militant who took part in a spectacular breakout from an Israeli gaol in 1987 under cover of thick fog, went on the run, but was now back in prison, where he had switched allegiances to Hamas. While Jehad maintained filial telephone contact with his father, he was now an adamant opponent of factions including Hamas, whose 'crazy ideas' he regarded as 'far away from reality', and also of Israeli policy towards Gaza. Though he and Lara had thought of leaving before, Jehad decided 'after the 2014 war – what I have witnessed from Israelis, from Palestinians, from everyone – for sure we can't stay here anymore'.

In Jehad's view, the younger generation didn't want to do as their parents had and work for decades for enough money to buy or build a house – what Jehad called the 'the holy idea' to Palestinians of a home – because they had seen what could happen. 'In [a] war between Hamas and Israel, that house went in a moment. Everyone wants to leave, no one wants to save money for these houses, no one wants to build his family.' When I agreed I hadn't found many educated young people during 2016 who wanted to stay in Gaza, Jehad shot back: 'I haven't found a single person.'

That was an exaggeration. But Yasmin Dawwas, secular and in her twenties like Jehad and Lara, was also determined to leave. In the summer of 2016 Yasmin qualified as a doctor and was assigned to work for a year as an intern at Shifa hospital. She had spent the previous night sewing up accident victims in ER when we met one afternoon on the elegant terrace of the Deira hotel, overlooking the sea. Dark-haired,

pretty, highly intelligent, ambitious, a good English speaker, Yasmin
had courage: both physical – she had taken part-time work as a fixer/
translator in Gaza, helping foreign journalists in dangerous times and
places – and moral. She refused, as a Muslim in a highly conservative
society, to wear the hijab despite the slighting remarks or downright
abuse this could incur, believing it should be a matter of personal choice.
She was determined to get away from Gaza.

She had wanted to be a doctor from an early age. Her father,
Mohammed, had suffered from a progressive and unusual autoimmune
disease over a long period, and the shortage of medical experts in Gaza
had always 'annoyed me, that you have to go outside. It's sad and it's
haunting me. It started very mild but he can barely walk now. I'm not
used to seeing something which I can't change, to be really helpless
about it and not do anything.'[3]

To compound her father's problem, Yasmin's beloved, lively and very
clever youngest sister Hala, nine, was badly injured in a car crash in
2011, and although recovered, has long-term uterine complications,
which could probably only be tackled with a so far prohibitively expensive trip to the UK or the US.

Yasmin had been disappointed by the lack of postgraduate opportunities in Gaza for specialisation, and the fact that 'they need doctors but
they can't employ enough because of the situation with Hamas and the
PA and no one is paying salaries; you get a quarter of your salary every
three months. It's not worth even starting a career here.'

In one field, of course, the medical skills of Gaza, if not the facilities,
are for the bleakest of reasons as good as anywhere: emergency medicine and the treatment of war injuries. But Yasmin's dream was to
become a cardiac surgeon and to be involved in international medical
research. 'Maybe I'll come back after twenty years or something, to do
some work. I wouldn't mind coming every year if I can to help and to do
whatever people need here. But not to live here.'

All this, Yasmin knew, was easier said than done. She would need a
place, a scholarship, a visa and, of course, all the necessary permissions
to travel through Egypt or Israel and Jordan. But her appetite was whet-
ted in the autumn of 2015 when finally, after a four-month delay, she got
the necessary permission to take a course at University College Hospital,
London. She worked hard at UCH, but also she felt a new sense of
freedom.

There was also another factor: the difficulty of being different in a conservative and closed society. 'When I go to some areas I feel like an alien. It's like they are asking people like me to accept their beliefs, their traditions and I have no problem with that. But at the same time I expect to be treated no differently from other people, who are wearing the hijab, for example.' To her irritation, she was routinely assumed to be a Christian. 'In Ramadan they think I am not fasting [she does fast], and they would ask my name and when I say Yasmin Mohammed Dawwas, they say "oh you're a Muslim." It's weird . . . these things are private, they shouldn't be an issue.'

According to Yasmin, a 'huge majority' of women wearing the hijab did so 'because of their families, I believe they are being forced to by their brothers or fathers because they don't want people to stare at them. And some people wear it in some places and not others, like if they go to [the highly traditional town of] Rafah because they don't want to be harassed.'

Yasmin, both middle class (her mother was an UNRWA school-teacher) and from a refugee family, incidentally cast a sharp eye on Gaza's social gradations, and how, seventy years after the *nakba*, the better known Gazan – i.e. not refugee – families 'just get married to each other . . . when it comes to marriage they wouldn't allow their children to go outside. They would look down at me because my family is not originally from Gaza.' One of these families had been particularly horrified when their daughter wanted to marry a Bedouin, a snobbery Yasmin saw as 'pathetic'. One of her friends, she said, had told her how her grandmother had asked what Yasmin's name was and on being told, 'she would say "Dawwas, where do you meet these people? Is she even from Gaza?" And my friend would say "but grandma, she's a doctor" to try and convince her, but she would have to justify her friendship – it's crazy.'

But this was much less fundamental than the pressure to get married. Before Yasmin graduated, 'relatives, friends, neighbours, whatever' would find excuses for why she was not married. 'But now they can't find an excuse. I feel I'm young, but compared to standards here, they think I'm not young and I'll lose my chances of getting married. You go to some weddings and you find the bride is eighteen, nineteen and I'm like an aunt. It's crazy. The only time I felt my age was when I was in London. People were treating me like I'm a kid! When I say it's not a priority for me to get married, that I'm ambitious and I want to travel and I want to get more degrees and be good at what I am, they say "OK, but you can do this with a husband."'

Yasmin was also irritated by the ban on contact between unmarried young men and women enforced by Hamas. There had been no recent repeats of a harrowing case in Beit Lahiya in April 2005, before Hamas was even in power, when armed and self-appointed moral enforcers from the faction shot dead twenty-one-year-old Yusra al-Azami as she returned in a car driven by her fiancé from an outing to the beach with his brother and his fiancée – who was also Yusra's sister. Both couples were to be married the following weekend. Hamas eventually admitted that the perpetrators were members of the organisation, and said they had not known the couples were engaged: 'There was suspicion of immoral behaviour,' said the faction's then spokesman Mushir al-Masri.[4]

Young couples would still risk clandestine contacts; a fairly unfashionable city centre hotel has a secluded roof terrace often used for trysts. But according to Yasmin if an informer or busybody (depending on your point of view) told the authorities that an unmarried man and woman are in an apartment together, the police would probably turn up, throw the couple out, tell the parents and require the pair to marry.

Yasmin doubted she could ever form a serious relationship in Gaza. 'I don't want to be surrounded with all these restrictions. I don't want to feel like I'm doing something so wrong.' During her stay in London, she said, 'it felt so good, I was not being judged for what I wear, I was not being judged for anything I do.' Like Kanafani's Mustafa, she couldn't see herself cutting ties completely. Her dream was to establish a scholarship fund for ambitious young students to travel abroad. 'People here have energy, they can be very creative, they have a lack of chances and I would love to help someone like this.'

Also like Kanafani's Mustafa, however, Yasmin had a good friend who was in Gaza to stay. Aya al-Wakil was a smart, practical and socially conscious twenty-six-year-old lawyer at the Palestinian Centre for Human Rights. She would happily travel abroad for a further degree, but it would be specifically 'to help the Palestinian cause . . . and to help people here when I come back'.[5]

Aya, unmarried, a top law student in her year, and wearing the hijab, unlike Yasmin or Lara, tended to avoid the 'negative energy' around those of her friends who talked continually of leaving. For her the dilemma was not whether to stay or go, but whether to specialise in international law or in women's rights. Part of her job was to help compile a dossier of alleged Israeli war crimes, accusations which PCHR and three other human rights agencies had submitted to the International Criminal Court. The other was the *pro bono* representation of women who were victims of domestic violence or struggling to negotiate a divorce law heavily weighted against them. And while she strongly believed in challenging Israel at the ICC, she acknowledged that it was as a women's lawyer that she saw 'results every day'.

In Palestinian law, divorce was vastly easier for men than women. Usually, divorced Gazan women had the right to retain custody of boys until the age of nine (fifteen in the West Bank) and girls until eleven, when they pass to the father. Although, as Aya explained, 'sometimes the father does not get the children if he is not responsible enough, or a criminal or psychologically unstable. If a woman becomes a widow, then she can keep the children, unless she gets married, when the husband's family get the children.' And women all too often didn't know that the law gave them rights to see their children when they were under the father's care. The rights of widows to keep their children – provided they stay single – was a 2010 reform in Gaza, which Aya said was enacted in the interests of the large number of women widowed by Operation Cast Lead.

Women could only initiate divorce through often lengthy Sharia court proceedings, and then only under certain conditions, including domestic violence if it could be proved. A big part of Aya's work lay in persuading the courts that the conditions were met. She and others were campaigning for another change, which she said is accepted in Islamic religion, that would allow women to secure a divorce by simply waiving all their rights to property, money and custody of the children. Discriminatory as this sounds, Aya was convinced that, if it were applied in Gaza, 'half of the divorce problems would be solved'.

But the Hamas government opposed this, said Aya, on the grounds that 'because women are more emotional, most families will get divorced when a small problem happens; the man is more wise'. She thought the very opposite. 'As far as I've seen, the man is always less wise, and nervous and aggressive. He would divorce a woman any minute that he's angry, for silly reasons. But the woman will think about everything; the family, the house, the children, everything. That's a . . . reason why many women keep silent about violence towards them . . . because they want to keep their families together.'

Most husbands in Gaza did not beat their wives, of course, whatever the correct reading of the infamous verse in the Qur'an which seems to sanction it in cases of spousal disobedience.[6] But while Aya believed that consciousness-raising by women's organisations had probably increased the willingness of women to report it, thus pushing up the numbers, she was sure the real incidence was also increasing, much of it generated by pressures which had sharply increased in the previous ten years – the feeling of powerlessness to protect the family; the traumatising effects of war, especially in cases where the family has lost its home; and levels of unemployment among the highest in the world.

A 2006 Human Rights Watch report excoriated the Palestinian Authority police for doing little or nothing to help battered women,[7] but Aya said, perhaps surprisingly, the Hamas police in Gaza had since adopted a more positive role, arresting men or compelling them to sign an agreement that if it recurs they will go to gaol.

Sometimes, she said, she 'can't sleep at night' because of the violence she heard about. Divorce was a remedy, but it could take from six months to a year in court, and the beating was often difficult to prove. 'Sometimes we have to send a woman back to her husband to get evidence, like a medical or police report, or like running out of the house so that neighbours will see what's happening.' While her job was often painful, it was a big part of what made her determined to stay in Gaza:

I feel like I'm making a change every day, I'm doing something important for my people and for my country, especially in the women's field. You can't imagine how happy I feel when I take a case to court and make life better or fairer for one of the women.

But . . . there is another reason: war. I cannot be a person who watches what's happening from the outside . . . I know a lot of people live outside [Gaza], and during the war it's really difficult for them. For me, if anything happened to my family during a war and I wasn't here with them, that would make me go nuts. I have younger brothers and sisters, and I am an active member of the family and give them psychological support during the war. I'm the oldest sibling still at home.

Quite apart from the fact that both her parents had been ill and she didn't want to leave them, Aya said she would miss her many friends in Gaza who are 'supporting me all the time. I'm sure that I couldn't replace the people I know here if I went outside. I would feel lonely.' She claimed that 'ninety per cent of my friends abroad are not really happy. I don't think they will ever be able to live the life they want as normal people and isolate themselves from what is happening here. They will always miss home.'

IT'S NOT SURPRISING, GIVEN THE MASS displacement of 1948, that exile and return are such a pervasive theme in Palestinian fiction. Aya's last point was reflected in the opening passage of a short story by Atef Abu Saif,[8] who, unlike Kanafani, is a Gazan. The protagonist, Ramzi, drives the forty kilometres from the north to Rafah, 'the lengthiest journey any resident of Gaza can make', on a mission: to meet his older brother who had decided to come back from Italy after thirty years because he 'could no longer stand living so far from home'. Ramzi was five when his brother left; he only knows his face through Skype.

His brother gives up after three frustrating attempts to cross the border; for three days he had queued at the Egyptian barrier, 'where thousands of travellers pushed and shoved as they exited through the iron gate in a surreal, nauseating scene'. Instead, Ramzi meets by accident another returnee, his old university friend Samir, who has worked for ten years as an accountant in Dubai, earning enough money to put his brothers through school, for the family to build a new home in their refugee camp and to pay for his sister's wedding. Up to now he has resisted coming back, because of the journey through Sinai, 'which he loathed', the hours of waiting on the Egyptian side of the crossing – if it was open – and the thought of the return journey; the days or weeks of waiting before performing 'the miracle of leaving Gaza'. But Samir was determined to succeed where Ramzi's brother failed, and see his own mother before she died. Ramzi's mother had died the year before, 'remembering that rainy March morning when his brother left the house and the Peugeot 405 took him through the muddy streets to the border'.

These individual backstories, elegiacally conjured by Abu Saif, were instantly recognisable to thousands of Gazan families. They embodied a national paradox: that the ever-increasing difficulties of passing freely in and out of Gaza made it all the more tempting to leave for good if the chance arose. But they also got to the heart of an unresolvable contradiction even for those keenest to leave: Gaza as a prison to escape from, but also forever home.

15

THE LONG-DISTANCE RUNNER OF BEIT HANOUN: SIEGE AND *SUMMOUD*

T HE FLOODLIGHTS WERE ON, THE FENCES were in place, the riders had walked the course, the waiters were pausing with their orders of coffee, tea and fresh mango juice for the tables scattered round the ground; the judges were in their front-row seats. On a warm spring evening in 2016 at the fashionable Al Jawad Equestrian Club, the spectators stopped chattering for a few minutes. Thirteen-year-old Mohammed al-Saadi, in white breeches, black helmet and hacking jacket, completed a clear round. There was a round of generous applause from an audience of around a hundred children, men and women, a significant number of the latter with bare heads and dressed in elegant but casual Western-style jeans and tops. Welcome to Gaza's *haute bourgeoisie* at play.

Despite years of siege and three devastating military onslaughts, horse riding was 'booming' in Gaza, according to owner Ashraf al-Yazouri. He had been persuaded to start the business by his children, opening it just a month before the launch of Operation Protective Edge in August 2014. During the conflict's brief ceasefires, staff had to rush to the club to tend to the horses. Forty horses, all imported through Israel from Europe, were kept and trained at the club stables – nineteen it owned, and twenty-one belonging to individuals paying 540 shekels a month in stable fees on top of up to 20,000 shekels (around £4,200) for each animal.

Al-Yazouri was a busy man, working at his IT training company from 8 a.m. to 5 p.m. on weekdays and coming to the club in the evenings. He thought its success stemmed from people's need 'to relieve stress', a sentiment echoed by clients. He admitted its appeal was limited to those who could afford it: twenty shekels (just over £4) for a forty-five-minute lesson was trifling compared to prices in a European riding school, but well beyond the reach of Gaza's majority.

It was also a place where men and women, admittedly mostly attached to families, seemed able to socialise freely. Had Hamas sought to interfere as they had at another Gaza riding club, insisting that boys and girls were trained separately? Well, said al-Yazouri, Ministry of Interior officials had met twice with the club's managers and investors. The first time they were 'aggressive', but 'at the second they saw it was for sport and that there was not going to be any "troubles" arising from the mixing of girls and boys here'.[1]

Lubna Bseiso, twenty-eight, had been coming for riding lessons three or four times a week. 'Every time I come here I find myself getting rid of all the stress,' she said. 'You don't feel you are in Gaza. And it's a great place for social life.' Rafiq Mussalam, a forty-seven-year-old lawyer who came regularly to the club with his two sons and two daughters, said: 'It's somewhere safe for my children to come, and they can do something healthy rather than get into trouble.' Once it had been possible for better-off Gazans to go abroad for holidays; now the riding school was an alternative, especially in summer.

Al Jawad stood at one end of Gaza's socio-economic spectrum, El Zohor, on the edge of the Khan Yunis refugee camp, at the other. Perhaps there were poorer places in the Gaza Strip. One of its residents, Adham Yusef Zorob, twenty-two, believed there were workers in Gaza who earned even less than he did. For driving rubble to a local cement factory on a donkey cart, he was paid, as the sole wage earner in a household of five adults and four children, around fifteen shekels (less than £3) a day. But if not the poorest, this dilapidated little shanty town of seventy to eighty families living in breeze-block and zinc-roofed shacks was surely one of the most neglected. At one end it was overlooked by a mountainous and regularly replenished municipal rubbish dump; in the middle, barefoot children played on the sand around a pyramid of rusting and twisted car chassis awaiting export as scrap metal to Egypt and Israel. The makeshift hamlet was hard to find; maybe its official designation as El Zohor – or 'flowers' – was a city hall joke. No one in Khan Yunis seemed to have heard of it, perhaps because nine years earlier it didn't exist; it was only after the siege began to tighten that families no longer able to pay their rent decided to jerry-build their own shelters on this forsaken wasteland. Until 2013 Zorob worked in the smuggling tunnels under the Egyptian border, earning – for Gaza – genuinely good money: 700–800 shekels (£150–£170) a week. But when the Egyptians started to destroy the tunnels, often by flooding them with seawater, the work fell off. By 2016, he didn't even own a donkey cart; to shift the rubble he had to pay to use someone else's. The life of his household – his wife, their young son and daughter, his parents, his divorced sister and her two younger children – was 'below zero', he said. The family subsisted on lentils, beans and some vegetables, with chicken once a fortnight if they were lucky. Would the family vote in local elections, scheduled (but later cancelled) in six weeks? 'I don't believe any of the factions will help me in the future,' said Zorob. 'I want to find something to eat. I don't care about politics or believe in it. I don't bother.'[2]

If the Gaza Strip was cut off from the outside world, El Zohor seemed somehow cut off from the rest of the Strip; Gaza's Gaza. Visitors were rare; in June 2016 a Palestinian aid worker who had brought Saudi-financed bags of food for the *Iftar* – the evening meal which breaks the Ramadan fast – was 'shocked' at the families' situation. Further into the hamlet, and opposite a five-metre-high pile of scrap metal, lived Almaza Zorob, whose weathered face creased into lines under her headscarf when she smiled, which was often. She had married into the large Zorob clan and lived in a house similar to Adham's, outside which women of the village bantered about men and marriage, surrounded by their shoeless children. One heavily pregnant woman, surely no more than thirty-five, was determined that this baby – her tenth – would be the last. Was it sensible to have so many children when incomes were so low? 'There's nothing else to do,' interjected Almaza's thirty-four-year-old married son Mahrous to general laughter. Almaza, no longer smiling, insisted on taking us into a dark room at the back of her house, where her paralysed and epileptic adult daughter was lying on a bed, apparently asleep but with her open palms making jagged, uncoordinated motions. The room smelled strongly of urine.

The sick woman's brother, Mahrous Zorob, was more upbeat than his friend and distant relative at the other end of the hamlet, although in the same business. 'Each day is worse than the one before,' he said, jokingly adding: 'We used to have a nice view but now we look at garbage. But at least no one is having to pay rent.' He too had built his own house; one room for him, his wife Nisrin, twenty-seven, and their five children, a cramped little kitchen where the family's clothes were stored, and a 'bathroom' where the lavatory was a hole in the ground and there was no shower; the family washed themselves with water from a red plastic jug. There were holes in the roof which he had no money to fix. But Mahrous and Nisrin Zorob had not given up, or even come close to it. Two trees, one olive and one lemon, which the couple had planted several years earlier in their small front yard, would be bearing fruit any year now.

Was it too fanciful to see the couple's trees as a symbol of endurance and hope? Or to think that, for all the differences, they had something in common with the equestrians of Al Jawad? El Zohor, of course, was far more representative of Gaza than the small, well-off minority who could afford to ride. While the riding club's members had a vastly easier life than their compatriots in El Zohor – and most of Gaza's other two million inhabitants – both in their own way sought to establish a corner of normality in abnormal circumstances; as if to demonstrate that even the inmates of 'the big prison' aspired to a quality of life that so many of those outside it took for granted.

The Arabic word *summoud*, though often rendered in English as 'steadfastness', is not easily translatable. Since 1967 it has been used by Palestinians, including Yasser Arafat, in an almost strategic sense of non-violent resistance to the Israeli occupation, for example by those continuing to cultivate – and refusing to leave – their land even when force was applied to make them do so. But while it signified a patriotic duty, it could be as simple as, 'given the current circumstances, just waking up every morning with the determination to carry on with one's daily routine and to hold fast to one's humanity in spite of the challenges and dangers.'[3]

Of course not everyone in Gaza was able to rise above 'current circumstances'. Data on suicide (deeply frowned upon in Islam) was hard to pin down, but NGOs said it was on the rise in 2016. It had even been one of the reasons the teacher Jehan al-Okka had been against the inclusion of *Romeo and Juliet* as a set text in the high school matricula-tion exam. One informal estimate was that ninety-five Gazans took their own lives in the first quarter of the year, an abnormally high figure.[4] One was Asmi Yunis al-Burim, who bought a two-litre can of petrol at a roadside garage, poured it over his clothes and set himself alight at the busy Bani Sheila junction outside Khan Yunis on the main north–south Saladin road, in full view of shoppers at a nearby green-grocer's. Although bystanders rushed to cover him with a blanket and swiftly called an ambulance, he died in hospital eight days later. When we went to see his extended family, fifty-five men, women and children in a single dilapidated house in the eastern Khan Yunis suburb of Bani Sheila, my Palestinian colleague and interpreter Mariam Dawwas asked his younger brother Omar why Asmi had killed himself. 'Are you from Gaza? Then you know,' he replied. 'Had he been depressed?' we asked. 'We are all depressed,' he said wearily.[5] Asmi was unemployed, like forty-two per cent of Palestinians in Gaza. He had had recurrent prob-lems with his back since falling four floors while working on a building site seven years earlier, and was trying to get to either Egypt or Israel for further treatment. The Egyptian border was mostly closed, and while a local doctor had promised to get him a referral by the Palestinian Authority in Ramallah to a hospital outside Gaza – an essential precon-dition of obtaining an exit permit from the Israeli military – 'nothing happened,' said Omar. His mother, Zeinab, said there were 'many reasons' why her son had killed himself. 'He was depressed because there was no work. He couldn't get money for medical treatment. He couldn't afford to get married. Thirty-one is a bit old not to be married. He looked to his brothers who were married and had children. And they couldn't help him. They could hardly get by themselves. He had no hope that anything was going to change,' she said. Before we left, a posed photograph of Asmi, a strikingly handsome man with swept-back black hair and a faint resemblance to Prince, was produced. 'The best of his age,' said Zeinab al-Burim, crying for the first time since we had arrived.

PAM BAILEY, AN AMERICAN HUMAN RIGHTS activist and former jour-nalist who started a Euromed-funded project 'We Are Not Numbers', giving young Gazans a platform to write about their experiences, carried out a contributors' survey using nine questions designed by the British NHS. She found that fifty-three per cent of her sample were 'likely' to suffer from clinical depression, with 'half having lost one or more family members or close friends in a past Israeli assault'; a third felt 'they are a failure or have let their family down'; and one in five believed 'they'd be better off dead, or contemplate hurting themselves, nearly every day or on more than half the days'. The reasons cited were: inability to travel out of Gaza (seventy-seven per cent), power outages (sixty-five per cent), inability to get a job at all or one that pays fairly (sixty-one per cent), Israeli attacks/surveillance (fifty-five per cent).[6]

It wasn't surprising to find 'power outages' figuring so high in Pam Bailey's straw poll of young adults' anxieties. For a decade, one of the most intensely discussed topics among Gazans, at least between wars, had been the chronic power cuts which by the spring of 2017 had reduced supply to four hours on and twelve hours off. Many middle-class families have become adept at dealing with outages, rushing to the microwave to exploit the few minutes every hour when the caretakers of the better class of apartment blocks switch on fuel-guzzling generators to allow the lifts to work, or getting up in the middle of the night to study for exams, or put on the washing machine or charge their phones.

The precariousness of life in a city with a chronic shortage of power was exemplified by a tragedy in May 2016. One Friday – a day of family recreation as well as prayer – Mohammed al-Hindi, thirty-one, his wife and five small children went to the fishing port where Gazans frequently congregate at weekends to buy cheap sweetcorn and coffee and enjoy the view of the Mediterranean. It was a peaceful, enjoyable afternoon; the children had their faces painted and their father bought sandwiches for supper. On the way back to the Beach refugee camp, Mohammed stopped to buy candles because the electricity was off; once home, he lit three and the children were put to bed in the single bedroom before Mohammed went out again on an errand. Within fifteen minutes, a candle had ignited straw matting and a mattress. 'The fire was in the doorway,' Mohammed said. 'When my wife tried to get in she was burned in her face. She started to scream so the neighbours came. They couldn't get into the room.'[7] By the time neighbours had battered a hole in the wall, his three youngest children were dead.

The children's deaths were a painful symbol of a decade-long power crisis, for which Gazans blamed pretty well everybody. While the implosion of the economy because of an Israeli blockade – and the denial of access to natural gas – was at the root of the problem, many Palestinians in

Gaza tended to point the finger at Hamas and Fatah, and the split between them. The two factions were locked in a dispute over who should pay for Israeli fuel for Gaza's ageing and bomb-damaged single power station, and for electricity from Israel's grid, which supplied sixty per cent of Gaza's electricity. In particular the PA in Ramallah insisted on taxing the fuel for the power station at a punishing rate of up to 170 per cent, so the diesel bought by the PA for 2.3 shekels a litre was being sold on in early 2017 to the (Hamas-run) Gaza arm of the electricity generating authority at the top taxed price of 5.7 shekels. The result was that the power station shut down in April 2017. The Gaza office of the Palestinian Power, Energy and Natural Resources Authority had insisted that it could produce up to 60MW from the power station if the fuel were tax-free.[8] Even that was well below the orginally planned 140MW. One reason was limited relay capacity; but another was repeated bombardment of the the plant, most recently in 2014, and the difficulty of bringing spare parts into Gaza to repair the war damage.

Then in 2017 Mahmoud Abbas took his own steps to force Hamas into surrendering its control of Gaza. Whether or not, as one of his PA colleagues claimed,[9] he had been acting under pressure from Washington, the result, as invariably with such measures, was to put the burden on the Gaza public. Abbas cut back the salaries of tens of thousands of PA public servants who had been paid for more than eight years to stay at home, with an immediate adverse effect on Gaza's already stricken economy. He severely reduced the payments for electricity supplied by Israel at normal commercial rates; Israel duly cut the supply to 80MW, threatening the operation of hospitals and sewage pumping stations as well as squeezing domestic supplies even further. And he reduced the medical insurance coverage for patients seeking treatment in the West Bank and Israel, worsening an already dire situation in which Israel was anyway denying over half of patients' applications for exit permits.[10] The British NGO Medical Aid for Palestinians said that six cancer patients had died in the first half of 2017 after being refused permits, pointing out that Gaza lacks radiotherapy or specialised chemotherapy provision.[11] Unsurprisingly the UN described daily life in Gaza as becoming 'more and more wretched'.[12] This was yet another climax to a chronic crisis endured by Gaza for a decade. Suffering it was a kind of *summoud*, albeit involuntary, on a national scale.

In the face of all this it's impossible not to be impressed by Gazan resilience. 'Ordinary people' is an objectionable enough term at the best of times. But in Gaza's extraordinary circumstances, there don't seem to be any ordinary people. Not Khaled Abu Ahmed, who ran a white goods shop in Jabalya, and who cheerfully dramatised his regret for voting Hamas in 2006 by slipping off one sandal and beating himself around the head with it. 'We wanted change and reform,' he said. 'We thought they would bring prosperity.' Or Adel Khail, a six foot six giant of a man who used to work in Israel for good money but now rose at 5 a.m. every day for 1,600 shekels (£350) a month to perform 'mission impossible' by clearing the streets of rubbish with his horse and cart – and who tenderly cradled the head of his mare Yusra when she was frightened by one of the city's few garbage trucks. Or Abu Tawfiq, the old falafel seller near the Pasha Palace in Gaza's old city who liked to reminisce that he never did better business than during the First Intifada, when the hungry *shabab* took a breather from throwing stones and Molotov cocktails; and now voiced his contempt for both Hamas and Mahmoud Abbas, saying he thought Marwan Barghouti should lead the Palestinians.

Meanwhile, Nader al-Masri, the athlete from Beit Hanoun, was still running. No one would choose Gaza as the place to train for the Olympics, yet that's what al-Masri had still been doing, seven days a week in the early morning and evening, undaunted by his failure to get out to Qatar for the work that might have helped him qualify for London 2012. During Operation Protective Edge his house had been destroyed, like so many others in Beit Hanoun, by Israeli forces. In May 2016, a corner of the living room of his father's house in Beit Hanoun was festooned with the cups and medals al-Masri had amassed since first starting to run seriously in 1998, recovered from the wreckage of his home after the war.

Yet he had been refused permission by Israel in the spring of 2016 to leave Gaza to take part in the annual Palestinian marathon in Bethlehem, which he had expected to win. He had been depressed at losing the chance to set a new Palestinian record: 'Because of my winning the marathon, they considered this as a success for Hamas government in Gaza. I think the Palestinian Olympic Committee didn't want anyone from Gaza to participate. The last thing [it] wants is me winning the marathon. They don't want anything to do with Gaza, they forgot about it after the split in 2007.'

An event in Derry, Northern Ireland, was crucial for al-Masri's hopes for running in Rio in August 2016. It would have made him the first ever Palestinian to qualify for an Olympic marathon and at thirty-six it was probably his last chance.

It never happened. This time it was the British immigration authorities who refused al-Masri a visa, apparently on the grounds that he might not return to Gaza – inconceivable for a devoted family man like al-Masri, who warmly credited his wife Sawsan's support for the fact he kept running. After protests, including from the late Deputy First Minister Martin McGuinness, the British relented, but too late for him to get the visa in time to travel. A less determined athlete would have given up, but al-Masri kept on running every day, and had prepared determinedly for the 2017 Bethlehem marathon and for a major track event in Azerbaijan.

Al-Masri did not get his Israeli exit permit for either event. 'This doesn't happen anywhere else in the world,' he said. 'You can't find an athlete or player in another country, training all this time, this hard and at the same time not knowing if they'll be able to go.' Yet, incredibly, this still super-fit thirty-seven-year-old continued to run twenty to twenty-five kilometres a day. As an ex-PA employee his salary, too, had been cut by thirty per cent as a result of Abbas's measure, a problem, he said, because he had to buy expensive vitamin drinks to replenish lost energy. But he would not quit. The running 'relieved stress' and, besides, he was doing a 'national job' training to represent his people if and when the opportunity finally arose.

IF NADER AL-MASRI REFLECTED ONE KIND of *summoud*, Souad al-Quraya embodied quite another. It had been Souad who had wept continuously back in 2006 as she described the struggle to feed her family when the international aid boycott was first biting in the aftermath of Hamas's election victory.[13] Yet in 2016 she had emerged as a capable, graceful woman in her early forties, proud of having single-handedly brought up her polite and self-confident children; the older ones were far better educated than she had ever had the chance of being, having left school at thirteen despite her obvious intelligence. She now wrote poetry, mainly for herself, but some of it she published on Facebook, and some of it had been recited at an event held by the Turkish charity for children who had lost a parent and which had helped the family from time to time, supplementing the small 700 shekels a month pension she had got from the PA for her late husband.

Not that life had been easy in the intervening years. The family was still poor. The oldest two children had been forced to drop out of university because there was no money to pay the fees, but her son was earning 'pocket money' playing semi-professional football with a local club and her daughter was working in a clothes shop, hoping to make enough to cover her university fees. Her second son Mohammed, twenty, had been working in a sofa factory until he was laid off in 2014 because there hadn't been enough work to keep the payroll intact.

Widowhood could also be problematic in a conservative and poorer area of Gaza City. When her husband had died, his family, as is often customary, had suggested she marry one of his unmarried brothers. She had refused; bringing up her children had been the priority. Instead, she said, 'life taught me to be strong. I had to change the clothes of a woman and put on the clothes of a man.' What did not come with that, however, was a man's relative freedom.

She hadn't, for example, felt able to go out to work to support her children – even supposing there was a job to go to. After her husband died, she had moved into a first-floor apartment in her brother's house. In the 2008–9 war the families heeded Israeli warnings to leave the area and she moved in with her father; her brother's house was destroyed and she and her children lost all their furniture and belongings. With the help of the Turkish charity, and another Qatari one, she was able to buy a plot of land opposite her father's house and he had helped her build a new three-room home 'brick by brick' over the next eight years.

When her father, who lived across the road, was not present, Souad put her complicated relationship with him into perspective: 'He is a very conservative man, and he does not allow me to go out most times under the pretext that I am still young and beautiful so I would be a target for men. My father keeps asking me every time I go out about where I go and why . . . If my father acts this way, can you imagine what other people say. I know that his attitude and pressure come from a place of care, but it affected me negatively.' Unsurprisingly, Souad had received several proposals of marriage. That had been 'positive' – it made her feel 'that I am a woman. But others saw it as a negative sign that I am still wanted for marriage.' As Souad knew, this attitude, embedded in the more conservative sectors of Gazan society, was not the product of Islam, which permits a widow to remarry. But many of her neighbours saw her as 'vulnerable', as she put it, to 'men's seduction'. She had written in one of her poems of such busybodies as 'human wolves'. She reflected that technological progress – with widespread use of smart phones and the internet – had not been matched by similar progress in 'society's perception of women'.

It was hard not to see the oppressive conservatism that Souad – and other women – had encountered as part of what Jawdat al-Khodary had called the 'mental siege'. A society closed off from the outside world tends to turn in on itself. Yet her reflections were not born of bitterness. This charming and hospitable woman had risen valiantly above her lack of formal education. The Palestinian journalist Hazem Balousha, who visited her with me three times during 2016, was struck by how correct her Arabic was for someone who had only reached eighth grade. Had she subsequently been to university, he asked her. No, she said, but she had helped her children with their homework and 'learned at the same time'. Meanwhile her eldest son snorted with supportive derision at people like his grandfather who thought that his mother should never marry again, saying it was 'completely normal' for her to do so. It seemed like a modest hope for the future – both Souad's and Gaza's.

If anyone still typified the dogged determination of Palestinians in Gaza to eke out a living whatever the odds, it was the Aziz brothers. Given how dejected the clothing manufacturer Abed Rabbo Aziz seemed back in 2007, when he still thought the embargo might be short-lived, it was striking that in early 2016 he was still – just – working, optimistically producing a small volume of jeans for the heavily depressed local market. While Abed Rabbo had tended to melancholy over the last decade, his younger brother had seemed perpetually cheery, constantly on the lookout for alternative means of supplementing the business he was taking care of in Abed Rabbo's absence. 'Sometimes my brother gets desperate and disappointed,' explained Aziz Aziz, 'but then he finds me still working and comes back.' But while he was employing on pittance wages a handful of workers in January 2016 – including his own sons and nephews – Abed Rabbo explained he couldn't hire more because there was 'no consumption'.

But the brothers weren't giving up. Three months earlier they had diversified into producing wire cages for battery chickens, something hitherto unknown in Gaza, but proposed by Aziz after an internet trawl. Having established there was a market, the brothers decided to venture into the chicken business themselves. That very morning they had sold 1,000 battery chickens to a local wholesaler at a profit of around 6,000 shekels (almost £1,000) – a red-letter day in a period of deepening economic gloom. The brothers took me to what had previously been their storehouse for imported cloth, where a few dozen of the creatures were still in the cages made in the factory, and several of which were barbecued for our lunch. Abed Rabbo Aziz saw the venture as a stopgap to fill the vacuum left by the blockade. At one point, as we sat round a brazier on a cold January day sipping tea and coffee, Abed Rabbo hit out at everybody: 'I understand that Israel has the upper hand, to do whatever it wants. It's politics. They want to separate Gaza from the West Bank. It's not my guilt as a citizen. I inherited the business from my father and I want to pass it on to my sons. Why are they punishing me? Why are they making me think about different products like chickens? But it's not my fault we have a problem with the Israeli government. It is the responsibility of Hamas and Abu Mazen to solve it.'[14]

So why were the brothers so determined to keep going? 'This is my life,' said Abed Rabbo. 'It's the only thing I can do. I can't let my children work with Fatah or Hamas.' He had personally seen the drift of young men from productive employment to the Hamas payroll, both civilian and military, some of whom had been killed. Alam, twenty, one of Aziz's sons, described how for five months he had prayed regularly at a local mosque that happened to be aligned with Islamic Jihad. One day a member of the faction had sidled up to him and invited him to 'follow us and work with us'. Alam said: 'I told him I had a job and I was doing a lot of bodybuilding. I said no. Now I pray at home.' But one of his friends who prayed at a different, Hamas-affiliated, mosque had succumbed to a similar overture. 'He joined and then he was killed in the last war. He was with me that day, and then two hours later he was dead. He was a fighter.' Alam's unemployed friends had often begged him to get them work, he added. 'Sometimes they get work here for twenty shekels a day [around £4], which is all there is.'

It was impossible to know how many young men joined the factions out of conviction and how many out of financial despair. Basil Abu Qamer's was a rather different case from Alam's, if a fairly common one. He was born in 1983 into a poor family of refugees. His father – who had originally worked in Israel, but had also been a Fatah activist who was released from an Israeli gaol because of illness – had been unable to work; as a result Basil left school at twelve (exceptionally early even in poor families) for various factory jobs; in 1997, aged only fifteen, he had started work at the Aziz factory. Since the beginning of the Intifada, and with a family chronically short of money, he had showed up whenever the work was available. Abed Rabbo, he said, had treated him 'like one of his children and sometimes even apart from my salary he was giving me money because he knew my situation'. But coming from a militant Fatah family, he had also fallen in with its military wing, the al-Aqsa Martyrs' Brigades. It had started in his teens with stone throwing at Israeli troops across the border early in the Intifada, when he was injured by a bullet in the knee. In 2003, at the age of twenty, he was recruited for a shooting attack on the Gaza settlement of Netzer Hazani. Mahmoud Abbas was Prime Minister and Fatah militants were supposed to be observing a ceasefire; Palestinian intelligence had been tipped off about the plan and arrested the unit. Basil was held for seven days and then released.[15]

Then he was engaged as an al-Aqsa Martyrs' Brigades fighter to confront the major incursion launched by Israel into Jabalya in the first week of October 2004. 'I was in the back, I wasn't in the front, I was patrolling in the streets, if they came further I would shoot at them. But they didn't and I didn't.'

By 2005 Basil's work at the Aziz factory had dried up, and he was persuaded to get through the fence into Israel by a friend who knew both how and where to cut it and to deactivate its electric sensors. The friend had relatives on the Israeli side, in Beersheba, which they intended to reach on foot. This time, the mission was to find work and not to launch an attack. After two days they were picked up by troops from the border.

This was bad news for Basil, because the Israeli military had information – from two other earlier Palestinian detainees, Basil thought – about his part in the planned 2003 attack on Netzer Hazani. Held in Ashkelon prison, Basil denied it. But Israeli intelligence resorted to a well-tried technique by sending 'birds' – slang for Palestinian collaborators who mingle incognito with detainees – to goad him by accusing him of collaborating with Israel. To prove he hadn't, Basil mentioned the 2003 operation – and the Israelis had their 'confession'. Basil was gaoled for three years, a sentence he served mainly in Nafha prison in the Negev desert. He was released before the 2008–9 war. Basil had found prison 'difficult' but there was one compensation: his family were receiving from the PA the prisoner's 'salary' of 1,800 shekels a month, and his father was saving most of it; he had enough money – including for the dowry* – to get married on his release.

By now Aziz had laid all his employees off. Basil took day work here and there when it was available, but by late 2015 he no longer cared whether he 'lived or died'. He had joined a series of weekly protests in late 2015 at the Erez crossing during heightened violence in the West Bank and Jerusalem. It was dangerous – two Palestinians were killed at Erez by live fire at one of the protests, on 17 October. And Basil was by now motivated less by nationalism than despair. 'I was very desperate, I was disappointed and pessimistic about everything. There was no work, nothing to do and I had two kids and with my wife living with my family, all of us were living in one room . . . and I thought if I left and was killed they would get something from the government so they could live on it . . . So to die with honour was better than to commit suicide.'

Instead Basil was seriously, though not critically, injured in the head by an Israeli tear gas canister. As he recovered consciousness in Shifa hospital, he began to repent of his kamikaze mission. In January 2016, when I first met him round Abed Rabbo's brazier, a slight figure in jeans and beanie hat, he had not yet got his job back. But as business picked up somewhat in advance of the 2016 Eid al-Adha festival, Basil was back on the Aziz payroll. He managed to rent a small apartment and, though things were still tough, he felt happier. He had relatives who were paid members of one of the armed factions, but he had no desire to join them. 'I have a family now,' he said. 'I take care about my kids.' But what if he lost his job again? 'Of course. If there is no choice, yes.'

Abed Rabbo Aziz wanted to keep Basil on – 'a good worker' – if he could. As Basil had said, Aziz tended to treat his employees as family, and by late 2016 he was determined to make the best of the slight easing on export restrictions which Israel had at last permitted, in the hope of selling once again to Israeli customers. It was a struggle: to remain legitimate, the goods first had to go to Hebron so that VAT could be levied

---

* Traditionally a Palestinian groom or his family pay a sum for the wedding and the bride's clothes, jewellery etc., as well as furnishing the home where the couple will live.

from the Ramallah-run West Bank and not from 'hostile' Gaza. And Aziz needed to share a truck to transport the goods with several other traders, otherwise the 4,000-shekel cost of shipping would be prohibitive. There had been problems; he had managed to sell a consignment of women's trousers to Tel Aviv wholesalers as a kind of pilot, but it took too long, and the trader said he couldn't start working with Gaza again.

Nevertheless, Israel was the market to which he wanted to return. A pair of trousers that would sell to a retailer in Gaza for five shekels would fetch him fifteen in Israel, before being sold on to shops by the Israeli dealer, Aziz said, for forty to fifty shekels, and then to the individual customer for seventy. A long time ago, before the Intifada, Aziz had the capital to import whatever cloth he wanted; since then he had been dependent on deals whereby the Israeli trader supplied the cloth and Aziz returned the finished product. Between 2007 and 2016, that, too, had been impossible because no exports were allowed out. Now there was a slim chance that he could at least recover a portion of his earlier business. One Gazan company had resumed making yarmulkes for a religious Israeli wholesaler. And compared with a negligible average of 14.7 trucks leaving Gaza every month between June 2007 and the end of 2014, the monthly average for the first eight months of 2016 was more than 160 trucks. But this was still well under a fifth of what it was pre-June 2007,[16] and the proportion of unspecified 'security blocks' on businessmen leaving Gaza for Israel – essential for fruitful negotiations with customers and clearing logistical hurdles – had doubled since 2013. Finally Aziz had found that his former Israeli partners were wary of switching back from current suppliers – mainly in the West Bank and Jordan – to Gaza because of the possibility of another war, or the reimposition of blanket restrictions that had prevailed for the previous decade. 'The Israelis are now afraid of sending work to Gaza,' he said.

But Aziz was going to keep trying. His dream was still to have the factory back to what it had once been, when he had 100 workers and the Arab music over the loudspeakers competed with the din of the sewing machines.

THE SPIRIT WHICH HAD KEPT the Aziz brothers going through a decade of siege was articulated by another businessman who operated on a much larger scale. One morning in early August during the 2014 war, the Australian journalist Ruth Pollard and I were travelling back from

Khan Yunis when two tank shells struck an apartment building on each side of Gaza's main north–south Saladin road just ahead of us. As our driver accelerated out of the line of fire, we passed the large, blackened al-Awda food processing factory, the largest in the Strip, engulfed by flames after being attacked earlier by artillery shelling. What was burning was 300 tonnes of margarine along with sugar, cocoa, vanilla, cartons, paper, flour and a range of finished biscuits and other food products; the total damage came to $18m. The owner Mohammed al-Tilbani had been in Saudi Arabia for the first thirty days of war; he was in the West Bank and on his way back to Gaza when he saw the television pictures of his factory, which employed around 400, going up in smoke. Once back in Gaza he waited until a ceasefire to go to the factory at Deir el Balah to assess the damage and remove what could be rescued from the fire. It was then, he would say later, that he had started to receive 'threatening texts' from the Israeli authorities warning him to keep away from the factory. One had said, 'Be careful: this time we targeted it with shells, next time it'll be an air strike.' Al-Tilbani, a self-made businessman and the son of a refugee farmer from Beersheeba, was religious; he fasted every Monday and Thursday. He was also proud of his humble origins; on the wall of his office at the factory was a recent picture of the Meghazi camp football team, which he sponsored. And he set about restoring the factory as soon as the war was over. 'I have a very strong will to keep working,' he said. 'If you are defeated, then you lose everything.'[17]

16

'WE LOVE LIFE, IF WE FIND A WAY TO IT'

Two passengers board an early morning train at a clean, modern railway station in the northern West Bank city of Jenin. One is a Palestinian businessman heading for a meeting in Cairo who will be whisked in less than ninety minutes to Gaza International airport, a new Middle East hub. The other, a female academic, will take the line all the way after it loops back north towards Gaza City, where she is due to attend an international conference on genetics.

On the way south they both savour the changing landscape through the train window – the mountains of Jordan to their left, the skyscrapers of Tel Aviv in the distance to the right. They both note with satisfaction the aqueduct running along the railway tracks that had finally solved at a stroke the desperate water shortages facing their people.

The electrified service is universally known as 'the arc', even though officially the term also applies to the power lines, natural gas pipes, fibre optic cables and even hiking trails which run along the same 130-mile corridor. When the train stops at Nablus and Hebron the passengers gaze out at the imaginatively planned new neighbourhoods, each with their green spaces, and many housing refugees who have returned, albeit not to their ancestral homes, to Palestine from Jordan or Syria.

After the airport, as the train turns north to its next stop at Khan Yunis, the academic observes the California-style urban rapid bus system speeding passengers to the centre of town. It's early summer; as the train approaches Gaza City, she idly watches the Western tourists to her left already gathering on the beach and then the cranes loading Maersk containers of fruit, flowers, clothing and furniture onto Europe-bound ships docked at Gaza's modern new seaport. She glances at her watch; on the way home she will visit her ageing mother in East Jerusalem, now the undisputed capital of the independent Palestinian state, as West Jerusalem is Israel's.

Laughably implausible as this utopian vision seems, it is no more than an extrapolation from a $2m Rand Corporation study published in 2005.[1] The report, which Rand itself accurately described as the 'most comprehensive recommendations ever made for the success of an independent Palestinian state', envisaged the arc as the centrepiece of an infrastructure and housing programme costing $33bn over ten years.

It is hardly surprising that when the report's main author, the American architect Doug Suisman, presented it to PA ministers in Ramallah, he was met with a stunned silence. It was only broken when the Gazan Jihad al-Wazir, then the Deputy Planning Minister, said: 'I have tears in my eyes.' Al-Wazir was Fatah aristocracy: his father was Abu Jihad, Yasser Arafat's long-time comrade from the Kuwait days, assassinated by Israel in Tunis during the First Intifada. A few days after the meeting, he said that Suisman's presentation had a kind of 'American naivety', which might be just what was needed to nourish hopes of a Palestinian state. 'I was very moved,' he said. 'You know, you are dealing all the time with the nitty gritty of the conflict and then someone comes from LA who has a vision, who has thought out of the box.'

More than a decade later Rand's thinking was, of course, still as 'out of the box' as ever. But the report conveyed something important: a sense of how, after a century of occupation by the British, by Jordan and Egypt, and by Israel, an independent Palestine with democratic leadership and a peace agreement with Israel had the human and natural resources to emerge as a modern, outward-looking state. It's a process in which Gaza, as its main international access point – by sea and air – would play a pivotal part.

Indeed, by stressing a new airport and seaport in Gaza – the one maritime part of a future Palestine – as a *sine qua non* of a successful independent state, the Rand team were in a long line of outside observers to grasp the terrritory's potential. Back in 1918 a learned Anglican monk and former army chaplain revisited the city after the ravages of the war between the British and the Turks the preceding year. Father Philip Napier Waggett told his readers in the *Church Times* that 'anyone . . . must realise how great for a long time yet the need will be of fostering care if Gaza is to recover its former prosperity. And it ought, of course, to go far beyond that, in a new and renovated Palestine. But here, as everywhere, the hope is in the security and regular work of the inhabitants, not in favour and gifts.'[2]

Gaza had a brisk trade before 1914 exporting barley for English breweries. But Fr Waggett was almost certainly casting his mind back further when he referred to its 'former prosperity': the several periods in Gaza's long history, ancient Egyptian, Roman, Byzantine, Otttoman, when, frequently fought over as it was, Gaza had been able to exploit its position on the ancient 'Way of the Sea' between Egypt and Syria, as a busy commercial port and entrepôt. Yet his main point was as relevant today as it was then: that Palestinians in Gaza would always choose economic freedom over man-made aid dependency.

Nor was he alone. Three years later, Sir Herbert Samuel, the first High Commissioner of the British Mandatory authority in Palestine, reported back to the Foreign Office in 1921 that postwar Gaza was still comparable to 'the devastated areas in France and Belgium'. In a request that would also echo down the decades, Sir Herbert said he hoped ministers would help 'to restore the prosperity of a town whose past history bears eloquent testimony to its potentialities'.[3]

To have a twenty-first-century sense of those 'potentialities' – not to mention Gaza's ingenuity in surviving an economic blockade – you could do worse than visit Work Without Borders (WWB). A fast-growing offshore IT company, it deployed some of the Strip's brightest young people on high-calibre, high-tech outsourced work for clients abroad, notably, but not solely, in Saudi Arabia. WWB was in the vanguard of cross-border commerce from a Gaza under siege, almost a legal cyber-equivalent of the smuggling tunnels at Rafah. Its quiet, open office in a Gaza City high-rise was far from the stereotypical international image of Gaza. Two of its products were a management system for a Saudi property and lettings company and an online grocery shopping platform developed in Gaza for a Riyadh-based company.[4]

With a dismal sixty-five per cent of recent university graduates unemployed,[5] WWB could afford to be choosy about whom it recruited. As a non-profit, it performed as a normal business, but sought to

maximise employment and invest in expansion. The staff outsourced by
WWB to companies outside Gaza were mostly graduates, but not necessarily in IT. One young man with a Master's in chemistry worked as a
web designer; an architectural student had become an animator; and
another qualified in civil engineering was working on social media.
Seed funding for the start-up came from a Saudi benefactor, and a
Qatari charity had provided a modest $7,000 grant for solar panels,
crucial because of repeated power cuts. Alaa el-Shurafa, WWB's director, said the company, which launched in 2011 with three workers, was
now approaching break-even point, greatly helped by the reputation of
Palestinians throughout the Arab world for their high standard of
education, commitment and loyalty as employees. 'I told all of our
customers, "don't give work to us because [you think] we need the work,
we're hungry, we haven't any money; no, please deal with me as a business, business-to-business."'

Women made up about a third of WWB's 112-strong workforce.
Mirvat Bkheet, twenty-seven, confident and ambitious, was in charge of
a team of eight men carrying out work for Innosoft, a Saudi company
providing 'technological solutions' for the private and public sector. A
graduate in information technology systems, she combined her full-
time job with a business MA at Gaza's Islamic University, which she
hoped to follow with a scholarship-funded business PhD in Europe.

Her boss was optimistic that WWB could continue to grow and
wryly revealed a paradox. On the one hand, 'I know that many companies are afraid of Gaza. Gaza means closure.' But on the other, unlike
companies elsewhere which lose some of their best staff to international corporations in the US or Europe, that was much less of a risk
in Gaza for the simple reason that it is hard to leave. Laughing,
el-Shurafa said: 'So sometimes the closure helps us. I'm very sad to say
it, but it's true.'

WWB functioned throughout the fifty-one days of the 2014 war, a
testament to the determination of its staff. A promotional video for the
firm showed scenes of destruction interspersed with WWB professing
their commitment. In it, Wafah Abu Rahma sat at home with her laptop,
announcing: 'We have been living with war for several days. There is a
lot of bombing and lots of destruction. Most activities stopped in the
Strip, but I did not stop working for a single day.' Something of Gaza's
potential permeates the video; it was impossible to watch without

thinking how much more these resourceful and committed young people could achieve in benign conditions.

Nor, even after what had been, literally and metaphorically, Gaza's darkest decade, was this stubborn creativity evident only in businesses like this. The artists Maha al-Daya and her husband Ayman Eissa had started to enjoy success even though, thanks to the economy, the local art market was next to zero and decent paints were still hard to come by. Both of them had exhibited abroad, which had helped them with foreign sales, art being one export to which the embargo did not apply. The couple had moved out of their apartment in the bleak high-rise with a lift shaft but no lift to an elegant old first-floor apartment with a wrought-iron balcony in the heart of Gaza City. And there had been another war, during which Maha had once again felt unable to pick up a paint brush.

Maha had won a scholarship – and more importantly the necessary visa and permits – to spend a fertile four months in Paris. There, instead of the Gaza boats she found herself painting among much else an evocative image of a *bateau mouche* on the Seine at night. She returned from France two days before Operation Protective Edge. 'It was crazy for me. I came to a war, it was horrible.' Maha kept her children occupied throughout the war, naturally with paper and paint. But at least this time the family were all together.[6]

She had started making dresses, gorgeously embroidering them in floral and abstract designs of vivid reds, greens and purples. A small conservatory was a riot of flowers, house plants, fruit, cacti – material for a hundred still lifes. She continued to paint Gaza landscapes and meticulously executed abstracts built around complex symmetrical patterns, which characterise some Islamic art. She had no wish either to paint or live outside Gaza. A lot of this had to do with the subjects to which she was repeatedly drawn, of course; but for a sophisticated and highly intelligent woman she cited another touchingly simple reason: 'It's not easy living abroad, especially with children. If your child was lost abroad, you wouldn't find them. Here in Gaza it's easy to find them!'

But while Maha continued to paint Gaza landscapes, Ayman's works were of people. 'Ayman doesn't just paint people, he paints women,' Maha was quick to point out, laughing. Indeed, most of his paintings are of women, often voluptuous but all in a highly distinctive style, usually clothed but including some nudes, which he can hardly exhibit in Hamas-run Gaza. When he last showed such a painting in Gaza in 2002, it had been surreptitiously scratched by an irate religious sheikh.

Social conservatism, this time partly reinforced by Hamas, had taken its toll on cinema in once movie-mad Gaza. Now there are only relics. But by clambering through a gap in a wire fence you can see the remains of the burned-out old al-Amer cinema, in the 1970s a welcoming, luxurious venue. In 2016, the detritus included rolls of old film stock; a single beer bottle on the floor of what had been the stalls; smashed tiles and porcelain of the lavatories on either side of an ample foyer, which would once have been lively with chatter; the tiered floor of what had been the dress circle; faded posters advertising Indian films like *Disco Dancer*.

The Amer had been one of several cinemas in Gaza, some of which survived well into Israeli occupation. Only at the end of the 1970s and during the 1980s did Islamist objections begin to threaten their survival. The biggest and best known of the picture theatres was al-Nasr in Omar El Mukhtar Street. In 2016 it was still a Gaza landmark, its curved neo-classical portico and large sign proclaiming 'Cinema' in English partly hidden behind trees; unlike the Amer, it was bricked up and impossible to enter.

Sami Efrangi, the seventy-four-year-old former manager, recalled the time before the Six Day War when the films came from the golden years of Egyptian cinema: mainly romances, dramas, comedies and musicals with stars like the singer Abdel Halim Hafez. Even in the 1960s there was some segregation in the auditorium. Maybe, he mused, there had been a little kissing and holding hands between couples because it was dark when the film was on 'and we couldn't observe everybody'. But mainly 'It was like a picnic for the families, a place to hang out. If you wanted to please your wife or your fiancée you would take her to the cinema.'[7]

Efrangi took a considerable risk by agreeing to rent the 1,350-seat Nasr from its owner for a sizeable $20,000 a year. The experiment did not start well; for the first two months films were playing to half-empty houses. Then an acquaintance who had visited the US told him about *Commando*, an Arnold Schwarzenegger vehicle; an Israeli distributor called him about it. Efrangi immediately got a taxi to Tel Aviv; those were the days, of course, when business was constantly being made across the Israeli–Gaza border.

Thirty-five years later Efrangi was still proud of the way he bargained the price down. 'So he says "Come on! You can ask anyone. This film is a big hit in the United States!" And I say, "Yeah, it can work in the US but that doesn't mean it will in Gaza."' Finally they agreed on $1,500. 'The day of the first show I was sleeping at home. I got a call from the workers at the cinema by seven thirty, eight o'clock in the morning, and they said: "The students are not going to their schools, they are surrounding the cinema." The picture house was full for the 10 a.m. showing and people were paying for standing room. And so it remained for the rest of the week with the cinema 'more than full' mornings, afternoons and evenings, said Efrangi. The reputation of the Nasr was made – thanks in large part to Arnold Schwarzenegger.

By 1987, as the First Intifada took hold, audiences plummeted, and Efrangi closed the Nasr. But in the optimistic period after Arafat's return and the formation of the PA, the new Ministry of Culture suggested he reopen it as Gaza's only cinema. It thrived for another decade. Then, in 1997, during a demonstration called by Islamists, a breakaway group advanced on the empty and non-operating al-Galla cinema. PA officials warned Efrangi that they might come to the Nasr next. He swiftly evacuated the audience.

'I locked all the doors [but] they stormed the cinema, they broke the doors. I was watching, moment by moment, minute by minute and I saw they were looting, burning, taking everything from inside, so I started to have tears. Everything was looted, stolen, in front of my eyes. A friend of mine came with his car, and he pushed me into the car and he says "don't worry you can make the money again." And I returned home.'

He recovered quickly from the losses, and within a week was planning his next move, a grocery business. But he added sadly: 'When I pass the cinema, I remember everything.'

After the 2014 war, however, film production and, to a severely limited extent, public showings were making a comeback. An art feature film made by Khalil al-Mozayen, one of several directors now working in the Strip, was chosen for the Dubai International Film Festival. Although a fictional portrayal of a woman ritually abused by her brother for shaming the family honour, it included a real-life sequence portraying the destruction of his entire film archive when his office in the Basha tower was bombed in the war. The scene, he proclaimed, highlighted 'the ability of the Palestinian people to rise from the ashes like a phoe-nix'.[8] But al-Mozayen was also the moving spirit behind the first two annual 'red carpet' Gaza film festivals. It was an innovation that needed careful negotiations with the reluctant Hamas authorities. The 2016 festival opened with the Gaza premiere of a biopic which could hardly have been closer to its audience's hearts.

For many Palestinians, not only but especially in Gaza, Mohammed Assaf shows what can be achieved with talent, determination and a bit of luck. The story of him winning *Arab Idol*, the Middle East's equiva-lent of *Pop Idol*, had been made into a film and in 2016 the free screen-ing drew a capacity crowd to the Shawa Centre's auditorium.

The young man from Khan Younis refugee camp, with charm, an impressive singing voice, a wonderfully Gazan backstory and massive determination, had been propelled in 2013 to international fame by his win. Tens of thousands of people erupted in firework-lighting, car-horn-honking, dancing celebrations, not only in Gaza, but across the West Bank. It was a rare moment of pure national pride and joy.

Many in Hamas had acute reservations, not only about the glitzy and irredeemably secular world of showbiz, but also about the winning song. 'Raise Your Keffiyeh', which honoured Palestinian prisoners, had been associated with the Arafat-led PLO and banned at Gazan weddings by Hamas. Before an ecstatic audience in Beirut and to millions watch-ing on TV, he had turned it into an anthem of Palestinian unity.

So Hany Abu-Assad's glossy feelgood biopic of the singer was not just any film. Which is why a packed house, families and friends, male and female, were prepared to sit through (as usual) a few too many speeches before watching its first showing in Gaza. During the film they clapped and cheered his difficult path to victory: the Hamas emigration officer at the Rafah crossing who, when Assaf arrives with fake papers, lets him through to Egypt after hearing him sing; Assaf scaling a high wall to get into the hotel where first-round auditions were being held when he arrived without the right ID; a fellow Gazan competitor giving up his place for Assaf when he arrives to get a place in the queue.

As the screening's organiser, Khalil al-Mozayen had been obliged to sign a Ministry of Interior document prohibiting 'intermingling' of women and men in the audience. Most of the film was shown with the house lights on, with the centre's private security guards patrolling the aisles. Half an hour into the movie, there was more clapping and cheering when the lights actually went down, but ten minutes later they went up again on the instructions of a young Hamas security man who said: 'No theatre in Gaza can be completely dark during the screening of a film to avoid immoral acts happening in the dark.'

A highlight of the lengthy preamble to the showing had been a musical interlude, including a piece played by a sixteen-year-old pianist from Gaza's Edward Said Conservatory. She was Sara Akel, the girl I had heard play a Bach Polonaise at the school four years earlier. Now it was 2016 and Sara was completing Grade 8, qualifying her for entry to study music at university level. She came to our meeting at the conservatory with her mother Ibtisam, a warm, engaging doctor who had been educated and trained in Algeria. Ibtisam chatted in precise, accentless French about how Gaza had become more conservative since she arrived in the 1980s to take up a job as the only female hospital consultant in the entire Strip. There were patients who did not want to be treated – or even for their wives to be treated – by a woman.

Sara spoke an almost equally faultless English that made her sound like any Anglophone teenager, her speech punctuated with 'like' and an American accent probably, she said, picked up by downloading films on the internet. Yet she was bi-cultural. Her first love was still Bach – whereas her mother's was Chopin; 'we're always arguing about it!' – but she also played regularly in an oriental orchestra.

In a way Sara's was a typical Gaza story – exceptional talent having to overcome obstacles that few of her peer group elsewhere could imagine. She had to wait seven years for a second-hand piano at home, not because of a lack of money but a result of the shortage of the instruments in Gaza during the blockade. When she first played it was on a toy keyboard, then she mostly practised on a Yamaha 'virtual piano'. So when she took part (by video, because she and her fellow competitors from Gaza had not been allowed out) in her first national Palestinian competition (she came third), she first had to practise at the conservatory so that she could perfect the use of the pedals.

But now Sara wasn't sure what she wanted to do after completing the *tawjihi* exam at the Christian-run Holy Family School, much favoured by Gaza's middle class, in the summer of 2017. She couldn't imagine life without a piano: 'If you stop playing for a while then your hands will lose what your mind gives them . . . This is so cheesy and clichéd, but your instrument kind of becomes a part of you. You can't just get it out of you.'[9]

Sara had got a permit to leave through Israel in 2015 for an 'awesome' two-week ensemble training course in the UK, organised for a handful of Palestinians by the Choir of London, a charity helping to fund outstanding musicians from the Occupied Territories, which included a master class at the Royal Academy of Music. A year later she had been invited to play at a choral festival in the West Bank. 'But we couldn't, because we didn't get permits. And this thing just keeps on happening.' Israel's separation of the two Palestinian territories was inviolable.

She had also become interested in the production side of recorded classical music. To pursue that, as well as to study further classical Western music, she would need to leave Gaza, something it was clear that she was increasingly minded to do. 'But I'm not saying this because I hate it in here. Ever since I was little, I always thought that if I ever get out of here then I'll probably come back because I'll miss it and my family's here. But now because I see it in a clearer way, I know that if I stay here then I probably wouldn't get the chances that I might get if I get out of here.' For her mother Ibtisam, however, Sara's ambition was the source of a painful dilemma, shared by the parents of many of the brightest children in Gaza, an intensely family-oriented society: to let them go or not. '*Je suis prise entre deux feux*,' Ibtisam said, using the more elegant French phraseology: between a rock and a hard place.

The Rand study had not covered culture, education or, indeed, human resources. But an earlier 2004 report, *Building a Successful Palestinian State*,[10] had tackled two more tangible, and interlinked, issues: water and energy. It said that while Israel had diverse water sources, the Palestinians had access to very few; in Gaza they were limited to the much degraded Coastal Aquifer, a primary reason why the UN had foreseen that Gaza might be 'uninhabitable' by 2020. And unlike many of its Arab neighbours neither Israel, nor, of course, the Occupied Territories, had oil, the subject of the 1970s Labour Prime Minister Golda Meir's famous joke that Moses 'took us forty years through the desert in order to bring us to the one spot in the Middle East that has no oil'. What Rand pointed out, and what Golda Meir could not have foreseen, was that natural gas had now been discovered in the Eastern Mediterranean coast – 3.5 trillion cubic feet of it, according to 2004 estimates. Among much else the gas could be used to power energy-guzzling desalination plants, which could in turn provide clean water. Much of it was off the coast of Israel; but some of it was found on Gaza's doorstep.

It's scarcely credible that 36 miles off the coast of a territory facing a catastrophic electricity shortage is what should be its greatest asset, one that could not only transform the Palestinian economy, but meet Gaza's energy needs at a stroke: the trillion cubic feet Gaza Marine natural gas field. Its discovery, some 600 metres below the Mediterranean's surface, by the BG Group in 1999 had been another great moment of hope for Gaza, in whose territorial waters the gas had been found. Yasser Arafat, with his customary eye for the spectacular, had visited the exploration platform in a fishing boat in September 2000, just before the Second Intifada broke out. Against a telegenic background of a huge gas flame shooting into the air, he declared the discovery 'a gift from God to us, to our people, to our children. It will provide a solid foundation for our economy, for establishing an independent state with holy Jerusalem as its capital.'[11]

For once, Arafat was not wildly exaggerating, at least about its economic potential. According to the Palestine Investment Fund, the field would save more than $60m a year in the PA's energy bill and provide $2.5bn direct revenues over its probable twenty-year gas-producing lifetime.[12] The gas could be shipped to Egypt or Israel to be liquefied, and then redistributed to Israel and the Occupied Territories, including Gaza, through the Israeli grid. There had been detailed nego-tiations between BG, the PA and Israel about the latter course in the early years of the century, but they had foundered first on haggles over the price – Israel was demanding access to the gas at well below market price[13] – and then on the grounds that 'funds flowing to the PA would be used to support terrorism'.[14] Because of its control of Palestinian territorial waters as the occupying power, Israel's cooperation would be needed ahead of any peace deal. But by the end of 2010 Israel knew that it had two large natural gas fields off its own coast, Tamar and Leviathan; it now no longer had the same vested interest in Gaza Marine, which has remained undeveloped ever since.

In an astute analysis of the issue, Simon Henderson, a leading expert on the Eastern Mediterranean energy market, pointed out that given the 'enmity' between the parties – not only Israel and Hamas, but also the PA and Hamas – a successful breakthrough on Gaza Marine was likely to 'require continuing diplomatic encouragement by outside parties like the European Union and the United States'.[15] The gas would not only supply Gaza, where the need is critical, but the

West Bank, in the process greatly easing the European and US burden of funding the PA.

One of the ironies of Gaza Marine lying fallow is that the war-damaged and spare parts-starved Gaza power station, currently dependent on diesel fuel from Israel charged at normal commercial prices, was actually designed in 2002 to run on (much cheaper) natural gas from the Marine field. A plan developed in 2016 by Israel and Qatar – which had been allowed by Israel to play an active part in Gaza housing reconstruction, and was an occasional paymaster for the diesel fuel for Gaza – was to reconvert the station to natural gas supplied on a pipeline running along the Gaza–Israel border from Israel.

Besides the failure to develop Gaza Marine, the planned import at commercial prices of natural gas from Israel and parallel proposals for a new 25MW high voltage link to Israel's electricity grid would be expensive stopgap measures which would still fall woefully short of meeting Gaza's energy needs. Yet even these had not borne fruit by mid-2017. Whether or not as part of its attempt to squeeze Hamas – pursued, as usual, at the expense of Gaza's civilian population – the PA in Ramallah had refused to sign off on them.[16]

The lack of a continuous and reliable source of power was one of the obstacles in the way of international plans to build a $500m large-scale water desalination plant on Gaza's coast. If it ever happened, it would be the largest construction project in the Palestinian territories and would go a long way to easing Gaza's chronic water crisis.

Some experts would argue that the plant would not be necessary if Israel had not restricted Palestinians' access to their own water sources. While the rapid growth in Gaza's population was a major factor so were the arrangements in the Oslo agreement which had the effect of making Gaza responsible for meeting most of its own water needs, as though it was a separate country and not an occupied part of one of the region's most water rich areas, in which Israel has declared a water surplus.[17] The agreement provided for the Israeli water company Mekorot to sell 5 million cubic metres (mcm) of water per year to the PA for Gaza, recently increased to 10mcm, and with an offer by Israel to increase its sale to 20mcm. (Local estimates suggest that Gaza needs 180mcm for domestic and agricultural use and that the deficit is around 100mcm.)[18] But Oslo did not provide for any joint management of the Coastal Aquifer, and therefore put no restrictions, for example, on Israel using its upstream position along the aquifer from siphoning the supply before it reaches Gaza; according to one independent expert the result was that Gaza was obliged increasingly to rely on local water sources when it was the one Palestinian area unable to do so.[19]

But a large-scale seawater desalination plant – similar, as it happens, to the one thirteen miles up the coast in Ashkelon (one of five operating in Israel) – would provide work as well as clean water. According to Bo Scheck, the Gaza operations director of UNRWA, responsible for the welfare of Gaza's refugee population, the project was not only 'indispensable for the well-being of the people', ensuring access to potable water and creating much-needed jobs, but a powerful symbol of hope. 'If you can see the first spade being put into this programme, it would have such a positive effect on the situation here, away from all its misery, which . . . might diminish the number of people who only see hope in radicalisation.'[20]

In its favour was widespread international agreement on paper by the Euromed countries for development and promises of investment. Against it, however, was donor fatigue, and the fear among Western and Arab governments that the plant could be destroyed in another war. Israel would also have to cooperate to an unprecedented extent by permitting huge amounts of construction material to enter Gaza, along with the provision of continuous energy, albeit supplemented by giant solar panels on site, to ensure 24/7 operation. Even though Israel had said it backed the project in principle, there was still great scepticism in Gaza that a project talked about for twenty years would actually happen, requiring as it would a decisive modification of Israel's siege policy over the last ten years.

One fine late January afternoon in 2016, the construction magnate Jawdat al-Khodary drove me up the coast north of Gaza City to watch the sun set over the Mediterranean and see his latest diversion: a garden, spread out like a gigantic natural multi-coloured quilt across two acres. He dreamed of one day turning it into Gaza's version of Kew Gardens. 'If I took you here blindfolded, would you know you were in Gaza?' he asked. The place was a colourful riot patchwork of plants, trees and what seemed like an infinite variety of al-Khodari's favourite cacti that the well-travelled and erudite businessman had brought back from all over the world.

He cited a small factory he had owned, employing between thirty-five and fifty workers, which had made foam mattresses for the local market until four years before. Necessary chemicals that al-Khodary imported through Israel from the multinational Dow Company were then proscribed as 'dual use', meaning that in the view of the Israeli authorities they could be used by Hamas or another armed faction for explosives or other military purposes. Al-Khodary said the Israeli agent for Dow had produced documentation seeking to show that had not been the case, but to no avail. Back in 2012 the smuggling tunnels under the Egyptian border were operating at their peak, but al-Khodary couldn't consider getting the foam that way because, as a frequent contractor for the UN, he was required to abide by international policy. He shut the factory and laid off his workers. Now he bought ready-made mattresses from a West Bank manufacturer. He reeled off commodities that were classified as 'dual use': large planks of wood, glue, steel. As we munched freshly picked carrots from the garden, al-Khodary said sadly, 'I have become a distributor for one of my competitors.' He echoed the remark he had made to me five years earlier: the siege had 'punished the wrong people'.

Al-Khodary had a point, if a familiar one: it wasn't easy to see how the blockade had assisted Israeli security. In a population growing by four per cent a year, it had helped to create a growing pool of young unemployed men all too susceptible to the 'radicalisation' that Bo Scheck feared. Did it make another war more or less likely? Israel's head of Military Intelligence, Herzl Halevi, gave a fairly stark answer to this question in February 2016: saying that Hamas was making efforts to stop other groups firing rockets, but that postwar reconstruction was proceeding 'very slowly' and Gaza's 'rehabilitation' was a key to avoiding further conflict, he told Knesset members, 'The humanitarian condition in Gaza is progressively deteriorating, and if it blows up, it'll be in Israel's direction.'[21]

Against such a background, it was striking how grudging – and reversible – were the few incremental easings of the siege that Israel announced from time to time. Back in early 2016 the civil society leader Raji Sourani recalled the old Jewish joke about the poor man who gets married, has several children and lives in only one room, and then visits his rabbi to complain that life had become intolerable. It's a long joke, and Sourani told it well; but to cut it short, the rabbi suggests that what he needs to do is to buy a goat and bring it into the house. As the man becomes progressively more distraught on subsequent visits, the rabbi advises him to do the same first with a cow, and then a donkey, by which time the man is suicidal. Week by week, the rabbi advises him first to get rid of the cow, then of the donkey. Gradually he feels better until, when he has finally also rid himself of the goat, he tells the rabbi, 'It's fantastic. I have nothing to complain about.' Sourani added with a flourish: 'The Israelis brought the entire zoo to our house.'

ONE JUNE MORNING IN 2016 I took the lift up to see Basil Eleiwa at his restaurant Level Up on the eleventh floor of the modern Zafer Tower. Before, I had been there only at night, when, if it weren't for the breathtaking views of the city and the sea, it would be difficult to believe you were in Gaza. Level Up felt like a popular hangout in Dubai or Sharm El Sheikh, only classier; you could understand why it was frequented by Gaza's middle class. Young men and women gossiped over ice cream and coffee, or sucked on water pipes filled with sweet smelling tobacco brought by a *narghila* man in a fez. Families enjoyed Caesar salad or pepper steak served by waiters in impeccable black tunics. From the terrace, the lights of Israel twinkled to the north and the east, so near and so unreachable for the vast majority of Gaza City's 700,000 inhabitants.

Sipping chilled strawberry and fresh lemonade cocktails that summer morning in the air-conditioned restaurant, it was hard not to be infected by Eleiwa's optimism, a necessary characteristic for a serial owner of fashionable hotels and restaurants in a market imploded by war and economic blockade. Late in 1991 he had started a small beach restaurant as a hobby, at a time when it could only open for a few hours because of an Israeli-imposed curfew. 'The [First] Intifada was still going; people needed to breathe, to be able to live their lives.'[22]

Twenty years on they still did. Eleiwa opened Level Up in 2014, just before the third and bloodiest of all the Gaza wars. Three weeks in, the building's developer Mohammed Abu Mathkour was phoned by an Israeli intelligence officer and told to take down a communications antenna that had been installed on the roof by Hamas. Caught between two colliding enemies, Mathkour said he couldn't do that without the permission of Hamas's Interior Ministry. The next day, Israeli tank shells hit the upper floors of the building, causing serious damage in the first of two attacks, but not so serious that it could not be quickly repaired and reopened after the war. It was an instant success with a clientele that Eleiwa insists is not 'elite' but 'middle and even lower middle class'. And while most Gazans could not afford to go to Level Up, Eleiwa said he kept his prices as low as possible while just making a modest profit. The pepper steak may be £10, but hummus or baba ghanoush and tea were £1.60 each, coffee or a freshly squeezed juice £1.90, and pizzas and filling club or smoked chicken sandwiches less than £3.

His first hotel, the once famous five-star Windmill Hotel, went up in smoke (literally) in October 2000 when Islamist protesters attacked it for allowing guests to drink their own alcohol on the premises. It may have lacked the charm of the much older and still flourishing city centre Marna House, with its shady, secluded terrace, but the Windmill set a trend followed by others, including the Deira, built in red-brown adobe brick with Moroccan arches, vaulted ceilings and a spacious seafront terrace; Roots, an upmarket seafront hotel which makes much of its money from weddings; al-Khodary's al-Mathaf, with another magnificent terrace; or al-Mashtal, a 220-room five-star resort hotel which Mövenpick started to build in the optimistic post-Oslo 1990s.

Now he was planning a new hotel on the beach (alcohol-free, of course). But why would Eleiwa embark on another one when bed occupancy in the city was only twenty per cent? 'Because it's my business and in this line of business, if you excel, if you distinguish yourself, based on better service and better quality you will have your share of the market.' Beyond this borderline management-speak, he had another more emotional response. 'This is my Gaza. I belong to this place. And one day Gaza will have its opportunity in this line of business and I assure you it will compete with the region. Because we have the basic factors for this industry to excel. We have wonderful weather. We have a wonderful beach. And most of the Gaza people enjoy hospitality by nature.' But even supposing political circumstances were miraculously transformed, wouldn't it take forever to restore the city's infrastructure, clean its coastal waters, heavily polluted with sewage, and market Gaza as the most improbable of all holiday destinations? Wasn't the city's fate to be continually, as the poet Mahmoud Darwish had described Palestine, 'a country on the verge of dawn' – but on a night that never ended?

'Palestinian people have sacrificed a lot throughout the last six decades and at one point we might get a leadership that will light this candle at the end of the tunnel for us,' said Eleiwa. Yes, Israel was 'the main factor in our misery', but the absence of an effective leadership that could heal the catastrophic split between the two main factions was also 'a fundamental problem of the Palestinian people'. 'If we reach a political settlement with the Israelis and have a leadership with vision, I doubt we would still need donors because the Palestinian people are very hard-working people with dignity.'

He added: 'Until that happens we are . . . maintaining good service standards that could be the basis of our competition with the region and the world . . . we're working for our future generation' – one which, with 18,000 graduates every year hunting for a handful of jobs, had been left 'with no hope'. In the meantime, he was ensuring that at least one corner of its economy did not go dark. 'Even if the business gets worse and I'm still able to pay my suppliers and my staff, that's more than enough.'

Meanwhile, it looked as though the customers, whatever their hardships and fears of another war, would keep coming to Level Up. For all their pain, Eleiwa insisted, enjoyment was embedded in Gazans' 'coastal culture'. Every Friday, for example, 'you will go to the beach and you will see the very simple poorest people are there with their small sandwich and a cup of tea. We love to live our lives.' That last sentence was a conscious echo of another line Eleiwa liked to quote from Darwish: 'We love life, if we find a way to it.'

It was easy here, high above the city, to forget the harsh facts of Gaza life. But Eleiwa's stubborn belief in the capacity of his own people also made it easy to imagine what they would achieve if they were ever allowed to realise the futuristic Rand vision that a decade earlier had brought tears to the eyes of Jihad al-Wazir.

Conclusion

MAHMOUD AL-BAHTITI, WHO, BACK IN EARLY 2003, had joked in front of the smouldering ruins of his workshop about Arafat's promise that Gaza would become 'Singapore', was the first Palestinian I ever met in Gaza. Almost fourteen years later I went back to Zeitoun to find him. It came as a surprise to discover that this wiry figure, looking younger than his sixty-six years with a neatly trimmed beard, blue open-neck shirt and the same dry sense of humour, was still in Al Basateen Street and still fixing car and truck engines, as he had been doing for half a century. But, he said, business had never been slower. He had stopped complaining about the Hamas government because of the shortage of electricity; thanks to the scarcity of work, the interruptions hardly mattered anymore. 'They can cut it as much as they like,' he said. 'Gaza is like heaven. There is no work in heaven either.'[1]

Al-Bahtiti had first learned his trade when he left school at fifteen, two years before the Six Day War, and started out on his own five years later. Those were the years of open borders when it was almost as easy for Palestinians to travel out of the Strip as it was for Israelis to travel in to buy fresh fish – or have their engine cylinders, camshafts and turbochargers fixed a good deal more cheaply than in Israel, and just as reliably 'I am not praising Israel, I am just saying that it was a fair life back then.' Business had been all right during the Arafat years after Oslo, he said, but it had got gradually worse and worse. As it happened, he had suffered exceptionally bad luck; his workshop had been destroyed or badly damaged not just in 2003 but in each of the three wars since then. In 2012 he had moved to Tel el Hawa where his premises were collaterally damaged in a strike on a nearby office of the Ministry of Interior.

'They never forget me,' he said wryly. Did the Israelis think he still made rockets? 'No, they do it just for revenge. To destroy the economy of course. They use building rockets as an excuse to destroy the economy.'

Al-Bahtiti still stood by his gibe at Arafat from that cold afternoon in January 2003. He admitted he wasn't to know it would get as bad as it had, he argued, with Hamas in charge. In fact, as a supporter of neither Hamas nor Fatah, he hadn't even voted in the 2006 parliamentary elections. But after the three wars and nine years of economic siege that followed Hamas's takeover of Gaza, he thought maybe he had judged the Palestinian Authority established by Arafat too harshly. After the elections, 'Hamas was not only rejected, but also hated, by most of the governments in the world. Subsequently, the Palestinian people in Gaza were treated in the same way Hamas was treated. We're all prisoners in Gaza, not only because of Israel, but Egypt and Jordan as well.' Al-Bahtiti reached back to the lines of a song from his teenage years by the greatest of all twentieth-century Egyptian singers, Umm Kulthum: 'Give me again my freedom, and let go my hands.'

Then he asked me a question. Given that Britain had issued the Balfour Declaration a century ago and 'we are still suffering as a result of that declaration', wouldn't an apology from the British government be in order? No, he wasn't trying to get what was now Israel back for the Arabs. He recognised that 'the Jewish people took their rights after Hitler committed massacres against them. But who will give us our rights? Germany still supports Israel till now, but Britain gave our lands to the Israelis and they never cared to give us our rights.'

Agree with him or not, al-Bahtiti touched a raw nerve. He was not wrong to trace the Palestinian experience back to the events of twentieth-century history, culminating in the genocide of European Jews in the Holocaust. Nor was al-Bahtiti wrong to internationalise the problem by implying that other countries as well as Israel bore a responsibility for solving it, very much including the British who occupied Palestine, and then abandoned it to a conflict that remains unresolved seventy years later. It is not a responsibility those countries have exercised with distinction over the past decade.

During a thoughtful speech in Monterey less than a year before the US–British invasion of Iraq, the then US Deputy Defense Secretary Paul Wolfowitz suggested: 'To win the war against terrorism and, in so doing, help shape a more peaceful world, we must speak to the hundreds of millions of moderate and tolerant people in the Muslim world, regardless of where they live, who aspire to enjoy the blessings of freedom and democracy and free enterprise. These are sometimes described as "Western values", but, in fact, they are universal.'[2]

It is striking that 'the blessings' identified in that unimpeachable doctrine were precisely those denied to Palestinians in Gaza. The international boycott imposed after the 2006 election result was hardly a ringing endorsement of democracy. The prolonged blockade, ostensibly aimed at Hamas for refusing to comply with the conditions laid down by Israel and the Quartet, afflicted the civilian population far more than Hamas itself. Despite protestations to the contrary, this made it all the harder for Israel to escape the charge that it was collectively punishing Palestinians in Gaza for their electoral choice, however varied their reasons for making it and however lacking in opportunities they were for reversing it. In Gaza it was a classic case, in Sara Roy's memorable description, of sanctions being applied against the occupied rather than the occupier. But it was also a reminder that for fifty years Palestinians have had no say in choosing the government that ultimately controls their lives, whether by having a state of their own or by being given the vote in a single, bi-national state.

The freedom of Gazans, and indeed all Palestinians under occupation, to travel, as well as to import and export goods, had been curtailed long before Hamas's election victory, of course. But it had been much more tightly restricted over the last decade than at any time since the Six Day War. When the British carried out their ferocious bombardment of Gaza City in 1917, those fleeing were at least able to get to other parts of Palestine. That possibility was not open to the vast majority of Palestinian civilians facing the three military onslaughts of 2008–9, 2012 and 2014.

But it was the crushing of 'free enterprise' that was perhaps the most striking consequence of an economic blockade of Gaza, which the Quartet approach helped to legitimise. The creation of a 300-metre (at least) buffer zone and the imposition of a three- or six-mile limit in Gaza waters wrought a devastating effect on both agriculture and the fishing industries. It is difficult to see how the collapse, mothballing, or – in wartime – outright destruction of hundreds of manufacturing companies, many owned by people with no love for Hamas and who had enjoyed close relationships with Israeli customers and suppliers, helped Israeli security. Let alone the consequential drift of the unemployed into jobs with Hamas, including its armed and paramilitary wings, as well as those hired to dig tunnels that were seen as a security threat to Israel.

There was a tendency, especially in the early years of the blockade, to depict conditions in Gaza as a purely 'humanitarian' crisis; to reduce the debate to one about whether aid reaching the Strip was enough to ensure its residents had enough to eat. This was an argument that Israel was normally able to win. There was world-class poverty – as well as some wealth – in Gaza. Begging, often by children, by 2016–17 was notably more common than during the Second Intifada; and in a society which put an exceptionally high premium on education, children were increasingly being forced by economic circumstances out of school in their early teens, in some cases to become the main wage earner. But people were not starving in the streets; malnutrition was a serious concern, but famine, thanks in large part to international aid covering up to eighty per cent of the population, was a fate Gaza had so far been spared. What was missing, in an instinctively entrepreneurial society, was an economy which could provide not only incomes but a measure of human dignity.

The point is underlined when older Palestinians talk, as al-Bahtiti did, about the 'golden' time before Oslo for Gazan businesses and workers. On the face of it, there was not much golden for Gaza between 1967 and 1993. It was an era often characterised by round-ups, arrests, bulldozing of homes and citrus groves, lethal firefights, the seizure of land and water for Israeli settlements, the army's house-to-house sweeps of the refugee camps, and all the other pressures which accompanied the constant physical presence on the streets of a military occupation. But al-Bahtiti's nostalgia for the period when Israel was directly running Gaza powerfully illustrates how far conditions, especially economic, have deteriorated since then. Israel placed severe limits on the Gazan economy in those first two and half decades of occupation, making it wholly dependent on theirs. But Moshe Dayan's strategy after 1967, partly in order to subdue Palestinian nationalist sentiment, was to allow many tens of thousands of Gazans to work in Israel, and for businesses to trade with it. From the early 1990s this relative openness was gradually replaced by a policy of separation, culminating in a twenty-first-century blockade, which left Gaza with virtually no economy. Finally the de-development was completed by three military assaults on the Strip within six years; they failed to dislodge Hamas but had a devastating impact on the civilian population, in deaths, injuries, destroyed property and infrastructure. Without a major rethink of Israeli and international policy, the assaults could well be repeated.

It is nevertheless too easy to blame Israel alone – as al-Bahtiti recognised. If Gaza were an open prison, Israel was not the only gaoler. Gazan Palestinians had also been forsaken by Egypt – especially by President Sisi's prolonged closures of Rafah and the destruction of the smuggling tunnels – and Jordan through the strict transit restrictions it imposes on Gazan (but not on West Bank) residents. They had been betrayed by the chronic failure of Fatah and Hamas to resolve their differences, subordinating the interests of Gaza's public to their own in a conflict made especially disheartening because the power they were struggling for was so heavily circumscribed by Israel. And, perhaps least discussed of all, they had been abandoned by the international community and Western governments in particular.

The Quartet, which in practice meant the US and the EU, could say that it had frequently called for the easing of the blockade. So it had; and after the *Mavi Marmara* episode in 2010, in which Israeli commandos killed nine people aboard the Turkish Gaza-bound aid ship, it persuaded the Netanyahu government to allow in a much wider range of consumer goods. But this did next to nothing to revive Gazan industry because exports were still banned. Nor was there any lifting of the restrictions that closed off Gazan residents' access to the outside world. In fact, there was no sign of either the EU or the US applying serious leverage on Israel to end the isolation of the Strip. In practice, Gaza seemed to share with North Korea the status of a territory where the civilian population was suffering but nothing – beyond providing the humanitarian minimum – could be achieved as long as a pariah government was in charge.

That pariah status was itself conferred by Israel's and her Western allies' boycott of Hamas after it won free elections in 2006. The international denial of contacts and funding then persisted for more than a decade despite an increasing realisation, at least among some of the Europeans who had originally decided on it, that it had been a mistake. The question for the international community that resounded after ten years in which most of civilian Gaza lived in fear, poverty and despair while its rulers' political and military control remained intact, was not so much 'why talk to Hamas' as 'why not'? Maybe Hamas's previous oscillation between violent insurgency and the exercise of political power makes it hard to assess with certainty what the outcome of engagement would have been. But for the Quartet to set more realistic conditions – for example, a long-term truce with Israel – would not have precluded the imposition of sanctions if Hamas had violated them; indeed, it would have afforded Western governments the leverage over Hamas's conduct that it had conspicuously lacked. Exactly what had been the gains to Israeli, Palestinian, regional and global security from this policy? And why was it not re-thought in the light of Hamas's first official and public espousal of a Palestinian state on 1967 borders in May 2017? It may even be that Yahya Sinwar's assumption of the Gaza leadership of Hamas reinforced that opportunity, since he had a good chance of bringing Hamas hardliners behind a rapprochement with the West in return for greater moderation. But if Sinwar's elevation turned out to be a triumph of the militarists over the pragmatists, as some Israeli commentators suggested, then was that not at least an indirect result of an approach by the international community which for so long shunned those in the movement who had made more pragmatic overtures?

But, of course, the plight of Gaza cannot be separated from that of the wider Israeli–Palestinian conflict. First, there can be no lasting end to that conflict, let alone the creation of a Palestinian state, without Gaza. Gaza, with its two million Palestinians and its economically all-important coastline has to be a part of it. It's also worth reflecting that Hamas, now running Gaza, did not come from nowhere. Back in 1995, fearing the unravelling of the Oslo accords, Haidar Abdel Shafi, the most revered of all Gazans, remarked that Hamas would not dare to disrupt a 'credible peace process'.[3] Abdel Shafi was underlining that Hamas's strength – beyond its bedrock of its minority support – had risen in direct relation to the failures of serial peace negotiations with the PLO. It would be rash to presume that Israel and the West can now indefinitely postpone a 'credible' peace process without in turn strengthening the more extreme forces – whether looking towards ISIS or not – which Hamas has so far contained in Gaza.

One of the most pervasive – and baseless – myths about the conflict is that a peace process can only work if the two parties want it, and that no external force can bring them together if they don't. The opposite is the truth. An end to conflict will simply not happen unless the outside world not only demands it but puts irresistible pressure on the parties – or, rather, the strongest party and the one that believes it has the greatest interest in maintaining the status quo, namely Israel – to reach an agreement.

It was impossible in 2018 to be optimistic about the consequences of Donald Trump's presidency for the Middle East. Unless Trump is prepared to apply real pressure and not mere exhortation to the parties, his chances of pulling off the 'ultimate deal', which has eluded all his predecessors, are next to zero. The US's insistence that it would not recognise the PLO until it recognised Israel was no doubt effective in helping to force Arafat into the 'historic compromise' by which he made a state on 1967 borders the Palestinian goal. But after the liberation of Kuwait from Iraq by the US-led coalition in 1991, George Bush also dragged a deeply resistant Yitzhak Shamir to the Madrid summit by suspending the US's multi-billion-dollar loan guarantees to Israel. The ensuing process did not, finally, succeed; but it was a now all too rare indication of the traction open to a determined US administration. 'The United States could stop [the settlements] so easily,' the liberal Israeli novelist A. B. Yehoshua told me in Haifa in 2005. 'Since the Six Day War they were saying they were against the settlements, and they have done nothing.' Instead Washington, in common with the rest of the international community, has largely contented itself with ritual criticisms of Israeli settlement policy while using 'the peace process', and the need not to disrupt it, as an excuse not to take firmer action to enforce its own stated objectives for the Middle East. The US interest in subsidising Israel by more than $3bn a year without exacting conditions is questionable, to put it mildly. No one sane thinks that the current global terrorist threats facing the West – like that posed by ISIS – were generated by the Israeli–Palestinian conflict. But in 2013 a former US general remarked that he 'paid a military price every day' when he was in charge of US Central Command 'because the Americans were seen as biased in support of Israel' and that the 'moderate Arabs who want to be with us ... can't come out publicly in support of people who don't show respect for the Arab Palestinians.' This was James Mattis, appointed by President Trump as Defense Secretary in 2017.[4]

This is not the place to spell out the historic reasons for that 'bias', including the influence, exercised through its funding of US political campaigns, of the American Israel Public Affairs Committee. But AIPAC has always been more representative of successive Israeli governments than it has of American Jewry. Indeed, one prospect of change in the longer term lies with indications both of a gradual fraying of bipartisan support for 'Israel right or wrong' among US Democrats, whom most American Jews support, and of a markedly more critical attitude towards present-day Israeli government policy among some younger American Jews.

But Mahmoud al-Bahtiti was also right to focus on the Europeans. The EU has stolidly continued to channel aid – at least €6bn since 1994 – to the Palestinians to ameliorate the impact, in the West Bank at least, of a policy with which it says it disagrees but over which it has made no attempt to exercise any real influence. The EU's effective subsidy of the occupation by ensuring the PA's obligations under Oslo, for example, to provide healthcare and education are met, however imperfectly, gave it a duty as well as a right to exercise some leverage, beyond pious restatements of its belief in a two-state solution. The EU could have actively supported a coalition government after the Palestinian elections in 2006, after the short-lived Mecca agreement in 2007 and in the early summer of 2014, when it might have prevented the 2014 war.

Similarly on finance and the distribution of revenues generated in Gaza. When the tunnels were open Hamas was able to levy taxes on imports through Egypt. With the tunnels closed, Gaza now depended wholly on goods from Israel, all the taxes on which were were remitted by Israel to the PA in Ramallah. The EU colluded with the rest of the international community by allowing the PA to spend an ever-decreasing proportion of those revenues in Gaza itself. Indeed, the Europeans stood placidly by when Mahmoud Abbas in April 2017, as part of his power struggle with Hamas, intensified the misery of Palestinians in Gaza with sanctions of his own. If the excuse for this European inertia was obeisance to a US administration constrained by legislation as well as politics from any action held to help a Hamas administration, then it underlined the case for formulating a Middle East foreign policy distinctive from that of the US, a task that became at once more urgent and more palatable during Trump's presidency.

For the EU also has leverage on Israel. When in April 2017 Netanyahu warned the German Foreign Minister Sigmar Gabriel he would not meet him if he also met the anti-occupation army veterans group Breaking the Silence, the minister commendably chose the latter. Commenting approvingly on the minister's decisions, the eminent Israeli academic Zeev Sternhell suggested the incident underlined 'that the only way to influence Israeli politics is through external pressure. In other words, what doesn't work with pressure will work with more pressure.'[5] Gabriel's stance was merely symbolic. But whether intentional or not, it was a subliminal reminder that Europe was Israel's biggest trading partner, accounting for about a third of the latter's foreign trade, worth around $30bn, covered by free trade agreements which exempted Israeli exports to Europe from tariffs. Yet without even re-erecting such barriers, let alone boycotting Israel, the EU could make a sharp impact by differentiating – but robustly – between Israel proper and Israeli settlements in the West Bank and East Jerusalem, regarded by the EU as illegal in international law, including by a ban on imports of goods from the settlements. When a London think tank, the European Council for Foreign Relations, merely *suggested* in 2015 that EU member states reviewed their relationships with financial institutions doing business in the West Bank settlements,[6] and it was thought (wrongly) the idea had been taken up by the European Council, the Tel Aviv banking index dropped by 2.46 points. Indeed, secondary sanctions of the sort that worked so well when applied by the US on Iran could be applied on any banks and businesses operating in the settlements. As Sternhell wrote in the same article: 'As long as it is still possible to export goods from [settlements in] the [occupied] territories, openly or otherwise, the protests in Europe's capitals will be ineffective.'

Why has this not yet happened? Here it is impossible to escape the legacy of the Holocaust. In grasping Israel's overriding preoccupation with security, Europe has an historic responsibility to understand Jewish fears of such a spectre ever being raised again. There is also little doubt that too few in the Arab world yet share that understanding. One Arab who did, however, was the late Edward Said, a passionate Palestinian nationalist, but also a determined advocate of a two-state solution when many others were still questioning the right of Israel to exist. Said's most lucid expression of that legacy was written on the eve of the Madrid Conference over a quarter of a century ago. But most of it resonates as strongly today, and the most strident promoters of anti-Israel slogans in the West would do well to note it. Said argued:

What Israel does to Palestinians, it does against a background not only of the long-standing Western tutelage over Palestine and the Arabs ... but also against an equally long-standing ... anti-semitism that ... produced the Holocaust of the European Jews. We cannot fail to connect the horrific history of anti-semitic massacres to the establishment of Israel; nor can we fail to understand the depths, the extent and the over-powering legacy that informed the postwar Zionist movement.

Palestinians, Said went on, however, were 'the victims of the victims' and are 'kept in this position to a great extent by Europe and the United states both of whom look away and excuse Israeli behaviour because Israel is seen as a state of survivors'.[7]

Wholly justified shame and sympathy related to the Holocaust is surely part of what, over the decades since 1967, muffled challenges by European governments to Israel's oppression of the Palestinians. Yet a different conclusion can be drawn from Europe's responsibility for the unspeakably dark history that accelerated the creation of Israel – namely that the conflict with the Palestinians is one which they have a historic duty to resolve, the unfinished business left over from the last century. For the Israeli–Arab conflict, in the historian Eugene Rogan's telling phrase, was 'made in Europe'. And it was the Palestinians and not the Europeans who were obliged to bear the indirect consequences of that history. The deep preoccupation of Israelis with security and the fears embedded by that same history – evident in the weeks before the Six Day War in 1967 – deserve absolute recognition. But Israel, a strong state with a flourishing economy, nuclear weapons, a well-trained and equipped army, is not facing 1938 all over again, however much Netanyahu has tried to persuade his voters it is. You do not have to agree with the Israeli writer and former politician Avraham Burg's radical assertion that Israelis have transferred 'our anger and revenge' from 'one people to another' – living comfortably with Germany as an ally while treating the Palestinians 'as whipping boys to release our aggression, anger and hysteria'[8] – to accept that the Palestinians have yet to escape the secondary aftermath of a European trauma in which the overwhelming majority of them played no part. Germany no doubt bears a responsibility for ending that secondary trauma; but so does Britain, whether it still sees itself as European or not, because of both the Balfour Declaration and its abandonment of Palestine in 1948. A century after the Declaration, Britain had amply fulfilled its first commitment to 'the establishment in Palestine of a national home for the Jewish people', but it had wholly failed to live up to the second – ensuring that 'nothing shall be done which may prejudice the civil and religious rights of existing non-Jewish communities in Palestine'.

To fulfil – finally – the Balfour Declaration's broken promise would be vastly more difficult were a just end to conflict not in Israel's interests as well as that of the Palestinians. The more extreme champions of the Israeli and Palestinian causes like to claim this is a zero sum game, in which every gain for the Palestinians is a loss for Israel, and vice versa. But it isn't. Since 2002 the Arab League has offered Israel full recognition, with all the accompanying benefits, including economic, that would entail, in return for a peace agreement with the Palestinians based on an end to the occupation it began fifty years ago. Israel, for the first time since 1967, would have internationally recognised borders. The major Sunni Arab states are eager for such an agreement because they believe that, with nuclear-armed Israel as an ally, they can together form what they see as a necessary counter-weight to Iranian power in the region. Characteristically, Netanyahu appears to have been testing whether he could secure such a regional alliance without reaching a fair agreement with the Palestinians. Such an outcome was unlikely (though by no means impossible; such betrayals have happened before). But even were he to fulfil what still looks like a fantasy, it would not douse the flame of Palestinian nationalism and the quest for independence and freedom.

And a positive outcome to that quest itself remains – contrary to what the Netanyahu government believes – an Israeli as well as a Palestinian interest. A resolution would bring an end to the morally corrosive effects of the occupation on Israeli society, including on the young soldiers obliged to enforce it. It would address the increasing hostility to Israel that the occupation breeds abroad, and resolve the patent injustice of denying Palestinians civil and political rights. Experience does not support the doctrine that military force, as opposed to a peace agreement, is able to provide the long-term security that Israelis crave. But even if it did, the dilemma highlighted by successive leaders from Barak to Olmert is inescapable: either it grants Palestinian independence on terms that a Palestinian leader can – literally – live with; or it casts itself increasingly in the eyes of the world as an apartheid state, facing increasing demands by Palestinians for equal human and political rights in a single state which would mean the end of Israel as it is now. As long it prefers to 'manage' the status quo – i.e. subjugation of the Palestinians – it's hard to resist the conclusion that in the very long term the greatest existential threat to Israel is not Iran or ISIS, let alone Hamas, but Israel itself. But in the meantime the alternative to a concerted and if necessary sanctions-based US/European effort to resolve the conflict is decades of bloodshed, more dispossession and degradation of the Palestinians, an uninhabitable Gaza, more settlements and more embarrassment – if it is embarrassable – for the international community.

But if a peace agreement is not concluded, then after fifty years the Palestinians cannot simply be told to go on waiting for relief until some mythical future when it will be. And that means applying genuine pressure on Israel to grant them some of the rights – economic rights to begin with, though that will never be enough without political rights – that they have so long been denied. This applies to all Palestinians, but Gaza, facing the direst conditions of all, is the right place to start, whether or not Israel or the PA agree. No doubt aid needs to be more equitably shared between Gaza and the West Bank, and it is difficult to see how it can be truly effective in the absence of international engagement with Hamas. But in the longer term what Gaza has always wanted and needed is not aid but an economy; the recovery of its capacity to make, cultivate and trade.

A new seaport for Gaza, which could attract substantial private-sector investment, is only one instance. It would not only at least begin restoring the territory as a trading hub again, and provide hundreds if not thousands of jobs while it was being built, but in the words of one of Israel's more hard-headed securocrats, ensure that 'during that process Hamas would have a good incentive not to open fire on Israel, which would risk this international project'.[9] The seaport is a good example because part of the reason it has so far been rejected – despite some support even within the Israeli Cabinet – is that it was one of Hamas's demands at the end of the 2014 war. A rethought international policy towards Gaza needs to abandon, in the interests of its people, the childish notion that nothing must be done for which Hamas could conceivably claim some credit.

The alternative to such a rethink could well be another war or wars. In the spring of 2017 the talk in Gaza and Israel was once again of war breaking out within months, and not only for the sake of military advantage. The two most calamitous wars had both been linked to the siege; the rocket fire that Israel cited as the reason for its assault in 2008 could have been prevented if the siege had been lifted. And in 2014 Hamas, backed into a corner by the failure of its agreement with Fatah, its political isolation after Morsi's fall in Egypt, the arrests of its activists in the West Bank after the murder of the three Israeli teenagers, the killing of seven of its Gaza militants and above all the dire conditions in the Strip, opted for a war 'that had a chance, however slim, of loosening the squeeze'.[10] On most counts the economic and humanitarian conditions in Gaza in early 2018 were much worse than those which formed the background to the 2014 war.

So the siege was the key factor when Gaza did erupt on 30 March 2018, albeit in a wholly unexpected way: the first unarmed mass protests in the Strip since the First Intifada. Tens of thousands – often entire families – of Gazans gathered near the border while hundreds more, mainly young men, some throwing stones, Molotov cocktails and launching flaming kites, advanced on the border fence, coming under live Israeli sniper fire from the other side. At least 120 Palestinians were killed, 62 of them on the climactic day of the weekly protests, 14 May, just as Jared Kushner and Ivanka Trump were inaugurating the new US embassy in Jerusalem, transferred from Tel Aviv in defiance of long-standing international consensus and the Palestinians' dream of a shared capital in that bi-national city. On the Gaza side of the border you could see the white plumes of tear gas against the thick black smoke of burning tyres, and hear above the screaming sirens of ambulances, their red lights flashing, the cracks of sporadic gunfire. But fifty miles away at the Jerusalem ceremony, an exultant Netanyahu, seemingly oblivious to the mounting toll of deaths, the highest on a single day since the 2014 war, or of injuries to over 2,500 Palestinians (and one Israeli soldier), celebrated the embassy move on 'a great day for peace'.

Although it did not originate the protests – they were the idea of some local Palestinian graduate students – Hamas then organised them; from policing and the provision of field hospitals to the demagogues urging the young men towards the fence from the tents strung along the border. Hamas, too, threatened – somewhat ambitiously – that the protesters were ready to surge across the fence. Some of those killed and injured were its own activists. But many others were not, and it is inconceivable that the protest – also backed by Fatah in an all too rare display of unity

– would have attracted such numbers were it not for Gaza's dire conditions. It was called 'the Great March of Return', an assertion of the 1948 refugees' descendants' 'right to return' to their ancestral homes in what was now Israel. This theme was as alarming to Israelis as it was unifying in Gaza, where well over half the population were refugees. But that mirrored the equally unbending Israeli insistence on Jerusalem as an 'undivided and eternal' capital of Israel, which Palestinians believed the US embassy move had endorsed. It reflected the failure over three decades to reach the two-state deal for which most Palestinians had long hoped and which would have included an honourable compromise on refugees. After all, as the PCHR's Raji Sourani said early in the protests, the families of those now being killed had, in 1993, been those who 'danced for Oslo... gave carnations and Gaza hugs to the Israeli soldiers'. In repeated interviews the jobless young men – 'hopeless people with nothing to lose' as the Fatah-supporting Gaza writer Atef Abu Saif put it – routinely echoed the 'return' mantra. But it became swiftly clear that what they wanted most was 'to make our dreams come true, find a job and have the crossings open', in the words of one Mahmoud Mansour, twenty-three, his elbow bandaged from an injury during a previous protest.

What was less clear was whether the international outcry over the shootings, echoing that during the 2014 war when Hamas was actually firing back, would help to ensure that dream would indeed come true. Certainly it was hard to think of a better way of preventing, at least in the medium term, a further escalation. For another war could not be ruled out. The deaths in spring 2018 also triggered criticism from a minority of Israelis appalled that live fire, rather than less lethal crowd control methods, had been used against the protesters. But the relative ease with which many, perhaps most, Israelis accepted the deaths as inevitable matched the majority – 90 percent in one poll – support for Operation Protective Edge, support which had gone far wider than Netanyahu's natural base on the right, including many who saw themselves as liberal or on the centre-left.

True, mainstream Israeli media coverage, with the notable exception of *Haaretz*, one of the world's best newspapers, was highly supportive in the 2014 war. The revelation of the Hamas tunnels constructed under the border no doubt helped to sustain the war fever. But was the closure of Gaza itself a factor? Apart from soldiers in combat, most Israelis knew little of Gaza from the inside. Even those kind Israelis (and there were quite a few) who volunteered to drive to Erez to ferry sick Palestinians to hospitals in Jerusalem or Tel Aviv inevitably had little idea what lay on the inside. In her fine book about living in the Strip in the 1990s, the Israeli journalist Amira Hass wrote 'the Israeli point of view is best summed up by the local variant of "go to hell" which is quite simply "go to Gaza" '.[11] Yet even since then there had been an eleven-year ban, ostensibly on security grounds, by the Israeli government on Israeli journalists reporting from inside the Strip, as many – Hass and her *Haaretz* colleague Gideon Levy among them – used to with distinction. It made Gaza seem even more unfathomable and dangerous to its neighbour than it once had. It was tempting to wonder if the story of Samson, his deception and capture in Gaza at the hands of the Philistines and his final destructive act, had re-emerged from the depths of Israel's collective subconscious; a biblical allegory to be played out again and again.

Certainly the right-wing Israeli commentators who blithely described wars in Gaza as 'mowing the grass' depicted them as a routine event, necessarily repeated every few years. When in Milton's *Samson Agonistes* the messenger arrives with the news that Samson – in perhaps the world's first recorded suicide attack – has killed the elite of Philistine society by pulling down the temple of Dagon, the chorus glorifies him for dying 'conjoined . . . with thy slaughter'd foes in number more/Than all thy life had slain before'. Such an epitaph may be bleakly accurate for IDF soldiers sent into Gaza and unlucky enough not to come out alive. But was it really one that Israel intended to keep writing for its young conscripts by regularly sending them to 'mow the grass'?

War in Gaza was avoidable. There had been several public warnings from within the Israeli military that deteriorating humanitarian conditions in Gaza could 'blow up' at any time, and it was fair to assume those arguments were made even more forcefully to Israel's political leadership in private. And the obverse was that radical improvement in those conditions was the best means of preventing such an explosion. Gaza may not yet become Singapore, or want to. But it still has the talent, education, resources and geography to recover over time. If the international community, with or without the US, were to use the capacity it undoubtedly has to influence events, it could start by reaching for the one outcome for Gaza that hasn't been attempted: lifting the siege and restoring a measure of enterprise, liberty and respect for democracy to its beleaguered and imprisoned people: 'Give me my freedom and let go my hands.'

Notes

CHAPTER 1: FROM OTTOMANS TO OSLO, 1917–1995

1. Eugene Rogan, *The Fall of the Ottomans*, p. 350.
2. Quoted in Natasha Gill, 'The Original "No": Why the Arabs Rejected Zionism, and Why it Matters', *Middle East Policy Council*, 19 June 2013. Gill lays out fully the case for Arab rejection on the 1947 partition resolution.
3. Rogan, *The Arabs*, p. 253.
4. Mustafa Abdel Shafi, *Would They Ever Learn?*, p. 118.
5. Reuters, 28 October 2011. Accessible on http://www.reuters.com/article/us-palestinians-israel-abbas-idUSTRE79R64320111028. Abbas said in interview on Israel's Channel Two: 'I know, I know. It was our mistake . . . It was an Arab mistake as a whole. But why do they punish us for this mistake [for] 64 years?' His comments broke a taboo and were controversial among Palestinians.
6. Abdel Shafi, *op. cit.*, p. 397.
7. Uri Avnery, *Gush Shalom* journal, 10 May 2008.
8. Ibid.
9. Interview with Uri Avnery, April 2008.
10. Benny Morris, *The Birth of the Palestinian Refugee Problem Revisited*, p. 467.
11. Interview with Attia Hijazi, April 2008.
12. US diplomat quoted in Morris, *op. cit.*, p. 468.
13. Gerald Butt, *Life at the Crossroads*, p. 181.
14. Abdel Shafi, *op. cit.*, p. 230.
15. D. C. Stevens quoted in Butt, *op. cit.*
16. See Avi Shlaim, *The Iron Wall*, p. 135.
17. Ibid. See also Jean-Pierre Filiu, *Gaza: A History*, p. 90.
18. In a major sweep initially intended to 'root out' out Palestinian guerrillas during the operation Israeli troops were accused by the UN of carrying out two mass executions in Khan Yunis after rounding up males over the age of fifteen.

UNRWA later produced a list of 275 people either machine-gunned to death in the town's central square, or shot in the refugee camp. Nine days later there was another mass shooting, in Rafah, of what Israel claimed were rioters incited by the Egyptians; the UN again produced a list of 111 names of those killed. Filiu, *op. cit.*, pp. 97–9. See also Joe Sacco, *Footnotes in Gaza*, 2009.

19. See Yezid Sayigh, *Armed struggle and the Search for State*, pp. 116–18.

20. See Filiu, *op. cit.*, p. 117.

21. Shlaim, *op. cit.*, p. 252.

22. Ibid., p. 258.

23. Interview with Mohammed Kardash, June 2007.

24. Interview with Fathi Sabbah, 26 January 2016.

25. Shlaim, *op. cit.*, pp. 711–12.

26. Morris, *op. cit.*, p. 256.

27. Interview with Theodor Meron, April 2007. See *Independent Magazine*, 26 May 2007.

28. Butt, *op. cit.*, p. 218.

29. Beverley Milton-Edwards and Stephen Farrell, *Hamas: The Islamic Resistance Movement*, p. 45.

30. Sara Roy, *Hamas and Civil Society in Gaza*, pp. 27–8.

31. Alexander Haig, *The Atlantic*, 26 April 2011.

32. Haidar Abdel Shafi opening speech at Madrid accessible online at http://www.pac-usa.org/speech-madrid.html.

33. See Shlaim, *op. cit.*, p. 529.

34. But for a much more nuanced view of Khartoum see Shlaim, *op. cit.*, pp. 276–7.

35. Arafat declared that 'Soon Palestinian flags will fly on top of every minaret and church.' Saïd K. Aburish, *Arafat: From Defender to Dictator*, p. 261.

36. Interview with Mahmoud Zahar, 29 August 2016.

37. Aburish, *op. cit.*, p. 256.

38. Ibid.

39. Interview with Haidar Abdel Shafi, 'The Oslo agreement', *Journal of Palestine Studies*, Vol. 23, No. 1, Autumn 1993.

CHAPTER 2: PEACE CANCELLED: FROM HOPE TO INTIFADA, 1995–2003

1. See Shlaim, *op. cit.*, p. 577.

2. Ibid.

3. See Amira Hass, *Drinking the Sea at Gaza*, p. 77.

4. Interview in Donald Macintyre, *Independent on Sunday*, 10 June 2007: 'General Gazit helped redraw the borders of Israel. He says the road map to peace is a lie'.

5. Jimmy Carter, 'Don't Give Up on Mideast Peace', *New York Times*, 12 April 2012.

6. See Shlaim, *op. cit.*, p. 686.

7. Amid the immense literature on Camp David and subsequent negotiations, see Dennis Ross, *The Missing Peace*, for the standard version underpinning the Clinton/Barak blame on Arafat. But for alternative views see Robert Malley's review of Ross, *New York Review of Books*, 7 October 2004; Daniel C. Kurtzer and Scott B. Lasensky, *Negotiating Arab-Israeli Peace*; and Aaron David Miller, *The Much Too Promised Land*.

8. Dennis Ross at Soref Syposium 2001, the Washington Institute. See also Shlaim, *op. cit.*, p. 681.

9. Amos Malka in Akiva Eldar, 'Popular Misconceptions', *Haaretz*, 11 June 2004: 'We assumed that it is possible to reach an agreement with Arafat under the following conditions: a Palestinian state with Jerusalem as its capital and sovereignty on the Temple Mount; 97 per cent of the West Bank plus exchanges of territory in the ratio of 1:1 with respect to the remaining territory; some kind of formula that includes the acknowledgement of Israel's responsibility for the refugee problem and a willingness to accept 20,000–30,000 refugees. All along the way . . . it was MI's assessment that he had to get some kind of statement that would not depict him as having relinquished this, but would be prepared for a very limited implementation.'

10. See Shlaim, *op. cit.*, p. 696, and Morris, *One State, Two States*, pp. 145–6.

11. See Ahron Bregman, *Cursed Victory*, pp. 248ff.

12. Israel Radio, November 1998.

13. See Bregman, *op. cit.*, pp. 246–7.

14. Ibid., p. 250.

15. David Landau, *Arik: The Life of Ariel Sharon*, p. 344.

16. Email to Cindy Corrie, 27 February 2003, available on the website of the Rachel Corrie Foundation: http://rachelcorriefoundation.org/rachel/emails.

17. Associated Press, 29 January 2006.

18. Israel insider, 30 January 2006, quoted in Milton-Edwards and Farrell, *op. cit.*

19. Landau, *op. cit.*, p. 445.

20. Ibid., p. 421.

21. Ibid., p. 443.

22. Ibid., p. 446.

23. Private conversation with Israeli diplomat, June 2003. See also Ethan Bronner, *New York Times*, 30 May 2003.

24. Martin Gilbert, *Israel: A History*, p. 212.

25. Amos Harel, *Haaretz*, 15 August.

26. Suzanne Goldenberg, *Guardian*, 22 August 2003.

27. Associated Press, 21 August 2003.

28. Vered Levy-Barzilai, interview with Dan Halutz, *Haaretz* magazine, 22 August 2002.

29. PCHR, *Weekly Report on Israeli Human Rights Violations in the Occupied Palestinian Territories*, 4 September 2003.

30. Chris McGreal, *Guardian*, 22 August 2003.

31. Landau, *op. cit.*, pp. 402–3.

32. Ibid. p. 452.

33. Private conversation with senior Fatah adviser to Abbas, January 2005.

34. Kurtzer and Lazensky, *op. cit*, p. 63.

35. See Macintyre, 'Hamas exacts revenge as suicide bombs kill 14 in Jerusalem and Tel Aviv', *Independent*, 10 September 2003.

36. *Intifada, Closures and Economic Crisis*, World Bank, May 2003.

37. See Macintyre, 'Dramatic split in Fatah blamed on Arafat's "follied" PA leadership', *Independent*, 16 December 2005.

38. See John Daniszewski, 'Remarks on Terror Become Fighting Words in Israel', *LA Times*, 11 March 1998.

39. B'Tselem *Fatalities Statistics*: http://www.btselem.org/statistics/fatalities/before-cast-lead/by-date-of-event. However, the gap between Israeli and Palestinian deaths is much wider if the figures are taken between September 2000 and December 2008. In that period 4,906 Palestinians and 1,063 Israelis were killed. Among the total of Palestinian deaths – nearly five times as great as that of Israelis – 3,002 were killed in Gaza alone, and all *before* December 2008 and the launching of the first of the three major Israeli military operations in the Strip.

40. Palestinian Centre for Human Rights (PCHR) letter to B'Tselem, 9 September 2001.

41. Interview with Noam Hayut, member of *Combatants for Peace*, 5 April 2006.

42. Charlotte Halle, 'She isn't just another statistic', *Haaretz*, 13 August 2001.

CHAPTER 3: 'NOT A JEW LEFT IN GAZA': DISENGAGEMENT, 2004–5

1. Ariel Sharon, 'By the end of 2005 there will not be a single Jew left in the Gaza Strip', Knesset Foreign Affairs and Defense Committee Meeting, 2 June 2004.

2. Shlaim, *The Iron Wall*, p. 777.

3. See Jewish Virtual Library, accessible on http://www.jewishvirtuallibrary.org/compensation-for-jews-who-lost-homes-in-disengagement.

4. Landau, *op. cit.*, pp. 456–7.

5. Ibid.

6. Ibid.

7. Elliott Abrams, *Tested by Zion*, p. 88.

8. Ibid., p. 778.

9. Ari Shavit, 'The Big Freeze', *Haaretz*, 8 October 2004.

10. Landau, *op. cit.*, p. 467.

11. Ibid., p. 486.

12. Ex-Mossad chief Ephraim Halevy quoted in Associated Press, 14 March 2004.

13. Shlomi Eldar, *Getting to Know Hamas* (Hebrew), pp. 62–3, cited by Shlaim, *op. cit.*, pp. 772–3.

14. Steve Weizman, 'Latest losses fuel Israeli calls to get out of Gaza', Associated Press, 14 May 2004.

15. 'Razing Rafah: Mass demolitions in the Gaza Strip', Human Rights Watch, 14 October 2004.

16. David Shearer and Anushka Myer, 'The dilemma of aid under occupation', in *Aid, Diplomacy and Facts on the Ground: The Case of Palestine*.

17. Abrams, *op. cit.*, p. 124.

18. The UN calculated that in the twelve months up to July of the previous year, nearly 50,000 teacher days were lost in its Gaza schools, at a cost of just under $1m because of delays at Abu Houli. *Report of the Commissoner General United Nations Refugee and Works Agency in the Near East*, General Assembly, 59th session, Supplement No. 13.

19. Palestinian Centre for Human Rights, 12 September 2005.

20. McGreal, *Guardian*, 13 September 2005.

21. Landau, *op. cit.*, p. 526.

22. Ibid., p. 453.

23. Interview with Sir John Jenkins, 23 June 2016.

CHAPTER 4: 'THE DREAM TURNED INTO A NIGHTMARE': POST-DISENGAGEMENT, 2005–6

1. Landau, *op. cit.*, p. 520.

2. Milton-Edwards and Farrell, *op. cit.*

3. Gideon Levy, *The Punishment of Gaza*, p. viii.

4. The figures post-2005 would be far lower still but for Operation Protective Edge in 2014. The 140 includes sixty-seven Israeli soldiers and five civilians killed in that war. Avishay Ben Sasson-Gordis, 'The Strategic Balance of Israel's Withdrawal from Gaza (2005–16)', *Molad: The Center for the Renewal of Israeli Democracy*, p. 10.

5. *Disengagement, the Palestinian Economy and the Settlements*, 13 June 2004, and *Stagnation or Revival? Israeli disengagement and Palestinian Economic Prospects*, World Bank, 1 December 2004.

6. Ora Cohen, 'Eiland: Full Economic Disengagement, Too', *Haaretz*, 1 November 2004.

7. James Wolfensohn, *A Global Life*, Chapter 7.

8. Steven Erlanger, 'Israeli Settlers Demolish Greenhouses and Gaza Jobs', *New York Times*, 15 July 2005.

9. See Abrams, *op. cit.*, p. 140.

10. Interview with Ayed Abu Ramadan, 23 January 2016.

11. Interview with Omar Shaban, 3 May 2016.

12. Wolfensohn, *op. cit.*, p. 419. An estimated 800 of the 4,000 greenhouses were left unusable by the looting. See https://www.jewishvirtuallibrary.org/israel-transfers-gush-katif-hothouses-to-palestinians-september-2005.

13. Wikileaks 'Secret' cable from US Embassy Tel Aviv, 14 June 2006.

14. Abrams, *op. cit.*, p. 149.

15. Ibid., p. 148.

16. Wolfensohn, *op. cit.*, p. 427.

17. Ibid., p. 450.

18. Interview with Raji Sourani, 24 November 2015.

19. 'The Agreement on Movement and Access: One Year On', UN Office for Co-Ordination of Humanitarian Affairs, November 2003.

20. Macintyre, 'Palestinian talks put on hold after suicide attack', *Independent*, 9 December 2005.

21. Abrams, *op. cit.*, p. 201.

CHAPTER 5: 'A BEAUTIFUL PICTURE TO THE WORLD': ELECTIONS, 2006

1. Macintyre, 'Hamas plays on its welfare credentials in historic elections', *Independent*, 25 January 2005.

2. Molly Moore, 'In Gaza, New Hamas-Dominated Council Attends to Basics', *Washington Post*, 16 May 2005.

3. WikiLeaks, Tel Aviv Political Officer Cable on 27 January meeting with Palestinian contacts, 1 February 2005.

4. Landau, *op. cit.*, p. 453.

5. Abrams, *op. cit.*, p. 164.

6. Milton-Edwards and Farrell, *op. cit.*, p. 255.

7. Private interview with EU diplomat, June 2016.

8. Morris, *op. cit.*, p. 171.

9. Interview with Mahmoud Zahar, 28 August 2016.

10. This was the 'Additional Member' system – broadly equivalent to that used in Germany and for the Scottish Parliament – in which electors have two categories of votes, one for a party and one for local representatives from their constituencies.

11. Unpublished report Kevin Lee and Scarlett MccGwire, *Palestinian Election Campaign Visit 15–20 January 2006.*

12. Graham Usher, 'The Democratic Resistance: Hamas, Fatah, and the Palestinian Elections', *Journal of Palestine Studies*, Vol. 35, No. 3 (Spring 2006), pp. 20–36.

13. WikiLeaks, cable, US Embassy, Tel Aviv, 9 January 2005.

14. Lee and MccGwire, *op. cit.*

15. Milton-Edwards and Farrell, *op. cit.*, p. 251.

16. Quoted in Usher, *op. cit.*

17. WikiLeaks, cable US Embassy, Tel Aviv, 13 January 2006.

18. Abrams, *op. cit.*, p. 152.

19. See Aburish, *op. cit.*, p. 155.

20. Milton-Edwards and Farrell, *op. cit.*, p. 254.

21. Interview with Bassem Naim, 4 June 2016.

22. Interview with Mahmoud Zahar, 29 August 2016.

23. Macintyre, 'United by courage, Palestinian women seize opportunity to assert their rights', *Independent*, 5 January 2005.

24. See Milton-Edwards and Farrell, *op. cit.*, pp. 254–5.

25. See Aburish, *op. cit.*

26. WikiLeaks, cable, Jacob Walles US Consul General, Jerusalem, 26 January 2006.

27. Usher, *op. cit.*

28. Macintyre, 'Hamas scores stunning win, but what now?', *Independent*, 27 January 2006.

CHAPTER 6: 'IT'S THE WRONG RESULT': INTERNATIONAL RESPONSE TO HAMAS'S VICTORY, 2006

1. Abrams, *op. cit.*, p. 163.

2. Ibid., p. 166.

3. Minute from the UK Representative to EU Office e-gram 1837/06, 27 January 2006, (redacted) released to author under Freedom of Information Act 2016.

4. E-gram from Jerusalem Consulate General, 27 January 2006, released to author under FOI 2016. A 27 January UK Department for International Development Minute also suggested – somewhat optimistically – that 'Hamas and Israel will need to find a way to work together', pointing out that at a municipal

level they already did. It suggested that it would be 'difficult' 'in the short term' for Hamas to renounce 'its commitment to the destruction of Israel and its support for terrorism'. The document, also released under the FOI, is so heavily redacted that it is impossible to be certain of its exact thrust, but in what appears to be a call for a more gradualist approach by the international community it says: 'ultimately Hamas's participation in the realities of political responsibility might bring out Hamas's transformation to a political rather than terrorist organisation'.

5. Álvaro de Soto's 'End of Mission Report', available via Rory McCarthy and Ian Williams, 'UN was pummelled into submission says outgoing Middle East special envoy', *Guardian*, 13 June 2007: https://www.theguardian.com/world/2007/jun/13/usa.israel1.

6. Private exchange with EU diplomat, June 2017.

7. Condoleezza Rice, *No Higher Honor*, p. 419.

8. See Álvaro de Soto valedictory.

9. Steven Erlanger, 'US, Israelis are said to talk of Hamas ouster', *New York Times*, 14 February 2006.

10. See Khaled Hroub, '"A New Hamas" through Its New Documents', *Journal of Palestine Studies*, Vol. 35, No. 4 (Summer 2006), pp. 6–27. This sections draws heavily on Hroub's analysis of Haniyeh's speech.

11. Ibid.

12. Interview with Omar Shaban, 3 May 2016.

13. Interview with Ahmed Yousef, 30 August 2016.

14. Interview with Ghazi Hamad, 9 May 2016.

15. Interview with Sami Abdel Shafi, 28 September 2016.

16. John Burns, 'Britain resumes talking with Hezbollah', *New York Times*, 5 March 2009.

17. Jack Straw, *Last Man Standing*, p. 461.

18. Foreign Office minute released under FOI.

19. Straw, *op. cit.*, p. 461.

20. Interview with Tony Blair, 16 January 2017. Blair did not elaborate on the informal contacts but the reference is almost certainly to limited and unpublicised contacts between British intelligence and Hamas officials from the period of Alan Johnston's kidnap.

21. Interview with Jonathan Powell, 19 February 2017.

22. Harry S. Truman Research Institute for the Advancement of Peace at the Hebrew University of Jerusalem and the Palestinian Center for Policy and Survey Research in Ramallah, September 2006.

23. Abrams, *op. cit.*, p. 167.

24. Interview with Mahmoud Zahar, 29 August 2016.

25. Abrams, *op. cit.*, p. 176.

26. See Macintyre, 'Ehud Olmert: "I can't afford to make mistakes",

Independent, 9 June 2006. Full transcript of Macintyre/Morris interview at http://www.geneva-accord.org/mainmenu/ehud-olmert-interview-june-6-2006. Olmert also laid considerable emphasis in the interview on the document's reference to the 'right of return' for 1948 refugees and their families.

27. See Macintyre, 'Hospital casts doubt on Israel's version of attack that killed seven Palestinians', *Independent*, 17 June 2006, and McGreal, 'The battle of Huda Ghalia – who really killed girl's family on Gaza beach?', *Guardian*, 17 June 2006. The exact cause was a mystery. Hospital records and the testimony of the first ambulanceman called to the scene did not bear out the Israeli investigation's contention that an IDF artillery barrage had stopped when the family was killed. One possibility is that the ground impact of the shelling detonated an unexploded shell lying in the sand.

28. Filiu, *op. cit.*, p. 295.

29. Gershon Baskin, *The Negotiator: Freeing Gilad Shalit from Hamas*.

30. Ibid., p. 296.

31. Ibid.

32. *West Bank and Gaza Update*, World Bank, March 2007.

33. Filiu, *op. cit.*, pp. 296–7.

34. Wolfensohn, *op. cit.*, pp. 437–8.

35. Interview with Souad al-Quraya, 12 May 2016.

36. Alex Fishman, *Yedhiot Ahronot*, 9 November 2006.

37. For a fuller account, see Macintyre, 'Gaza children cannot escape as Israel mounts its bloodiest attack in months', *Independent*, 9 November 2006; and 'Immersed in grief and unable to move on', *Independent*, 11 November 2006.

38. B'Tselem Fatalities before Cast Lead accessible on http://www.btselem.org/statistics/fatalities/before-cast-lead/by-date-of-event.

39. Milton-Edwards and Farrell, *op. cit.*, p. 224.

40. Ibid., p. 266.

41. Eric Westervelt, 'Abbas gets money, Support – and Distrust', National Public Radio, 19 January 2007.

CHAPTER 7: 'SO MANY HARD TIMES AHEAD': CIVIL WAR, 2007

1. See International Crisis Group, 'Inside Gaza: The Challenge of Clans and Families', 20 December 2007.

2. Interview with Alan Johnston, 11 July 2016.

3. Alan Johnston, *Kidnapped and Other Dispatches*.

4. Interview with Alan Johnston, 11 July 2016.

5. Abrams, *op. cit.*, p. 219.

6. Interview with Ghazi Hamad, 6 June 2016.

7. Amnesty International, 'Occupied Palestinian Territories: Torn apart by factional strife', 24 October 2007. See the report for a detailed account of the atrocities committed in the intra-Palestinian fighting, accessible at https://www.amnesty.org/en/documents/mde21/020/2007/en/.

8. Interview with Ahmed Yousef, 12 September 2016.

9. Milton-Edwards and Farrell, *op. cit.*, p. 288. Israel kept foreign reporters out of Gaza during the June fighting, but these authors provide a vivid reconstruction.

10. Ibid., p. 290.

11. David Rose, 'The Gaza Bombshell', *Vanity Fair*, March 2008.

12. See Macintyre, 'How "national unity" has been soured by suspicions about outside interference', *Independent*, 18 May 2007.

13. Milton-Edwards and Farrell, *op. cit.*, pp. 285–6.

14. Palestine Papers (leaked to Al Jazeera), 'Palestinian security plan – United Kingdom Project Synopsis', Military Liaison Office Jerusalem, 2 May 2005.

15. Milton-Edwards and Farrell, *op. cit.*, p. 287.

16. Abrams, *op. cit.*, p. 229.

17. Ibid., pp. 229–30.

18. Milton-Edwards and Farrell, *op. cit.*, p. 285.

19. WikiLeaks, Tel Aviv cable, 22 May 2006.

20. *Evening Standard*, 4 July 2007.

21. Private conversation with UK diplomat.

22. Cam Wilson, 'What If Israel Talked to Hamas?', *Wall Street Journal*, 1 August 2007.

23. *Jerusalem Post*, 19 July 2007.

24. WikiLeaks, cable, US Embassy, Tel Aviv, 13 June 2007.

25. Jean-Pierre Filiu, *op. cit.*, p. 343.

26. Interview with Ghazi Hamad.

27. Amnesty International report: 'Occupied Palestinian Territories: Torn apart by factional strife', 24 October 2007.

28. PCHR statement: 'PCHR Condemns Excessive and Lethal Use of Force against Civilians in Gaza', 13 November 2007.

CHAPTER 8: THE GAZA DIET: SIEGE, 2008-9

1. 'As Rice arrives, Israel calls Gaza "hostile territory"', *New York Times*, 19 September 2007.

2. *Economic Monitoring Report to the Ad Hoc Liaison Committee*, World Bank, May 2008.

3. UNRWA report: 'Prolonged crisis in the occupied Palestinian territory: Socio-economic developments in 2007', July 2008.

4. 'Israeli "Economic Warfare" to Include Electricity Cuts in Gaza', *Washington Post*, 28 January 2008.

5. Macintyre, 'A fight for life in a power struggle', *Independent*, 30 January 2008.

6. B'Tselem statistics accessible at http://www.btselem.org/statistics/fatalities/before-cast-lead/by-date-of-event. These are the numbers reported as not 'participating in hostilities' when they were killed; they include seventy-five minors and seventeen women.

7. Robert Pastor, *Memorandum of Conversation March 17–18, 2008, 11:30 pm–3:30 am – Damascus, Syria*. For copies of these and all other documents written by Robert Pastor about this period I am greatly indebted to Professor Avi Shlaim, Emeritus Professor of International Relations, Oxford University.

8. 'Summary of rocket fire and mortar shelling in 2008', Meir Amit Intelligence and Terrorism Information Center (Israel).

9. Meir Amit Center, *op. cit.* At Rafah, where 279 Palestinians had been leaving every day on average in the first half of 2007, the daily exits from June to October 2008 were, month by month, 7, 14, 108, 84 and 1.

10. See 'IDF Operation in Gaza: Cast Lead', Israel Ministry of Foreign Affairs, 21 January 2009: http://www.mfa.gov.il/mfa/foreignpolicy/terrorism/palestinian/pages/aerial_strike_weapon_development_center%20_gaza_28-dec-2008.aspx.

11. Meir Amit Center, *op. cit.*

12. Shlaim, *op. cit.*, p. 801.

13. Pastor memo to R. J. Goldstone, 6 December 2009. (The memorandum was sent to Judge Richard Goldstone.) Pastor's version of the June 2008 ceasefire, as shown him by Hamas said:

> 1. Mutual agreement on stopping all military activities by the start of the 'zero hour' on Thursday the 19th of June 2008 at 06:00 am.
>
> 2. Ceasefire period for six months according to what has been agreed nationally among the political parties under Egyptian auspices.
>
> 3. The ceasefire will be implemented under national consensus and under Egyptian auspices.
>
> 4. After 72 hours of the start of the ceasefire, crossing points will be opened and there will be a 30% increase in goods entering the Gaza Strip.
>
> 5. After 10 days all goods (quantity and quality) that were banned/restricted will be allowed to go into Gaza.
>
> 6. Egypt will work to expand the ceasefire into the West Bank later.

14. WikiLeaks, US Consulate General, Jerusalem cable, 16 December 2008.

15. See Macintyre, 'Chronic malnutrition in Gaza blamed on Israel', *Independent*, 15 November 2008.

16. Quartet Statement, 24 June 2008.

17. WikiLeaks, US Consulate General, Jerusalem cable, 2 December 2008.

18. Israel Ministry of Foreign Affairs, 'EU ministers vote to upgrade diplomatic dialogue with Israel', Statement, 9 December 2008.

19. Wikileaks, US embassy Tel Aviv 'Secret' cable, 22 December 2008.

CHAPTER 9: 'NOT A HAIR WILL FALL OF A SOLDIER OF MINE': OPERATION CAST LEAD, 2008–9

1. PCHR, 'Weekly Report on Israeli Human Rights Violations in the Occupied Palestinian Territory', 7 May 2008.

2. Breaking the Silence, *Our Harsh Logic: Israeli Soldiers' Testimonies from the Occupied Territories, 2000–2010*, testimony catalogue number: 188758.

3. See Macintyre, 'Israel should be proud of the open criticism democracy provokes', *Independent*, 21 December 2015, and Peter Beaumont, 'Israel sunk in "incremental tyranny", say former Shin Bet chiefs', *Guardian*, 6 April 2017.

4. Accessible online at http://www.breakingthesilence.org.il/about/organization.

5. UN letters in author's possession.

6. B'Tselem, 1 January 2011: http://www.btselem.org/gaza_strip/castlead_operation.

7. Ben Lynfield, ' "We are going wild," says Foreign Minister', *Independent*, 13 January 2009.

8. Mohammed Dawwas, 'Life in Gaza: "Hungry, freezing, and terrifying" ', *Independent*, 4 January 2009.

9. Fares Akram, 'The death and life of my father', *Independent*, 5 January 2009.

10. Maysaa Samouni testimony accessible at http://www.btselem.org/testimonies/20090108_soldiers_kill_and_wound_members_of_a_Samuni_family.

11. MAG Legal Opinion: Al-Samouni Family Incident, accessible online at http://www.law.idf.il/163-5080-en/Patzar.aspx.

12. Report of the United Nations Fact-Finding Mission on the Gaza Conflict, 5 September 2009.

13. Richard Goldstone, 'Reconsidering the Goldstone Report on Israel and War Crimes', 1 April 2011.

14. Norman Finkelstein, *Method and Madness*, pp. 62–3.

15. Yoram Dinstein, 'The Conduct of Hostilities Under the Law of International Armed Conflict', p. 117 (quoted in Finkelstein, *op. cit.*, p. 63).

16. Breaking the Silence, *Breaking the Silence: Soldiers' Testimonies from Operation Cast Lead, Gaza 2009*, p. 46.

17. 'White Flag Deaths Killings of Palestinian Civilians during Operation Cast Lead', Human Rights Watch, July 2009.

18. 'The Spirit of the IDF', accessible at https://www.idfblog.com/2011/11/02/the-spirit-of-the-idf/.

19. Moshe Halbertal, 'The Goldstone illusion', *New Republic*, 6 November 2009.

20. Asa Kasher and Amos Yadlin, 'Military Ethics of Fighting Terror: An Israeli Perspective', *Journal of Military Ethics*, Vol. 4, Issue 1, 2005. Available from http://www.tandfonline.com/toc/smil20/4/1.

21. Avishai Margalit and Michael Walzer, 'Israel: Combatants and Civilians', *New York Review of Books*, 14 May 2009.

22. Amos Harel, 'The philosopher who gave the IDF moral justification in Gaza', *Haaretz*, 6 February 2009.

23. Margalit and Walzer, *op. cit.*

24. MAG, 'IDF Military Advocate General Takes Disciplinary Action, Indicts Soldiers Following Investigations into Incidents during Operation Cast Lead', 6 July 2010. On Juhr al-Dik, the IDF said the soldiers had spoken of an incident on 5 January, the Palestinians of one on 4 January, which, as the first day of the ground invasion, was not one the family was likely to misremember. When I went back to Juhr al-Dik after the MAG report was released in 2011 two of Majda's brothers said records would show their telephone calls to the ICRC trying to summon an ambulance on 4 January. The investigation into the killing of the women was never reopened; nor was the soldier – or the mysterious 'unknown individual' supposedly killed on 5 January – ever identified.

25. Recorded testimony of Jodie Clark in a play, *I Am a Warehouse*, written and performed by Chris Gunness, Director of Communications, UNRWA, 2009. The IDF claimed to have deployed white phosphorus to provide a smokescreen protecting its tanks from Hamas anti-tank fire; UNRWA officials questioned whether there was anti-tank fire in the area at the time.

26. Gabi Siboni, 'Disproportionate Force: Israel's Concept of Response in Light of the Second Lebanon War', *Israel Institute for National Security Studies*, 2 October 2008.

CHAPTER 10: 'THEY'RE PUNISHING THE WRONG PEOPLE': SIEGE, 2008–12

1. Hass, '2,279 Calories per Person: How Israel Made Sure Gaza Didn't Starve', *Haaretz*, 12 October 2012.

2. Nicholas Pelham, *Palestine Speaks*, appendix. Pelham's is the most detailed analysis of the growth of the tunnels industry.

3. UN World Food Programme, *Economic and Food Security Survey, West Bank and Gaza Strip, occupied Palestinian territory 2010*.

4. Portland Trust, *The Private Sector in Gaza*, December 2010.

5. 'Assessment Of Restrictions On Palestinian Water Sector Development', World Bank, April 2009.

6. 'Let it Flow', *Ewash*, March 2016.

7. 'Protecting children from unsafe water in Gaza', UNICEF, March 2011.

8. *Ewash, op. cit.*

9. Gisha, 'Hand on the Switch – Who's responsible for Gaza's infrastructure crisis?', 26 January 2017. Available from http://gisha.org/publication/5780.

10. World Bank, *op. cit.*

11. Roy, *The Gaza Strip*, 1995, (p. 162 in 2016 edition).

12. See Zafrir Rinat, 'Mekorot launches program to save the coastal aquifer', *Haaretz*, 31 July 2009.

13. C. Messerschmid, 'Water in Gaza – Problems & Prospects', Birzeit University, Birzeit, 2013, quoted in Elisabeth Koek, 'Water For One People Only', Al-Haq, 2013.

14. Roy, *op. cit.*, p. l.

15. British proposal: 'Lifting Gaza's closure'. (I am grateful to Nicolas Pelham for sharing this paper with me.)

16. 'Dashed Hopes – Continuation of the Gaza Blockade', survey by twenty-two aid agencies.

17. Clyde Haberman, *New York Times*, 4 July 1994.

18. Roy, *op. cit.*, (p. 233 in 2016 edition).

19. Ibid., p. li.

20. Interview with Ayed Abu Ramadan, 23 January 2016.

21. Filiu, *op. cit.*, p. 337.

22. Interview with Assad Saftawi.

23. Filiu, *op. cit.*, p. 322.

24. See Mazal Muslem, 'Ben-Eliezer: Israel Should Free Barghouti, He Is Next PA Leader', *Haaretz*, 25 September 2007. The call for the release of Barghouti, who was serving five sentences for murders and other acts allegedly committed by Fatah militias, by Benjamin Ben Eliezer, then Labour Infrastructure Minister, was also made by the Kadima (and ex-Likud) Environment Minister Gideon Ezra.

25. This was neatly summarised as: 'near daily mortar or rocket attacks by mostly non-Hamas Palestinian militants, and weekly Israeli incursions, together with more frequent machine-gun strafing of Palestinians entering a 300–1,500 metre-wide Israeli-imposed "buffer zone", naval fire against Palestinian fishermen travelling outside a three-nautical mile limit, shelling of areas close to the Gaza–Israel border and aerial strikes against Gaza militants'; 'Israel and Hamas: fire and ceasefire in a new Middle East', International Crisis Group, 22 November 2012.

26. Aluf Benn, 'Israel Killed Its Subcontractor in Gaza', *Haaretz*, 14 November 2012.

27. *Times of Israel*, 29 May 2012.

28. *Economic Monitoring Report to Ad Hoc Liaison Committee*, World Bank, March 2013.

29. *An Analysis of the Economic Restrictions Confronting the West Bank and Gaza*, World Bank, September 2008, cited in Roy, *op. cit.*, p. xxvi.

CHAPTER 11: 'WELCOME TO THE
BIGGEST PRISON IN THE WORLD'

1. Gisha, 'Gaza Up Close', December 2016.

2. Interview with Nabil Shurafa, 25 April 2016.

3. Alan Johnston, 'Years of delays at Gaza airport', *BBC News*, 15 April 2005.

4. Gisha report on Rafah crossing, 2 June 2016.

5. Joseph Federman, 'Israel increases interrogations of Gazan travellers', Associated Press, 22 September 2016.

6. Barak Ravid, 'Israel Should Reduce Use of Administrative Detentions for Palestinians, Top Official Says', *Haaretz*, 3 May 2012.

7. Gisha factsheet, '"Security blocks" restricting exit from the Gaza Strip disrupt the lives of thousands', December 2016.

8. Interview with Ayed Abu Ramadan, 6 February 2016.

9. Interview with Bilal Abu Daher, 16 August 2016.

10. See Gisha, *op. cit.*

11. Interview with Mariam Dawwas, 17 August 2016.

12. Palestinian Public Opinion Poll No. (62), *Palestinian Center for Policy and Survey Research*, 13 December 2016.

13. Peter Beaumont and Patrick Kingsley, 'Devil and the deep blue sea: how Mediterranean migrant disaster unfolded', *Guardian*, 1 October 2014.

14. Fishman, 'Gaza: a human time bomb', *Yedhiot Ahronot*, 8 February 2016.

15. 'Fatal shooting of Palestinian man caught on video', Al Jazeera, 27 December 2015. Available online: http://www.aljazeera.com/news/2015/12/fatal-shooting-palestinian-man-caught-video-151226132048015.html.

16. Interview with Amna Hassan and family members, 7 May 2016.

17. Interview with Bilal al-Amar, 8 May 2016.

CHAPTER 12: 'LET'S NOT DIE TOGETHER':
OPERATION PROTECTIVE EDGE, 2014

1. Interview with Mohammed al-Rifi, 10 August 2016.

2. Interview with Tareq al-Rifi, 12 August 2016.

3. OPE fatalities accessible at http://www.btselem.org/statistics/fatalities/during-cast-lead/by-date-of-event. B'Tselem does not use the term 'civilian' but 'not participating in hostilities' for non-combatant casualties.

4. UN OCHA, 'Gaza: One Year On': http://gaza.ochaopt.org/2015/06/key-figures-on-the-2014-hostilities/_ftn15.

5. UN OCHA, Monthly Humanitarian bulletin, November 2016.

6. US NGO American Near East Refugee Aid (ANERA), 'Rebuilding Gaza', Vol. 6, August 2016: http://www.anera.org/wp-content/uploads/2015/07/Rebuilding-Gaza-Humanitarian-and-Reconstruction-needs.pdf.

7. Assaf Sharon, 'Failure in Gaza', *New York Review of Books*, 25 September 2014. See also Nathan Thrall, 'Hamas's Chances', *London Review of Books*, 21 August 2014. This section leans heavily on their analysis.

8. See Shlomi Eldar (Israeli commentator and Hamas expert), 'Accused Kidnappers Are Rogue Hamas Branch', *Al-Monitor*, 29 June 2014. Also see Amos Harel and Chaim Levinson, 'One Year After West Bank Murder-kidnapping: What Israel's Security Forces Got Wrong', *Haaretz*, 12 June 2015, which covers the claim by the senior Hamas figure Saleh Arouri in Turkey that the faction's military wing *had* been responsible. According to the report, the Israeli defence establishment, after exhaustive, and at times ruthless inter-rogation of local Hamas operatives, regarded the claim by Arouri as an 'empty boast'.

9. Eldar, 'Has Israel recognized link between Gaza blockade, security threat?', *Al-Monitor*, 1 March 2017. Available from http://www.al-monitor.com/pulse/originals/2017/03/israel-gaza-war-2014-state-comptroller-report-blockade.html.

10. Norman Finkelstein (*Method and Madness*, pp. 138–9) argues that Netanyahu deliberately timed the ground invasion hours after the shooting down of the Malaysian airline, in order to minimise international attention. If so it was not that successful since the Gaza operation attracted widespread cover-age, notably in Europe. Moreover, unlike in 2008–9 foreign journalists and TV crews had not been prevented from entering Gaza.

11. Roy, *op. cit.* (2016 edition), p. 396.

12. Mohammed Daraghmeh and Karin Laub, 'Hamas claims "victory for the resistance" as long-term truce is agreed with Israel', Associated Press, 26 August 2014.

13. Herb Keinon, 'Netanyahu: Hamas suffered its greatest blow since it was founded', *Jerusalem Post*, 27 August 2014.

14. July 2014 Peace Index, Israel Democracy Institute. Available at https://en.idi.org.il/press-releases/12790.

15. 'IDF official: Gaza underground wall should be done in months', *Times of Israel*, 25 September 2016.

16. See Sharon, *op. cit.*

17. Available from https://www.youtube.com/watch?v=uw5z4an-Nhw.

18. B'Tselem, 'Black Flag: The legal and moral implications of the policy of attacking residential buildings in the Gaza Strip, summer 2014', accessible on http://www.btselem.org/publications/summaries/201501_black_flag.

19. See Nathan Thrall, 'Hamas's Chances', *London Review of Books*, 21 August 2014.

20. I was much criticised by pro-Israeli social media users for a passing reference to Mohammed Badran in a long dispatch from Gaza to the *New Statesman* about the war which wrongly reported that his entire family had been wiped out in the Nusseirat bombing. They had been alerted to the error by a correction which I immediately made online when I found his mother and injured sister with him at Shifa hospital a few days later. But one of these, the British blogger Tom Grossman, was wrong to blame me – and other Western journalists – for 'rely[ing] on Hamas's misinformation and distortion of casualty figures' and doctors. The report had been based on information relayed in good faith by Ghassan Abu Sitta, a plastic surgeon living in Beirut with an international reputation and nothing to fear from Hamas; when he examined Mohammed in the chaos of the Shifa emergency room, exceptionally in a tight-knit Gazan family, there had been no family members with the boy. In the mayhem he had been mistaken, or misinformed, about the reason, which turned out to be that the other injured family members had been taken to the Deir el Balah hospital. I was also later criticised for not reporting on the day of his death, what I did not then know but also corrected when I did, that Nidal Badran had been in the Qassam Brigades.

21. *New Statesman*, 22 July 2014.

22. Christopher F. Schuetze and Anne Barnard, 'Resisting Nazis, He Saw Need for Israel. Now He Is Its Critic', *New York Times*, 14 August 2014.

23. See https://www.youtube.com/watch?v=ACgwr2Nj_GQ.

24. Interview with Mohammed Bakr, 2016.

25. Beaumont, 'Witness to a shelling: first-hand account of deadly strike on Gaza wall', *Guardian*, 16 July 2014.

26. IDF Military Advocate General, 'Operation Protective Edge: Investigation of exceptional incidents', update 4 accessible on http://mfa.gov.il/MFA/ForeignPolicy/IsraelGaza2014/Pages/Operation-Protective-Edge-Investigation-of-exceptional-incidents-Update-4.aspx.

27. Geneva convention Arts 50 (1) and 52 (1), Additional Protocol I, quoted in Report of the Independent Commission of Inquiry on the 2014 Gaza Conflict, UN Human Rights Council.

28. Beaumont, 'Israel exonerates itself over Gaza beach killings of four children last year', *Guardian*, 11 June 2015.

29. Landau, 'The moral case for Israel's Ground Invasion', *Haaretz*, 21 July 2014.

30. Israel adamantly denied it was responsible. I arrived about thirty minutes after the strike, but witnesses immediately after the attack saw militants moving in to clear debris.

CHAPTER 13: 'FROM THE MIDDLE AGES TO THE NINETEENTH CENTURY': HAMAS SHIFTS ITS GROUND

1. *Washington Post*, table updated 20 September 2016, available from https://www.washingtonpostcom/graphics/world/israel-palestine-deaths/.

2. This was first noticed by the journalist Amira Hass: see Hass, 'Somebody in Hamas got scared and this sentence was deleted', *Haaretz*, 3 May 2013.

3. Hamas, 'A Document of General Principles and Policies', accessible on http://hamas.ps/en/post/678/a-document-of-general-principles-and-policies.

4. '"The situation in Gaza is much worse than prior to the war in 2014": an interview with Giora Eiland', *Fathom*, May 2017, accessible at http://fathomjournal.org/the-situation-today-is-much-worse-than-prior-to-the-war-in-2014-an-interview-with-giora-eiland/.

5. Milton-Edwards and Farrell, *op. cit.*, p. 82.

6. In author's possession.

7. The 'vision' set out in the document states: 'Hamas is a national liberation movement that conducts its activities only within Palestine's borders.

1. Having an Islamic background and moderate ideology, Hamas believes in positive dialogue between different civilisations with no recourse to violence or oppression.

2. Hamas has nothing to do with any sectarian, ethnic or political conflict in the region.

3. With high respect for all religions and faiths, Hamas believes the Palestinian struggle is a struggle against the Israeli occupation not against Judaism per se.

4. We seek to restore unalienated rights of the Palestinian people, believing if the political way achieves such objective, it would be the best.

5. Believing in democracy and peaceful transition of power, Hamas cherishes respect for human rights in general and rights of women in particular.

6. Over the last months, Hamas has taken all necessary measures and made concessions needed for reconciliation.'

8. Lally Weymouth's interview with Ismail Haniyeh, 'We do not wish to throw them into the sea', *Washington Post*, 26 February 2006.

9. Interview with Mahmoud Zahar, 29 and 30 August 2016.

10. Interview with Ayman Aloul, 12 March 2016.

11. Filiu, *op. cit.*, pp. 334–5.

12. PCHR: http://pchrgaza.org/en/?cat=45.

13. Fares Akram and Isabel Kershner, 'Gaza Killing of Italian Activist Deals a Blow to Hamas', *New York Times*, 15 April 2011.

14. Interview with Ahmed Yousef, 30 August 2016.

15. Erlanger, 'From Hamas Figure, an Unusual Self-Criticism', *New York Times*, 26 August 2008.

16. Eldar, 'Sinwar and Dahlan's Cairo face-to-face', *Al-Monitor*, 14 June 2017.

17. Interview with Mohammed El-Emadi, 16 June 2016.

18. Tony Blair speech to Herzliya conference, 21 June 2017.

19. Benjamin Netanyahu speech to the UN General Assembly, 29 September 2014. The full quote was: 'ISIS and Hamas are branches of the same poisonous tree. When it comes to their ultimate goals, Hamas is ISIS and ISIS is Hamas. And what they share in common, all militant Islamists share in common.'

20. 'Islamic State threatens to topple Hamas in Gaza Strip in video statement', *Reuters* report in *Guardian*, 30 June 2013.

21. Barak Mendelsohn, 'Al-Qaeda's Palestinian Problem', *Survival: Global Politics and Strategy*, Vol. 51, No. 4 (August–September 2009).

CHAPTER 14: 'THEY WILL ALWAYS MISS HOME'

1. Ghassan Kanafani, 'Letter from Gaza' (1966), London, Tricontinental Society, 1980 (English). Available online at https://kanan48.wordpress.com/ghassan-kanafani/letter-from-gaza/.

2. Interview with Jihad Saftawi, 23 July 2016.

3. Interview with Yasmin Dawwas, 28 August 2016.

4. Macintyre, 'Hamas admits its gunmen shot betrothed woman in "honour killing"', *Independent*, 13 April 2005.

5. Interview with Aya al-Wakil, 21 August 2016.

6. 4:34 in N. J. Dawood (trans.), *The Koran*, p. 370.

7. 'A Question of Security: Violence against Palestinian Women and Girls', Human Rights Watch, November 2006.

8. Atef Abu Saif, 'A Journey in the Opposite Direction', in *The Book of Gaza*.

CHAPTER 15: THE LONG-DISTANCE RUNNER OF
BEIT HANOUN: SIEGE AND *SUMMOUD*

1. Interviews at Al Jawad Equestrian Club, August 2016.

2. Interviews with Zorob residents, 23 August 2016.

3. Jean Zaru, 'Occupied with Non-Violence: A Palestinian woman speaks', quoted in Timothy Seidel chapter 'Development as Peacebuilding and Resistance: Alternative Narratives of Nonviolence in Palestine-Israel' in *Non-Violent resistance in the Second Intifada: Activism and Advocacy*.

4. Mohammed Omer, '"The smell of death hangs everywhere": Blockade drives Gazans to suicide', *Middle East Eye*, April 2016.

5. Interviews with al-Burim family, 5 May 2016.

6. Ms Bailey revealed these figures at a conference organised by the Gaza Community Mental Health Programme in April 2016.

7. Interview with Mohammed al-Hindi, 12 June 2016.

8. Unpublished Gaza Power and Energy Resources Authority letter to European diplomatic missions, 2 May 2017 (in author's possession).

9. Private conversation with PLO executive member, 23 April 2017.

10. WHO, Occupied Palestinian Territory, *Monthly Report*, May 2017.

11. Medical Aid for Palestinians, 'Gaza in Darkness', July 2017.

12. UN News Centre, 11 July 2017, accessible at http://www.un.org/apps/news/story.asp?NewsID=57157#.WWoj71GEbIU.

13. See Chapter Six.

14. Interviews at the Aziz factory, 29 June 2016.

15. Interview with Basil Abu Qamer, 23 June 2016.

16. Gisha, 'Gaza in numbers', December 2016.

17. Interview with Mohammed al-Tilbani, 7 January 2016.

CHAPTER 16: 'WE LOVE LIFE, IF WE FIND A WAY TO IT'

1. 'The Arc: A Formal Structure for a Palestinian State', RAND Corporation, 1 December 2005. Accessible at http://www.rand.org/pubs/research_briefs/RB9119.html.

2. *Church Times*, 15 November 1918.

3. Butt, *op. cit.*, p. 159.

4. Interviews with Work Without Borders, 25 June 2016.

5. This may be a conservative estimate; overall graduate unemployment among Palestinians, according to the Palestinian Central Bureau of Statistics, is fifty-one per cent and the rate of unemployment among all Gazans – forty-two per cent in 2016 – is over twice as high as in the West Bank, eighteen per cent.

6. Interview Maha al-Daya, 20 January 2016.

7. Interview Sami Efrangi, 20 August 2016.

8. Khaled Alashqar, 'Gaza cinema struggles amid post-war ruins', *Al Jazeera English*, 13 December 2014

9. Interview with Sara Akel, 30 August 2016.

10. Accessible at www.rand.org/content/dam/rand/pubs/monographs/2007/RAND_MG146-1.pdf.

11. 'Arafat Hails Big Gas Find Off the Coast of Gaza Strip', *New York Times*, 28 September 2000.

12. Palestine Investment Fund annual report 2012 cited in Simon Henderson, 'Natural Gas in the Palestinian Authority: The Potential of the Gaza Marine Offshore Field', German Marshall fund of the United States *Policy Brief*.

13. See Victor Kattan, 'The Gas Fields off Gaza: A Gift or a Curse?', *Al-Shabaka*, 24 April 2012.

14. Simon Henderson, *op. cit.*

15. Ibid.

16. Unpublished letter to Robert Piper from Maj. Gen Yoav (Poli) Mordechai, Co-ordinator of Government Activities in the Territories, 13 April 2017 (in author's possession).

17. Ziyaad Lunat, 'The "Economic Peace" Model in the Palestinian Water Sector', cited in Roy, *op. cit.*, p. lv.

18. Munther Shiblak, head of the Coastal Muncipalities Water Utility, quoted in *Al-Monitor*, 31 May 2015.

19. J. Selby, 'Cooperation, domination and colonisation: The Israeli–Palestinian Joint Water Committee', *Water Alternatives*, Vol. 6, No. 1 (February 2013), pp. 1–24.

20. Interview with Bo Schack, Operations director, UNRWA, 22 November 2015.

21. 'IDF intel chief warns despair in Gaza could explode toward Israel', *Times of Israel*, 24 February 2016.

22. Interview with Basil Eleiwa, 24 June 2016.

CONCLUSION

1. Interview with Mahmoud al-Bahtiti, 29 September 2016.

2. 'Bridging the Dangerous Gap between the West and the Muslim World', speech by Paul Wolfowitz, 3 May 2002. Available at http://www.au.af.mil/au/awc/awcgate/dod/s20020503-depsecdef.htm.

3. *Journal* of *Palestine Studies*, Vol. 25, No. 1 (Autumn 1995), pp. 76-8.

4. Lazar Berman, 'Ex-US general: We pay a price for backing Israel', *Times of Israel*, 25 July 2013.

5. Zeev Sternhell, 'Europe is beginning to tire of Israel', *Haaretz*, 5 May 2017.

6. Hugh Lovatt and Mattia Toaldo, 'EU Differentiation and Israeli settlements', European Council on Foreign Relations, 22 July 2015, available from http://www.ecfr.eu/publications/summary/eu_differentiation_and_israeli_settlements3076.

7. Edward Said, *The Politics of Dispossession*, p.169.

8. Interview with Avraham Burg in Macintyre, 'Israel's New Prophet', *Independent*, 1 November 2008.

9. Giora Eiland interview in http://fathomjournal.org/the-situation-today-is-much-worse-than-prior-to-the-war-in-2014-an-interview-with-giora-eiland/.

10. Nathan Thrall, 'Hamas's Chances', *London Review of Books*, 21 August 2014.

11. Hass, *Drinking the Sea at Gaza*, p. 9.

Acknowledgements

M Y FIRST THANKS ARE TO THE people of Gaza who have been repeatedly generous with their time and hospitality – and fearless about expressing their very diverse views – over the fourteen years I have reported from the Strip. I owe a profound debt to two great Gazan friends, Sami Abdel Shafi and Fares Akram, for sharing their deep insights and knowledge over many years. Thanks too for all I have learned over the last decade from Jawdat al-Khodary, Raji Sourani, the late Eyad Sarraj, Mahmoud Daher, John Ging, Chris Gunness, Omar Shaban, Hamdi Shakkura and more recently – including for generously welcoming me with their families into their homes – Mohammed Sabbah and his brother Fathi. As translators and fixers, Mohammed Dawwas, his intrepid daughters Yasmin and Mariam, and, especially during several months in 2016, Hazem Balousha, all helped me far more, I suspect, than they realise, at least to begin understanding a society that is far more complex than it appears at first sight. As did Munir Dweik, Ashraf al-Masri, and Abeer Ayyoub.

Much of the book stems originally from my reporting for the *Independent* for the eight years after I was appointed full-time Jerusalem correspondent in 2004 by Simon Kelner, whose interest in the Israeli–Palestinian story – and Gaza in particular – was unwavering.

For allowing me two terms as an academic visitor at St Antony's College, Oxford, I am grateful to the Warden, Margaret MacMillan, and the fellows, including Professor Eugene Rogan, Director of its Middle East Centre, and above all Professor Avi Shlaim, whose encouragement, advice and generosity in sharing his unrivalled knowledge and some important documents has been invaluable. I am also grateful to Dr

Tareq Baconi for reading the manuscript and making numerous helpful suggestions. This is probably the place to make the far from ritual point that those listed here bear no responsibility for my errors or wrong conclusions.

For discussions outside Gaza over the years my thanks to Tony Lawrence, Antonia Caccia, Karen Kaufman, Sarah Helm, Michael Neuwirth, Rami Dajani, Daniel Levy, Shai Grunberg, Sari Bashi, the late Eric Silver, Ross Allen, Sir Vincent Fean, Tim Williams, John Edwards, Sir John Jenkins, Sir Tom Phillips, Harriet Matthews, Kim Sengupta, Fuad Bateh and, for his understanding of what the occupation means for Israel as well as the Palestinians, to the inspiring Yehuda Shaul.

Thanks are due to the consistent support and encouragement of four foreign editors of the *Independent*, Katherine Butler, Archie Bland, Alistair Dawber and David Wastell, as well as of my eminent former *Independent* colleagues, Robert Fisk and Patrick Cockburn. I have benefited enormously from the knowledge and comradeship of the correspondents I have worked with in Gaza since 2003. Until 2006, when Israel stopped Israeli and East Jerusalem Palestinian journalists from entering Gaza, these included my two close friends, mentors and *Independent* colleagues, Quique Kierszenbaum and Said Ghazali. And, from other organisations, Chris McGreal, Stephen Farrell, Heidi Levine, Rory McCarthy, Harvey Morris, Alan Johnston, Ben Lynfield, Ruth Pollard, Tobias Buck (who first suggested I write a book about Gaza), Nicholas Pelham, Ana Carbajosa, Alberto Stabile, Conal Urquhart, David Blair, Tim Butcher, Catrina Stewart, Adrian Blomfield and Harriet Sherwood. To Harriet I owe an especially great debt for unstintingly using her skills as a former *Guardian* foreign editor to unpick and cut down to size a horribly unwieldy original draft and for providing huge moral support during the whole project. Heartfelt thanks are also due to Scarlett MccGwire who not only read the manuscript and made many helpful suggestions (and excisions), but also generously provided encouragement when the task seemed hopeless. My thanks to my friend of half a century Nigel Williams for his perceptive comments on the early draft.

For invaluable research as well as often difficult transcription of taped interviews, I am especially indebted to Misha MccGwire and Jack Saville; but also to Roba Salibi, Lawrence Speelman and James Macintyre.

I have tried to identify sources in the endnotes wherever appropriate.

Passages and quotations for which there is no such reference usually stem from events I personally witnessed or interviews I conducted at the time. Of the many books I have consulted and listed in the bibliography I would particularly recommend for further reading on Gaza: Jean-Pierre Filiu's and Gerald Butt's two histories of Gaza, Beverley Milton-Edwards and Stephen Farrell's on Hamas, Sara Roy's masterful account of Gaza's de-development, Atef Abu Saif's outstanding picture of what it was like for a Palestinian to live through the 2014 war, and Amira Hass's unmatchable account of living in Gaza in the 1990s, as resonant now as it was when it was published in 2000.

I am especially grateful to my publisher Oneworld and its astute and long-suffering non-fiction editor Sam Carter, whose numerous suggestions were invariably for the better, and to his assistant Jonathan Bentley-Smith; my thanks, too, to my agent Gordon Wise for his indispensable help in bringing this project to fruition.

Select Bibliography

Abrams, Elliott. *Tested by Zion: The Bush Administration and the Israeli-Palestinian Conflict*. New York, Cambridge University Press, 2013

Aburish, Saïd K. *Arafat: From Defender to Dictator*. London, Bloomsbury, 1998

Baskin, Gershon. *The Negotiator: Freeing Gilad Shalit from Hamas*. Jerusalem, The Toby Press, 2013

Blumenthal, Max. *The 51 Day War: Ruin and Resistance in Gaza*. London, Verso, 2015

Breaking the Silence. *This is How We Fought in Gaza: Soldiers' Testimonies and Photographs from 'Operation Protective Edge'*. Jerusalem, Breaking the Silence, 2015

–––– *Our Harsh Logic: Israeli Soldiers' Testimonies from the occupied territories 2000–2010*. New York, Picador, 2012

Bregman, Ahron, *Cursed Victory: A History of Israel and the Occupied Territories*. London, Penguin Books, 2015

Butt, Gerald. *Life at the Crossroads: A History of Gaza*. Nicosia, Cyprus, Rimal Publications, 1995

Dawood, N. J. (trans.). *The Koran*. London, Penguin Books, 1974

Dayan, Major-General Moshe. *Diary of the Sinai Campaign 1956*. London, Sphere Books, 1966

Dothan, Trude. *Deir el-Balah*. Jerusalem, The Israel Museum, 2008

Filiu, Jean-Pierre. *From Deep State to Islamic State*. London, Hurst and Company, 2015

–––– *Gaza: A History*. London, Hurst and Company, 2014

Finkelstein, Norman G. *Method and Madness*. New York and London, OR Books, 2014

Gazit, Shlomo. *Trapped Fools: Thirty Years of Israeli Policy in the Territories*. London, Frank Cass, 2003

Gilbert, Martin. *Israel: A History*. London, Black Swan, 1999

Gisha. *Disengaged Occupiers: The Legal Status of Gaza*. Tel Aviv, Gisha, 2007

Hass, Amira. *Drinking the Sea at Gaza*. New York, Metropolitan Books, 1999

Helm, Sarah. *The Aftermath: A correspondent's return to Gaza* (ebook). Newsweek Insights, 2015

Hirst, David. *The Gun and the Olive Branch: The Roots of Violence in the Middle East*. London, Faber and Faber, 1977

Hoke, Mateo and Malek, Cate. *Palestine Speaks: Narratives of Life under Occupation*. London, Verso, 2015

Johnston, Alan. *Kidnapped and Other Dispatches*. London, Profile Books, 2007

Kurtzer, Daniel C. and Lasensky, Scott B. *Negotiating Arab-Israeli Peace*. Washington, DC, United States Institute of Peace Press, 2008

Landau, David. *Arik: The Life of Ariel Sharon*. New York, Alfred A. Knopf, 2014

Lawrence, T. E. *Seven Pillars of Wisdom*. Ware, Wordsworth Editions, 1997

Levy, Gideon. *The Punishment of Gaza*. London, Verso, 2010

Matar, Dina and Tawil-Souri, Helga. *Gaza as Metaphor*. London, Hurst Publishers, 2016

Miller, Aaron David. *The Much Too Promised Land*. New York, Bantam Dell, 2008

Milton-Edwards, Beverley and Farrell, Stephen. *Hamas: The Islamic Resistance Movement*. Cambridge and Boston, Polity Press, 2010

Mishal, Shaul and Sela, Avraham. *The Palestinian Hamas*. New York, Columbia University Press, 2006

Morris, Benny. *One State, Two States*. New Haven, Yale University Press, 2009

---- *1948: A History of the First Arab-Israeli War*. New Haven, Yale University Press, 2008

---- *The Birth of the Palestinian Refugee Problem Revisited*. Cambridge, Cambridge University Press, 2004

Omer, Mohammed. *Shell-Shocked: On the Ground under Israel's Gaza Assault*. New York and London, OR Books, 2015

Pappe, Ilan. *A History of Modern Palestine: One Land, Two Peoples*. Cambridge, Cambridge University Press, 2004

Prashad, Vijay (ed.). *Letters to Palestine*. London, Verso, 2015

Reinhart, Tanya. *The Road Map to Nowhere: Israel/Palestine since 2003*. New York and London, Verso, 2006

Rhoades, Peter and Shlaim, Avi. *Gaza: An Artist's Response*. London, Skyscraper Publications, 2016

Rice, Condoleezza. *No Higher Honor: A Memoir of My Years in Washington*. London, Simon & Schuster, 2012

Rodgers, James. *No Road Home: Fighting for Land and Faith in Gaza*. Bury St Edmunds, Abramis Academic Publishing, 2013

Rogan, Eugene. *The Fall of the Ottomans*. London, Penguin, 2016

–––– *The Arabs: A History*. London and New York, Allen Lane, 2009

–––– and Shlaim, Avi. *The War for Palestine*. New York, Cambridge University Press, 2007

Ross, Dennis. *The Missing Peace: The Inside Story of the Fight for Middle East Peace*. New York, Farrar, Straus and Giroux, 2004

Roy, Sara. *The Gaza Strip: The Political Economy of De-Development*. Washington, DC, Institute for Palestine Studies, 2016

–––– *Hamas and Civil Society in Gaza*. Princeton, Princeton University Press, 2014

Sacco, Joe. *Footnotes in Gaza*. London, Jonathan Cape, 2009

Said, Edward W. *The End of the Peace Process*. London, Granta Books, 2002

–––– *The Politics of Dispossession: The Struggle for Palestinian Self-Determination 1969–1994*. London, Chatto & Windus, 1994

–––– *The Question of Palestine*. New York, Vintage Books, 1992

Saif, Atef Abu. *The Drone Eats With Me*. Manchester, Fasila, 2015

–––– *The Book of Gaza*. Manchester, Comma Press, 2014

Segev, Tom. *1967: Israel, the War and the Year That Transformed the Middle East*. New York, Metropolitan Books, 2007

Seidl, Timothy. *Non-Violent Resistance in the Second Intifada: Activism and Advocacy*. London, Palgrave Macmillan, 2011

Shafi, Mustafa Abdel. *Would They Ever Learn?*, Vol. 1. Mustafa Abdel Shafi, Palestine, 2000

–––– *Would They Ever Learn?*, Vol. 2. Mustafa Abdel Shafi, Palestine, 2000

Shafi, Sami Abdel. *Realigning EU Policy in Palestine: Towards a Viable State Economy and Restored Dignity*. London, Chatham House, 2015

Shepherd, Naomi. *Ploughing Sand: British Rule in Palestine 1917–1948*. London, John Murray, 1999

Shlaim, Avi. *The Iron Wall: Israel and the Arab World*. London, Penguin, 2014

–––– *Israel and Palestine*. London, Verso, 2009

Straw, Jack, *Last Man Standing: Memoirs of a Political Survivor*. London, Macmillan, 2012

Tawil-Souri, Helga and Matar, Dina [Edited]. *Gaza as Metaphor*. London, Hurst Books, 2014

Wolfensohn, James, *A Global Life: My Journey Among Rich and Poor, from Sydney to Wall Street to the World Bank*. New York, Public Affairs, 2010

Index